MODERNISM AND THE CELTIC REVIVAL

In *Modernism and the Celtic Revival*, Gregory Castle examines the impact of anthropology on the work of Irish Revivalists such as W. B. Yeats, John M. Synge, and James Joyce. Castle argues that anthropology enabled Irish Revivalists to confront and combat British imperialism, even as these Irish writers remained ambivalently dependent on the cultural and political discourses they sought to undermine. Castle shows how Irish modernists employed textual and rhetorical strategies first developed in anthropology to translate, reassemble, and edit oral and folk–cultural material. In doing so, he claims, they confronted and undermined inherited notions of identity which Ireland, often a site of ethnographic curiosity throughout the nineteenth century, had been subject to. Drawing on a wide range of post-colonial theory, this book should be of interest to scholars in Irish studies, post-colonial studies, and modernism.

GREGORY CASTLE is Professor of British and Irish Literature at Arizona State University. He is the editor of *Post-colonial Discourses: A Reader*. He has published articles in *James Joyce Quarterly*, *Genre*, *Twentieth-century Literature*, *European Joyce Studies*, and *Theatre Journal*. He was awarded the Gerald Kahan Scholar's Prize in 1998 by the American Society for Theater Research for an essay on John M. Synge's *Playboy of the Western World*.

MODERNISM AND THE CELTIC REVIVAL

GREGORY CASTLE

DAMAGED

CAMBRIDGE
UNIVERSITY PRESS

PUBLISHED BY THE PRESS SYNDICATE OF THE UNIVERSITY OF CAMBRIDGE
The Pitt Building, Trumpington Street, Cambridge, United Kingdom

CAMBRIDGE UNIVERSITY PRESS
The Edinburgh Building, Cambridge CB2 2RU, UK
40 West 20th Street, New York, NY 10011–4211, USA
10 Stamford Road, Oakleigh, Melbourne 3166, Australia
Ruiz de Alarcón 13, 28014 Madrid, Spain
Dock House, The Waterfront, Cape Town 8001, South Africa

http://www.cambridge.org

© Gregory Castle 2001

First published 2001

Printed in the United Kingdom at the University Press, Cambridge

Typeset in Baskerville 11/12.5pt   System 3b2   [CE]

A catalogue record for this book is available from the British Library

ISBN 0 521 79319 x hardback

Contents

Acknowledgments

This book has taken several years and gone through many refinements. I would like to take this opportunity to acknowledge the criticism and support I have received while working on it. I am grateful to have worked with two extraordinary editors at Cambridge University Press, Ray Ryan and Rachel De Wachter, who guided this project throughout with patience, respect, good humor and genuine concern that it shape up to its potential. Equally supportive and helpful was my copyeditor, Gillian Maude. Many colleagues and friends were, wittingly or not, helpful contributors in the process of writing this book. I thank especially my mentor and good friend John Paul Riquelme, whose support for this project has been generous and unstinting. I owe to him whatever clarity and felicity my style may possess. I thank Joseph Valente, who read an early draft of *Modernism and the Celtic Revival* and whose comments guided me in an early stage of revision. In the same vein, I thank the readers at Cambridge University Press whose reports proved helpful in final revisions. Several people have read parts of this book and I acknowledge their role in making it better than it might have been. Nicholas Grene was generous with his time and knowledge about Synge, and Richard Finneran's remarks on an embryonic conference paper on Yeats and ethnography proved singularly important. Peter Costello patiently helped me in my search for information on Irish Catholicism and introduced me to Anthony Roche, whose delightful remarks about Irish drama helped me understand the tangle of reactions to Synge's plays. Conversations with Patrick McGee, Colleen Lamos, Bill Mottolese and other Joyceans have, over the years, helped to shape my attitudes toward Joyce and his relationship to colonialism, anthropology and the Revival. In a similar fashion, my graduate students at Arizona State University tolerated me patiently as I began to make the arguments for this book and in the process gave me opportunities to revise or expand on my own views. Amanda Yeates' efforts as a research assistant were indispensable and she was, in many ways, my first reader. I thank my parents, Ralph and Donna Castle, who gave me unconditional support and encouragement, and my dear friend Kristi Van Stechelman, who made my life beeter as I worked on this project. Finally, to my daughter, Camille, whose love has inspired and sustained me, I dedicate this book:

M'iníon, aon searc is grá mo chléibh

Abbreviations

A	*Autobiographies*
CA	*The Cutting of an Agate*
CT	*The Celtic Twilight (1902 edn)*
E	*Explorations*
EI	*Essays and Introductions*
FFT	*Fairy and Folk Tales of Ireland*
L	*Collected Letters of W. B. Yeats*, vol. I
OB	*On the Boiler*
Plays	*The Collected Plays of W. B. Yeats*
Poems	*The Poems of W. B. Yeats: A New Edition*
SR	*The Secret Rose* (1897)
SRH	*Stories of Red Hanrahan / The Secret Rose / Rosa Alchemica* (1914)
TL	*The Tables of the Law; and The Adoration of the Magi* (1914)
UPI	*Uncollected Prose*, vol. I
AI	*The Aran Islands* in *J. M. Synge, Collected Works*, vol. II
MS	*Synge Manuscript Collection, Trinity College, Dublin*
Playboy	*The Playboy of the Western World, J. M. Synge, Collected Works*, vol. IV
SH	*Stephen Hero*
D	*Dubliners*
P	*A Portrait of the Artist as a Young Man*
U	*Ulysses*

CHAPTER I

The Celtic muse: anthropology, modernism, and the Celtic Revival

ETHNOLOGY, n. The science that treats of the various tribes of Man, as robbers, thieves, swindlers, dunces, lunatics, idiots and ethnologists.

Ambrose Bierce[1]

Modernism and the Celtic Revival emerged out of the necessity of finding a way to teach W. B. Yeats's *Mythologies*. In pursuing the implications of Yeats's role as a folklorist, I was led to anthropology and its influence on the Celtic Revival as well as to the conclusion that very little critical work had been done in this area. To be sure, critics like Philip Marcus, Mary Helen Thuente, Edward Hirsch, and Deborah Fleming have explored the aesthetic and political implications of folklore, legend, and myth in the production of Revivalist texts; but no one has explored in any extensive way the influence of anthropology on the way Revivalists represented Irish culture and the Irish people. This study attempts just such an exploration, beginning with a consideration of the work of two prominent Anglo-Irish Revivalists, Yeats and John M. Synge, before moving on to consider the Catholic-Irish writer, James Joyce, whose work can be read as a critique of the anthropological assumptions of the Celtic Revival. My contention is that for each of these writers the desire to revive an authentic, indigenous Irish folk culture is the effect of an ethnographic imagination that emerges in the interplay of native cultural aspirations and an array of practices associated with the disciplines of anthropology, ethnography, archaeology, folklore, comparative mythology, and travel writing.

It is my chief contention that the relationship between anthropology and the Celtic Revival is an important feature of modernism as it developed in the Irish context. As Terry Eagleton has recently argued, Ireland is unique among European nations in that "as a whole [it] had not leapt at a bound from tradition to modernity.

I

Instead, it presented an exemplary case of what Marxism has dubbed combined and uneven development."[2] On the one hand, this uneven development led to a situation in which modernization occurred in some spheres (parliamentary politics, colonial administration, the arts) but was retarded in others (industry, agriculture, education); but, on the other hand, it also created the conditions for a dynamic modernist artistic culture, especially among Anglo-Irish Revivalists who, because of their own ambiguous social position as members of a dominant ruling class *and* as proponents of nationalist self-determination, were perhaps better able to appreciate the contradictions inherent in a society mutually determined by the tension between what Eagleton calls the archaic and the modern. This may explain the conservative – indeed, at times anti-modern – tenor of much of Revivalist discourse.

Following Perry Anderson's analysis of the relationship between modernity and revolution, Eagleton notes that there are three preconditions for a flourishing modernism:

The existence of an artistic *ancien régime*, often in societies still under the sway of an aristocracy; the impact upon this traditional culture of breathtakingly new technologies; and the imaginative closeness of social revolution. Modernism springs from the estranging impact of modernizing forces on a still deeply traditionalist order, in a politically unstable context which opens up social hope as well as spiritual anxiety. Traditional culture provides modernism with an adversary, but also lends it some of the terms in which to inflect itself.[3]

For Eagleton, the agonistic relationship between the archaic and the modern creates ideal conditions for the emergence of modernism; and these conditions exist most dramatically not in the metropolitan center, which lacks the key criteria of "breathtakingly new technologies" and social revolution, but on the colonial and decolonial margins: "the 'no-time' and 'no-place' of the disregarded colony, with its fractured history and marginalized space, can become suddenly symbolic of a condition of disinheritance which now seems universal."[4] Irish modernism, then, while it seeks to accommodate new technologies and revolutionary energies, is at the same time very conservative: "If there is a high modernism, there is little or no avant-garde," and this is so because the Anglo-Irish monopolized modernism by translating political dispossession into cultural production. The deracinating effects of land legislation and an increasingly cynical Liberal party that seemed willing to abandon its client ruling class to its own ineffectuality left the Anglo-Irish feeling acutely their ambivalent position between colonizer and colonized. Eagleton notes that this "in-betweenness" was "a version of the hybrid spirit of the European modernist, caught between diverse cultural codes" and that the Anglo-Irish Revivalists' recourse to "the celebrated formalism and aestheticism of the modernists" was an effective and defiant "rationalization of their own rootless condition."[5]

Eagleton's argument that Irish modernism emerged in the estranging contact of modernity with a traditional or archaic culture finds support in a consideration of the role anthropology played in the development of the Celtic Revival's modernist aesthetic of cultural redemption. This aesthetic is one of the most controversial elements of the Celtic Revival, in part because the anthropological authority behind it renders it internally contradictory, at once complicit with and hostile toward a tradition of representation that sought to redeem Irish peasant culture by idealizing or essentializing its "primitive" social conditions. This is true especially for writers like Yeats and Synge, whose meditations on Irish culture employ theories of cultural difference and discursive techniques and strategies borrowed from, or analogous to those found in, anthropology. Whereas the English or European modernist might regard anthropology as a way of integrating non-Western sensibilities and perspectives into an essentially Western frame of reference, the Revivalist must contend with the possibility of colluding with a discipline that in significant ways has furthered the interests of imperialism by producing a body of authoritative knowledge about colonized peoples. It is an abiding assumption of this study that an analysis of the role played by anthropology in the Revival may help us to understand the rhetorical and imaginative force of a specifically Irish form of anthropological modernism that seeks to transform indigenous materials into new cultural texts. However, given the uneasy relation of tradition to modernity in colonial Ireland, this task is complicated by the ever-present potential of complicity with the very discourses of nationalism, colonialism, and anthropology that invoke a binomial distinction between the primitive and the civilized in order to argue for the cultural and racial inferiority, political impotence and historical irrelevance of the native Irish people.

At the *fin de siècle*, the Revival was a complex and multifaceted movement, comprising a variety of approaches to the representation of Irish cultural. As Mary Helen Thuente argues, in *The Harp*

Re-strung: The United Irishmen and the Rise of Irish Literary Nationalism, the origins of Revivalism lie in the late-eighteenth-century United Irishmen movement. Another line of development, originating in the Young Irelanders of the 1840s, produced a form of Revivalism associated with the Gaelic League and Irish–Ireland nationalism. This development reaches a culmination in the 1890s with men like Sir Charles Gavan Duffy, Dr. George Sigerson, and Douglas Hyde, whose essays and speeches disseminated an ideology of "racial" self-improvement and national education and whose vision of Revivalism had a strong reformist orientation and sought principally to restore a belief in the essential piety and nobility of the Irish people. In a 1892 speech to the Irish Literary Society, Duffy held up the generation of the 1840s as a model for the present:

A group of young men, among the most generous and disinterested in our annals, were busy digging up the buried relics of our history, to enlighten the present by a knowledge of the past, setting up on their pedestals anew the overthrown statues of Irish worthies, assailing wrongs which under long impunity had become unquestioned and even venerable, and warming as with strong wine the heart of the people, by songs of valour and hope; and happily not standing isolated in their pious work, but encouraged and sustained by just such an army of students and sympathizers as I see here to-day.[6]

Hyde and Duffy were quick to point out just how far the Irish people had come from this "golden age," which the famine and penal laws had obscured from the people's memory. "What writers ought to aim at, who hope to benefit the people," Duffy asserts, "is to fill up the blanks which an imperfect education, and the fever of a tempestuous time, have left in their knowledge, so that their lives might become contented and fruitful."[7] It is the "native" artist's responsibility to rediscover the "natural" harmony of Ireland: "to be wise and successful," writes Duffy, "the proper development of Ireland . . . must harmonize with the nature of the people, and correct it where correction is needful."[8] The belief in cultural or racial essence, together with a belief in moral and cultural reform, led Hyde, echoing Duffy and Sigerson, to complain that "[w]e have at last broken the continuity of Irish life" and that "the present art products of one of the quickest, most sensitive, and most artistic races on earth are now only distinguished for their hideousness."[9] These complaints and the general goal of racial self-improvement underscore the extent to which Irish–Ireland nationalists had internalized anthropological and colonialist assumptions about the Irish "race."

One of the chief concerns of *Modernism and the Celtic Revival* is to examine the issues raised above from the perspective of Anglo-Irish Revivalists like Yeats and Synge, as well as from the perspective of Joyce, whose critique of Revivalism effectively guaranteed its continued relevance as a context for Irish artistic production. There has been a great deal of work on the Revival in the last thirty years or so, beginning with Phillip Marcus's *Yeats and the Beginning of the Irish Renaissance* and, a little later, Richard Fallis's *The Irish Renaissance*. These texts are important for establishing the main lines of literary and historical descent and, in Marcus's case, for placing Yeats at the center of Revivalist theory and practice. However, as with any attempt to construct a genealogy, there are dangers of mystification and misrepresentation. Robert O'Driscoll's characterization of Revivalism, rooted in Yeats's conception of a "war of spiritual with natural order" (*SR*, vii), exemplifies a tendency to regard the Revival as absolutely resistant to Empire. He argues that the "imposition of an imperialist ideal was rejected by the writers of the Celtic Revival long before the political and military leaders created a physical body for the spiritual principles." Further, he maintains that "[t]he Celtic Revival was deliberately created as a counter-movement to the materialism of the post-Darwinian age" and that the Revivalists did not believe "that literature was a criticism of visible life, but that it was a revelation of an invisible world."[10]

Now, it may be true that the Celtic Revival was anti-imperial in its general orientation. But the claim that it rejected an imperial ideal is not always supported by Revivalist practice, especially when that practice is influenced by anthropology. This is not to say that Revivalists acted in willful collusion with imperial authorities, though some nationalists, like D. P. Moran, were fond of making such accusations. In recent years, books like Seamus Deane's *Celtic Revivals* and Declan Kiberd's *Inventing Ireland* have taken a more critical approach to Revivalism and its nationalist aspirations, paying careful attention to the problematic position of the Anglo-Irish Revivalist in a nationalist movement that often demanded racial as well as ideological authenticity.[11] Kiberd poses the problem in terms that underscore its anthropological dimensions:

The plaque which now stands on Shaw's cottage in Dalkey may well in its inscription speak also for Yeats: "The men of Ireland are mortal and temporal, but her hills are eternal." Behind such an aphorism lies a familiar strategy of the Irish Protestant imagination, estranged from the community, yet anxious to identify itself with the new national sentiment. While Roman Catholic writers of the revival period seemed obsessed with the history of their land, to Protestant artists that history could only be, as Lady Gregory insisted, a painful accusation against their own people; and so they turned to geography in the attempt at patriotization.[12]

The condition of estrangement from a community that issues a "painful accusation" against them forced many Anglo-Irish Revivalists into ambivalent positions suggestive of those taken by ethnographers who stand both inside and outside the culture they investigate, striving for a balance between participation and observation. The "turn to geography" that Kiberd notes is an attempt to shift the grounds of Irish identity from race to locality and to make a virtue of ambivalence. As Leopold Bloom tells the citizen, in Joyce's *Ulysses*, "A nation is the same people living in the same place" (*U,* 331).

Of course, Bloom's notion of national identity does not appease the citizen, and Bloom is left feeling as ambivalent as ever. The same is frequently true of the Anglo-Irish Revivalists who turn to geography – and, I might add, to the folk culture of a people for whom the land is of signal importance – in order to find a ground for national identity or, to use Kiberd's term, "patriotization." Unlike Bloom, however, their considerable social authority makes them vulnerable to the charge of perpetuating certain forms of discursive violence against the Celtic (i.e., Catholic) Irish. This was certainly the charge leveled at Synge during the controversy over *The Playboy of the Western World,* and it was leveled at Yeats as well, whose lack of Irish was often pointed out as evidence of his inability to say anything meaningful about Irish folk culture. The importance of a book like Kiberd's is that it examines this ambivalent position from a perspective informed by postcolonial theory (especially the work of Frantz Fanon) which allows us to understand, at least in part, how it might be understood as a form of resistance. It is my belief that the charge of complicity can properly be weighed and evaluated only when we recognize that the authority of the Revivalists who established the Abbey Theatre, and worked legend and folklore into the fabric of a modern Irish literature, was essentially anthropological. Moreover, I believe it is important to recognize the extent to which this authority governs an ethnographic imagination capable of transforming complicity with primitivist discourses into more or less critical revisions of the concepts of "tradition" and the "peasant."[13]

It is equally important to recognize that this work of revision was conducted by intellectuals who were not, strictly speaking, "native." Thus the problematic status of the Revivalist as a "native intellectual" makes the Irish situation a difficult one to analyze, for it lies outside the limits of a Manichean opposition that pits native against colonialist and "primitive" peasant against "civilized" participant–observer.[14] Two important facts need to be acknowledged. The first is geographical. Ireland is an "internal" colony, which means it is situated in close proximity to the metropolitan center. This proximity creates problems of administration and social control that are not to be found in other colonies of the Empire. As a result, the standard model of core–periphery interaction, in which the core (i.e., London and the Home Counties) "dominates the periphery politically and . . . exploits it materially,"[15] applies to Ireland in ways that are significantly different from its application in South Asia or Africa. The term "metropolitan colony" best describes the unique position of Ireland in the Empire, since both Ireland and England shared the same language, legal code, urban culture and geopolitical location.

But this proximity ought not to lead us to believe that Ireland somehow suffered less profoundly the violence of imperialism. Indeed, the very lack of discernible racial difference led to an especially pernicious, because discursive, form of violence. Matthew Arnold's *On the Study of Celtic Literature*, in an effort to resolve the problem of racial similarity, posits a Celtic "element" that, though part of the British national character, is nevertheless inferior to a stronger Teutonic one. The burden of assimilation was therefore greater on the Irish than elsewhere in the Empire, in part because assimilation was perceived as natural and inevitable. "Let the Celtic members of this empire consider that they too have to transform themselves," Arnold admonished. "Let them consider that they are inextricably bound up with us."[16] The anthropological modernism of the Revival seeks both to counter and to rewrite a discourse in which, as David Cairns and Shaun Richards argue, "the Irish were racially and culturally located to a subordinate position in the Imperial community through, amongst other elements, [Matthew] Arnold's typifications of 'Celtic' personality as feminine, irrational, impractical and childlike, and social-darwinist stereotyping of the Irish as inferior racially to the Aryan Anglo Saxons."[17]

The second important fact is historical. The proximity to the metropolitan center produced two distinct, and distinctly dominant, socio-political groups: the English imperialists and the Anglo-Irish. Historically, the Anglo-Irish, in addition to holding most of the land, served also as regional governors, parliamentary representatives, and managers of major businesses and industries; as a ruling class (and here we might speak of the "Protestant Ascendancy"), the Anglo-Irish had long provided the political and economic links to England and its representatives in Ireland.[18] A singular situation thus developed in which a relatively small group of non-Irish settlers, over a considerable period of time, transformed itself into something like a native Anglo-Irish class quite different from, say, the Anglo-Indian enclaves of the sub-continental colonies. Herein lies the crux of the problem for the student of the Revival, for, despite their political and economic affiliation, the English and the Anglo-Irish were not always allies; the curious sense of nativity that developed among the Anglo-Irish from the time of the Old English settlements in the early seventeenth century, while frequently manifesting itself in colonialist terms, just as frequently resulted in the fervent adoption of Ireland as a homeland and source of patriotic pride. But the pride and fervor, and most of all the confidence of the men and women who rallied around the United Irishmen in 1798 and later around the Young Irelanders, foundered on sectarianism, which for some revisionist historians was artificially fomented in order to drive a wedge between the Catholic Irish and their Anglo-Irish sympathizers.[19] By the end of the nineteenth century, many of the Anglo-Irish began to feel isolated and marginalized, a condition that Roy Foster attributes to land reform, the inevitability of Home Rule and the rise of both Catholic nationalism and an increasingly powerful and vocal Catholic middle class.[20] It is easy to see why an Anglo-Irish intellectual, isolated equally from the Ascendancy ruling class and from an emergent Catholic nationalism, might feel his or her position as ambivalent. Acutely self-conscious of their marginal status as intellectuals in a colony moving inexorably toward some form of Catholic self-determination, Revivalists like Yeats and Synge were burdened by questions of political and cultural authenticity. And, while Joyce, raised and educated in Catholic institutions, may be less burdened by these questions, he nevertheless faced some of the same problems of isolation and marginalization, the same sense of being both inside and outside culture, that led Yeats to Sligo and Galway and Synge to the Aran Islands. In part because he lacked the characteristic ambivalence of the déclassé Anglo-Irish intellectuals and in part because he wrote at an exilic remove (both literally and figuratively) from the culture that nevertheless occupied his imagination, Joyce remained aloof from the Revival; he was critical of it but did not repudiate it, and precisely in this way he succeeded in redefining it.

I have suggested above that the ambivalence felt by the Anglo-Irish Revivalists is analogous to that which we find in the ethnographic situation, which is not surprising given the remarkably similar investments in strategies of cultural observation and textual production. If Revivalists courted the possibility of duplicating the anthropological project of creating a "total" picture of the Celtic "race," it is because they could not always effectively escape the disciplinary authority of anthropology when they appropriated its techniques of cultural observation and analysis (e.g., collecting and editing folklore, conducting fieldwork, writing up accounts from fieldnotes, and the like that are taught in universities and practiced on academic- or state-sponsored anthropological missions) or when they adopted the model of a unitary or "sovereign" subjectivity, presupposed as foundational for the ethnographic participant–observer, as a justification for their own experiential authority. We should not be surprised, then, to discover that the danger of collusion with anthropology was not only unavoidable but to some degree constitutive of their various projects of cultural redemption.

However, while the Celtic Revival is historically coeval with the new metropolitan "sciences" of anthropology and ethnography, and though it borrowed some of their characteristic theories and textual practices, it was far less bound up in the institutional structures of power that determined the work of academically trained anthropologists like A. C. Haddon, A. R. Radcliffe-Brown, and Bronislaw Malinowski, and it had a different relationship with imperial authority. Thus, Revivalists were in a position to resist anthropology's foundational theories of culture and some of its more egregious assumptions about primitive peoples. The contradictions inherent in these assumptions and in the emergent methods of scientific ethnography were either deeply repressed – a gesture that accounts for the ontological and epistemological self-assurance of a discipline that derived cultural universals from the perspective of a superior race – or examined only in unofficial contexts, like Malinowski's posthumously published *A Diary in the Strict Sense of the Term*. In literary texts like Yeats's *Celtic Twilight* and Synge's *Aran Islands*, which make use of anthropological theories of culture and employ ethnographic methods, the contradictions are readily apparent, indeed they constitute a signal feature of Revivalist writing about Irish culture. Because Revivalist writers had no professional stake in the discipline of anthropology, they were free to exploit the contradictions inherent to the discipline (which did not itself recognize the existence of such contradictions); but the absence of a professional stake did not prevent Revivalists from adopting forms of participant observation and modes of cultural translation by which native texts and practices were reproduced for and consumed by a metropolitan audience. The *un*disciplined use of ethnographic methods and anthropological theories of culture led to a style of representation that was at once scientific (or pseudo-scientific) and literary. Thus, conflicting authorities – aesthetic and anthropological – governed a discourse of cultural redemption that strove both to represent *and* to invent Irish culture.

As I suggested above, the argument that the Celtic Revival was complicit in a discourse of primitivism gains some credence when we consider the historical coincidence of the Revival and modern anthropology, both emerging almost simultaneously in the late-nineteenth century in response to quite different imperial pressures. In some important ways, Revivalists were engaged in anthropological work similar to that which was going on in Ireland under the auspices of British universities and learned societies. *The Celtic Twilight* and *The Aran Islands* might be regarded as part of a tradition of anthropological inquiry that had reached a culmination in the same decade (the 1890s) in which A. C. Haddon, the principal investigator of the British Association's Ethnographic Survey of the British Isles, conducted fieldwork in the West of Ireland. For it is undeniable that, just when legendary and folkloric texts were becoming available in translation, when scholars and collectors were beginning to find an audience, when the Royal Academy of Ireland and the Royal Anthropological Institute of Great Britain and Ireland were turning their attention to the West of Ireland – just at this time, Anglo-Irish Revivalists emerged with their desire to redeem an authentic Irish culture that was deemed incapable of self-preservation and in need of "civilized" or "advanced" outsiders to represent them and to serve as "custodian[s] of an essence, unimpeachable witness[es] to an authenticity."[21] Countering "anthropological fictions" like the "purist notion[] that native cultures resist history, or that they disappear in its presence,"[22] the Revivalists strove to relocate Irish folk culture in an Irish context and to create new, affirmative, and liberatory anthropological fictions of their own.

One of the questions this study will raise is, to what extent does the historical concurrence of anthropology and the Celtic Revival create the conditions in which Anglo-Irish Revivalists could acquire discursive power over the Catholic-Irish whose lives and folkways are the subject of a redemptive anthropological discourse over which they have little or no control? As Malinowski said of the Trobriand Islanders, "[t]he natives are not, of course, capable of a consistent theoretical statement,"[23] a convenient assumption for the ethnographer, whose analytical skill alone can unveil the secret functioning of a culture. But it is equally important to indicate the extent to which this discursive power can be read as a form of resistance both to anthropology and imperialism. In this sense, Revivalist complicity with anthropological theories and practices edges very close to the concept of "mimicry" as it is theorized by Homi Bhabha and other postcolonial theorists. But, no matter how we construe the relationship between Revivalism and anthropology, historical concurrence is not identity. Therefore, I want to insist that Revivalists are *not* ethnographers, at least not in the sense that they are trained in the disciplinary protocols of anthropological theory and ethnographic practice; nor should their texts be understood to have the same form or authority as those produced by university-trained ethnographers. Rather, I contend that the long history of Ireland's subjection to anthropological inquiry provided the Revival with an historical opportunity to create (through strategies of appropriation and resignification) new representations of Irish culture and to resist the *mis*representations generated by British colonialists and anthropologists and Irish–Ireland nationalists. Though recent critics of the Revival have condemned its ambivalent relationships with these groups, I submit that it was this very ambivalence that enabled Revivalists and their critics to make such varied critical interventions in the debates on Irish national identity and the right to represent it. *Modernism and the Celtic Revival* is an attempt to reevaluate this ambivalence and the anthropological modernism that crafted it into a progressive mode of cultural critique.

It would be instructive to consider some of the main features of British anthropology as it developed in the period with which I am concerned in this study, from the 1890s to 1922, the period encompassing the major works of Yeats, Synge, and Joyce. I want to emphasize, however, that the Revivalists did not move in a kind of developmental lock-step with anthropology; my argument is simply that in some cases Revivalists adapted anthropological techniques and practices that were available to them at the time they wrote, while in other cases they anticipated anthropology in their strategies of representing Irish peasant culture. Indeed, in at least one case – W. Y. Evans-Wentz's *Fairy-Faith in Celtic Countries* (1911) – the situation is reversed, and an anthropologist cites Revivalists like Yeats, Lady Gregory, Hyde and AE (George Russell) as authorities on Irish mysticism and fairy-faith. If, as I contend, certain problems in anthropology, especially those which concern the ethnographic participant– observer, are homologous to problems that arise in the work of the Celtic Revivalists, then this homology warrants our attention and can help us better understand how modernity impinges on tradition in Ireland and how this impingement creates a uniquely Irish modernist sensibility.

In recent years, anthropologists and ethnographers have begun exploring the problems of writing about culture, problems which have existed in anthropology since the time of E. B. Tylor, considered by many to be the founder of the discipline. This trend toward revisionism has often taken the form of an exposé in which deconstructive analysis uncovers contradictions in anthropological theory and ethnographic method. In many respects, this has been a salutary trend, but it is not necessarily a new one; for a deconstructive impulse has always motivated the development of anthropology as it moved from one dominant theoretical perspective to another, from evolutionism to diffusionism to functionalism to structuralism and beyond. At each stage of development, new techniques and theories were put into place, and theorists and practitioners alike decried the inadequacy of what came before. Just as Malinowski criticized evolutionists and diffusionists – "the 'survival' monger, the 'origin' hunter, and the dealer in 'cultural contacts' "[24] – so Lévi-Strauss criticized Malinowski and his followers in the functionalist school for "find[ing] salvation in their asceticism and, by an unheard-of miracle, do[ing] what every good ethnographer must do and does."[25]

But, having said that revisionism in contemporary anthropology is nothing new, that it is coeval with the development of the discipline, I do not mean to imply that contemporary critiques of anthropology can offer us nothing that has not been offered before. Contemporary theories reflect contemporary attitudes toward culture, cultural difference, language, nationalism, race, gender – the whole constel-lation of problems that concern anthropology and literary studies today. New theories can alert us to problems in the development of anthropology that were not addressed by earlier generations, prob-lems like racism, gender relations, or the relationship between language and national identity. Moreover, intellectuals of emergent postcolonial states have produced discourses that overlap in many ways with those of anthropology, and the rise of "indigenous" ethnographers has reframed many of the problems of anthropology, especially that of the participant–observer. These problems and concerns are new to the extent that they are increasingly self-evident to the anthropologist and ethnographer, and are held up for criticism and revision in monographs and theoretical works; but they are hardly new from the point of view of practice. Malinowski's *A Diary* is a famous proof of my point, for in that text the ethnographer confronts the limits of his own objectivity, betrays a brutal strain of racism ("On the whole my feelings toward the natives are decidedly tending to '*Exterminate the brutes*'") and of misogyny (he notes "the perennial whorish expression of the Kiriwina women"), and suggests that ethnography's disinterestedness is a fragile thing indeed: "I get ready; little gray, pinkish huts. Photos. Feeling of ownership: It is I who will describe them and create them."[26]

For many contemporary critics of colonialism, anthropology developed as a "human science" within a context of imperial expansion and domination. Edward Said puts it this way: "[I]t is anthropology above all that has been historically constituted and constructed in its point of origin during an ethnographic encounter between a sovereign European observer and a non-European native occupying, so to speak, a lesser status and a distant place."[27] The desire for an ethnographic encounter is bound up with the idea of Empire, as evidenced by the remarks of E. W. Brabrook, president of the Royal Anthropological Institute of Great Britain and Ireland who, in 1897, argued that "[a]n empire like that of the United Kingdom ought certainly to possess some central establishment [an Ethnographic Bureau] in which a knowledge of the races of the empire might be acquired."[28] A few years earlier, John Beddoe, then president of the Institute, called for the support of all those who believed in the supremacy of the British Empire and its anthropological mission:

The Institute requires the active aid of all its friends, if it is to maintain the position that should be occupied by the only purely Anthropological Society in the greatest empire of this and of all time . . . It needs new men . . . who will not only follow out the old lines, but invade new territories, or rather cultivate those corners of our territory which have been partially neglected, for instance, psychology, if indeed that great domain may be spoken of as a corner.[29]

At the back of such statements are three governing assumptions about culture: (1) the sovereign belief in the superiority of white Europeans, specifically Britons of a certain class and education; (2) the self-assurance of a positivist science; and (3) the right to possess or "acquire" the cultural knowledge of other races in the name and in the language of Empire.

The imperative to develop an Ethnographic Bureau stems in part from a desire to institutionalize the relationship between amateur collectors of ethnographic data and colonial administrators. "Of all the modern social sciences," Said writes, "anthropology is the one historically most closely tied to colonialism, since it is often the case that anthropologists and ethnologists advised colonial rulers on the manners and mores of the native people."[30] We get a sense of the importance of such advice in the *Journal of the Anthropological Institute of Great Britain and Ireland*. In his Anniversary Address for 1896, Brabrook commended the Reverend Godfrey Dale's ethnographic work, particularly his "Account of the Principal Customs and Habits of the Natives inhabiting the Bondei Country [E. Africa]," compiled mainly for the use of European missionaries:

[I]t is especially valuable as a record of the researches of a keen and well-equipped observer, who had acquired a remarkable mastery of the language of the natives, and had so secured their confidence as to be able to obtain full details of their practices in regard to male and female initiations, witchcraft, and the like, showing striking resemblances and at the same time marked divergences when compared with similar customs recorded as prevailing in Australia and elsewhere.[31]

The influence of such amateurs, and the missionaries and colonial officials they sometimes advised, on the formation of colonial policy is hard to discern with any confidence. But some revisionist critics of anthropology feel more confident about the role played by amateurs in the development of ethnography as a discipline.

Mary Louise Pratt, for example, argues that ethnography, as it developed into a modern scientific discipline, defined itself by contrasting its theory and praxis to those of "older less specialized genres, such as travel books, personal memoirs, journalism, and accounts by missionaries, settlers, colonial officials, and the like."[32] However, as Pratt argues, ethnography, particularly its "opening narratives" of arrival, "display clear continuities with travel writing." Significantly, this continuity is repressed once "ethnography blinds itself to the fact that its own discursive practices were often inherited from these other genres and are still shared with them today."[33]

The precise nature of this inheritance – personal experience without any theoretical basis or principles governing practice – meant that ethnography's origins lay in a subjective and well-nigh literary tradition of "unscientific" reflections on culture. Thus it was imperative for anthropology to develop disciplinary protocols that would distinguish their work from that of amateur travel writers and colonial officials. This imperative was recognized by E. B. Tylor, whose *Primitive Culture*, published in 1871, provided the foundation for a modern scientific anthropology. "It is wonderful," Tylor writes, "to contrast some missionary journals with Max Müller's Essays, and to set the unappreciating hatred and ridicule that is lavished by narrow hostile zeal on Brahmanism, Buddhism, Zoroastrism, besides the catholic sympathy with which deep and wide knowledge can survey those ancient and noble phases of man's religious consciousness."[34] Tylor's scientific approach to culture was characterized by a method of comparative ethnology with a theoretical grounding in evolutionism. His primary goal was to place on a firm empirical footing a discipline that had hitherto stumbled in the quagmires of historical ignorance and theoretical inconsistency. Refuting the evidence for cultural degradation (that is, the process by which "civilized" cultures revert or fall into a "primitive" state), Tylor insists that, despite isolated instances of degradation, culture develops generally and inexorably toward higher forms of civilization:

The thesis which I venture to sustain, within limits, is simply this, that the savage state in some measure represents an early condition of mankind, out of which the higher culture has gradually been developed or evolved, by processes still in regular operation as of old, the result showing that, on the whole, progress has far prevailed over relapse.[35]

A progressive, evolutionary model of cultural development can be established, Tylor argues, only by careful observation of native customs, practices, beliefs, and ceremonies and by equally careful extrapolation from archaeological research. The insistence on the localization of cultural phenomena is a refutation of the idea that innovations in primitive societies, when evidence for evolution or diffusion are absent, can be explained as instinctual or innate elements of human nature, what Tylor calls "transcendental wisdom." Rather, ethnographic evidence consistently points to the existence of "rude shrewd sense taking up the facts of common life and shaping from them schemes of primitive philosophy."[36]

Tylor's influence on the early development of modern anthropology was enormous. Perhaps his most significant contribution was the definition of culture that he offered in the first sentence of *Primitive Culture*: "Culture or Civilization, taken in its wide ethnographic sense, is that complex whole which includes knowledge, belief, art, morals, law, custom, and any other capabilities and habits acquired by man as a member of society."[37] The elucidation of this "complex whole" became the principal activity of anthropologists and ethnographers who approached the project of cultural analysis with a wide array of methods and techniques. Franz Boas, for example, rejecting the evolutionism and diffusionism of Tylor and his immediate successors, put forward a theory of the "culture concept" which argued for a plurality of cultures, each of which was historically determined. For Boas, different civilizations had their own developmental histories, and he thus formulated a method in which localized knowledge was analyzed in historical contexts.[38] The "history of the fleeting moment" that for Lévi-Strauss constitutes an important part of Boas's contribution to anthropology,[39] underscores the near-impossibility of arriving at anything like a definitive historical account of cultures without reliable historical records. As Radcliffe-Brown writes, referring to the period 1908–9, "ethnologists were mostly thinking in terms of origins and history," and he began his study of the Andaman Islanders with a view toward making "a hypothetical reconstruction of the history of the

Andamans and the Negritos in general." However, during the course of his work, Radcliffe-Brown discovered that "a systematic examination of the methods available for such reconstructions of the unknown past convinced me that it is only in extremely rare instances that we can ever approach demonstrable conclusions and that speculative history cannot give us results of any real importance for the understanding of human life and culture."[40]

A quite different development takes place in enterprises like the British Association's Ethnographic Survey of the British Isles, which began work in the early 1890s. Headed by A. C. Haddon, the Association's ethnographers employed anthropometric instruments in order to measure cranial size, "nigrescence" and other physical characteristics of peasants in the West of Ireland. Though rigorously empirical and objective, the anthropometric method could lead the ethnographer into comical situations that underscored the extent to which the psychological and sociological elements of native cultures were ignored or deemed irrelevant. In his *Study of Man*, Haddon quotes John Beddoe to illustrate some of the difficulties of fieldwork. Beddoe, after noting "the necessity and frequent difficulty of obtaining the consent of the owner of the head to be examined" (and this with the textual equivalent of a straight face), goes on to detail some of the ruses by which he got "unsuspecting Irishman" to submit to having their head-measurements taken.[41] Though toler-antly indulged by the ethnographer, the behavior of the Irish subjects was regarded as little more than the expected reaction of a simple, primitive people; no attempt was made to understand the social psychology of the Irish subjects' reactions to subterfuge. I will discuss Haddon's scientific ethnography at greater length in chapter three of this study, but suffice it to say at this point that his methodology, and that of others of the Cambridge school, like W. H. R. Rivers and C. G. Seligman, in part because of its origin in the natural sciences, led to the development of a realistic style. This would become the "dominant mode of ethnographic prose," a mode that Stephen Tyler refers to contemptuously as the "easy realism of natural history," which is finally illusory because it promotes "the absurdity of 'describing' nonentities such as 'culture' or 'society' as if they were fully observable, though somewhat ungainly, bugs" and "the equally ridiculous behaviorist pretense of 'describing' repetitive patterns of action in isolation from the discourse that actors use in constituting and situating their action."[42] And, while there is some truth to

Tyler's claim about the self-assurance of ethnographers with respect to the realistic mode of representation, their methods of description are not as bound to naturalistic procedures as he makes them out to be – and this is due primarily to the development of a functional method that takes human psychology, especially insofar as it is manifested in social psychological behaviors, into account.

Radcliffe-Brown, a student of Haddon and Rivers, was one of the first to embrace what would become known as the functionalist method and to recognize the importance of social psychology and of the interpretation of social customs, rituals and myths. He was interested primarily in "social functions," which "denote the effects of an institution (custom or belief) in so far as they concern the society and its solidarity or cohesion." His analysis of the "ceremonial customs" of the Andaman Islanders revealed that their specific social function was "to maintain and to transmit from one generation to another the emotional dispositions on which the society (as it is constituted) depends for its existence."[43] Only through intensive fieldwork can the ethnologist arrive at correct interpretations of such customs:

> Living, as he must, in daily contact with the people he is studying, the field ethnologist comes gradually to "understand" them, if we may use the term. He acquires a series of multitudinous impressions, each slight and often vague, that guide him in his dealings with them. The better the observer the more accurate will be his general impression of the mental peculiarities of the race.[44]

As will become evident below, Radcliffe-Brown's description of the field ethnologist and his understanding of social function served as a foundation and point of departure for the work of Malinowski, whose functionalist method, empirical and ahistorical, emerged in the 1920s and became the dominant mode of field-ethnography – a mode which enabled the exploration of social institutions and the "mental peculiarities" of natives as well as the development of totalizing, synthetic representations of native cultures created through the careful employment of scientific methods for the collection, translation, and analysis of ethnographic data.

The desire for a "complex whole" that subtends Tylor's famous definition of culture remained a constant in anthropology, though Malinowski's functional method redefined the ways anthropologists conceived of cultural totalities. "Functional anthropology," he writes, holds "that the cultural process is subject to laws and that the

laws are to be found in the function of the real elements of culture."
These elements are "institutions, customs, implements and ideas."[45]
The conception of culture that emerges from functional anthropology is based not on any historical understanding but on the
observation of these elements and the behaviors associated with
them: "Culture is then essentially an instrumental reality which has
come into existence to satisfy the needs of man in a manner far
surpassing any direct adaptation to the environment."[46] For
Malinowski, culture is concerned primarily with secondary or
derived needs, which constitute extensions of primary physiological
needs (shelter, food, procreation); institutions develop in order to
fulfill these derived needs and make up the "complex, many-
dimensional medium of cultural interests" that is the object of
ethnographic analysis.[47] It is out of this medium that the functional
anthropologist constitutes, through scientific observation of empirical phenomena, the totality of culture.

The functional method, as it is enunciated in and exemplified by
Malinowski's *Argonauts of the Western Pacific*, involves the analysis not
only of easily observable phenomena associated with social institutions, but also of those aspects of native culture that Malinowski calls
"*the inponderabilia of actual life*," a category that includes all manner of
routine, mundane details, conversational tones and affective displays:
"the subtle yet unmistakable manner in which personal vanities and
ambitions are reflected in the behaviour of the individual and in the
emotional reactions of those who surround him." These inponderabilia are accessible for scientific formulation and documentation,
but not by means of any "superficial registration of detail," nor "by
questioning or computing documents, but have to be observed in
their full actuality." The ethnographer must make "an effort at
penetrating the mental attitude expressed in them."[48] The functional analysis of social institutions like the ceremonial Kula exchange lays bare the structure of the institution as well as the
constellation of attitudes, behaviors, and relationships that the Kula
calls forth and organizes. The ethnographer "has to study the
behaviour of the native, to talk with him under all sorts of conditions,
and to write down his words. And then, from all these diverse data,
to construct his synthesis, the picture of a community and of the
individuals in it."[49] Once the ethnographer has penetrated to the
depths of the native's mental attitudes, he then steps back and
"take[s] in the whole institution with one glance, let[s] it assume a

definite shape.''[50] Lévi-Strauss criticizes this position of authority and the general truths that the ethnographer intuits through a process of "inner meditation," arguing that the functionalist is disdainful of historical records or comparative studies with neighboring cultures because he does not want "to spoil the wonderful intuition" that enables him to grasp dubious "eternal truths" through "an abstract dialogue with his little tribe."[51]

But Malinowski believed that such comparative approaches detracted from the more important business of understanding a single society in the present. For him, a synthetic picture of a native culture can only be drawn from the perspective of the field-ethnographer who seeks through empirical observation and analysis to grasp the totality of behaviors, attitudes, and relationships that constitute the complex function of a social institution. In this regard, Malinowski's work is of signal importance, for it established the norm of intensive immersion in the field as the *sine qua non* of a scientific ethnography:

> What is then this ethnographer's magic, by which he is able to evoke the real spirit of the natives, the true picture of tribal life? As usual, success can only be obtained by a patient and systematic application of a number of rules of common sense and well-known scientific principles, and not by the discovery of any marvellous short-cut leading to the desired results without effort or trouble.[52]

The ethnographer's ability to draw "true pictures" of tribal life, to evoke the "real spirit" of natives, turns out to be not so very magical. The principles of scientific method to which Malinowski alludes were not clearly defined in the work of early ethnographers like Radcliffe-Brown, who readily admitted the limitations of an imperfect scientific method: "My failure fully to comprehend the Andamanese system was partly due to the difficulties of the language, in which I did not have time to become expert, and partly to the nature of the Andamanese terms, of which it is by no means easy to discover the meaning, even with careful observation."[53] Less then ten years later, Malinowski was able to establish quite precisely the goals of a scientific ethnography that could overcome these obstacles: first, the ethnographer "must possess real scientific aims, and know the values and criteria of modern ethnography"; second, he ought to "live without other white men, right among the natives"; and third, "he has to apply a number of special methods of collecting, manipulating and fixing his evidence."[54]

A corollary to the methodological assurance that the ethnographer carried into the field is a conviction that the natives themselves were incapable of producing a "true picture" of their own culture because they lacked the ability to theorize their own social existence. If a native were asked to give an overview of the structure of the Kula exchange, for example, he would give only his own subjective views. "Not even a partial coherent account could be obtained. For the integral picture does not exist in his mind; he is in it, and cannot see the whole from the outside." (To give him credit, Malinowski does suggest that the same could be said of "civilized" societies.) But it is not simply a matter of being inside the structure being analyzed, for the natives are, at bottom, incapable of "consistent theoretical statement."[55] If they could articulate the function of their own social institutions, if they "could furnish us with correct, explicit and consistent accounts of their tribal organization, customs and ideas, there would be no difficulty in ethnographic work."[56] Because the native lacked theoretical self-reflection, the ethnographer must set out to "grasp the native's point of view, his relation to life, to realise *his* vision of *his* world."[57]

But the norms of fieldwork embodied in Malinowski's *Argonauts of the Western Pacific* – the "scientific aim" of participant-observation, the selection and analysis of data governed by scientific principles, the use of native informants – are prey to internal contradictions that threaten not only the integrity of the norms themselves but the scientific nature of the results they are supposed to guarantee. These contradictions are rooted in the intersubjectivity that subtends the ethnographer's participation in cultural activities and the establishment of rapport with native informants; both activities create opportunities for identification, empathy, hostility, erotic desire, and a host of other x-factors that must be suppressed in order to achieve the unbiased and objective point of view of the scientific observer.

The precise nature of these contradictions becomes clear when we examine Malinowski's attitude toward his native subjects and the kind of representations he wished to make of them. On the one hand, the ethnographer's attempt to "grasp" the native's point of view is accompanied by a desire to represent more accurately the nature of the native's mental attitudes. In this way, science "kills" the false picture of natives that had emerged in previous anthropological work (Tylor, for example, referred to "primitive" peoples as "lower races"), offering for the first time a "true" representation: "The time when we could tolerate accounts presenting us the native as a distorted, childish caricature of a human being [is] gone."[58] We may quarrel with Malinowski's assertion that he offers a "true picture," but we sense that the attempt has at least brought him closer to an understanding of the concrete social reality of native peoples and of the value of that reality. On the other hand, this picture, even as it corrects invidious notions of native psychology and social life, appears at the same time to mark a kind of regression. To be sure, Malinowski's discovery of a "primitive knowledge of an essentially scientific character"[59] – which reminds us of Tylor's discovery that the "savage" possesses a "rude shrewd sense" that "tak[es] up the facts of common life and shap[es] from them schemes of primitive philosophy"[60] – suggests an enlightened attitude toward primitive peoples. However, Malinowski's claim that certain "queer and sordid customs" have "a core of rational and practical principle" strikes Lévi-Strauss as a "return to the eighteenth century, but to its worst aspect."[61] Presumably that aspect is the idealization of native peoples as "noble savages," projections of Western nostalgia for simplicity, sincerity and "naturalness." What Lévi-Strauss could not have known when he wrote these words was the quite different picture, in *A Diary in the Strict Sense of the Term*, of Malinowski's ambivalent, often violent attitude toward the natives: at times, "the *niggers* don't exist," while at other times, the ethnographer feels a petulant, murderous rage toward them: "The natives still irritate me, particularly Ginger, whom I could willingly beat to death. I understand all the *German and Belgian colonial atrocities*."[62] (We hear in this second remark an echo of Malinowski's incessant novel reading, specifically Joseph Conrad's *Heart of Darkness*.[63])

As these remarks clearly indicate, Malinowski had mixed feelings about his motives for pursing ethnographic inquiry. However, I do not think this ambivalence arose from any serious doubt as to the scientific validity of ethnography; rather, it seems to have arisen as the effect of psychological conflicts, often articulated in terms of nearly uncontrollable sexual longing, that undermined his concentration: "I am strong enough physically to overcome my lack of concentration and control states of mind I don't approve of."[64] "[P]otential lechery" and "chasing skirts" are consistently linked, in the *Diary*, with his incessant novel reading, and the combination throws him into a "Dostoevskian state" which is alleviated only by reminders of the importance of "eliminat[ing] *elements of worry out of*

my work. To have a feeling *of the ultimate mastery of things.*"[65] This
mastery over his work is something the ethnographer gains by an
appeal to disciplinary authority: "I *should* read ethnographic
works."[66] But *A Diary* reveals a more troubling "element of worry,"
for the sexual longing Malinowski feels for his fiancée and the
fantasies he has about native women become inextricably associated
with his ethnographic work, a psychic reality that is condensed, like
the language of a dream, into the repeated image of mosquito
netting, which serves as a metonymy for the ethnographer's
isolation in the field. In one particularly evocative example, Malinowski writes of the intense longing he feels for his fiancée: "I
missed her – I wanted to have her near me again. Visions of her
with her hair down. Does intense longing always lead to extremes?
Perhaps only under mosquito netting."[67] The implication here is
that the ethnographic situation fosters a state of psychological crisis
that would not exist if the ethnographer did not have to "live
without other white men, right among the natives." Perhaps the
inverse is also true, and the ethnographer cannot achieve the
scientific aims he sets for himself without the "Dostoevskian state"
that continually forces him to reexamine those aims and to clarify
how best to achieve them.

The ambivalence of the participant–observer, here interpreted in
terms of sexual longing and despair about getting his work done,
may be more than simply unavoidable; it may, in fact, be a crucial
determinate for productive anthropological work, but one that must
be suppressed in the interest of science. James Clifford has remarked
that the "ironic stance of participant observation" was rendered
normative and "scientific" by Malinowski: "By professionalizing
fieldwork anthropology transformed a widespread predicament into
a scientific method."[68] What I am suggesting is that this irony is
determined in large measure by the kinds of ambivalence associated
with psychological crises centering on sexual longing and a sense of
dissociation or dehiscence of the self. The "predicament" to which
Clifford refers could therefore be regarded as the inevitable bypro-
duct of a "modern" phase in the development of anthropology, a
phase which was ambivalently split between an impulse toward
modernization and one toward *modernism*. In a process of modernization, the empiricism of A. C. Haddon, which had been grounded in
the categories of the natural sciences, and the early efforts of people
like A. R. Radcliffe-Brown to formulate a functional method of

cultural analysis were refined into a principled scientific endeavor
with new techniques for the collection and analysis of data from the
field and new sociological categories for the interpretation of that
data. But new fieldwork techniques meant new kinds of relationships
with native subjects – relationships which were often complicated by
the long-term immersion now required of ethnographers – and new
categories meant that new kinds of data could now be considered,
for example *"the inponderabilia of actual life"* and the "mental attitudes" that so occupied Malinowski in *Argonauts*. Because we have
access to his field diary, we can see to what extent these new
relationships and new categories of data brought the ethnographer
perilously close to a modernist recognition of what Marlow, in *Heart
of Darkness*, calls his "distant kinship" with "savages." Consequently,
Malinowski feels a sense of estrangement from his own "kind" (a
feeling he records in his diary) and an ambivalent desire for
identification with his native subjects, which replicates similar
feelings of estrangement and similar desires just beginning to emerge
in Western modernist writing. The difference, of course, is that
Malinowski's modernist experience occurs under conditions that are
supposed to be governed by principles of scientific detachment,
conditions that ordinarily guaranteed the authority and stability of
his sovereign, autonomous selfhood.

In Malinowski's *Diary*, the tension between the *modernizing* impulse
of new ethnographic techniques and the *modernist* nature of the
ethnographer's relation to his informants comes into sharp relief and
reveals one of the facets of his work that is quintessentially modernist:
the idea that alienation and dissociation are the conditions of
modernity and that these "inauthentic" conditions can be overcome
by an appeal to the authenticity of the "primitive." As the chapters
that follow will demonstrate, this appeal is a common enough strategy
for Celtic Revivalists. Like the ethnographic participant–observer,
the Revivalists felt acutely their ambiguous and ambivalent position
between the primitive and the civilized, between the colonizer and
the colonized. Where the Revivalists differ from Malinowski, and
from ethnographers in general, is in their capacity to explore the
critical potential of *in*authentic representations in the ongoing
struggle for national self-determination and self-identification.

A modernist vision of the primitive suffuses both *Argonauts* and *A
Diary*. The motif of lost innocence, of *tristes tropiques*, recurs in the
many allusions to the "olden days" when tribal life was more

intensely ritualized and dangerous. "Much of native belief and custom has been undermined," Malinowski writes, by the "wanton interference" of Westerners whose "narrow-minded application of our sense of morality and propriety" has "cut the taproot of [the native's] vitality."[69] It is unclear whether the ethnographer regards his own work as part of this interference. For, despite his claim that the time was gone when anthropologists could create a "childish caricature of a human being" and pass it off as credible science, despite his claim to be offering instead of this caricature a "true picture," the evidence of *Argonauts* suggests that Malinowski's "true" representations of the pure primitiveness of Trobriand society were strongly determined by literary techniques and desires. "This island," Malinowski writes in *A Diary*, "though not 'discovered' by me, is for the first time experienced artistically and mastered intellectually."[70] The ethnographer's artistic experience of the Trobriands is plainly evident in a number of ways in *Argonauts*. To begin with, there is the arrival scene, narrated in a manner that points up its imaginary character: "Imagine yourself suddenly set down surrounded by all your gear, alone on a tropical beach close to a native village, while the launch or dinghy which has brought you sails away out of sight."[71] Malinowski returns to this motif of an "imaginary first visit"[72] several times in the first fifty pages, and we are strongly impressed not simply with the literary manner of its presentation but the admission, not to be mentioned again, of the ethnographer's vulnerability in this strange place that he can conjure only by inviting his reader to imagine it. Thus he speaks of a "feeling of hopelessness and despair" attendant upon his failure to come "into real touch with the natives." He mentions periods of "despondency, when [he] buried [him]self in the reading of novels, as a man might take to drink in a fit of tropical depression and boredom."[73]

It is significant that these preliminary admissions are folded into an "imaginary" narrative, ultimately to be negated by the discovery, within a page or two, of "the secret of effective field-work."[74] Indeed, throughout the rest of the text, there is no attempt to separate the "imaginary" element of his experience from that which is properly scientific. Thus Malinowski's frequent references to the picturesque aspect of the islands and the importance of making his impressions of them striking for the reader are part and parcel of a "scientific" account. Here we see a strategy that characterizes

Synge's representations of the Aran Islands, for at the same time that Malinowski vouches for the accuracy of every detail in his descriptions of the Kula districts, he asserts that his descriptions "have been given with a few light touches in order to produce a vivid and so-to-speak personal impression of the various type of natives, and countries and of cultures."[75] Clifford Geertz's remarks about Malinowski's "literary" impulse are relevant here:

Malinowski reports having recourse to Wells, Shaw, Stevenson, Swinburne, Brontë, Hardy, Thackeray, Kipling, Conrad and Conan Doyle, amongst others, whilst in the field – even as he kept promising himself he would not – as vital counterweights to the "the wretchedness of life" being "imprisoned" on the Trobriand Islands. Meanwhile, his own published writing has been likened by [James] Clifford to that of Zola, both being "naturalists," intent on heightening the facts they were reporting by adding "atmosphere."[76]

This "heightening" of the facts to which Geertz refers is rather subdued in *Argonauts*, but the ethnographer's intentions, as they are recorded in *A Diary*, suggest that he perceived his role in terms of the "psychic heroism" Yeats celebrated in Synge's sojourns on Aran. Speaking of his intention to impress his fiancée, Malinowski writes of, "Desire for heroic, dramatic experiences, so I can tell her about them."[77] But later he will admonish himself, denying his desire for heroism even as he recasts the imperative to work – "My main task now must be: work. *Ergo*: work!"[78] – in terms of a playful, well-nigh spiritual "plunge": "*Work easily, without effort and heroism. Work ought to be for you a matter of course and a matter of play. You ought to love to see your papers round you, plunging into the depths of work.*"[79] Malinowski's scientific motivations are often imbued with a kind of spiritual fervor, a compulsion "to plunge my spirit into reality. Something greater than curiosity and more essential than thought."[80]

Connected to this compulsion and to a general modernist impulse toward self-reflection and self-reflexiveness is Malinowski's interest in the "mental attitudes" of natives, which, as I have indicated above, is directly addressed in *Argonauts*.[81] More pertinent for an understanding of the Celtic Revival's projects of cultural redemption is the expression of this interest in *A Diary*, where the participant–observer manifests the kind of inner divisions and conflicts that characterize the modernist sensibility in literature, and does so in terms of a discourse of primitivism that is deployed simultaneously as a scientific means of understanding a native culture and as a means for working through a psycho-sexual crisis. Malinowski asserts that his diary is a mode of "self-criticism" and "self-analysis" and that it enables him to record "changes in life's course, *readjustment of values*," the ongoing "conversation with oneself."[82] And, while many of the reflections he records in his diary are personal, a good deal of them refer to his ethnographic work, a habit he regrets does not characterize the English.[83]

In the self-analytical mode of the *Diary*, Malinowski reflects on his alienation from the culture in which he does his work and his dissociation from any sense of a coherent, stable selfhood. Over against what he *should* feel – "I should clearly and distinctly feel *myself*, apart from the present conditions of my life, which in themselves are nothing to me" – he finds himself feeling instead a sense of "imprisonment in existence symbolized by the island," which ethnographic work does little to ameliorate besides offering an opportunity "to run away from oneself."[84] One solution, which confronts the ethnographer with an insuperable dilemma, is to identify with the Other, to find in the Other's experience something of his own essence: "What is the deepest essence of my investigations? To discover what are his [the native's] main passions, the motives for his conduct, his aims . . . His essential, deepest way of thinking. At this point we are confronted with our own problems: What is essential in ourselves?"[85] As we will see in my discussion of Yeats and Synge, this desire for what is essential about oneself, mediated through an ethnographic inquiry into primitive "passions," governs the expression of modernist concerns for the nature and stability of the self. The difference, of course, is that, whereas Malinowski contains this expression in a private diary, the Revivalist could incorporate transgressive expressiveness as *autoethnography*, a form of transculturation "in which colonized subjects undertake to represent themselves in ways that *engage with* the colonizer's own terms . . . in response to or in dialogue with . . . metropolitan representations."[86] (I will return to this alternative in my discussion of Synge in chapter 3.) This is not to say that Malinowski completely suppresses his realization of the intersubjective relations of native and ethnographer; but it is the case that, when he does allow for such relations in his ethnographic and theoretical works, he does so in order to alert ethnographers to the necessity of restricting oneself to *behaviors*, to that which can be observed. "It remains true, however," he has to admit, "that in current and intuitive practice we react and respond to the behavior of others through the mechanism of our own introspection."[87]

It is in *A Diary* that this mechanism of introspection is allowed full sway over the ethnographer's attitudes and the results are, as we have already seen, sometimes shocking. I want to conclude this discussion of Malinowski's texts by returning to the persistence of "lecherous thoughts" in order to underscore the way identification with native "passions" slides into a desire for erotic possession that parallels similar strategies in Revivalist practice, especially in Synge's and Joyce's exploitation of the erotic and voyeuristic aspects of participant observation. The basis for this mode of desiring the Other is a psychological state of perpetual crisis: "Yesterday during the afternoon I tried to understand my *Stimmung* and to analyze *in flagrante* my psychological state during my *feverishness*; naturally, emptiness and sluggishness, weak grasp of reality; shallow associations or absence of thoughts; total absence of metaphysical states."[88] It is hard to tell if Malinowski refers to physical illness here (he is constantly medicating himself against a hostile environment) or to the frenzy of anxiety over his "lecherous thoughts," since both tend to have the same debilitating, self-lacerating effect. Thus when the noises of his surroundings "get horribly on [his] nerves," Malinowski notices that "[t]he moral tonus" lowers and he experiences "[e]motional bluntness":

Resistance to lecherous thoughts weaker. Clarity of metaphysical conceptions of the world completely dimmed: I cannot endure being with myself, my thoughts pull me down to the surface of the world. I am unable to control things or to be creative in relation to the world. Tendency to read *rubbish*.[89]

Elsewhere, as I have noted above, Malinowski regards this tendency for his thoughts to be pulled down to earth as a compulsion "to plunge my spirit into reality. Something greater than curiosity and more essential than thought."[90] But this more positive evaluation of his desire to merge with the world occurs only when he feels most self-assured, most capable of possessing "the sea and the stars and the universe."[91] More often, he finds himself longing to *be* the native Other in order to assuage his feelings of alienation and dissociation through sexual possession. Thus, when he sees "a pretty, finely built girl" walking ahead of him, he muses on "her figure, her legs, and the beauty of the body so hidden to us, whites" and then confesses:

"At moments I was sorry I was not a savage and could not possess this pretty girl."[92]

Malinowski's desire to express the truth of a primitive society and thereby to redeem it from "interference," one of the express goals of *The Argonauts of the Western Pacific*, contrasts dramatically with his desire for the Other, his sexual longing and self-lacerations, his perhaps unconscious need for a psychological feverishness that will prod him into productive labor, all of which find expression in *A Diary in the Strict of the Term*. As I have argued in the previous section, Malinowski's experience, as it is recorded in both *Argonauts* and *A Diary*, evinces an essentially modernist sensibility, not unlike that of T. S. Eliot, whose interest in comparative anthropology and the primitivism of Lucien Lévy-Bruhl reveals an underlying affinity between anthropology and modernism.[93] But the anthropological modernism of the Celtic Revival bears only a passing resemblance to the modernism of Eliot and others, like E. M. Forster and Conrad, who were interested in "primitive" non-Western people and societies. The point I want to emphasize here is not that a literary impulse in Malinowski's work links it to modernism; but rather that the necessity for that impulse emerged out of a conflict between a civilized observer and a primitive society, a conflict which we find in no European modernist context save that of the Anglo-Irish Revivalists, for colonial and anthropological interventions in Ireland created entirely different social conditions from those found in New York, Paris, or London. This is especially true for Yeats and Synge, for, by approximating (when they were not duplicating) the subject-position of the participant–observer, they tended to embrace not only the norms, but also the contradictions of ethnographic inquiry, exploiting them (if not always consciously or systematically) in their analysis of a traditional society in which they felt they were a part and from which they felt they were excluded by virtue of their modernity. Insofar as they desired to redeem or represent a primitive Catholic-Irish peasantry, Yeats and Synge mapped the anomie and deracination of their own subject-position onto that of the participant–observer. It is for this reason that we might take Malinowski rather than, say, Eliot as a possible model for understanding the peculiar tensions and contradictions confronting Revivalism and Irish modernism.

In my discussion of Malinowski, I have emphasized certain

psychic displacements characteristic of modernism that arise earlier and more acutely in a colonial Irish than in a metropolitan context. In view of Terry Eagleton's thesis that Ireland's colonial status, together with its strong traditional social organization, created ideal conditions for the formation of a *conservative* modernist sensibility, the role of anthropology in the Celtic Revival becomes pivotal, since both sought to conserve the pristine social conditions of primitive societies and both had to contend with the tensions and contradictions that arise when a traditional culture comes into contact with a modern – that is to say, *civilized* – observer. This is certainly the case in Synge's ethnographic account of the Aran Islands and Yeats's folklore collections and folkloric fictions, for both Yeats and Synge presupposed certain key elements of anthropological theory having to do with primitive cultures and employed, however inconsistently or even unwittingly, techniques of participant observation. But other features of modernism, specifically narrative self-reflexivity and plurivocality, are less evident in early Revivalist writing, in part because of the conservative tendency of Anglo-Irish literary production. When we do see these features – for example, in Synge's "exaggerated" realism and in Joyce's experiments in style and point of view – they signal a commitment less to an ethnographic imagination than to a critique of that mode of imagining. Joyce's work (and, to a lesser extent, Synge's) serves as a salutary self-criticism of the Revival's reliance on a redemptive discourse that purports to offer a pro-nationalist representation of traditional Irish culture, while at the same time it assimilates that culture into an essentially anthropological frame of reference. The chief difference between the participant observer and Revivalists like Synge and Joyce with regard to self-reflexivity and narrative plurivocality lies in the fact that the former must repress the desire for subjective response and "counter-narratives" in the production of a primary, authoritative ethnographic text (relegating the expression of such desires, when they arise, to unofficial or private texts), while the latter is free to incorporate such desires into a primary text, having no disciplinary pressures to suppress subjective responses or the fragmentation and multiplication of narrative perspective.

In fine, then, the importance of ethnographic participant observation as a paradigm for understanding the anthropological modernism of the Celtic Revival is two-fold: on one level, it helps us to understand more clearly the ambivalent social position of Anglo-

Irish Revivalists pursuing a project of cultural redemption; on another level, it allows us to see how Revivalism, precisely because it lacked disciplinary constraints, was able to resolve the problems such a project entails in a way that guaranteed the Revival's continued participation in the debates on Irish national self-determination. The resolution of these problems, however, entailed a recognition that representations of the Irish peasantry, whether they emerge out of Revivalist, colonialist, anthropological, or nationalist contexts, are ultimately more or less critical anthropological fictions.

I want to conclude this introduction by sketching briefly the perspective of what is now called "new" or "revisionist" anthropology and suggest how this perspective can further an analysis of the anthropological modernism of the Celtic Revival. One of the most important issues to emerge from this revisionist orientation – one that, not incidentally, refocused attention on the colonial dynamics of anthropology – was the problem of intersubjectivity, specifically of the ambivalent and often contested rapport between Western ethnographers and native subjects. The impression we get throughout Malinowski's *Argonauts* and in his theoretical writings is that the ethnographer's authority stems primarily from his being in the field, directly observing social and cultural phenomena; thus, his scientific account reflects no "empty programme" but rather "the result[s] of personal experience."[94] James Clifford, like other revisionist ethnographers, envisions a mode of ethnographic authority that would deconstruct the sovereign Western observer's personal experience in the interplay of multiple and divergent voices. The ambivalence of the participant–observer's position with respect to the native society he or she observes is given a new, more positive value based on its ability to expand the theoretical and methodological limits of anthropology and to enable a movement *between* cultures. In this way, ethnography can "survey the full range of human diversity or development" and embrace a state of perpetual displacement, "a form both of dwelling and of travel in a world where the two experiences are less and less distinct."[95] Rather than see ambivalence and dialogic interplay as weakening ethnographic authority, revisionist ethnographers tend to regard them as new modes of authority that rupture and destabilize traditional balances of power in which the fieldworker represents a native society in a discourse foreign to its members.[96]

The influence of literary and critical theory in this revisionist trend has been a cause of some alarm for some anthropologists.

Francesco Loriggio regards this influence as a kind of "disciplinary reciprocity" that "'produces' self-reflexivity or the recovery of tradition [and] enhances the value of an approach routed through anthropology or literature."[97] Sensing the resistance to such influences, David Chioni Moore has urged anthropology to cease worrying about incursions at its borders: "The main point is, finally, that anthropology should stop worrying about metaphysical foundations (or lack thereof) and should learn to love interpretation, at least in theory, because that's all there ever is, and it's not such a bad thing at that."[98] However, a good deal of revisionist work, no matter how useful heuristically for puzzling over problems of textual production in anthropology, tends to remain frustratingly rhetorical and impractical. For example, Stephen Tyler, a self-proclaimed post-modernist ethnographer, rejects "the ideology of 'observer-observed,' there being nothing observed and no one who is observer";[99] but elsewhere he notes that in participant observation the "absence of dialogue signifies the subordination of participating to observing and the use of participation as a deception, as a means of establishing a position from which to observe."[100] It would seem that the categories of observer/observed are simply too persistent to be deconstructed out of existence. And the alternative – "a polyphonic text, none of whose participants would have the final word in the form of a framing story or encompassing synthesis"[101] – does not sufficiently acknowledge that deconstructionist strategies to avoid the ontological and epistemological certainties of anthropology entail the use of what many postcolonial theorists and revisionist ethnographers now recognize as classically Western models of language and discourse.[102] Kamala Visweswaran admits as much when she argues that, while "[d]econstructive ethnography attempts to disrupt [the] process of identification, often through recourse to a fractured, multiply positioned subject," while it seeks "to abandon or forfeit its authority," it must acknowledge in the end "that it is impossible to do so."[103]

According to Edward Said, it is precisely the "problematic of the observer" that remains "underanalyzed," even in revisionist anthropology.[104] Despite the theoretical gains made by "meta-anthropological scholars" like Clifford, Said still discerns "a genuine malaise about the sociopolitical status of anthropology as a whole," an unwillingness, as he puts it, to "explicitly call[] for an end to anthropology."[105] By refusing this call, Said argues, revisionist anthropology refuses history, for it cannot see (or will not take seriously) that the origin of the crisis in anthropology is precisely the crisis of decolonization, when imperial styles and genres are appropriated and transformed by native intellectuals striving, against colonialist misrepresentations, for new modes of expression. One of the reasons for this refusal, which frustrates any sustained and principled critical analysis of either anthropology or imperialism, is "the constitutive role of the observer, the ethnographic 'I' or subject, whose status, field of activity, and moving *locus* taken together abut with embarrassing strictness on the imperial relationship itself."[106]

At the same time that he indicts revisionist anthropology for its failure to address the ideological implications of ethnographic observation, Said stresses the importance of "emergent" or "indigenous" ethnographers. He argues that native intellectuals, especially when they turn their efforts to anthropology, address the political implications of anthropology directly but are often ignored by Western specialists who may perceive (correctly) that a "native point of view" would be hostile to their own traditional methods:

The native point of view, despite the way it has often been portrayed, is not an ethnographic fact only, is not a hermeneutical construct primarily or even principally; it is in large measure a continuing, protracted, and sustained adversarial resistance to the discipline and the praxis of anthropology (as representative of "outside" power) itself, anthropology not as textuality but as an often direct agent of political dominance.[107]

Said's adversarial nativism, critical of anthropology on the basis of its unexamined affiliations with imperialism, suggests the near inevitability of a constitutive struggle between anthropology and its colonized "interlocutors."

Especially relevant for the present study is the emphasis on native intellectuals and their relations to nationalism – relations that can be defined as either complicity with or resistance to imperialist discourses. In his essay "Third World Intellectuals and Metropolitan Culture," Said addresses "the remarkable outpouring of literature and scholarship emanating from the postcolonial world" and focuses on a "fairly discrete aspect" of what he calls a "powerful impingement":

[T]hat is, the work of intellectuals from the colonial or peripheral regions of the world who wrote not in a native language but in an 'imperial' language, who felt themselves to be organically tied to a mass effort at resisting imperial rule, and who set themselves the specifically revisionist and critical task of dealing frontally with the hegemonic culture in new, radically provocative ways. These figures address the metropolis using the techniques, the discourses, the very weapons of scholarship and criticism once reserved exclusively for the European, now adapted either for insurgency or revisionism at the very heart of the Western center.[108]

It is this quality of an immanent critique that characterizes both revisionist anthropology and postcolonial theory.[109] Arising from this struggle is a new ethos of textual production in which knowledge hitherto suppressed or ignored – originating both in native cultures and in the culture of the ethnographer – is brought to light and articulated in a hybrid discourse. For revisionist ethnographers and postcolonial intellectuals alike, "writing culture" is not a process of discovering essences or universals, of tracking down origins; rather it is a process of cultural translation that produces "new originals" or, as Talal Asad puts it, "transformed instances of the original, not authoritative textual representations of it."[110]

Asad's distinction between transformative instant and representation indicates a common ground for revisionist anthropology and postcolonial theory, which has been especially prolific in developing non-mimetic models of anti-colonial discourse, the most influential of which is the mode of transformative instantiation called "restaging" or "colonial mimicry." Echoing Asad, Benita Parry argues that "when the scenario written by colonialism is given a performance by the native that estranges and undermines the colonialist script," the result is not "a copy of the colonialist original, but a qualitatively different thing-in-itself."[111] Homi Bhabha's conception of colonial mimicry seeks a similar kind of estrangement in which the dialectical relation of native to colonialist is destabilized, and difference is installed as the productive mark of native identity. For Bhabha, "colonial mimicry is the desire for a reformed, recognizable Other, *as a subject of a difference that is almost the same, but not quite.*" This "recognizable" Other, because it suggests the proximity of the Other to that which it is not, "poses an immanent threat to both 'normalized' knowledges and disciplinary powers."[112] The colonizer's uneasiness springs from the recognition that the colonized is not a being occupying a fixed position but rather a monstrous, unstable shifting potentiality – *almost the same, but not quite.*

It is important to note, however, that Bhabha's theory of colonial mimicry, like other similar theories, emerges out of a specific context (for Bhabha, British India) characterized by a Manichean structure of colonial domination; it is, in fact, as anyone can see from Bhabha's theoretical debt to Frantz Fanon, a theory of racial difference. As such, it has proven invaluable in the study of colonial situations where Western colonizers discriminate against and disavow subaltern races. Because a clear racial difference does not exist in Ireland, and because a Manichean structure is frustrated by the existence of an intermediate social group of Anglo-Irish Revivalists, theories like Bhabha's, even while they may be suggestive conceptually, have limited applicability. This is not to say that postcolonial theory has nothing to offer the student of the Celtic Revival; on the contrary, as critics like Declan Kiberd and David Lloyd have recently demonstrated, postcolonial critique can be quite useful in the analysis of modern and contemporary Irish culture. Since the texts I discuss in this study were produced in an era of decolonization – which, as Fanon writes, entails "a complete calling in question of the colonial situation," a revolutionary process that "transforms spectators crushed with their inessentiality into privileged actors, with the grandiose glare of history's floodlights upon them"[113] – the work of postcolonial theory may sometimes prove useful, particularly when the concepts and structures of power that such a theory criticizes exist in the Irish context. It is imperative, therefore, that the specific conditions of colonialism in Ireland, especially the unique role played by the Celtic Revival, always be kept in view. Thus sufficiently cautioned, it is possible to regard Revivalists like Yeats and Synge as harbingers of what Said calls the "revisionist postcolonial effort to reclaim traditions, histories, and cultures from imperialism," "to reclaim, rename, and reinhabit the land."[114] But this reclamation, as Said himself realizes, is always complicated by the kind of social and political ambiguities that bedevil Anglo-Irish intellectuals like Yeats, whose "loyalties were confused, to put it mildly, if not in his case quite contradictory." He concludes, however, by reminding us of the revolutionary potential of Yeats's "confused loyalties" and his manipulation of Catholic-Irish culture: "Because Yeats's Ireland was a revolutionary country, he could use its backwardness as a source for a radically disturbing, disruptive return to spiritual ideals lost in an overdeveloped modern Europe" – a return that "underline[s] the colonial predicament . . . of a culture indebted to the mother country for its own self and for a sense of 'Englishness' and yet turning toward the colony."[115]

Frantz Fanon is often adduced in discussions of the revolutionary potential of Irish writing. Especially pertinent is his description of the development of the native intellectual. In the first of three phases, he "gives proof that he has assimilated the culture of the occupying power." In the second phase, "[p]ast happenings of the bygone days of his childhood will be brought up out of the depths of his memory; old legends will be reinterpreted in the light of a borrowed aestheticism and of a conception of the world which was discovered under other skies." In the third phase, the native intellectual produces a "a fighting literature, a revolutionary literature, and a national literature"; "[i]nstead of according the people's lethargy an honoured place in [their] esteem," they turn themselves into "awakener[s] of the people," "introducing into their readers' or hearers' consciousness the terrible ferment of subversion."[116] Fanon's emphasis on revivalism, specifically on a "borrowed aestheticism" that has the potential of furthering revolutionary aims, has clear relevance in the Irish situation.

What the Celtic Revivalists reveal in their complicit relationship with anthropology is a quintessentially modernist dilemma – the gap between experience and its representation – which in an Irish context takes on a conservative character that threatens to transform the revolutionary energies of the Revival into a reactionary nostalgia for "archaic," pre-colonial origins. There is, therefore, always the danger described by Fanon that the native intellectual will "fail[] to realize that he is utilizing techniques and language which are borrowed from the stranger in his country" and will "content[] himself with stamping these instruments with a hallmark which he wishes to be national, but which is strangely reminiscent of exoticism. The native intellectual who comes back to his people by way of cultural achievements behaves in fact like a foreigner."[117] I submit that Revivalism manages, at considerable pains and by no means completely, to skirt this danger of exoticism when it redeploys the techniques and strategies of anthropology, folklore, and ethnography in order to collect, translate, preserve, and thereby redeem an indigenous Irish folk culture. I submit further that the Celtic Revivalists create a "contact zone" in which a traditional or "archaic" folk culture enters into a productive and, at times, critical dialogue with the modernizing tendencies of anthropology. It is this capacity for productive, critical dialogue that constitutes the foundations of an anthropologically inflected and singularly Irish modernism.

Each of the chapters in *Modernism and the Celtic Revival* explores a different manifestation of this engagement and the ways in which it enables the creation or critique of Revivalist discourse. Chapter 2 is concerned chiefly with Yeats's early journalism, folklore compilations, and folkloric fictions, though a brief consideration of his later work (specifically, the poetry and the miscellany *On the Boiler*) will illustrate the shift from an ethnographic imagination that seeks "fair equivalents" for cultural essences to an imagination driven by the desire to reinstate the Anglo-Irish intellectual tradition as an authentically Irish one. Yeats's concern in the early work with creating a more inclusive notion of the Irish "race" is transformed into a new interest in eugenics that reflects his isolation from the confessional state that came into being in 1922.

Chapters 3 and 4 feature the work of Synge, which I believe to have been decisive in the development of the Revival and its strategies of cultural invention and redemption. In chapter 3, I examine Synge's *Aran Islands*, which develops the theme of "vanishing cultures" that resounds so pervasively in the modern era of ethnography. But, because it straddles the borderline between ethnography and autobiography, between scientific and imaginative representation, it is able to destabilize if not entirely to unseat the primitivism and racialism that authorized the kinds of ethnographies produced at the same time by such eminent anthropologists as A. C. Haddon. Chapter 4 is concerned with Synge's most famous play, *The Playboy of the Western World*, and the riots that followed its first performance in Dublin. In this chapter, I draw on the theory of social drama put forward by anthropologist Victor Turner to explore how *The Playboy* contributes to and complicates the debate among nationalist factions on the representation of national self-determination and national identities. For Synge's attempt to translate traditional folklore into stage drama altered the nature of the dialogue by suggesting that the crucial issue was not the *right* representation but rather the *right to represent*. His self-critical, anti-realistic style limned what we might call a "poetics of inauthenticity" that Joyce would elaborate throughout his career.

Chapters 5 and 6 explore the ways that this elaboration of a poetics of inauthenticity contributes to a critique of the Celtic Revival's ethnographic projects. Chapter 5 considers the development of Joyce's critique of Revivalism in *Dubliners* and *A Portrait of the Artist as Young Man*, focusing on the native intellectual who unwittingly accepts a primitivist discourse and thus unwittingly misrepresents his "own" culture. Though Joyce did not have to contend with the charges of elitism or irrelevance that were often lodged against Yeats and Synge, he recognized that his own position as a college-educated Catholic Dubliner put him at a considerable distance from rural Ireland. Stephen Dedalus's reaction to an old man from the West of Ireland eloquently captures the ambivalence that even Catholic intellectuals experienced: "I fear him. I fear his redrimmed horny eyes. It is with him I must struggle all through this night till day come, till he or I lie dead, gripping him by the sinewy throat till . . . Till what? Till he yield to me? No. I mean him no harm" (*P*, 252; Joyce's ellipsis). The dilemma Joyce faces in the early fiction is the inverse of that which confronted Yeats: the representation of an experience of *in*authenticity that turns out to be the only authentic representation that he can produce. Chapter 6 concentrates on *Ulysses*, beginning with an examination of Stephen's growing critical awareness of his own complicity in both primitivism and Revivalism. I then consider the figure of Leopold Bloom as an alternative, but not necessarily a privileged one, to the dead-end of Stephen's cynical rejection of nationalism. His flagrant and self-legitimizing ethnographic voyeurism leads to the production of anthropological fictions or private fantasies of Otherness; this productivity illustrates the persistence of anthropological categories and discourses about culture, and serves as another example of the paradoxical authenticity that Joyce derives by representing the experience of *in*authenticity. In *Ulysses*, Stephen's and Bloom's experiences together anatomize and parody the ambivalent positions of participant–observer and Anglo-Irish Revivalist.

By proffering a critique of the Celtic Revival, by exploring its ideological investments in anthropological discourses about an Other culture, Joyce's texts work out explicitly and coherently a tendency toward self-criticism that is implicit, inconsistent, and sometimes contradictory in Yeats and Synge. At the same time, they exemplify the further unfolding of a modernist impulse that is Irish in orientation and strongly committed to cultural self-analysis, an impulse that emerges out of the convergence of an "archaic" native culture and the "modern" technologies of anthropology. *Ulysses* proves especially significant, for it contextualizes Joyce's critique of the Revival's redemptive ethnographic imagination within the larger framework of a critique of realism and the Western novelistic tradition. But, far from signaling a break with the Celtic Revival,

Joyce's anthropological modernism constitutes something like the inevitable result of a movement whose chief concern was the "invention" of Ireland. The absence of any discussion of *Finnegans Wake* in this study might be understood as a kind of negative proof of this invention, for, while it incorporates elements of Irish folklore and mythology, its near-total rejection of traditional novelistic realism, and thus of the kind of discourse that characterizes much of traditional ethnographic writing, results in an authentically Irish text: hybrid, contestatory, shifting along the boundary between representation and performance. If, as I suggest in chapter 6, Joyce's critique of the Revival in *Ulysses* succeeds in fatally undermining the anthropological assumptions subtending it, then the *Wake* makes meaning in a space beyond ethnography and the desire for cultural redemption, a discursive space that achieves what revisionism could only theorize, a space where there is "nothing observed and no one who is observer."[118]

CHAPTER 2

"Fair Equivalents": Yeats, Revivalism, and the redemption of culture

> We may go mad some day,
> and the enemy root up
> our rose-garden and plant
> a cabbage-garden instead.   W. B. Yeats[1]

In recent years, Yeats studies have witnessed a turn toward the politics of cultural production that is neatly epitomized in the title of Ann Saddlemyer's selection of the letters of Yeats, John M. Synge, and Lady Augusta Gregory: *Theatre Business*. As these letters attest, the principal Revivalists, in addition to penning works of extraordinary literary merit, at the same time ran a complex and often volatile business. Adrian Frazier and R. F. Foster, among others, have filled in the historical context of these letters, establishing beyond reasonable doubt that Yeats was the prime mover (for good or ill) behind the scenes of the various incarnations of the Irish Literary Theatre. Especially important is Foster's *W. B. Yeats: A Life*, which plainly indicates the depth of Yeats's commitment to Revivalist ideas and strategies and his willingness to modify them, especially after the meteoric success and early death of Synge. A related trend is the analysis of Yeats's "political identities" and the complex relationship between Yeats and nationalism.[2] It is significant that critics now speak of multiple political identities, for one of the things that new historical criticism has yielded is a more refined sense of Yeats's nationalist affiliations and loyalties which were, as I have suggested in the introduction, complicated by his Anglo-Irish background.

What is not evident in this critical and historical discourse on Yeats's politics is a consideration of the role of anthropology in his conception of Revivalism. There are instances, in fact, when the absence of this consideration is unaccountable. What, for example, do we make of a book like Stephen Myers's *Yeats's Book of the Nineties: Poetry, Politics, and Rhetoric*, which fails to mention (or mentions in passing) Standish O'Grady, Douglas Hyde, Lady Gregory and John M. Synge, all active in the 1890s and all influential in developing Yeats's Revivalist attitudes toward Irish folk culture?[3] Marjorie Howes's recent study of Yeats and nationalism scarcely mentions the Revival, much less the anthropological discourses that underwrite it. Concentrating on the gender and class dynamics of "Yeats's nations," Howes's study exemplifies the kind of progressive, political critique that Elizabeth Cullingford inaugurated with *Yeats, Ireland and Fascism*. But Howes's emphasis on Arnoldean Celticism in her examination of Yeats's early career fails to take into consideration the broader anthropological context in which that career took shape, a context in which Yeats's attitudes toward Catholic Ireland and his place in it are determined by Revivalist historians like Standish O'Grady, advanced nationalists like John O'Leary, academicians like Eugene O'Curry, folklorists and collectors like Patrick Kennedy, T. Crofton Croker, Lady Gregory, and Sir William and Lady Wilde, and Gaelic Leaguers like Douglas Hyde.

One powerful motivation for Yeats's folklore compilations and other work of the 1890s is a desire to preserve and thereby redeem an authentic Irish folk culture. His interest in the purity and preeminence of a folk culture can be credited in large measure to a belief in the innate spiritualism and mysticism of the Irish peasantry and the reality of what anthropologist W. Y. Evans-Wentz calls fairy-faith, a living faith that "depends not so much upon ancient traditions, oral and recorded, as upon recent and contemporary psychical experiences, vouched for by many 'seers.' "[4] Yeats's interest in fairy-faith is to some extent the effect of a powerful nostalgia for folk traditions that, while not yet lost, were rapidly losing their power. As Douglas Hyde puts it, in a short essay included in Evans-Wentz's study, these traditions "certainly still exist, and can be found if you go to search for them; but they often exist almost as it were by sufferance, only in spots, and are ceasing to be any longer a power."[5] The nostalgia for tradition, for an authentic peasantry characterized by spiritualism and a strong fairy-faith led Yeats to adopt, in the folklore projects of the late 1880s and the 1890s, a form of redemptive ethnography that strove to salvage "lost" or "vanishing" cultures; this mode of redemption consigns such cultures to an "ethnographic present" that seeks to redeem it from time, from modernity and, ultimately, from itself.[6] James Clifford describes this temporal displacement as an allegory of salvage: "The real or genuine life of tribal works always precedes their collection, an act of salvage that repeats an all-too-familiar story of death and redemption. In this pervasive allegory the non-Western world is always vanishing and modernizing – as in Walter Benjamin's allegory of modernity, the tribal world is conceived as a ruin."[7] For Malinowski, this world, "broken by the interference of Government officials and the influence of Mission work," can be recovered only in a kind of fantasy fulfillment in which "visions of a primeval, happy, savage life [are] suddenly realised, even if only in a fleeting impression."[8] The reality of "tribal disintegration"[9] led ethnographers like Malinowski to reconstruct tribal societies through painstaking analysis of social functions and relationships, a practice that presupposes the necessity of their interventions. "The other society is weak and 'needs' to be represented," notes Clifford, and so the ethnographer becomes "the recorder and interpreter of fragile custom," the "custodian of an essence, unimpeachable witness to an authenticity."[10] This will sound familiar to anyone who has read the work of men like Sir Charles Gavan Duffy or Dr. George Sigerson, Young Irelanders who argued that the preservation of Irish culture, in appropriate textual forms, was needed to stave off metropolitan corruptions; it will sound familiar, too, to readers of Yeats's early essays, reviews, and letters, which called for preserving folk culture for future Irish artists. In 1888, Yeats wrote, in a letter to Katharine Tynan, that his folklore collecting was meant to lead primarily to the preservation of old texts for the future production of *new* ones: "You will have to read straight through my book of folk-lore. It was meant for Irish poets. They should draw on it for plots and atmosphere. You will find plenty of workable subjects" (*L*, 88).

Yeats's approach to the problems of cultural representation aligned him in significant ways with the discourses of Celticism that in other ways he explicitly rejected. It is one of the virtues of Howes's study that this ambivalent condition is put under critical pressure. Her conclusions are worth citing here: "Yeats's Celticism was complicit with and dependent upon imperialism in a general and very important sense. But the shape of that generally complicit relation changed over time, and different aspects of Yeats's Celtic writings offered different forms of repetition, appropriation and critique in relation to imperialism."[11] Howes credits Yeats with a degree of self-reflection that issues in a challenge, "however partial, ambivalent, and implicit," to "the period's equation of viable political nationality with masculinity."[12] To the extent that Howes's argument focuses on issues of gender, masculinity, and nationality, her remarks make a good deal of sense and in the main support my own conclusions about Yeats and the Celtic Revival. What is missing in her account, however, and in those of other recent critics of Yeats's Celticism, is an analysis of the ways in which strategies of "repetition, appropriation and critique" characterize an anthropological modernism that redefines the relationship between tradition and modernity, a relationship in which "[t]raditional culture provides modernism with an adversary, but also lends it some of the terms in which to inflect itself."[13]

This chapter will explore how Yeats's engagement with anthropological discourses enabled a strategic exploitation of ambivalence that resulted not in authoritative ethnographic accounts but rather in the production of a modern native literature grounded in a traditional folk culture. The idea of ambivalence found in the work of postcolonial theorists like Homi Bhabha – something liberating and revolutionary, a monstrous, unstable shifting potentiality: *almost the same, but not quite*[14] – might serve as a useful starting-point for a consideration of the kinds of complicity with imperialism (and here I would want to include anthropology) that Howes and others have recently brought to light. If Yeats's ambivalence is potentially progressive, then the resemblance between his methods in the early work – especially the folklore compilations and folkloric fictions collected in *The Celtic Twilight, The Secret Rose, Stories of Red Hanrahan* – and those of anthropologists and ethnographers, must be considered along with the fact that he wished to serve *nationalist* interests rather than the Empire, the university, or the vogue for things primitive. As for the vexed question of Yeats's later (re)turn to the Anglo-Irish class that bore the brunt of his Revivalist polemics, suffice it to say that after 1907, the year Synge's *The Playboy of the Western World* premiered, he began to turn his attention away from the Irish-speaking peasantry to a new "indigenous" group, the Anglo-Irish or, as Yeats put it in "Under Ben Bulben," the "[h]ard-riding country gentlemen" (*Poems*, 327).

Seamus Deane argues that Yeats invented an Ireland "amenable to his imagination" but found Ireland "in reality" to be recalcitrant to his imaginary construct.[15] Deane has reservations about Yeats's nationalist politics, but, like a lot of critics, he cannot resist praising him for seeing the necessity of a cultural nationalism that posits nationhood as primarily a fictive process – a process, in other words, of *writing*. Accordingly, he reads Yeats's Revivalist project not in terms of the culture it seeks to represent, but in terms of a text that does not purport to represent anything, indeed one that triumphs precisely in the *failure* of representation. Essentially opposed to this textualist interpretation but proceeding from the same notion of an invented or (to use Benedict Anderson's phrase) "imagined community," is Edward Said's estimation of Yeats as a "poet of decolonization": "Like all poets of decolonization," writes Said, "Yeats struggles to announce the contours of an 'imagined' or ideal community, crystallized not only by its sense of itself but also of its enemy."[16]

But to speak of writing or inventing culture is at some level to reintroduce one of the foundations of modern anthropology: a concept of culture that "covers" or explains observable facts about a given community. E. B. Tylor, in 1871, defined culture as a "complex whole which includes knowledge, belief, art, morals, law, custom, and any other capabilities and habits acquired by man as a member of society."[17] Modern anthropology began with this notion of culture and assumed that the multitudinous parts of a "complex whole" could be described and analyzed in a satisfactory way; definitive ethnographic descriptions of cultures could then be produced which would affirm and sustain the theories that gave them legitimacy. Of particular importance in late-nineteenth-century theories of culture was the concept of the primitive, which had outgrown its Romantic origins in Rousseau and been redefined in terms of a rigid binomial opposition of civilized and primitive races. As one of the foundational concepts in modern anthropology, this binomial opposition strongly determined the role of the ethnographic fieldworker – and this is true whether we are dealing with academic professionals like A. C. Haddon, A. R. Radcliffe-Brown, and Malinowski or Revivalist amateurs like Synge and Yeats, for each subscribed to some form of the belief that only the Western or "civilized" observer can speak for a primitive or "savage" native people. Deborah Fleming draws our attention to this essentially anthropological authority when she argues that Revivalists like Yeats and Synge "sought to speak for people other than themselves, to 'represent' them to the world, and to use them in order to establish a new national culture and an audience for themselves."[18]

Until the landmark work of Claude Lévi-Strauss (especially *La Pensée Sauvage*) and the rise of structuralist anthropology, the civilized/primitive distinction was largely grounded in certain inherent features (skin color and physiological difference) or sociological factors (drunkenness, laziness, criminality) the presence of which determined conclusively that a particular race was primitive. Said sums up the extensive "historical and cultural circumstances" in which this distinction emerged:

> One of them is the culturally sanctioned habit of deploying large generalizations by which reality is divided into various collectives: languages, races, types, colors, mentalities, each category being not so much a neutral designation as an evaluative interpretation. Underlying these categories is the rigidly binomial opposition of "ours" and "theirs," with the former always encroaching on the latter (even to the point of making "theirs" exclusively a function of "ours"). This opposition was reinforced by anthropology, linguistics, and history but also, of course, by the Darwinian theses on survival and natural selection, and – no less decisive – by the rhetoric of high cultural humanists.[19]

Said's *Orientalism* draws our attention to the diverse ways in which the binomial opposition primitive/civilized governs the representation of native peoples, and subsequent work on the subject tends to follow Said's lead. Marianna Torgovnick, for example, regards the "primitive" not as an objectively measurable category of human social organization, but rather as a *discourse*; the non-Western world is structured by images and ideas that form "the basic grammar and vocabulary of . . . primitivist discourse, a discourse fundamental to the Western sense of self and Other."[20] Johannes Fabian makes a similar point when he remarks that "[e]xotic otherness may be not so much the result as the prerequisite of anthropological inquiry": "We do not 'find' the savagery of the savage, or the primitivity of the primitive, we posit them, and we have seen in some detail how anthropology has managed to maintain distance, mostly by manipulating temporal coexistence through the denial of coevalness."[21] The main point here is that the discourse of the primitive posits an imaginary object defined by stereotypes of the sort on which armchair anthropologists relied. It is a short step from this constructionist view to one that would argue for a direct link between primitivism and the kind of mystical self-fashioning that Declan

Kiberd discovers in Yeats's work. Torgovnick's analysis heads in this direction when she notes that a tropological approach to the primitive often ends with Western observers "adopting the tropes in their perception of self" – in short, "[w]e imagine ourselves through the primitive."[22]

Of course, Yeats was not the only modernist to draw on a primitivist discourse. Marc Manganaro argues that in the work of T. S. Eliot there is a "less than relativistic attitude toward the 'primitive,'" which arises out of "an intellectual interest in the new fields of anthropology and sociology," particularly the work of Lucien Lévy-Bruhl.[23] According to Manganaro, Lévy-Bruhl's notion of the primitive individual as "prelogical" or "mystical" led Eliot to formulate a conception of the sacred grounded in the primitive:

Though it is an explicitly Christian concept, the *verbum infans*, a central figure in Eliot's poetry from 1918 to 1942, is itself the ultimate ineffable, the "word within a word, unable to speak a word," the *mana* (the "primitive" spiritual essence discussed by then-current anthropology) that, like the holy thunder discussed in numerous anthropological texts, is at the source of sacredness and thus inexpressible.[24]

Torgovnick advances a similar argument when she asserts that "primitive beliefs and social relationships" in modernist and contemporary discourse are often viewed as equivalent to the "oceanic," that is, "to a dissolution of boundaries between subject and object, between all conceived and conceivable polarities."[25] But Yeats differed from modernists like Eliot in two important respects: one, his interest in the notion of the primitive emerged in the late 1880s and 1890s, much earlier than Eliot's; and, two, directly related to this early emergence, his ambivalent social status as an Anglo-Irishman in colonial Ireland and his involvement in the cultural nationalism of the Revival meant that his relationship to the primitive was far more complicated than it was for a metropolitan modernist like Eliot.

Yeats did resemble Eliot, however, by taking a mystical view of the peasant, a view which he fashioned by "correcting" the conventional wisdom about the "Celtic race" popularized by Matthew Arnold. Yeats seemed instinctively to understand that his own ideas about the Irish primitive had to be defined more or less overtly against those of Arnold and Ernest Renan. In his influential essay "Poetry of the Celtic Races," published in 1859, Renan sought to give "a voice to races that are no more" and characterized the Celtic temperament as feminine, childlike, given to messianism and a "transparent" or "realistic naturalism" that was the sign of "the love of nature for herself, the vivid impression of her magic."[26] The Celtic race (and by this he means the Breton and Welsh perhaps more than the Irish) "is faithful to its conquerors when its conquerors are no longer faithful to themselves." Renan is sympathetic toward the Celtic races, claiming Breton ancestry himself, and he recognizes that "[p]oor Ireland . . . was not destined to find grace in the eyes of English puritanism."[27] It is perhaps an unintentional irony that this destiny was in part determined by the tactic of feminization that had the effect of marginalizing Celtic races with respect to the patriarchal puritanism of English imperialists.

Renan's text creates the kind of gendered colonial space that imperialism required in order to regulate and control a subaltern people. With Arnold, a further development of this strategy transforms Renan's portrait of a feminized race forsaken by its conquerors into an imperial allegory of paternal appropriation. But first Arnold has to establish that this feminine and forsaken race is worth appropriating. He takes Renan to task for his depiction of the Celt as timid, shy and delicate, arguing that "however well it may do for the Cymri [i.e., the Welsh and Breton], [it] will never do for the Gael, never do for the typical Irishman of Donnybrook Fair."[28] Even as he allows that the Irish possess certain "typical" qualities of energy, dynamism, and turbulence – qualities which justify including the Irish in an imperial collective – Arnold manages to qualify his enthusiasm for them by insisting that the "Celtic nature" is inherently "sentimental," for the Celt was always ready, as he put it in a phrase borrowed from Henri Martin, "to react against the despotism of fact."[29] By sentimental, Arnold means many things: a lively personality, a keen sensitivity, sociability, hospitality, eloquence, but most important, a desire "to aspire ardently after life, light, and emotion, to be expansive, adventurous, and gay."[30] It is this sentimental nature that he finds not only attractive but in some ways desirable as a quality that might augment the English character, already dominated by Teutonic materiality and political strength. By welcoming into the imperial fold a sentimental, politically emasculated subaltern race, Arnold's conception of a Celtic/English hybrid invites comparisons with the kind of marital union Howes describes:

a happy patriarchal marriage between the feminine and attractive but inferior Celt and the masculine and superior Saxon, whose domination was natural and inevitable but whose own existence would be enriched by a feminine influence . . . The Celt alone was a specimen of maimed masculinity, of illness and lack, while the Celt coupled with the Saxon could become the angel in the British house of empire, sweetening and completing it.[31]

The characterization of the Celt as feminized and politically impotent serves well Arnold's thesis that the "Celtic genius of Wales and Ireland" "cannot count appreciably now as a material power." Though Celtic power "once was everywhere," it is now gone; instead of exercising its will in the political arena, the Celt must be content with becoming an object of modern science: "What it *has* been, what it *has* done, let it ask us to attend to that, as a matter of science and history."[32]

In statements like these, Arnold implies that political impotence has reduced the Celtic people to the status of an anthropological curiosity; and this reduction in status could only have come about because of racial inferiority. As Vincent Pecora notes, Arnold's "pseudo-scientific ethnological categories" in *Celtic Literature*, "are at times not that far from those of Joseph Arthur de Gobineau," the influential nineteenth-century racial theorist.[33] It is an irony, which Yeats will reformulate, that racial difference is what allows Arnold to include the Celtic people in an imperial "family." Quite explicitly, Arnold seeks to encourage the Celtic people to accept the cultural role that he assigns to them, a role designed to further the aims of imperialism at the cost of the Celt's native language and customs:

Let the Celtic members of this empire consider that they too have to transform themselves . . . Let them consider that they are inextricably bound up with us, and that, if the suggestions in the following pages have any truth, we English, alien and uncongenial to our Celtic partners as we may have hitherto shown ourselves, have notwithstanding, beyond perhaps any other nation, a thousand latent springs of possible sympathy with them.[34]

Arnold's philological evidence for this sympathy presents all sorts of problems, especially given the fact that he included extensive footnotes, added to the essay for his *Collected Works*, citing Lord Strangford ("less distinguished for knowing ethnology and languages so scientifically than for knowing so much of them"[35]), who calls his evidence into question.

Arnold's essay – which, Pecora notes, is "clearly a work of borrowed scholarship" that ultimately begins "to break apart into something like a scholarly collage"[36] – marshals the authority of philologists and ethnologists in order to co-opt the cultural energies of the Irish and other Celts by insisting that their cultural allegiance should be with the Empire and with the English language. But there is another side to Arnold's Celticism, one that is reflected in the nineteenth-century stereotype of the Irish as "undisciplinable, anarchical, and turbulent by nature."[37] In line with Renan, Arnold attributes this turbulence to the Celt's affinity with the wild magic of nature: the Celt "seems in a special way attracted by the secret before him, the secret of natural beauty and natural magic, and to be close to it, to half-divine it." This "special attraction," like the Celt's sentimentality, tempers any hint of masculine energy and suggests a creative receptivity – a "reverence and enthusiasm for genius, learning, and the things of the mind" – that is gendered feminine.[38] In Arnold's view, a "feeling for what is noble and distinguished," an "indomitable personality," and "sensibility and nervous exaltation" give the Celt access to nature's "weird power and . . . fairy charm."[39] The signal effect of Arnold's essay is to consign the Celtic people to a realm of magic naturalism that is at the farthest remove from cultural and political power: "Magic is the word to insist upon" (as he had earlier insisted on sentimentality), "a magically vivid and near interpretation of nature; since it is this which constitutes the special charm and power of the effect I am calling attention to, and it is for this that the Celt's sensibility gives him a peculiar aptitude."[40]

I have rehearsed what is perhaps a familiar story, Arnold's Celticism, because its very familiarity may tempt us to forget how important Arnold was in the development of Yeats's ideas about the Irish peasantry and its folk culture. Throughout the 1890s, Yeats fought against the stereotyped depictions of the Irish in countless articles, reviews, and letters to editors, friends, and fellow artists; and nowhere are we more impressed with Yeats's own social authority than when he responds directly to Arnold's *On the Study of Celtic Literature*. His response appears to grant Arnold's claims a certain legitimacy as a scholarly description of Celticism at the same time that it subtly reinterprets his central argument about the Celtic imagination and its relation to English literature and the British Empire. As R. F. Foster puts it, "[t]hough jeering at Matthew Arnold," Yeats "still apparently subscribed to the Arnoldean view of the Celt as dreamy, sensitive, and doom-laden."[41]

Yeats counts on his readers' familiarity with this view. At the beginning of "The Celtic Element in Literature," he cites several "well-known sentences" and then notes:

though I do not think any one of us who write about Ireland have built any argument upon them, it is well to consider [these well-known sentences] a little, and see where they are helpful and where they are hurtful. If we do not, we may go mad some day, and the enemy root up our rose-garden and plant a cabbage-garden instead. Perhaps we must re-state a little Renan's and Arnold's argument. (*EI*, 174)

The "well-known sentences" concern the Celt's "realistic naturalism" and "turbulent" reaction to the "despotism of fact." In his "restatement," Yeats challenges the cultural superiority of the English and offers a kind of prophylactic for the madness of colonial domination. That he does so without seriously questioning Arnold's primitivist assumptions indicates either a subtle strategy or a blind spot. Whereas Arnold had claimed that the Celt was unique in being able to "half-divine" natural magic, Yeats issues the counter-claim that this ability is not a racial trait but one characteristic of a people who were able to sustain contact with an "ancient worship of Nature": "I do not think that [Arnold] understood that our 'natural magic' is but the religion of the world, the ancient worship of Nature and that troubled ecstasy before her, that certainty of all beautiful places being haunted, which it brought into men's minds" (*EI*, 176). This is a very subtle strategy, one that does not so much deny the primitiveness of the Celt as revalue it by insisting on the Celt's ability to maintain in the present a connection with an ancient (that is to say, pre-historical) "religion of the world." In this way, Yeats reconfigures primitivism, shifting its *locus* from a racial to a temporal plane, in order to make a bold claim for the spiritual superiority of a "timeless" people.

Yeats does not quarrel with Arnold's attempt to prove a Celtic influence on English literature, nor with his famous conclusion that the Celtic sensibility can be defined as a "passionate, turbulent, indomitable reaction against the despotism of fact."[42] However, he is quick to clarify the nature of this influence and to refuse any racial stigma attached to the reaction against "facts." "All folk literature," Yeats writes, "and all literature that keeps the folk tradition, delights in unbounded and immortal things" (*EI*, 179). Like the great poets of the European tradition, who had not forgotten "the ancient religion" and who "were near to ancient chaos," the Celt reacted against "fact" in order to embrace that which was superior to facts, the timeless, spiritual substratum of folk traditions. Unlike Slavonic, Finnish, and Scandinavian traditions, "the Celtic alone has been for centuries close to the main river of European literature" (*EI*, 185). The effect of such statements is to refute on literary–historical grounds the subaltern status of the Celtic people that Arnold presupposes on racial grounds. Again, the primitiveness of the Celt, defined by Arnold in terms of racial essence, is redefined as a spiritual trait that links the ancient to the modern in a continuous, timeless unity. The memory of an "ancient religion" sustains the Irish people, who enjoy an ascendancy in the near future: "[A] new fountain of legends, and, as I think, a more abundant fountain than any in Europe, is being opened, the fountain of Gaelic legends" (*EI*, 186). Reversing Arnold's attempt to refuse the Irish people a share of historical agency, Yeats predicts that the Irish legends "may well give the opening century its most memorable symbols" (*EI*, 187).

Yeats subtly reverses Arnold's call for Celtic submission to the British Empire, but this reversal raises an important question: does it generate an anti-colonialist discourse capable of resisting the discriminatory effects of primitivism, or does it in fact fail to avoid a remystification of the Celt, thus reinscribing Arnold's strategies of binomial racial and cultural typing? Declan Kiberd has explained Yeats's rewriting of Arnold as an elaboration of his father's idea "of uniting Catholic imagination with Protestant efficiency." According to Kiberd, Yeats's "project of inventing a unitary Ireland is the attempt to achieve, at a political level, a reconciliation of opposed qualities which must first be fused in the self." I agree with his conclusion that "a potentially insulting cliché is retrieved . . . in a subtle and subversive fashion, to underwrite the very separatist claim that Arnold sought to deny"[43] However, I want to suggest that this subversion is by no means complete, that a residual reliance on primitivist discourse – implicit in his appeal, in "The Celtic Element," to an "ancient worship of Nature" and surfacing more explicitly in his folklore projects – prevents Yeats from offering a decisive critique of imperialist Celticism and its anthropological assumptions about the Irish "race."

Implicit in Yeats championing of the folk tradition of the Celtic people is an idealization of the peasant. Marjorie Howes has noted that "[w]hile [Yeats's] increased emphasis on the peasant appears to be a move away from the imperial feminization of the colonized and toward a more viable nationalism [grounded in a masculine ethos], a close examination of [his] peasant suggests that it brought him into greater harmony with the deep structures of colonial thought."[44] Certainly Yeats's position with respect to the imperialist ethnology typified by Arnold constitutes something more complicated than a "greater harmony with the deep structures of colonial thought." As I have suggested above, Yeats's assent to the binomial distinction between primitive and civilized peoples carries the proviso that the Irish Celts were neither pre-literate, having an intimate connection with a rich folk tradition, nor without history, having an equally intimate connection with an "ancient religion."

Where Yeats may be said to harmonize with colonial thought is in his construction of an idealized Irish peasant. As critics have noted, Yeats's peasant is no less "constructed" than the primitive native of anthropologists or the simianized subhumans of British satirists.[45] Richard Loftus has argued that "Yeats often uses a peasant mask when arguing his belief in the intuitive way of life"; but when he tries "to represent the rustic as a personification of simple nobility and dignity, the result is usually less than satisfactory."[46] And while we might argue with Loftus's conclusion that Yeats's peasant is a "powerful, although stylized, symbol of human vigor that seems to penetrate to the center of man's physical being," we can agree that the peasant is, at bottom, "a fabrication, the product of a poet's imagination."[47] Edward Hirsch concurs, arguing that for Anglo-Irish writers like Yeats and Synge, who felt keenly their separation from the Catholic Irish as well as from the Protestant middle class, "the Irish peasant not only represented some essential Irish identity but seemed wholly Other":

By mystifying an ancient, unchanging folk life, removed from the harsh realities of land agitation and social conflict in the countryside, they could treat the peasant as a romantic emblem of a deep, cultural, pastoral, and significantly anticommercial (or nonmaterialistic) Irish life . . . Country life was characterized by its orality, organicism, and closeness to nature.[48]

Yeats's representations of the peasantry, then, were as imaginary as the Ireland he thought he was reviving and preserving. But, while he may have made certain anthropological assumptions about the cultural and spiritual essence of the Irish peasantry, he ultimately comes to different conclusions than do imperialist Celticists and anthropologists. Ironically, his attempt to ennoble the peasantry by inducting it into a triumvirate including the poet and the enlightened aristocrat can be accounted for by the same logic that allowed Arnold to admit the Celtic sensibility into the English national character: the peasant has a natural connection to an ancient religion that offers the Anglo-Irish Revivalist a way to join the Catholic Irish in a "Unity of Being" that transcends cultural differences.

Throughout the 1890s, Yeats called for an Irish national literature and spoke often and passionately about what that literature ought to look like. In "Nationality and Literature," for example, he advocated a national literature that would seek its identity and substance not in the traditions of Europe but in Ireland's own folk tradition. The fundamental difference between Ireland and the rest of Europe, according to Yeats, was that Ireland was still caught up in an epic era, and that in such an era folk art formed the basis of a national literature: "All that is greatest in that literature is based upon legend – upon those tales which are made by no one man, but by the nation itself through a slow process of modification and adaptation, to express its loves and its hates, its likes and its dislikes" (*UP1*, 273). By associating the legendary phase of Irish literature with other great cultures – primarily Greek and Indian – Yeats implies that Ireland, by taking its folk culture seriously, will discover the same greatness possessed by "Homer, Aeschylus, Sophocles, Shakespeare, and even Dante, Goethe and Keats," who "were little more than folklorists with musical tongues" (*UP1*, 284).

That Yeats took seriously his role as a folklorist and that he regarded his versions of folklore as more authentic than those that had come before has been demonstrated in recent scholarship and criticism.[49] In the introduction to his *Fairy and Folk Tales of the Irish Peasantry*, Yeats is especially critical of Anglo-Irish compilers:

The impulse of the Irish literature [of T. Crofton Croker and Samuel Lover] came from a class that did not – mainly for political reasons – take the populace seriously, and imagined the country as a humorist's Arcadia; its passion, its gloom, its tragedy, they knew nothing of. What they did was not wholly false; they merely magnified an irresponsible type, found oftenest among boatmen, carmen, and gentlemen's servants, into the type of a whole nation, and created the stage Irishman . . . Their work had the dash as well as the shallowness of an ascendant and idle class. (*FFT*, 6–7)[50]

Yeats rejected the rationalizations and stereotyping that he found in the work of these compilers, believing that the essential element of folklore was all but extinguished: "As to my own part in this book, I have tried to make it representative, as far as so few pages would allow, of every kind of Irish folk-faith. The reader will perhaps wonder that in all my notes I have not rationalized a single hobgoblin" (*FFT,* 8).

Fairy and Folk Tales includes material previously collected by Crofton Croker, Samuel Lover, Patrick Kennedy, Lady Wilde, P. W. Joyce, Standish O'Grady, Douglas Hyde, William Carleton, Letitia McClintock, and others, as well as original poetry by Samuel Ferguson, William Allingham, and Yeats himself.[51] The dilemma Yeats faced in compiling this material was similar to that faced by the ethnographer: how to resolve the tension "between the urge toward fidelity to the received text and the impulse to transform."[52] For the ethnographer, this tension may be resolved by a method of line-by-line transliteration, as was the case in Malinowski's analysis of "magical texts," a method that allowed him to remain faithful to those texts and to minimize the possibility of transformation.[53] The resolution Yeats effected involved a process in which transformation played a much larger role, though not, at least in Yeats's view, to such an extent that fidelity to the "received text" was seriously compromised. Here it is important to emphasize that Yeats's ethnographic imagination has, finally, a literary end. His "program for Irish literature," according to Edward O'Shea, entailed "searching Ireland's proximate past for imaginative literature that was distinctively Irish, uncorrupted by the skepticism and scientism he perceived in England and by English stereotypes of Irishmen, but also a literature of respectable artistic merit."[54] Far from rationalizing the tales, Yeats's method was meant to evoke the "literature of a class for whom every incident in the old rut of birth, love, pain, and death has cropped up unchanged for centuries" (*FFT,* 5). The "unchanged" nature of the incidents with which folklore deals corresponds to the "ancient worship of Nature" that Yeats celebrated in "Celtic Literature"; in both cases, he invokes something like the timelessness of the ethnographic present, an escape from temporality that sustains the enduring value of a pristine primitive condition.

Yeats was aware that this work of preservation and translation transformed not only the nature but also the function of the original folklore. O'Shea sees this awareness as the motivating factor in the compilations: "Through judicious editing, which at times extended to the actual rewriting of his material, Yeats was able to isolate such a literature and present it to the Irish reading public and his contemporary writers as a testimonial to a distinctively Irish imagination and a model for the future."[55] Despite his tendency to rewrite some of his materials, Yeats believed he was being faithful to "the fundamentals of the story" (*UP1*, 174). In this respect, he attempted to maintain what O'Shea calls the "generic integrity" of the tales, a process that subordinated the accuracy in translation to the preservation of the *essence* of traditional material. The decision to rewrite some of the folktales, then, was grounded in a desire to redeem them from the kind of editorial misrepresentations that he found in previous compilations. According to Mary Helen Thuente, Yeats's method in *Fairy and Folk Tales* "reflects his search for an imaginative yet authentic depiction of Irish folklore which avoided the extremes of a ponderous scientific air on the one hand, and a bogus stage-Irish literary charm on the other."[56] As O'Shea and Thuente imply, Yeats's creative approach to the preservation of folklore redefined the way authenticity was conveyed in the representation of traditional cultural texts – it was no longer a matter of accurate transcription or translation but rather of evoking "fair equivalents" governed as much by an aesthetic as by an anthropological authority.

The evocative method of *Fairy and Folk Tales* and other texts of the 1890s is a function of an ethnographic imagination that posits an equivalence between cultural redemption and imaginative creation. In a letter replying to a critic of *Fairy and Folk Tales*, Yeats clarified his own position by praising a fellow Revivalist:

> To me, the ideal folk-lorist is Mr. Douglas Hyde. A tale told by him is quite as accurate as any "scientific" person's rendering; but in dialect and so forth he is careful to give us the most quaint, or poetical, or humorous version he has heard. I am inclined to think also that some concentration and elaboration of dialect is justified, if only it does not touch the fundamentals of the story. It is but a fair equivalent for the gesture and voice of the peasant tale-teller. (*UP1*, 174)

Curiously, in a review of Hyde's *Beside the Fire*, Yeats praises Hyde for just the sort of "scientific renderings" that a literary method is meant to improve upon, for having "caught and faithfully reproduced the peasant idiom and phrase. In becoming scientifically accurate, he has not ceased to be a man of letters" (*UP1*, 188). The inconsistency in Yeats's estimation of Hyde's folkloric methods is evident in his own compilations. On the one hand, Yeats condemned the purely scientific methods of professional folklorists like Alfred Nutt (who, he believed, wanted tales "full of little hooks, as it were, to hang theories on" [*L*, 89]): "They ['literary' folklorists] have made their work literature rather than science, and told us of the Irish peasantry rather than of the primitive religion of mankind, or whatever else the folk-lorists are on the gad after. To be considered scientists they should have tabulated all their tales in forms like grocers' bills – item the fairy king, item the queen" (*FFT*, 6). What Yeats condemns here is the taxonomic practices associated with professional folklorists like Nutt, John Rhys, and Henri D'Arbois de Jubainville who sought to assimilate Irish folklore and mythology into a universal system.

On the other hand, Yeats's organization of his material reveals a taxonomic system for ordering what he considers to be specifically Irish folklore that employs modes of classification and typology similar to those found in the work of Nutt and others who identify local tales with the universal type they instantiate.[57] The contradiction in Yeats's method surfaces in a note appended to one of Hyde's contributions to *Fairy and Folk Tales*: "I found it hard to place Mr. Douglas Hyde's magnificent story ["Teig O'Kane (Tadhg O Cathan) and the Corpse"]. Among the ghosts or the fairies? It is among the fairies on the grounds that all these ghosts and bodies were in no manner ghosts and bodies, but *pishogues* – fairy spells" (*FFT*, 23). Yeats's uncertainty reveals an anxiety about finding its proper place in a system that will in some measure authenticate it. Hirsch, noting this contradiction, finds it ironic that "the foremost polemicist of the so called 'literary' approach to folklore was intent on providing a taxonomy of the fairy world."[58] In developing this taxonomy, Yeats invokes an anthropological discourse of binomial stereotyping (Western folklorist/primitive folk); but rather than read this borrowing as a sign of bad faith with respect to traditional materials, we might regard it as the textual enactment of an ambivalent desire for a scientific method. By refusing to demystify the tales and explain away "hobgoblins," Yeats refuses the rationalizations of previous compilers; but, by developing a taxonomic system grounded in local distinctions between the various classes of folklore, he undermines the universalizing tendencies of professional folklorists. In this sense, the taxonomy in *Fairy and Folk Tales* is less scientific and empirical than it is creative and strategic. It represents an attempt to use scientific method in a subversive fashion in order to undermine prejudices and stereotypes about Ireland and the Irish.

One result of this evocative or *re*creative method was a redefinition of the *objects* that constituted the folk tradition, particularly with respect to the *sidhe*, which Yeats refashioned to reflect his own sense of social and cultural ambivalence. As Frank Kinahan points out, *Fairy and Folk Tales* reveals an ambivalence with respect to the *sidhe* best exemplified in Yeats's poem, "The Stolen Child":

> Away with us, he's going,
>   The solemn-eyed;
> He'll hear no more the lowing
>   Of the calves on the warm hillside.
> Or the kettle on the hob
>   Sing peace into his breast;
> Or see the brown mice bob
>   Round and round the oatmeal chest.   (*FFT,* 59)

In this poem, as in many other of Yeats's "fairy" poems, the "supernatural world" at times pulls Yeats "toward mystic depths"; but just as often "the influence wanes, and an earthly counterpull brings him, as it brought Oisin, back to the shores on which the frailer tents are pitched."[59] Kinahan notes further that a "more intricate" view of the *sidhe* depended on the fact "that Yeats not only believed in a world of the spirit but saw its pull as genuinely compelling," in large part because he believed that the supernatural was part of the natural or "real" world:

Yeats may not have seen the world of the sidhe as wholly joyful, nor again as a fit home for the heart of man. But he did see it as beautiful; and it is in this above all that he differed from the earlier Irish fairylorists who saw the land of faery as lamian in a more obvious sense of the term. Writers such as [William] Carleton, [Patrick] Kennedy and the Wildes saw the attractions of faery as dangerous because illusory. Yeats saw them as dangerous because real.[60]

Evans-Wentz provides us with an anthropological perspective on the reality of fairies which takes into account their psychic character: "[I]f fairies actually exist as invisible beings or intelligences, and our investigations lead us to the tentative hypothesis that they do, they are natural and not supernatural, for nothing which exists can be supernatural." This hypothesis is somewhat less tentative by the end of Evans-Wentz's study: "Fairyland, stripped of all its literary and imaginative glamour and of its social psychology, in the eyes of science resolves itself into a reality, because it is one of the states of consciousness co-ordinate with the ordinary consciousness."[61] Yeats's own remarks in *The Celtic Twilight* suggest that fairyland and fairy-faith were much more than enabling metaphors, were in fact "real" states of consciousness. And these remarks are echoed in "Swedenborg, Mediums, Desolate Places," in which Yeats praises Swedenborg for "the clearing-away of obscurities to unrecorded experience" (*E*, 35).

This, then, is the position Yeats took with respect to Arnold's mystification of the Celtic character: what for Arnold is "a magically vivid and near interpretation of nature"[62] is for Yeats *real*. The other-worldly is simultaneously *this*-worldly; and magic, far from being an eccentricity of the Celtic imagination, lay at the heart of Yeats's Revivalist project.[63] The *sidhe* and the fairy-lore associated with them came to represent for him the local manifestation of a ancient spiritual or mystical sensibility. And, while he continued to situate the peasant in an essentially binomial system of opposition to modern civilization, his assertion of the reality of fairy-faith and its connection with other mystical states of consciousness points to an inclusive "Unity of Being" that effectively dismantles the opposition.

In his *Autobiographies*, Yeats recalled the attitude toward culture he had developed in the 1880s and 90s: "I delighted in every age where poet and artist confined themselves gladly to some inherited subject-matter known to the whole people, for I thought that in man and race alike there is something called 'Unity of Being,' using that term as Dante used it when he compared beauty in the *Convito* to a perfectly proportioned human body" (*A*, 190). Though he later realized that a Unity of Being, "however wisely sought, is [not] possible without a Unity of Culture in class or people that is no longer possible at all" (*A*, 212), he began his career as a folklorist with the belief, as Deborah Fleming puts it, that "[t]he poet, peasant, and aristocrat were indissolubly and organically linked because they had nothing to do with the commercial bourgeois world, and the aristocracy became the means of holding onto hope for unity of culture in the face of increasing mercantilism."[64] This hope, R. F. Foster argues, fused Protestant mysticism with a claim on the land:

As his career developed from [the] marginalized base [of the Anglo-Irish in the 1890s], Yeats remade an Irish identity in his work and in his life. In the process he reclaimed Ireland for himself, his family and his tradition. He began by asserting a claim on the land – particularly the Sligo land – through its people: the discovery of folklore and fairy belief. Difficulties arose: he could, for instance, be attacked as incapable of interpreting Ireland religiously, as he was a *Protestant* mystic. But folklore and anthropological interests, besides being often connected in the 1890s with theosophical or occult investigations, opened a way into nationalism via "national tradition" (as Scott and others had shown long before).[65]

The occult revival of the 1890s served as a creative outlet for Anglo-Irish intellectuals and artists – Bram Stoker's *Dracula*, for example, comprises "seven years of Yeats-style research into folklore, myth, armchair anthropology, medieval history, magic – particularly diabolism"[66] – whose sense of deracination could not be assuaged by the discourse of unity that had emerged in the United Irishman movement in 1798 and that had lost its credibility among many nationalists after the fall of Parnell. Yeats would prove to be no exception.

In "Irish Fairies, Ghosts, Witches, etc.," an essay written in 1889 for a theosophical magazine, Yeats justified his recourse to an occult philosophy that to many seemed eccentric with respect to Irish folk culture:

When reading Irish folk-lore, or listening to Irish peasants telling their tales of magic and fairyism and witchcraft, more and more is one convinced that some clue there must be. Even if it is all dreaming, why have they dreamed this particular dream? Clearly the occultist should have his say as well as the folklorist. The history of a belief is not enough, one would gladly hear about its cause. (*UP1*, 130–1)

For Yeats, occultism is the best way to understand the cause and origin of folklore and the "universal mind" of which "the fairies are the lesser spiritual moods" and "wherein every mood is a soul and every thought a body" (*UP1*, 247). Irish writers who were urged to mine Irish folklore for poetic material were also urged to explore the occult since, as Phillip Marcus puts it, all "point toward the same conclusion: the spiritual, the visionary, the occult are fit subjects of concern for Irish writers because they are essentially related to the true Celtic nature."[67] Marcus's conclusions were anticipated by Evans-Wentz's claim that the Irish peasant's "mystic" consciousness made possible a belief in the existence of a "discarnate" conscious-ness that could "exhibit itself in various individual aspects as fairies."[68] However, Evans-Wentz makes clear that, while "Fairy-Faith is common to all classes of Celts, we do not state that it is common to all Celts." He also suggests that fairy-faith is stronger in some areas than others: "We have frequently emphasized how truly the modern Celtic peasant in certain non-commercialized localities has kept to the faith of his pagan ancestors, while the learned Christian scribes have often departed from it."[69] This is in accord with Yeats's views, though Yeats is inclined to posit a more universal mystic consciousness – rooted in a "universal mind" and an "ancient religion" – because he wants to close the gap that class and religious differences opened up between him and his peasant informants and to create a space in which he could work out the ambivalence of his deracinated social position.

As I have suggested above, Yeats's interest in spirituality and the occult was far from at odds with his folkloric work; indeed, the former seemed to justify the latter, for by occult means he hoped to go beyond compiling "the history of a belief" to discovering its cause, which is one way of describing the goal of anthropology with respect to native culture. "Clearly the occultist should have his say as well as the folklorist." Indeed, and throughout the 1890s, especially after meeting Lady Gregory in 1894, Yeats set about having his say by illustrating the spiritual and occult character of the Irish peasant in a series of articles, reviews, and stories. A second compilation, which capitalized on the first, was published in 1892, followed a year later by *The Celtic Twilight*. This latter text is important for a number of reasons. First, it contains stories Yeats himself collected in the field, and thus approaches the status of an ethnography of folk culture as opposed to a compilation of previously collected material; second, it combines literary and folkloristic conventions in such a way as to create a generally hybrid text; finally, it prepares the ground for the folkloric fictions of the late 1890s by lending a certain ethnographic authority to Yeats's insistence on a mystical or visionary strain in the Irish peasantry.

When Yeats goes into the field, collects tales from various informants (usually familiar inhabitants of County Sligo and County Galway), and publishes them together under his own name, he involves himself, notwithstanding his claim to literary authority, in producing the kind of "scientific text" Talal Asad describes:

It remains the case that the ethnographer's translation/representation of a particular culture is inevitably a textual construct, that as representation it cannot normally be contested by the people to whom it is attributed, and that as a "scientific text" it eventually becomes a privileged element in the potential store of historical memory for the nonliterate society concerned.[70]

When Asad speaks of "privileged" elements, he refers chiefly to the power conferred on ethnographic texts to translate the cultural artifacts of a native people into the language and genres of the metropolis, a process that creates an asymmetrical relation of discursive power. This act of translation cannot be contested, since the language of the ethnographer is usually foreign to the indigenous group under study, and this would certainly be true of those of Yeats's informants who knew little or no English. The question remains whether Yeats, in *The Celtic Twilight*, exploits this asymmetry in order to point up the patent misrepresentations that he found in both academic and popular folklore compilations and to avoid reduplicating the dominance inherent in the observer/observed dyad. In short, the question remains whether Yeats can speak with the authority of a native, despite social and religious differences that clearly mark him as an outsider.

While *The Celtic Twilight* can be regarded as a "privileged" text, a cultural translation that makes folklore available to a metropolitan audience, be it British or Anglo-Irish, it is also a text that aggressively seeks to assert a native vision of Ireland in which Anglo-Irish Revivalist and Catholic peasant find common cause in a mystical "Unity of Being." Unlike *Fairy and Folk Tales*, the chief purpose of which was to present folklore free of the corruptions of previous compilers, *The Celtic Twilight* combines the perspectives of the fieldworker and the storyteller, thus mediating two cultural perspectives: the Revivalist's and the peasant's. This mediation can be regarded as an essentially creative act in which Yeats redeems a primitive folk culture threatened by modernity at the same time that he seeks to present an original, native work of art. Edward Hirsch has noted that *The Celtic Twilight* is a generic anomaly, a "curious hybrid of the story and the essay, the accurate notation of the folklorist and the fictional reminiscence of the imaginative writer." The hybrid and anomalous quality of *The Celtic Twilight* allowed Yeats, according to Hirsch, to "invest[]the stories with his own supernatural and symbolist ideas. But he believed those ideas must be rooted in the 'thoughts of the generations.'"[71] While the tales in *The Celtic Twilight* reproduce to some degree the traditional topoi and narrative structures of *Fairy and Folk Tales*, there is a transformative

process at work by which Yeats recasts the tales he hears, deliberately
creating something new out of the act of translation, while at the
same time retaining the timeless quality of stories that are the
"thoughts of the generations." The generic hybridity of *The Celtic
Twilight*, then, reflects the demand for scientific accuracy at the same
time that it raises to prominence the demand for an evocative
literary authenticity.

In *The Celtic Twilight*, a subversive potential emerges within the
very ambivalence that signals its indebtedness to anthropology. The
first edition included a prefatory note that revealed a desire to
belong among the native Irish from whom he collected his material
even as it invoked objectivity and accuracy, those cardinal virtues of
ethnographic inquiry: "I have therefore written down accurately
and candidly much that I have heard and seen, and, except by way
of commentary, nothing that I have merely imagined. I have,
however, been at no pains to separate my own beliefs from those of
the peasantry, but have rather let my men and women, dhouls and
faeries, go their way unoffended or defended by an argument of
mine."[72] The prefatory note seeks to guarantee the disinterested
nature of the collection, to treat the tales in the way that oral
traditions are typically treated by folklorists – as authentic artifacts
recorded or captured as accurately as is possible in a written
medium. But his insistence on accuracy comports uneasily with the
solicitude, which is significantly linked to deception, he shows with
respect to his informants: "In these new chapters [added in 1902], as
in the old ones, I have invented nothing but my comments and one
or two deceitful sentences that may keep some poor story-teller's
commerce with the devil and his angels, or the like, from being
known among his neighbours" (*CT*, 2–3). Synge makes similar
claims, as does Lady Gregory, who expresses (in a parenthetical
remark in *Visions and Beliefs in the West of Ireland*) a desire to keep her
sources anonymous: "When I had begun my search for folklore, the
first to tell me he himself had seen the Sidhe was an old, perhaps
half-crazed man I will call Michael Barrett (for I do not give the real
names either of those who are living or who have left living
relatives)."[73] In these gestures that seek to preserve anonymity,
Revivalists assert their authority as protectors and preservers of folk
culture; but, at the same time, they assert a conflicting desire, rooted
in affectionate familiarity, not to offend those whom they regard as
neighbors.

Despite the claims he makes in the prefatory note, Yeats's textual strategies in *The Celtic Twilight* eschew accurate transcription and taxonomic organization. They also reflect a conscious refusal to cling to the protocols of participant observation. Traditional field-work, ethnographic and folkloric, is based on experiential authority grounded in rapport, "a 'feel' for the foreign context, a kind of accumulated savvy and a sense of the style of a people or place."[74] Establishing rapport entails the acquisition, as Radcliffe-Brown describes it, of "a series of multitudinous impressions, each slight and often vague, that guide [the ethnologist] in his dealings with [people he is studying]."[75] But, rather than use this rapport to establish relationships with informants that would further the crea-tion of a "scientific" text, Yeats followed out the other possibility ever-present in ethnographic rapport, one which we see in the desire for native women that Malinowski recorded in his field diary, a sense of intersubjective belonging and even possessiveness well beyond the conventional limits of fieldwork. Yeats seems to have understood that, as long as he remained socially and culturally estranged from the peasantry, his authority as a native folklorist and his aspirations to become part of a native literary tradition would both be under-mined. It was therefore necessary for him to find a common experiential ground on which to establish an intimate connection with his peasant informants. This process began in earnest in *The Celtic Twilight*, where Yeats's ethnographic imagination combines the desire for accurate cultural description with a reluctance to achieve the kind of distance that would allow for the separation of observer and observed. When he takes "no pains to separate [his] own beliefs from those of the peasantry," he could not be acting more unlike the ethnographer who seeks an objective point of view from which to study a native community. This ambivalent position is to be expected, given that Yeats relied heavily on informants from Sligo, including people who worked for or knew his family, people like Mary Battle, his uncle George Pollexfen's servant. His indebted-ness to Mary Battle is recorded (significantly, *post-facto*) in his *Autobiographies*, where he notes that "[m]uch of my *Celtic Twilight* is but her daily speech" (*A*, 70).[76]

Intimacy is fostered by this shared locality; but it also engendered some confusion about Yeats's position with respect to his informants. "A Knight of the Sheep" dramatizes this confusion. It tells of his visit to the home of "a strong farmer" and his conversation with him and a tax collector. Because Yeats's presence in large measure instigates the action in the tale, it is hard to tell whether he participates as folklorist or neighbor:

And then the two men parted, with an angry flush and bitter hearts, and had I not cast between them some common words or other, might not have parted, but have fallen rather into an angry discussion of the value of their dead sons. *If I had not pity for all the children of reverie I should have let them fight it out, and would now have many a wonderful oath to record.* (*CT*, 54)

Yeats's intervention in the dispute and his pity for the "children of reverie" point to his desire for (if not the reality of) an intersubjective connection that would allow an outsider to have an insider's perspective, free of any necessity for a scientific account. Also notable about this passage is that the italicized sentence, which plainly marks Yeats as the participant–observer in a position to exploit a situation for ethnographic material, is left out of editions after 1902. By making such excisions, he suppresses any textual evidence of his essentially ethnographic authority, while leaving the evidence of his intersubjective connection firmly in place.

Yeats refers frequently in *The Celtic Twilight* to his own experiences with and belief in fairy-lore and legend, and we can read these references as part of his attempt to compensate for being outside peasant society. In "The Sorcerers," for example, he speaks of the "darker powers" and the possibility of "communicating in states of trance with the angelical and faery beings" (*CT*, 63), while in "A Voice," he tells of his preoccupation "with Aengus and Edain, and with Mannanan, son of the sea" (*CT*, 115). His fairy-faith is most clearly marked in "The Old Town," which begins: "I fell, one night some fifteen years ago, into what seemed the power of Faery" (*CT*, 137). The significance of this tale lies in Yeats's willingness to identify himself with the mystic peasant milieu and to admit the provisional and subjective nature of his role as participant–observer. In fact, the experiences he shares with his informants have the effect of challenging the validity of what he sees:

We saw it all in such a dream, and it seems all so unreal, that I have never written of it until now, and hardly ever spoken of it, and even when thinking, because of some unreasonable impulse, I have avoided giving it weight in the argument. *Perhaps I have felt that my recollections of things seen when the sense of reality was weakened must be untrustworthy.* (*CT*, 138–9; my emphasis)

What he sees and what he remembers are unreliable; but equally significant is the fact that he admits as much in his text, thereby calling into question the experiential authority of his own ethnographic project. In another tale, "Regina, Regina, Pigmeorum, Veni," he relates a similar experience of falling "into a kind of trance, in which what we call the unreal had begun to take upon itself a masterful reality" (*CT*, 93). Here, too, he cannot "remember rightly" (*CT*, 93); and though what he sees and remembers is unreliable and he can find no confirmation among his friends whose "somewhat meager recollections" he compares with his own to no avail (*CT*, 139), he nevertheless establishes a commitment to his subjects and their milieu that goes well beyond the development of ethnographic rapport and begins to approximate an intimate, intersubjective union. By according his "friends" an equality that would permit them to compare notes with him, Yeats undermines the authority of the ethnographic observer that had given him access to the folk-life of the peasantry in the first place.

Yeats was able to develop a degree of intersubjective connection with people in County Sligo and elicit stories and anecdotes from them in part because he was, by the time of *The Celtic Twilight*, well known as a "national poet." What is interesting is that this fact is recorded in one of the tales, "An Enduring Heart," in which an old man who has just told a story urges his daughter, "Tell that to Mr. Yeats, he will make a poem about it." But both the daughter and the poet know better, and Yeats concludes the tale by lamenting: "Alas! I never made the poem, perhaps because my own heart, which has loved Helen and all the lovely and fickle women of the world, would be too sore. There are things it is well not to ponder over too much, things that bare words are best suited for" (*CT*, 60). What are we to make of these "bare words"? Perhaps Yeats meant to indicate that a "scientific person's rendering," which he had criticized in the introduction to *Fairy and Folk Tales*, might be preferable to a poetic treatment too traumatic for the poet to endure. This frank admission that the folklorist harbors subjective responses to the folklore he collects signals an ambivalent investment in ethnographic modes of inquiry.

The convergence of folklore and poetry occurs in a more complex, intertextual fashion in "A Visionary," which later becomes the basis for a poem, "The Lamentation of the Old Pensioner." In the poem, an old man laments that he has been forgotten by all those who once knew him:

The road-side trees keep murmuring,
Ah, wherefore murmur ye,
As in the old days long gone by,
Green oak and poplar tree?
The well known faces are all gone
And the fret lies on me.[77]

Yeats has written that "[t]his small poem is little more than a translation into verse of the very words of an old Wicklow peasant."[78] The incident in question is recorded in "A Visionary," which recounts a visit from AE who tells Yeats about meeting "an old peasant who, dumb to most men, poured out his cares for him": "and once he lamented that his old neighbours were gone, and that all had forgotten him: they used to draw a chair to the fire for him in every cabin, and now they said, 'Who is that old fellow there?'" (*CT*, 20). A kind of intertextuality emerges here, with poem and tale reflecting each other, fracturing and pluralizing ethnographic authority. It is worth noting at this point that Yeats relied on AE just as Evans-Wentz had: as a "reliable seer-witness."

Like many of the stories in *The Celtic Twilight*, "A Visionary" raises the question of authority that is at the heart of Yeats's Revivalist project: to what authority, aesthetic or ethnographic, does one appeal to succeed in redeeming an authentic folk culture? In traditional ethnographic encounters, according to Talal Asad, "it is not the personal authority of the ethnographer, but the social authority of his ethnography that matters."[79] As we have seen in *The Celtic Twilight*, the authority behind Yeats's desire to record "accurately and candidly much that I have heard and seen," is in some ways facilitated by his standing as "Mr. Yeats," the "national" poet. Unlike *Fairy and Folk Tales*, which relied uneasily on the authority of previous compilations and adopted a taxonomic organization, *The Celtic Twilight* relies instead on the personal authority of the poet to draw out or evoke an essence, a "fair equivalent for the gesture and voice of the peasant tale-teller" (*UP1*, 174). This is not to say, of course, that Yeats rejected entirely the primitivism to which so many folklorists subscribed; nor is it to deny a certain lingering indebtedness to traditional techniques of collecting, transcribing, translating, ordering and editing traditional materials. Such partial investments are characteristic of autoethnographic texts in which "subordinated or marginal groups select and invent from materials transmitted to them by a dominant or metropolitan culture."[80] The strategies of ethnographic inquiry that allowed Yeats to achieve rapport with his native informants were governed by the kind of social authority to which Asad alludes; but equally important were spiritual and aesthetic authorities that, while seeking the same goal of preservation, employed different means. Thus, *The Celtic Twilight* evinces a hybrid social authority; it hews to the protocols of disinterested observation at the same time that it sanctions mystical and visionary experiences not typically covered by ethnographers (Evans-Wentz is a notable exception).

In 1894, Yeats's interest in folklore developed in new directions, spurred by meeting Lady Gregory, whose aid he enlisted in collecting and translating tales. She was intellectually and artistically productive, and Yeats himself underscores the importance of the literary market for Revivalist work when he praises not only Lady Gregory's collecting abilities but also her ability to sell books: "From her came the great collection of folklore that, turned into essays for the monthly reviews, brought ten or fifteen pounds at a time" (*A*, 247). Lucy McDiarmid and Maureen Waters argue that Lady Gregory's authority in areas like folklore and translation was greater than Yeats's.[81] Her success was due largely to her knowledge of the Irish language and her willingness to allow native speakers to have a hand in translation. In her essay on the nineteenth-century poet, Anthony Raftery, for example, Lady Gregory writes that she "ha[d] been helped to put it into English by a young working farmer, sitting by a turf fire one evening, when his day in the fields was over."[82]

At the time he met Lady Gregory, Yeats was capitalizing on the publication the year before of *The Celtic Twilight* and "The Celtic Element in Literature" by writing reviews and articles that promoted the value and centrality of folklore for a national literature. In an 1894 review of William Larminie's *West Irish Folk Tales*, Yeats noted that "[t]he recent revival of Irish literature has been very largely a folklore revival, an awakening of interest in the wisdom and ways of the poor, and in the poems and legends handed down among the cabins" (*UP1*, 326). The year before, in a review of T. F. Thistelton Dyer's *The Ghost World*, Yeats had written that "Folk-lore is at once the Bible, the Thirty-nine Articles, and the Book of Common Prayer, and well-nigh all the great poets have lived by its light. Homer, Aeschylus, Sophocles, Shakespeare, and even Dante, Goethe and Keats, were little more than folklorists with musical tongues" (*UP1*, 284). In addition to reviewing, Yeats wrote a series of long articles that drew extensively on Lady Gregory's fieldwork in the Kiltartan area of Galway in order to define and exemplify different aspects of Irish folklore – the *sidhe*, pooka fairies, witchdoctors and the like – and to emphasize the peasant's mystical qualities. The articles included anecdotes, tales and other ephemera that Lady Gregory ultimately published in *Visions and Beliefs in the West of Ireland.* McDiarmid and Waters quote Colin Smythe who remarked that Lady Gregory's hand " 'was quietly in much that was published by Yeats in periodicals.' "[83] Though Yeats may not have concurred with this assessment, he was careful not to devalue the discoveries she made: "If she had not found those tales, or finding them had not found the dialect of Kiltartan, that past could not, as it were, have drawn itself together, come to birth as present personality" (*A*, 227). The articles that made use of Lady Gregory's material became part of Yeats's ongoing project of resistance to colonialist and anthropological stereotypes of the peasantry. They also served well his strategy to redeem the "organic vitality" of "a race held together by folk tradition,"[84] to restore "forgotten mythologies" and a folk art that is "the oldest of the aristocracies of thought," "the soil where all great art is rooted" (*CT*, 232–3).

Promotional copy for the 1895 edition of Yeats's *Poems*, which Allan Wade believes was "doubtless" inspired by the poet, sums up the kind of hybrid social authority that Yeats's texts asserted in the early 1890s:

Mr. Yeats has written of the beautiful and singular legends of Ireland, not from any archaeological or provincial ambition, but with the desire of moulding the universal substance of poetry into new shapes, and of interpreting, to the best of his power, the spirit of Ireland to itself. (*L*, 243)

The transformation of "beautiful and singular legends" into "new shapes" reflects Yeats's desire not simply to preserve the traditional materials that he collected and published but to create "new originals" that retained, as their essential element, the "universal substance of poetry." The desire related in the promotional copy, like that which animated Yeats's response to Arnold's *On the Study of Celtic Literature*, presupposes the "Unity of Culture" that was so important to Yeats in the 1890s. It is not surprising, then, that he was strongly drawn to the figure of the bard, who similarly fashioned and refashioned traditional materials in the creation of new traditional texts.[85]

The idea of the bard as a social authority resonated deeply with Yeats from the start. In 1890, in a review of Sophie Bryant's *Celtic Ireland*, he celebrated the bards as "the most powerful influence in the land," but he also underscored their isolation – they "kept by the rules of their order apart from war and the common affairs of men" – as well as their capacity to ride "hither and thither gathering up the dim feelings of the time, and making them conscious" (*UP1*, 163). It is their ability to bring the world of spirit into living consciousness that stands out for Yeats, the "one curious thing in ancient Celtic history" for which "the power of the bards" was responsible: "they all seem striving to bring something out of the world of thoughts into the world of deeds – a something that always eluded them" (*UP1*, 164). One of the most influential sources of information on the bardic tradition at that time was Standish O'Grady's two-volume *History of Ireland*, which appeared prominently on Yeats's list of thirty essential Irish books (*L*, 247ff.). Yeats claimed that it "ha[d] done more than anything else to create that preoccupation with Irish folklore and legend and epic which is called the Irish literary movement" (*UP1*, 368). Like Lady Gregory's *Cuchulain of Muirthemne*, O'Grady's *History* brought an imaginative version of the Irish past to a wide audience and, by the 1890s, according to Richard Fallis, "had become almost a bible for young Irish writers and nationalists. They found in it stirring retellings of the ancient tales, and they also found in his Cuchulain an exemplar of the Irish spirit, manly, courageous, extravagantly emotional, and genuinely noble."[86]

Yeats would have read in O'Grady's *History* that the bards were "not so much a class as an organization and fraternity acknowledging the authority of one elected chief. They were not loose wanderers, but a power in the State, having duties and privileges. The ard-ollav ranked next to the king, and his eric was kingly."[87] Subsequent studies support O'Grady's description of a powerful, hybrid social authority. Osborn Bergin, for instance, remarked, in a 1912 lecture before the National Literature Society in Dublin, that the bard (in Irish, *file* or *ollamh*) was "a professor of literature and a man of letters, highly trained in the use of a polished literary medium, belonging to a hereditary caste in an aristocratic society, holding an official position therein by virtue of his training, his learning, his knowledge of the history and traditions of his country and his clan."[88] Daniel Corkery, writing in 1924, adds that the bard performed functions akin to those of a journalist and was often "a public official, a chronicler, a political essayist, a keen and satirical observer of his fellow-countrymen . . . He might be a poet, too." So important were the bards in medieval Irish society that the bardic schools constituted "the university system of the nation – granting degrees, or what corresponded to such, and bestowing privileges on both professors and students simply because they were professors and students."[89] By the late 1890s, Yeats had discovered, in the Irish bardic tradition, a model for the native intellectual whose deracination and hybridity led ultimately to a new conception of social authority. And in the bard's isolation from "the common affairs of men," he discovered a precedent for the Revivalist who strove to bring to consciousness the spiritual realities he shared with the peasantry.

In *Stories of Red Hanrahan* and *The Secret Rose*, collections of folkloric fictions published in 1897, Yeats laid claim to a bardic authority, with a characteristic emphasis on the bard's mystical capacity. As Richard Loftus notes, "[a]ccording to Irish tradition, the ancient *filid* were not only technically accomplished in the art of verse-making, but also were possessed of *imbas forosna*, that is, second sight; and many of the Irish poets, including Yeats, seemed to have believed half-seriously that this unique faculty was theirs by right of inheritance."[90] I think we may say with confidence that Yeats was more than half-serious about his desire for affiliation with the bardic tradition, especially considering the role he wished the bard to play in his evolving project of Revivalist nationalism. According to Phillip Marcus, Yeats achieved a synthesis of diverse elements: "the mastery of the craft and esoteric wisdom of the bards, the language and modern Nationalist goals of the Young Irelanders, and subject matter that was national but not necessarily of any *obvious* and *immediate* political relevance."[91] It is this lack of any "*obvious* and *immediate* political relevance" that complicates our assent to Edward Said's claim that in Yeats "[t]he narrative and the density of personal experience are equivalent to the experience of the people."[92]

Our assent is complicated in a similar way by Yeats's desire for an élite "esoteric" literature. In a letter to John O'Leary, Yeats wrote of his desire, in *The Secret Rose*, to make "an honest attempt toward that aristocratic esoteric Irish literature, which has been my chief ambition. We have a literature for the people but nothing yet for the few" (*L*, 286). The idea of an esoteric literature was quite inimical to the populism of many Irish-Ireland nationalists, but it proceeded logically from Yeats's developing sense of the Anglo-Irish Revivalist as a bardic authority estranged both from the Ascendancy ruling class and an emergent, middle-class Catholic nationalism. The "few" to which Yeats alludes are the contemporary equivalent of the "intellectual aristocracy" in which the bard played a central role. Though it seems like an appeal for an exclusionary, mandarin literary tradition separate from that of the "people," Yeats's remark might better be read as an appeal for a newly energized, native folk tradition, capable of creating the conditions in which the peasant and the Revivalist could act in concert against the discursive domination of anthropological and colonialist discourses – the conditions, in other words, for what Frantz Fanon calls a "literature of combat," a literature that would "call[] on the whole people to fight for their existence as a nation."[93] If Yeats's esoteric literature failed to achieve the revolutionary goals articulated by Fanon, it achieved something perhaps more important, at least to Yeats's development as a modernist, for it refined his sense of a Manichean struggle between matter and spirit, a struggle that underscored the incommensurability of tradition and modernity. In his folkloric fictions, we see an emergent anthropological modernism that allegorizes the feelings of deracination and dissociation to which T. S. Eliot and other "high" modernists were to give expression twenty years later.

Ironically, while *Stories of Red Hanrahan* and *The Secret Rose* represent the "esoteric Irish literature" that Yeats longed to create, they also relate the history of the destruction of the very bardic class that inspired him.[94] These collections constitute a history lesson told in a series of interconnected allegories, parables, visionary tales, local histories, and folk-beliefs that take the reader from legendary times to the late nineteenth century. Throughout, a conception of time characteristic both of folk-belief and primitivism completely dominates the temporality of the stories. For example, in "The Heart of the Spring," an old man longs for "a life whose abundance would fill centuries." He has been taught by "Men of Faery" to believe in the reality of a moment that "trembles with the Song of the Immortal Powers" (*SRH*, 129). The "dream-distraught history" (*SR*, 2) that the bard Aodh sings to Queen Dectira inaugurates the first edition of *The Secret Rose* and is repeated in stories like "Proud Costello, MacDermot's Daughter, and the Bitter Tongue" where history, folktale and legend fuse: "[T]he country people still remember how when the night had fallen he would bid Duallach of the Pipes tell out, 'The Son of Apple,' 'The Beauty of the World,' 'The King of Ireland's Son,' or some like tale; and while the world of legends was a-building, would abandon himself to the dreams of his sorrow" (*SRH*, 177). Costello's search for Una becomes an alternative to historical progress and change, for he "cared only for the love sorrows, and no matter where the stories wandered, Una alone endured their shadowy hardships" (*SRH*, 177).

Costello's abandonment to sorrow is a quintessential expression of the "Celtic Twilight" mood – the dominance of "love sorrow," the vague unreality of wandering stories and "shadowy hardships" – that permeates early poems like "Who Goes With Fergus?" with its shadowy woods, dim seas and "dishevelled wandering stars," and "The Stolen Child":

> Where the wave of moonlight glosses
>   The dim grey sands with light,
> Far off by furthest Rosses
>   We foot it all the night,
> Weaving olden dances,
> Mingling hands, and mingling glances,
>   Till the moon has taken flight.   (*FFT*, 58)

The melancholy sense of something sacrificed or left behind – "He'll hear no more the lowing / Of the calves on the warm hillside" – and the general sense of a crepuscular mingling of boundaries and movements indicate less a realm of inconsequential insubstantiality than an alternative form of temporality, something closer to what Victor Turner calls liminality, a time "set apart from the ongoing business of quotidian life" that takes place in the subjunctive mood, "a world of 'as if,' ranging from scientific hypothesis to festive fantasy."[95] But we should also bear in mind Kinahan's and Evans-Wentz's insistence on the reality of the fairies: Yeats did not regard the "attractions of faery as dangerous because illusory," he "saw them as dangerous because real."[96] It is this reality that Yeats attempted to capture in *The Wind Among the Reeds*, in which the answer to the question – "What one in the rout / Of the fire-born moods / Has fallen away?" – would appear to be the *sidhe*, the "unappeasable host" that is "comelier than candles at Mother Mary's feet" (*Poems*, 56, 58).

Rather than depict "some moment of famous Irish history" – the proper stuff of "a really national poem or romance," as one of Yeats's "friends in Ireland" would have it (*SR*, vii) – Yeats preferred, in the *Stories of Red Hanrahan* and *The Secret Rose*, to write history allegorically as a "war of spiritual with natural order" (*SR*, vii). DeCourcey declares a truce with Fitzgerald (*SRH*, 100–1), monasteries are burned and rebuilt, the "customs of Elizabeth and James" (*SRH*, 163) arise and as quickly pass away. But what is really important for Yeats is the struggle between worldly forces (both secular and ecclesiastic) and the mystical peasantry. In "The Curse of the Fire and the Shadows," the *sidhe* and the bards join sides with the Church in order to combat the British army. Elsewhere, as in "The Crucifixion of the Outcast," the priests, with the peasants' assistance, attack the bard, in part because he appears to possess supernatural abilities not sanctioned by the Church. But, like the priest who starts out condemning the folk healer Biddy Early only to end up sending her his horse "that has a sore in his leg this long time, and try will she be able to cure him,"[97] the monks capitulate to a spiritual force beyond their reckoning. *The Secret Rose* is all about this force, the generative power of that "universal mind" whose existence alone can unite the Revivalist and the peasant.

The title poem prefacing the stories of *The Secret Rose* can be understood as an expression of this power that unifies:

> Far-off, most secret, and inviolate . . .
> > Thy great leaves enfold
> The ancient beards, the helms of ruby and gold
> Of the crowned Magi; and the king whose eyes
> Saw the Pierced Hands and Rood of Elder rise
> In Druid vapor and make the torches dim;
> Till vain frenzy awoke and he died; and him
> Who met Fand walking among flaming dew
> By a grey shore where the wind never blew,
> And lost the world and Emer for a kiss . . .
> And the proud dreaming king who flung the crown
> And sorrow away, and calling bard and clown
> Dwelt among wine-stained wanderers in deep woods. (*Poems*, 70)

Yeats invokes the Rose, Dante's sublime symbol of the presence of God, to signify a mystical unity-in-unfolding at the heart of Irish folk life "wherein every mood is a soul and every thought a body" (*UP1*, 247). The unifying symbol of the rose subsumes a host of mythical and legendary figures, recapitulating both the history of Christianity and that which Christianity excludes. It represents a play of doctrines, a plenitude of icons, a contradiction of belief, and

a resistance to the domination of any one doctrine, icon, or belief –
all within a general economy of signification that transforms ambivalence into a totalizing visionary experience. In *The Secret Rose*, well-
understood folkways suddenly emerge enshrouded in new significance. In the new mythology formulated here, which is tantamount
to a new historicism based on folklore and legend, Yeats appears to
leave behind the experiential authority of ethnographic redemption
and takes on the creative authority of the bard who mediates
between the spiritual or "magical" world of the Celt and the
material or "historical" world of Empire.

In *The Secret Rose*, the visionary supplants the world-historical,
spirituality triumphing over materiality in whatever form it might
take. The questing knight in "Out of the Rose," who represents a
spiritualized bardic figure, seems to move in a lost age of chaos that
in "the Ireland of today" still "murmurs like a dark and stormy sea
full of the sounds of lamentation" (*UP1*, 66). The historical world –
"outer order and outer fixity" (*SRH*, 108) – is found wanting, and the
knight searches for and finds "the wayward light of the heart" on
"this western isle" that is "fuller of wars and rapine than any other
land" (*SRH*, 108, 110). Bardic isolation is rewarded with visionary
peace, and this peace is the legacy he leaves to the people:

Thereat he began to sing in Latin, and, while he sang, his voice faltered
and grew faint. Then his eyes closed, and his lips fell apart, and the lad
[sent by the local villagers to collect their reward for helping the knight kill
"wood-thieves"] knew he was dead. "He has told me a good tale," he said,
"for there was fighting in it, but I did not understand much of it, and it is
hard to remember so long a story." (*SRH*, 111)

The knight's rejection of the material world is a rejection of
experience itself in favor of "discarnate" realities that seem to offer
little to the peasant boy, who is distracted by the crowing of a cock in
the valley below – little more, that is, than stories difficult to
understand and too long to remember.

As Yeats well knew, the bardic class described by O'Grady and
Bergin was already beginning to disappear in the mid-seventeenth
century due largely to the settlements and shifts in land occupation
that followed Cromwell's acceleration of the plantation schemes
begun in the previous century. Thus, a figure like Red Hanrahan
would have been an epigone, less a bard in the classic sense than an
untrained wandering poet, like the ballad singers Raftery and
Moran, the last gleeman, who declares descent from Homer, "a

poet, and a blind-man, and a beggar-man" (*CT*, 85). Nevertheless, Hanrahan is given an impressive genealogy: he is "the last of that mighty line of poets which came down unbroken from Sancan Torpeist (whom the Great Cat well-nigh ate), and mightier Oisin, whose heart knew unappeased three hundred years of daemonic love" (*SR*, 142). Despite this lineage, however, Hanrahan is closer in style and temperament to eighteenth-century bards like Eoghan Rua O Suilleabhain (Owen O'Sullivan, the Red) and Tadg Gaelach O Suillebhain (Timothy O'Sullivan, the Gaelic), the latter being, as Yeats puts it in "The Twisting of the Rope," an "ignorant rhymer" (*SR*, 144).[98] A hedge-schoolmaster in contact with "fairyland" (he calls up Cleena of the Wave, who then becomes his *Leanshee* or fairy mistress [see *FFT*, 76]), Hanrahan is a penurious bard, a balladeer who persists in regarding himself as "a king of the poets of the Gael and a ruler of the dreams of men" (*SR*, 160). After his bewitchment at the hands of an "old mountainy man" (*SRH*, 3), Hanrahan goes off wandering and meets four old women who possess the four sacred objects of Irish legend – cauldron, stone, spear, and sword (*SRH*, 15). Hanrahan's heroic "struggle for historical identity" and his "imaginative conquest of Irish history,"[99] ends in a moment of fairy transport, a moment come and gone in "a pulsation of the heart" (*SRH*, 63). His quest, by amalgamating elements of Christian tradition, mysticism, and folklore, provides an alternative to the traditional Grail story, with the quasi-legendary, quasi-mystic bard in place of the questing knight.[100]

More than any other figure in Yeats's work of the 1890s, Hanrahan comes closest to embodying the ancient Celtic bard who possesses "imaginative passions," who takes pleasure in "all folk literatures," "in unbounded and communal things" (*EI*, 178–9), who feels and sings the grief of the nation. His voice – disembodied, homeless, elemental – is associated with "the wind in a lonely place" (*SRH*, 40), the same wind that gives the *sidhe* its name. In "Red Hanrahan's Song about Ireland," the "wayward light of the heart" is manifested in Hanrahan's memorialization of the iconic figure of Cathleen ni Houlihan:

> The old brown thorn-trees break in two high over Cummen Strand,
> Under a bitter black wind that blows from the left hand;
> Our courage breaks like an old tree in a black wind and dies,
> But we have hidden in our hearts the flame out of the eyes
> Of Cathleen, the daughter of Houlihan.　　　　　　　(*Poems*, 81)

Hanrahan's song celebrates the undaunted courage and fortitude of the Celt, symbolized by the ritual flame of "Cathleen, the daughter of Houlihan." The bleakness of the landscape stems as much from the speaker's own mystical sensibility as from the "bitter black wind." "Red Hanrahan's Song about Ireland" repeats and ratifies the message of the folkloric fictions: the unifying embrace of the Irish landscape and its folklore, which can be verified only through non-rational, ritualistic or visionary experience. The implication, I think, is that Yeats the Anglo-Irish folklorist has donned the mantle of the bard he has created, with the effect (perhaps not consciously intended) of blurring the lines between anthropological facts and anthropological fictions. And it is this blurring, I submit, that constitutes one of the chief features of Yeats's evolving anthropological modernism.

In *Stories of Red Hanrahan* and *The Secret Rose*, Yeats appears to complete the movement toward a form of social authority that would legitimize a Revivalist project of cultural redemption in which folklorist and peasant commingle in a single emblematic figure, Red Hanrahan. However, the publication history of these texts tells another more complex and even contradictory story. Yeats intended to conclude the first edition of *The Secret Rose* with a suite of mystical stories – "Rosa Alchemica," "The Tables of the Law" and "The Adoration of the Magi" – but the latter two were left out at the publisher's request.[101] Around the same time that he revealed his desire for an esoteric literature to John O'Leary, Yeats made a similar revelation to Katharine Tynan. Referring to stories like "Rosa Alchemica," Yeats wrote, "I am now trying to do some wild Irish stories which shall not be mere phantasies but the signatures – I use the medium's term – of things invisible and ideas" (*L*, 253). In part, this statement reflects Yeats's increasing involvement in occult activities; but it also indicates a shift in his sense of what constitutes "Irish" stories and the "essence" that they ought to evoke. Rather than "fair equivalents," which reflected his interest in the mode of representing folklore, Yeats in these stories is more concerned with deriving, through alchemical transmutation, a "divine and imperishable substance" (*SRH*, 192), which suggests a greater interest in the nature of mystical consciousness itself, rather than the folkways of those who possess it.

To some extent, this development corresponds to and anticipates a shift in anthropology from the empiricism of A. C. Haddon to the "anthropo-psychological method" employed by Evans-Wentz in *Fairy-Faith in Celtic Countries*. Evans-Wentz's ethnography of fairy-faith, based on research and fieldwork done in 1907–9, was dedicated to AE and Yeats and reflects their mystical conceptions of Irish folklore as well as their interest in the relationship between folklore and psychic phenomena. Using his "anthropo-psychological method," Evans-Wentz sets out to examine Celtic fairy-faith "sympathetically as well as scientifically," drawing to his aid archaeology, anthropology and comparative mythology.[102] He also articulates a scientific method not unlike the functional analysis of social psychology that A. R. Radcliffe-Brown was developing at about the same time and that Malinowski would perfect shortly thereafter:

It is assumed as a working principle that each ethnic group has or tends to have an individuality of its own, and, moreover, that the members of such a group think, feel, and act primarily as the representatives, so to speak, of that ethnic individuality in which they live, move, and have their being. That is to say, a social as contrasted with an individual psychology must, it is held, pronounce both the first and last word regarding all matters of mythology, religion, and art in its numerous forms.[103]

Where Evans-Wentz differs from anthropologists like Radcliffe-Brown and Malinowski is in his interest in psychic phenomena, which he holds to be every bit as open to analysis as the more material aspects of social life. But, having said that, we might note that fairy-faith constitutes what Malinowski calls "the inponderabilia of actual life," which are accessible to scientific formulation and documentation, but not to "superficial registration of detail"; to get at these "inponderabilia," the ethnographer must make "an effort at penetrating the mental attitude expressed in them."[104] Significantly, Evans-Wentz uses similar language to describe his own ethnographic method: "to penetrate as deeply and in as natural a way as possible the thoughts of the people who believe in fairies and like beings, by living among them and observing their customs and ways of thought, and recording what seemed relevant to the subject under investigation."[105] Indeed, he appears to follow the lead of Radcliffe-Brown and Malinowski in concentrating on social organization: "The invisible Irish races have always had a very distinct social organization, so distinct in fact that Ireland can be divided according to its fairy kings and fairy queens and their territories even now."[106]

The parallel I am drawing here suggests once again that Revivalist literary practice either paralleled or anticipated developments in anthropology. And it was precisely the lack of disciplinary constraint that allowed Yeats to make the shift from "fair equivalents" to "divine and imperishable substance" in such a way as to facilitate a closer identification with the mystical consciousness that is hinted at in *The Celtic Twilight*. Significantly, the characters in the mystical stories are not peasants; they resemble instead the Revivalist mystic AE, upon whom Evans-Wentz drew as a "reliable seer-witness" and who offered "very rare and very important evidence," which served "to illustrate and to confirm" his own anthropological conclusions.[107] The "signatures" Yeats created in his "wild Irish" stories, aside from being more purely the products of his own literary imagination and less the effects of an ethnographic process, represent a growing conviction (amplified in the anti-realistic drama) that a native Irish literature need not rest on anthropological assumptions of racial or cultural difference and, moreover, that the lessons he had learned combating these assumptions would permit him to create something newly original, something "wildly" Irish, in competition with other notions of Irishness. There is also a greater openness to European mystical ideas such as theosophy that aligned Yeats more closely then ever before with the tradition of "Protestant magic," which R. F. Foster associates with "an insecure middle-class" seeking spiritual relief from the debilitating social changes that had marginalized the Anglo-Irish politically and economically, a class that possessed "a race-memory of elitism and a predisposition toward seeking refuge in the occult."[108] And, while the plays and poetry after 1897 still occasionally represent aspects of Irish folklore, Yeats is less and less concerned with ethnographic redemption, since the development of his occult interests led him increasingly toward symbolism and non-mimetic modes of representing spiritual or "discarnate" realities.

In the mystical stories, the bardic energies that animated *The Secret Rose* and *Stories of Red Hanrahan* are transposed to a more overtly occult level. "Rosa Alchemica," for example, focuses on Owen Aherne, who suffers from a "measureless desire for a world made wholly of essences" (*SRH*, 192). He has created a cordon sanitaire in his rooms in order to block out any trace of the external world, including the peasant who has disappeared almost completely from the text: "The portraits, of more historical than artistic interest, had gone; and tapestry, full of the blue and bronze of peacocks, fell over the doors, and shut out all history and activity untouched with beauty and peace" (*SRH*, 192–3). Aherne's interest in the alchemical "transmutation of all things into some divine and imperishable substance," of "the weary heart into a weariless spirit" (*SRH*, 192, 195), marks the transformation of the folklorist's desire for "fair equivalents" and cultural preservation into the mystic's desire for "divine substances," for an alchemical unity in which the material world of history and society is transubstantiated in a visionary experience articulated in the style of early modernist aestheticism. If these mystical stories reflect a greater involvement in such ideas, they also reflect the price Yeats had to pay for giving up the anthropological authority that urged him to revive folk culture in the first place.

Michael Robartes, the emissary of a realm "made wholly of essences," attempts to convince Aherne to join the mystic Order of the Alchemical Rose. The latter's refusal induces Robartes to cast a spell and envelope Aherne in illusions "caused by memory, and by the twilight of incense" (*SRH*, 202). Aherne resists this "indefinite world," invoking the greatness of a mind that "reflect[s] everything with indifferent precision like a mirror" as a kind of charm to ward off "the illusions that creep like maggots into civilizations when they begin to decline, and into minds when they begin to decay" (*SRH*, 205). The *"hysterica passio"* of Aherne's vision – a "sheer madness" that was "so powerful in its melancholy exaltation that I tremble lest it wake again and drive me from my new-found peace" (*SRH*, 209) – recalls Hanrahan's vision of the "ancient defeated gods": "And it seemed to [Hanrahan] that the little soft rose leaves as they went fluttering down into the valley began to change their shape till they looked like a troop of men and women far off in the mist, with the color of roses on them" (*SRH*, 58–9). Unable to resist an "indefinite world" that fills him with terror, Aherne falls into a visionary swoon in which he hears a voice telling him that " '[t]he mirror is broken into numberless pieces' ": "and then a multitude of pale hands were reaching toward me" (*SRH*, 206). The mirror, in which the world is reflected as it is, fractures and recombines into a totalizing vision:

I was being lifted out of the tide of flame, and felt my memories, my hopes, my thoughts, my will, everything I held to be myself, melting away . . . [T]hen I passed beyond these forms, which were so beautiful they had almost ceased to be, and, having endured strange moods, melancholy, as it seemed, with the weight of many worlds, I passed into that Death which is

Beauty herself, and into that Loneliness which multitudes desire without ceasing. (*SRH*, 206–7)

Aherne's vision expresses both the beauty of form and the formless beauty of "strange moods"; it is a vision that recalls the "Great Memory" of *Per Amica Silentia Lunae*, in which images are "mirrored in a living substance whose form is but change of form."[109] It also articulates the triumph, displaced into dream or fantasy, of spirit over matter, a triumph of the "Unity of Being" the folklorist advocated just a few years earlier, only achieved in the absence of any genuine "Unity of Culture." When Aherne is chased from the Temple of the Alchemical Rose, "set out on the very end of a dilapidated and almost deserted pier" in the West of Ireland (*SRH*, 211), by fishermen and peasants incensed by his idolatry, we are struck by the absence of a "Unity of Culture" and the distance Yeats has traveled from the villages of Sligo and Galway where he sought an intimate rapport with a visionary peasantry.

The intersubjective rapport that Yeats the folklorist had struggled to develop in his earlier work is, in the mystical stories, discarded in favor of an esotericism in which rapport has become thoroughly spiritualized. To some degree, the recourse to occult hermeticism, to the consolations of an "indefinite world," is meant to alleviate "the war that wages within" (*SRH*, 231), which had been the subject of the allegorical historiography of *The Secret Rose*. This war is also the subject of "The Tables of the Law" in which Owen Aherne's heretical beliefs lead to his expulsion from the providential narrative of Christian salvation: "I am not among those for whom Christ died, and this is why I must be hidden. I have a leprosy that even eternity cannot cure. I have seen the whole, and how can I come again to believe that a part is the whole? I have lost my soul because I have looked out of the eyes of the angels" (*TL*, 20). The "whole" that Aherne has seen, the vision that transports him beyond form to the realm of "strange moods," excludes him, as it had excluded the knight in "Out of the Rose," from the historical world. It is the desire to reunify these separate worlds that informs the last story of the mystical trilogy, "The Adoration of the Magi," in which three men receive wisdom from a woman who tells them "the secret names of the immortals" in "the Gaelic of their native country" and speaks of "the Sidhe of Ireland and of their love for the Cauldron, and the Whetstone, and the Sword and the Spear" (*TL*, 33). The narrator, after hearing their story, is uncertain whether the old men are not themselves "Immortals: immortal demons," but, in any case, he realizes that his path is not the same as theirs: "Whatever they were, I have turned into a pathway which will lead me from them and from the Order of the Alchemical Rose." He will lose himself now "among the prayers and the sorrows of the multitude," repeating "a prayer which was made I know not how many centuries ago to help some poor Gaelic man or woman who had suffered with a suffering like mine" (*TL*, 34–5). "The Adoration of the Magi" ends as *The Celtic Twilight* began, with an invocation to "the demons of the air" (*TL*, 35). And the reader is left wondering whether Aherne's spiritual journey has returned him to the world of Irish men and women he had abandoned and, if it does, whether he has learned anything in the process.

By 1897, the first phase of Yeats's modernist project of cultural redemption comes to a culmination in the figures of Robartes and Aherne, adepts in occult rituals, abstracted from the historical world in which the Irish people remain victims of colonialist and anthropological stereotypes and misrepresentations. As he entered into the next phase of his career, writing for and running the Abbey Theatre, Yeats began the process of redefining Revivalism under the influence of Synge's tragic heroism. At the same time, he was becoming uneasy with the specter of an independent Catholic Ireland and was beginning to formulate a more frankly Anglo-Irish conception of "Irishness." The first stage in this formulation was the reconstruction of the figure of Red Hanrahan in the years following the original publication of *Stories of Red Hanrahan*. I have already remarked on the new centrality Yeats gave the stories when he published them separately in 1905. In his preface to Synge's *The Well of the Saints*, he justified this strategy by saying that *The Secret Rose* "had separated my imagination from life, sending my Red Hanrahan, who should have trodden the same roads with myself, into some undiscoverable country" (*CA*, 112). Yeats, like Owen Aherne, had come to recognize that the spiritual need not be "indefinite" or "measureless," that it might adhere precisely in the materiality of an embodied personality, a recognition that would come to characterize his "high" modernist style. But what seems tentative in Aherne is more certain in Yeats, in large measure due to the influence of Synge and Lady Gregory.

A crucial stage in the evolution of Hanrahan took place in 1907, the year of the *Playboy* riots, when Yeats first began the process of revising *Stories of Red Hanrahan*. In a note to *Early Poems and Stories* (1925), Yeats recalls his collaboration with Lady Gregory:

We worked together, first upon that tale, and, after, upon all the others, she now suggesting a new phrase or thought, and now I, till all had been put into that simple English she had learned from her Galway countrymen, and the thought had come closer to the life of the people . . . Dr. Hyde had already founded the first Gaelic play ever performed in a theatre upon one of the stories, and but the other day Lady Gregory made a Hanrahan play upon an incident of her own invention.[110]

What is remarkable about Hanrahan is the sense of vertigo induced by the proliferation of possible authors and versions, a *mélange* of early modernist aestheticism and Celtic folklore. In the figure of Red Hanrahan, "originality" and "authority" are constantly multiplied, challenged, overturned. In acknowledging Lady Gregory's assistance in rewriting *Stories of Red Hanrahan*, Yeats confesses that their collaboration produced a language "nearer to the tradition of the people among whom [Hanrahan], or some likeness of him, drifted and is remembered" (*SRH*, 2). Declan Kiberd complicates our sense of Hanrahan's historical "reality" when he observes that Douglas Hyde "was described, with no exaggeration, as a scholar-in-waiting to the Irish renaissance, furnishing Yeats with the figure of Hanrahan and a host of other *personae*."[111] The proliferation of representations and models suggests that Hanrahan was less a specific historical individual or even a type of the Irish bard than an effect of a collaborative ethnographic imagination.

The result is a form of *in*authenticity; or, to put my point another way, a form of authenticity that inheres not in a faithful representation of folk culture but rather in the textual effects of the Revivalist's desire to resolve his own ambivalent social identity. As Yeats put it in a note to the first edition of *The Wind Among the Reeds* (1899), Hanrahan became a "principle of the mind": "It is probably that only students of the magical tradition will understand me when I say that . . . Hanrahan is the simplicity of an imagination too changeable to gather permanent possessions, or the adoration of the shepherds."[112] It is this "changeable" imagination that undermines Hanrahan's status as a cultural icon while simultaneously guaranteeing his relevance for Yeats's evolving Revivalist project of cultural redemption. For, though Yeats admits that Hanrahan is the product of a collaboration, he nevertheless insists on his authority as an autonomous creator: the figure that Yeats the Revivalist "redeemed" as part of an authentic folk culture becomes the creation or "thought" that the modernist poet lays claim to in "The Tower," published almost thirty years after *Stories of Red Hanrahan*:

> And I myself created Hanrahan
> And drove him drunk or sober through the dawn
> From somewhere in the neighbouring cottages.
> Caught by an old man's juggleries
> He stumbled, tumbled, fumbled to and fro
> And had but broken knees for hire
> And horrible splendour of desire;
> I thought it all out twenty years ago. (*Poems*, 196)

Although he is a fallen, ineffectual bard, Hanrahan still powerfully embodies the process of Yeats's self-fashioning. The double assertion of possession ("I myself") betrays the poet's desire for the singularity of an original act of creation, unassisted and unmediated by a folk tradition he helped create. The ethnographic ambivalence of his early Revivalist work, actuated by a desire to "achieve a folkloristic impersonality,"[113] is finally overwhelmed by the prerogatives of the modern artist for whom culture is indistinguishable from personality. Feelings of social and political displacement, which Yeats once thought he could overcome in a unity with the peasant mediated by a redemptive ethnographic imagination, give way to an emancipatory self-fashioning mediated by an equally redemptive style borne out of "solitary self-absorbed consciousness" that, according to Kiberd, "creates its own environment. Style so understood is war on the chancy and casual, on mere character and circumstance."[114]

The shift from the "fair equivalents" Yeats sought in his early folkloric work to the "divine substances" of the mystical stories might be understood, then, as a shift from a mode of more or less realistic representation to the rigorously non-representational style of plays like *The Green Helmet, On Baile's Strand* and *At the Hawk's Well* – a style better suited to the expression of "internal consciousness." As Kiberd argues, "the need to resort to non-representational art is obvious to those writers who seek to elaborate a landscape of internal consciousness rather than submit to a despised external setting."[115] Yeats's increasing involvement in dramatic writing after the turn of the century, together with his close association with Synge, led him to a reassessment of Revivalist aesthetics with a new emphasis on tragic heroism and, paradoxically, given Synge's fierce advocacy of the Irish peasantry, to a new sympathy with the Anglo-Irish intellectual tradition.

As I have suggested, Synge's life and work proved instrumental in the development of this "landscape of internal consciousness" and a concept of personality that moved Yeats closer to his mature modernist aesthetics.[116] The influence is marked in essays written between 1903 and 1910 – specifically in "Discoveries" and "John M. Synge and the Ireland of His Time," both reprinted in *The Cutting of an Agate* (1919) – where Yeats develops the idea of personality and redefines the virtues of the Revivalist artist. According to Robert O'Driscoll, personality was for Yeats a release of "energy . . . unique to an individual engaged in active life," "an energy that comes from the whole man, the spontaneous expression of a moment of intense life, "an eddy of life purified from everything but itself."[117] In "Discoveries," Yeats writes that we have lost, in literature, a sense of personality, a "delight in the whole man – blood, imagination, intellect, running together – but have found a new delight, in essences, in states of mind, in pure imagination, in all that comes to us most easily in elaborate music" (*CA*, 66). In order to regain this sense of personality, we must ascend "out of common interests, the thoughts of the newspapers, of the market-place, of men of science, but only so far as we can carry the normal, passionate, reasoning self, the personality as a whole" (*CA*, 74). It is the reality of conflict, "all that heightens the emotions by contest" (*CA*, 153–4), that makes possible the return of this "lost" personality: "Is it that all things are made by the struggle of the individual and the world, of the unchanging and the returning, and that the saint and the poet are over all, and that the poet has made his home in the serpent's mouth?" (*CA*, 97).

The controversy over Synge's *Playboy of the Western World* may have been the point at which Yeats realized that he had failed to capture the "essence" of Irish folk culture, and it may be that his new emphasis on personality was an attempt to bypass the political dimensions of his project of cultural redemption. In "On Those that Hated 'The Playboy of the Western World,' 1907," Yeats criticizes those who could not accept Synge's heroic attempt to do what he himself had done less effectively – that is, contest misrepresentations of the Irish peasantry in the assertion of his own right to advance an anthropological fiction that nevertheless revealed a truth that previous so-called "authentic" representations had missed:

> Once, when midnight smote the air,
> Eunuchs ran through Hell and met
> On every crowded street to stare
> Upon great Juan riding by:
> Even like these to rail and sweat
> Staring upon his sinewy thigh.   (*Poems*, 111)

This short poem crystallizes the argument, in "John M. Synge and the Ireland of His Time," that Synge was a tragic figure, "full of passion and heroic beauty," whose "discovery of style," purified of "insincerity, vanity, malignity [and] arrogance" (*CA*, 146, 142), resulted from his own alienation and loneliness – qualities that, according to Yeats, Synge found in abundance on the Aran Islands.

"On Those that Hated 'The Playboy of the Western World,' 1907," appeared in *Responsibilities*, a volume which marks a decisive turning point in the development of Yeats's project of cultural redemption. As I noted above, in talking about Yeats's "wild Irish" stories, a native Irish literature need no longer rest on anthropological assumptions of racial or cultural difference. What needs to be explored at this point is how Yeats came to reinvest his work with an acute sense of just such differences, and how this reinvestment determined the shape of his mature modernism. For it is clear that the anthropological tenor of Yeats's modernism is considerably attenuated in the poetry from about the time of *Responsibilities*, published in 1914, with the result that his concern for race and culture exhibits a quite different form of social authority from that which we see in the work of the 1890s. Yeats's Revivalist project until about 1897 was dedicated primarily to a method of creative evocation in which "fair equivalents" of folklore were the goal of a redemptive ethnographic project. As I have shown with respect to the "wild Irish" stories, a shift took place in which "divine substances" displaced "fair equivalents" as the object of a new social authority that combined the visionary capacity of the mystic with the modern artist's increasing interest in personality as the mediating filter for any representation of the "real" world outside the sovereign observer's consciousness. This process begins in earnest in the essay on Synge, where the emphasis on personality predominates; a few years later, in *Per Amica Silentia Lunae* (1917), the idea of personality is complicated by its integration into a mystical doctrine of psychic doubling that operates in the form of a dialectic of self and anti-self, which Yeats was to elaborate further in *A Vision*.

This shift registers in another way in "Swedenborg, Mediums, Desolate Places" (1914), an essay in which Yeats reconciles his folkloric work with Lady Gregory with his burgeoning interest in occultism. Speaking of Swedenborg's ideas of the separation of "the spiritual from the physical body" after death, Yeats develops a parallel that was implicit in *The Celtic Twilight*. "It is characteristic of his whole religious system, the slow drifting of like to like," he writes; and then, after noting the similarity of the afterlife to life on earth, he quotes Swedenborg: "for 'when what is spiritual touches and sees what is spiritual the effect is the same as when what is natural touches what is natural.'" The Swedenborgian vision of heaven is identical to the peasant vision of fairyland: "It is the other world of the early races, of those whose dead are in the rath or the faery hill, of all who see no place of reward and punishment but a continuance of this life, with cattle and sheep markets and war" (*E*, 34–5). In a sense, "fair equivalents" have not disappeared; it is simply that the objects for which Yeats sought to evoke equivalence had changed: no longer the Revivalist ethnographer seeking to evoke and thereby redeem the tangible folkways of the peasantry, Yeats had become the adept seeking through occult rituals and symbols to gain access to the *in*tangible experiences of "discarnate consciousnesses" – experiences that are not foreign to the tangible world itself. As Evans-Wentz notes, "in the Celtic scheme of evolution the Otherworld with all its gods, fairies, and invisible things, and this world with all its visible beings, form the two poles of life or conscious experience." Though it is a "mysterious land beyond the Ocean," the Otherworld is a place "where the dead find a new existence, and where [the Tuatha De Danann's] god-king Tethra ruled, as he formerly ruled in this world."[118]

That Yeats could still manage to reconcile his occult beliefs with the fairy-faith of the peasantry is not surprising, since in 1914 he had not yet come to identify the social consciousness of the peasantry with the Catholic ideology of the newly emergent confessional state of 1922. The dominant trend in Yeats's development after 1914 is toward a spiritualized conception of artistic personality which is not without a parallel in the thinking of anthropologists whose interest in social psychology led to an increased awareness of the relationship in their own experience between spirit and the external world. As I noted in chapter 1, Malinowski's modernism is to some extent determined by just such an awareness, for the experience of fieldwork was often characterized as a kind of spiritual fervor, a compulsion "to plunge my spirit into reality. Something greater than curiosity and more essential than thought."[119] This aptly describes Yeats's sense of the link between a spiritualized personality and the world of material relations and effects. But something else must be adduced in order to account for the direction Yeats ultimately took, a direction that many readers have found disturbing because it led him to advocate eugenics and population control. For his interest in occultism was in some ways balanced by a new conception of the "reality" of "race" that he was seeking to invent – or perhaps I should say *re*invent, because that reality was increasingly being associated by Yeats with an Anglo-Irish intellectual tradition.

This reinvention begins with *Responsibilities*, which includes several poems that respond to social events like the Dublin Corporation's refusal to build an adequate gallery for Hugh Lane's collection of Impressionist paintings. In "September 1913," Yeats excoriates the materialism of an emergent Catholic middle class and mourns the passing of "Romantic Ireland." In "Paudeen" he continues the critique in more patently stereotypical terms: "Indignant at the fumbling wits, the obscure spite / Of our old Paudeen in his shop, I stumbled blind / Among the stones and thorn-trees" (*Poems*, 109). The sense of disillusionment with respect to the aspirations of Irish nationalism and the philistinism that he regarded as the social concomitant of nationalist political radicalism led Yeats to a recognition of the problematic nature of his own commitment to nationalism, especially the way in which his conception of the peasantry reflected that commitment.

"Easter 1916" is an important poem in this respect, but one that reveals a lingering ambivalence concerning the martyrdom of those involved in the rebellion. On the one hand, the poem records a moment of transformation when the aspirations of Irish nationalists cease to resemble the farcical "fumbl[ing] in a greasy till" (*Poems*, 108) and begin to solidify into a tragi-comic tableau that encompasses the "vivid faces" coming "from counter or desk" and the poet himself. He is certain "that they and I / But lived where motley is worn" and that the "terrible beauty" of the sacrifice derived from and includes them all. On the other hand, the poet is critical of that very sacrifice, wondering if it was worth the surrender of social grace and artistic talent, wondering if it was worth it to see the heart's desire "[e]nchanted to a stone / to trouble the living stream." His ambivalence deepens in a surprising direction when he appears to admit that this "stony" sacrifice, while it troubles the "living stream," is nevertheless a part of that stream, for "the stone's in the midst of all" (*Poems*, 180–1). The ambivalence recorded here – of being caught between rebellion and criticism of the rebels, uncertain whether their sacrifice is a part of life's flow or an impediment to it – reflects Yeats's growing awareness that his early efforts at representing Irish folk culture had paid too little attention to the politics of representation. Kiberd argues that "Easter 1916" reflects a struggle between Yeats's "public, textual duty" and his "more personal urge" to question republican sacrifice:

[t]he poem speaks, correspondingly, with two voices, and sometimes enacts in single phrases ("terrible beauty") their contestation. The sanction for the first voice from bardic tradition was strong: but the force of the second was becoming more apparent to Yeats who increasingly defined freedom in terms of self-expression. He was abandoning the rather programmatic nationalism of his youth for a more personal version of Irish identity.[120]

I would add that this struggle is a repetition, in a more overtly political idiom of the "war of spiritual with natural order" (*SR*, vii) that animated the folkloric fictions of the 1890s, only now the "more personal urge" triumphs. The contestation enacted in the phrase "terrible beauty" and the ambivalence I noted above with respect to the "enchanted heart" are reenacted again and again throughout the later poetry and underscore the process by which Yeats, in developing his "personal version of Irish identity," redefined the goals of a Revivalist project of cultural redemption.

A "personal vision" of the kind Kiberd adduces entailed the reclamation of the artist's right to represent, which was, for Yeats, the right of possession. I have already shown how this right evolved in the revision of Red Hanrahan, a process of intertextual collaboration that installed Yeats as the autonomous artist orchestrating a singular creation: "I myself created Hanrahan," the poet emphatically states (*Poems*, 196). An earlier, more quietly programmatic instance of this right to represent, one that underscores the *in*authenticity of the representations that proceed from it, is "The Fisherman," a poem from *The Wild Swans at Coole* (1919), in which Yeats frankly admits the imaginary status of the peasant he had celebrated in the 1890s: he is a "man who does not exist," a man "who is but a dream," who stands as an emblem of a "cold / And passionate" poetry (*Poems*, 149). In repudiating the Arnoldean rustic of redemptive Celticism, Yeats appears also to be repudiating the idea of evoking "a fair equivalent for the gesture and voice of the peasant tale-teller" (*UP1*, 174). In the 1890s, Yeats's desire for an "imaginary Ireland" was grounded in the idea that the Revivalist's ethnographic imagination could restore the authenticity of the folk through an evocative equivalence. The kind of authenticity proffered by *Fairy and Folk Tales* and *The Celtic Twilight*, authorized by the Revivalist's commitment to a redemptive ethnography, is quite different from the ratification of the poet's artistic autonomy that we see increasingly in the later work. Synge's influence is notable here, particularly in Yeats's awareness of his own role in creating phantasmic constructions of a "wise and simple man" in "grey Connemara clothes"; but we also see it in the heroism of his attempt to use such constructions in order to confront those who would oppose his desire "[t]o write for my own race / And the reality": "The clever man who cries / The catch-cries of the clown, / The beating down of the wise / And great Art beaten down" (*Poems*, 148).

Given the context of "The Fisherman," a volume that commemorates the cultural influence of the Anglo-Irish Revival, we might regard the poet's confession to having constructed a phantasm, "a man who does not exist," as a claim to the kind of glory that he recalls in his elegy, "In Memory of Major Robert Gregory." This poem celebrates the "[d]iscoverers of forgotten truth" and those, like Synge, who "chose the living world for text," who were born to "cold Clare rock and Galway rock and thorn, / To that stern colour and that delicate line / That are our secret discipline / Wherein the gazing heart doubles her might" (*Poems*, 133–4). A significant shift occurs in these late poems from an interest in the "the gesture and voice of the peasant tale-teller" whose reality was deemed valuable and worthy of preservation to an interest in the heroic artist who bravely constructs images of that reality the very constructedness of which testifies to the "secret discipline" of the artist who gazes, whose heart "doubles her might." The ideal of ethnographic observation in the service of creating "fair equivalents," having achieved a kind of apotheosis in the mystical "wild Irish" stories, is now recast as the ideal of artistic discipline, or *re*vision and recreation. "New originals," to be sure, but with a greatly diminished share of the essence that the poet once celebrated as the root of both folk and civilized culture. Just as the "fair equivalents" of an ethnographic imagination gave way to "divine substances" of the mystic, so these substances, by virtue of their subordination to the authority of the autonomous and sovereign poetic creator, gave way to the singular ability of a heroic personality to produce imaginary communities, to help determine what an authentic Irish identity might be.

For Kiberd, Yeats's emphasis on personality and stylistic self-fashioning is part of larger social vision: "The project of inventing a unitary Ireland is the attempt to achieve at a political level a reconciliation of opposed qualities which must first be fused in the self. In other words, personal liberation must precede national recovery, being in fact its very condition."[121] It may be true that personal liberation must precede national recovery, but Yeats's changing conception of Revivalism and the role of the Anglo-Irish intellectual raise questions about the kind of nation that ought to be recovered. *The Celtic Twilight* and the folkloric fictions, in large measure because their hybrid forms tended to resist the process by which ethnographic texts acquire social authority over the native subjects they seek to represent, offered a vision of a "unity of being" forged in an intersubjective rapport with a mystical peasantry. In the later work, the problems of race, cultural authenticity, and national identity are reframed in terms of a heroic Anglo-Irish tradition that for Yeats was the bedrock of whatever was great about Irish culture. His famous Senate speech of 1925, to protest a bill that would make divorce illegal, marks the début of his project to rehabilitate that tradition, a project that entailed a reformation of his ideas about race and the relationship between primitive and civilized peoples:

I think it is tragic that within three years of this country gaining its independence we should be discussing a measure which a minority of this nation considers to be grossly oppressive. I am proud to consider myself a typical man of that minority. We against whom you have done this thing, are no petty people. We are one of the great stocks of Europe. We are the people of Burke; we are the people of Grattan; we are the people of Swift, the people of Emmet, the people of Parnell. We have created the most of the modern literature of this country. We have created the best of its political intelligence.[122]

The sentiments here, rendered in the form of a last will and testament in "The Tower," express a call for liberty; but, as Richard Ellmann notes, it is "the liberty of a privileged class" advocated by a man who "insisted upon speaking as a man of the world and Anglo-Irishman rather than as a man of letters or a man of conviction."[123]

Many important poems were to follow that combined the aspect of the Anglo-Irishman with that of the man of letters and the man of conviction; it is just that the subjects of the artist's vision and the particular nature of his convictions change. The high modernist's disillusionment with modernity, expressed so vividly in "Coole Park and Ballylee, 1931," seeks relief in tradition; but it is not the "[t]raditional sanctity and loveliness" that the Revivalists, those "last romantics" chose for a theme from "the book of the people." What the poet commemorates both as a value in itself and as an antidote to the "darkening flood" of modernity, is "ancestral trees / Or gardens rich in memory" that had once "glorified / Marriages, alliances and families, / And every bride's ambition satisfied" (*Poems*, 242). In these and in poems that followed, Revivalism is redefined in terms of the heroic triumph of the "indomitable Irishry." In "The Municipal Gallery Re-visited," Yeats sums up his mature vision of Revivalism in a manner meant to give it a kind of retrospective legitimacy:

> John Synge, I and Augusta Gregory, thought
> All that we did, all that we said or sang
> Must come from contact with the soil, from that
> Contact everything Antaeus-like grew strong.
> We three alone in modern times had brought
> Everything down to that sole test again,
> Dream of the noble and the beggarman. (*Poems*, 321)

In this and other poems of commemoration, Yeats redefines Revivalism as a campaign by an Anglo-Irish élite to "test" artistic personality against a "[d]ream of the noble and the beggarman," to single-handedly redeem from historical obscurity a déclassé ruling class, and to grant it the authenticity that had always eluded it.

In 1939, near the end of his life, Yeats published a miscellany, *On the Boiler*, that expressed his new ideas about the Irish "race" and the advisability of redeeming certain portions of it. Though there is scarcely any overt mention of the Catholic Irish, it is clear from the tone of the piece, and from the bitter sense of lost Anglo-Irish greatness recorded in the short play *Purgatory* included in *On the Boiler*, that Yeats's new interest in education and eugenics was a response to the isolation and irrelevance of the Anglo-Irish class within the Catholic confessional state that Ireland had become after Eamon de Valera's rise to power in the 1930s. Most important about *On the Boiler* is the way it redefines the anthropological tenor of Yeats's mature modernist vision. The primitivism that he struggled against in the 1890s and later, in the aftermath of Synge's *Playboy*, was fundamentally a discourse about racial essence; the primitivism that we find in *On the Boiler* is of a different and more complex sort, primarily because it seems to derive its power to distinguish among races less from the kinds of physiological differences that marked the "dark-skinned" native as inferior than from cultural differences that marked the socially "degenerate" as inferior. This shift in the ground of racial difference (notwithstanding the reliance of National Socialism on retrograde nineteenth-century ideas of race as a function of blood purity) is partly the result of anthropological theories that focused on the social institutions and material culture of primitive societies. Thus Malinowski, who contributed the entry on "culture" to the *Encyclopaedia of the Social Sciences* in the early 1930s, could write that "[t]he racial need of continuity is not satisfied by the mere action of physiological impulses and physiological processes but by the working of traditional rules associated with an apparatus of material culture."[124]

In *On the Boiler*, Yeats addresses the idea of the degeneration of racial continuity from a number of perspectives. He begins by recalling the Lord Mayor's attempt to return the Mansion House to "its eighteenth-century state." The problem for Yeats, evidently, is that "[a]ll Catholic Ireland, as it was before the National University and a victory in the field had swept the penal laws out of its bones, swells out in that pretentious front" (*OB*, 10). The implications of this statement are not altogether clear, but we might gather from subsequent statements that the public life of Catholic Ireland is of a very poor quality indeed when compared to that of the Anglo-Irish of the eighteenth century. Of the former, Yeats writes, "it seems probable that many men in Irish public life should not have been taught to read and write, and would not have been in any country before the middle of the nineteenth century" (*OB*, 11). In these remarks, Yeats reinscribes a primitivist assumption about the Catholic Irish, who would be better off with the penal laws still in their bones, subject to the social authority of their Anglo-Irish superiors. But, at the same time that Yeats criticizes the literacy of the public men, he condemns the educational system that breeds incompetence. As an "apparatus of material culture," this system is therefore partly responsible for maintaining racial health and continuity; its failure to do so is linked to a general degeneration of the body and mind that Yeats sees in the principal European nations (see

OB, 16–17). However, we cannot read these pages without seeing in them a covert attack against Catholic Ireland. Drawing on literature from the Eugenics Society and other sources on intelligence testing, Yeats notes that "[i]n almost all European countries, especially those where Catholicism encourages large families among the poor, there has been an equal or greater decline" than in England since 1873 (*OB*, 17).

In the evidence he marshals for his argument about the degeneration of culture, we see the ideal of cultural redemption transformed into a project of eugenics that calls, on the one hand, for an élite of "six or six thousand . . . the core of Ireland . . . Ireland itself" and, on the other hand, the restriction in education and social advancement of those who fail to maintain strong racial continuity. Taking as his text a passage from Robert Burton's *Anatomy of Melancholy*, which argues for the gelding or destruction of the sick and deformed "for the common good, lest the nation should be injured or corrupted" (*OB*, 16), Yeats argues that "[s]ooner or later we must limit the families of the unintelligent classes, and if our government cannot send them doctor and clinic it must, till it gets tired of it, send monk and confession box" (*OB*, 20). We see in this theory of eugenics an alternative solution to the dilemma posed by the contradiction between the traditional and the modern. Whereas in the early days of the Revival, as Terry Eagleton argues, "Traditional culture provide[d] modernism with an adversary, but also len[t] it some of the terms in which to inflect itself,"[125] Yeats now regards traditional culture, which references to "monk and confession box" clearly mark as Catholic, as an impediment to modernity:

We cannot go back as some dreamers would have us, to the old way of big families everywhere, even if the intelligent classes would consent, because that old way worked through lack of science and consequent great mortality among the children of those least fitted for modern civilisation. (*OB*, 20)

Yeats admits that "[a]mong those our civilisation must reject . . . exist precious faculties" like "clairvoyance, prevision, and allied gifts, rare among the educated classes" but which are "common among peasants" (*OB*, 26–7). It is striking how far he has traveled from the days of the early Revival when such gifts were evidence of a "unity of culture" that would include the peasant and the Anglo-Irish poet as equals. Yeats has not devalued the gifts of the

peasantry so much as shifted them out of the peasant's "mediumistic
sleep" and relocated them into the "wide-awake" consciousness of
the artist who appeals to "[e]ugenical and psychical research" as
"revolutionary movements with that element of novelty and sensation which sooner or later stir men to action" (*OB*, 27).

This is an up-to-date variety of primitivism that grudgingly accepts
the peasants' gifts but in the end finds the peasants themselves,
subsumed now among the "Irish masses," "vague and excitable
because they have not yet been moulded and cast." The élite who
should lead the "hundred men" who possess superior education and
"blood," are, of course, the Anglo-Irish intelligentsia, whose ranks
may ultimately include Catholics, once they have been properly
molded and cast (*OB*, 30). The eugenic argument concludes by
instating a new binomial distinction between Greek and Asiatic
cultures, the former represented by an ideal of statuary proportion,
the latter by a "multiform, vague, expressive Asiatic sea" (*OB*, 37).
Clearly, the "vague and excitable" Irish masses belong to the Asiatic
category, and equally clearly the distinction between Greek and
Asiatic is a return to the kind of racial typing that Yeats found in
Matthew Arnold's *On the Study of Celtic Literature* and that he attempted
to turn to nationalist advantage in his own "Celtic Element in
Literature." A late poem, "The Statues," articulates this distinction,
but does so in a way that conflates the categories of the traditional
and the modern as Yeats appeared to understand them in the 1890s:

> When Pearse summoned Cuchulain to his side,
> What stalked through the Post Office? What intellect,
> What calculation, number, measurement, replied?
> We Irish, born into that ancient sect
> But thrown upon this filthy modern tide
> And by its formless, spawning, fury wrecked,
> Climb to our proper dark, that we may trace
> The lineaments of a plummet-measured face.   (*Poems*, 337)

The "Asiatic vague immensities" referred to in "The Statues" and
On the Boiler emerge as the formless "spawn" of the "filthy modern
tide"; what once constituted a traditional culture (the "Irish
masses," the Catholic nationalists who fought with Pearse) over
against modernity is now figured as part of that modernity Yeats had
been criticizing at least since his 1925 Senate speech. We are not
given clear answers to the two questions that open this stanza, but
the weight of evidence in *On the Boiler* suggests that when the poet

refers to "we Irish" he is not referring to Pearse, and when he wonders what intellect would reply to Pearse's summons, it is not that of the "plummet-measured face" whose divine contours "gave to the sexual instinct of Europe its goal, its fixed type" (*OB*, 37).

At the end of his life, Yeats appeared to have betrayed the ideals he held in the early days of the Revival, ideals of cultural redemption that were grounded in the superior spiritual virtues of the peasantry. But perhaps we should not be so surprised, for we can find evidence of Yeats's interest in degeneration and eugenics as early as 1897. In "Rosa Alchemica," Owen Aherne accuses the mystical adept Michael Robartes of trying to "sweep me away into an indefinite world which fills me with terror": "I command you to leave me at once, for your ideas and phantasies are but the illusions that creep like maggots into civilizations when they begin to decline, and into minds when they begin to decay" (*SRH*, 205). What are we to make of this connection? That the illusions of the mystic have now become the reality of the Irish masses? Or is it that those illusions, once shared by adept and peasant alike, are given up now in favor of a more "wide awake" Protestant magic? As is so often the case when discussing Yeats's cultural politics, one must conclude with the rhetorical equivalent of an exasperated shrug.

In a sense, this is the only way of responding to the one-act play, *Purgatory*, that closes *On the Boiler*, for in it we find a singularly ambivalent picture of the Anglo-Irish class, an ambivalence that is more confounding given the fact that Yeats has so clearly elevated that class earlier in the text. The play is set against the backdrop of "[a] *ruined house and a bare tree*" and depicts a boy and an old man talking about the legends of drunken murderousness that surround the house's destruction. On the one hand, the play is an eloquent memorial to the Anglo-Irish Big House culture whose passing Yeats had been mourning for over twenty years:

> Great people lived and died in this house;
> Magistrates, colonels, members of Parliament,
> Captains and Governors, and long ago
> Men that had fought at Aughrim and the Boyne . . .
> They had loved the trees that he cut down
> To pay what he had lost at cards
> Or spent on horses, drink and women;
> Had loved the house, had loved all
> The intricate passages of the house.   (*OB*, 41)

In the space of a single passage, Yeats's memorialization slides into a condemnation of sensual excess and riotous living, for the master of the house, the old man's father, had himself "killed the house" and "to kill a house / Where great men grew up, married, died, / I here declare a capital offence." The irony, of course, lies in the fact that the old man was himself responsible for killing his father and burning the house; he is the murderer he himself condemns. The motive for his act, presumably his disapproval of the drunken sensuality that led to his begetting, is reenacted as the old man and boy stand before the ruins. He calls out to the ghost of his dead mother: "It is not true / That drunken men cannot beget / And if he touch he must beget / And you must bear his murderer" (*OB*, 43). In a travesty of the legend in which Cuchulain unknowingly kills his own son in single combat, the old man kills the boy, his son, out of a fear that he would continue a murderous legacy: "I killed that lad because [had he] grown up, / He would have struck a woman's fancy, / Begot, and passed pollution on" (*OB*, 45).[126]

We might say that both *On the Boiler* and Yeats's Revivalist career end on this ambivalent note. The spokesman for an Anglo-Irish élite appears, in an unsavory argument for the limitation and even elimination of unfit members of society, to betray the cause of Revivalist cultural redemption; but at the conclusion of that argument he offers an allegory of Anglo-Irish deracination that implicates the Anglo-Irish themselves in their own degeneration, the hereditary sensuality and murderousness that "pass[es] pollution on." The image offered by the boy of this deracinated class – "A dead, living, murdered man" (*OB*, 44) – neatly sums up the ambivalence of Yeats's cultural politics in the late 1930s. But the ever-present possibility that *On the Boiler* contains ironies of which even the poet himself was unaware, makes it very difficult to draw conclusions about how far Yeats really traveled from his early Revivalist attitudes. In the chapters that follow, we will see that Synge and Joyce confront the same ambivalence with respect to the value of cultural "purity" and the costs of cultural "degeneration." It may be the case that Synge's genuine affection for Irish folk life and Joyce's Catholic background disallowed any turn toward eugenics or any argument for the racial superiority of an Anglo-Irish élite. But, whatever the cause, their commitment to a mode of art that refused to make any simplistic assumptions about race and racial superiority led them to champion the liberatory power of the *in*authentic and the *in*essential. This mode of art – profoundly anti-realistic even as it seeks to discover what is real in experience – could only emerge in a scrupulous and interminable critique of the primitivism, that for Yeats, not only remained as a powerful determinate of his work, but in the end frustrated any clear message we might take from it.

CHAPTER 3

"Synge-On-Aran": 'The Aran Islands' and the subject of Revivalist ethnography

Islanders too
are for sculpting. Note
the pointed scowl, the mouth
carved as upturned anchor
and the polished head
full of drownings.
                    There
he comes now, a hard pen
scraping in his head;
the nib filed on a salt wind
and dipped in the keening sea.   Seamus Heaney[1]

In his Introduction to *The Aran Islands*, John M. Synge writes, "In the pages that follow I have given a direct account of my life on the islands, and of what I met with among them, inventing nothing, and changing nothing that is essential" (*AI*, 48). This disclaimer might well serve as an expression of the attitude toward culture that was emerging among anthropologists like A. R. Radcliffe-Brown and Bronislaw Malinowski in the first decades of the twentieth century. At the same time, it raises questions about representation that are central to ethnography and that deepen the difficulties of establishing rapport and credibility with native communities. Synge strove to establish himself among the Aran Islanders and managed to establish the distance proper to ethnographic observation and to write something like an ethnographic account. But this account is destabilized in ways that suggest a modernist sensibility at odds with the mode of ethnographic redemption that has been called into being as an anodyne for his sense of dissociation and alienation. In this respect, Synge's *Aran Islands* develops still further certain aspects of Yeats's Revivalist project. And if Synge differs in any significant way from Yeats it is because his text, more clearly grounded in fieldwork and ethnographic conventions of representation, explicitly reaffirms (by virtue of shared methods and perspectives) the authority and cultural assumptions of anthropological inquiry that are implicit in Yeats's folkloristic texts.

Synge's interest in peasant culture can be traced to his boyhood wanderings in County Wicklow and then through a diverse education in continental Celticism under the tutelage of Henri D'Arbois de Jubainville, whose lectures at the Sorbonne on Celtic culture and mythology Synge had attended while living in Paris, and the Breton writer Anatole le Braz.[2] As David Greene remarks, Ernest Renan "placed the problem of Celtic revivalism squarely before him."[3] He was also part of a European artistic milieu that was being electrified by new anthropological knowledge. "Like Yeats, Pound, and Eliot," writes Richard Fallis, "Synge employed a creative method related to the comparativist methods of nineteenth-century literary and anthropological scholarship. He studied philology and cultural anthropology at the Sorbonne, and the method he learned there 'took.'"[4] This method prepared him for his experience of the primitive Aran Islanders; and, while without such methods he could not produce the kind of ethnographic text he had in mind, he had no professional obligation to adhere to them in any deliberate or consistent fashion. But Synge's anthropological modernism, like Yeats's, involved more than simply borrowing a comparative method; it also involved the appropriation of an ethnographic attitude that was in significant ways undermined by an unscientific intersubjectivity – a desire to enter into an intimate, reciprocal rapport with the islanders – that revealed the fissures in the observer's own consciousness as well as in his ethnographic account.

In his essay "John M. Synge and the Ireland of His Time," Yeats noted that one of Synge's strengths as a writer about Irish culture was his habit of "unmeditative watching" and his desire for invisibility: "He told me once that when he lived in some peasant's house, he tried to make those about him forget that he was there, and it is certain that he was silent in any crowded room" (*CA*, 155, 145). On the Aran Islands, he wished to efface himself to such an extent that the islanders would simply forget him. However, his desire for invisibility, for an enabling distance, conflicted with his desire to establish an intimate rapport with his informants. The Forward to *The Aran Islands* captures this ambivalence:

As far as possible . . . I have disguised the identity of the people I speak of, by making changes in their names, and in the letters I quote, and by altering some local and family relationships. I have had nothing to say about them that was not wholly in their favor, but I have made this disguise to keep them from ever feeling that *a too direct use had been made of their kindness, and friendship*, for which I am more grateful than it is easy to say. (*AI*, 20; my emphasis)

Like similar disclaimers made by Yeats and Lady Gregory, this one reveals an ambivalence about Synge's role as a participant–observer, for in the same gesture it calls for the "direct use" of material garnered from informants and seeks to mitigate in advance the effects of any "excessive" use that might interfere with the rapport he had established with them.

But at the same time that Synge's work on the Aran Islands conforms in significant ways to the protocols of the emerging discipline of ethnography, it simultaneously subverts those protocols by dramatizing a desire for the Other that has no place in the ethnographer's scientific account. The subversive desire to *know* the islanders and their community from the inside, beyond the limits set by disciplinary convention, in one sense liberates both the observer and the observed from the discursive hegemony of ethnography by redefining the authority of experience and by making the partici-pant–observer both subject *and object* of an ethnographic text; but, because of the persistent influence of a Manichean discourse of primitivism subtending Synge's project of cultural and personal redemption, the Aran Islander ends up as a phantasm, an exotic projection of a sovereign and civilized European observer. To some extent, Synge resembles the ethnographic hero who, as Susan Sontag puts it, "submits himself to the exotic to confirm his own inner alienation as an urban intellectual" and ends "by aiming to vanquish his subject by translating it into a purely formal code."[5] In seeking to confirm "his own inner alienation as an urban intel-lectual," Synge submits himself to the "exotic" Aran Islanders; but unlike Claude Lévi-Strauss, the subject of Sontag's remark, he does not translate his experience into a "formal code." Given his ambivalent desire to identify with the islanders, to vanquish his subject would mean to vanquish himself. He must therefore retain the distinction between civilized and primitive, observer and observed that ordinarily gives anthropology its warrant to intervene in and redeem non-Western societies. In doing so, he retains a sense of difference from the islanders precisely in order that he might long for their primitive simplicity as a way to abolish that difference. Though he fails ultimately to deconstruct the position of participant–observer, his ambivalence with respect to the ethnographic authority that both distinguishes him from the islanders and proffers the opportunity to identify with them anticipates the destabilizing modernism we see in the work of Bronislaw Malinowski.

Like Yeats, Synge was caught up in an ambivalent relationship with the dominant discourses of anthropology, and his attitude toward peasant culture – he regarded the Aran Islanders as a wild and primitive, inherently noble people cut off from modern Europe – betrays an equally ambivalent investment in primitivism. To the extent that Synge's text translates native customs, rituals, and folklore into a foreign and dominant language, it becomes a "scientific text," whose "social authority," according to Talal Asad, derives from an imbalance of power between the ethnographic observer and the native under his or her observation.[6] But this social authority becomes fractured and hybridized by a literary style and an autobiographical structure; thus, ethnographic authority comes into direct conflict with literary authority in *The Aran Islands* and the result is a form of autoethnographic expressiveness that exploits the techniques of participant observation in order to redefine the relationship between observer and observed and to develop a mode of rapport that incorporates the desire for the native into a text unbound by scientific principles of objectivity and accuracy.

In this chapter, I argue that *The Aran Islands* furthers a Revivalist project of cultural redemption by appropriating and redeploying the techniques of ethnographic fieldwork, especially those which enable the development of rapport with native informants, in the interests of producing something like an indigenous ethnography. Further, I argue that this appropriation yields a critique of ethnographic authority by bringing that authority into contact with an autobiographical impulse that, for Synge, is deeply rooted in a desire for a meaningful and unambiguous Irish identity. Mary Louise Pratt's articulation of the practice of *autoethnography* can help us understand how Synge's complicity with anthropology can yield progressive results. According to Pratt, dominant and subaltern cultures meet and interact in a "contact zone" where processes of "transculturation" take place. "[S]ubordinated or marginal groups select and invent from materials transmitted to them by a dominant or metropolitan culture," she writes. "While subjugated peoples cannot readily control what emanates from the dominant culture, they do determine to varying degrees what they absorb into their own, and what they use it for."[7] Autoethnography is the term Pratt uses to indicate a specific process of transculturation "in which colonized subjects undertake to represent themselves in ways that *engage with* the colonizer's own terms. If ethnographic texts are a means by which Europeans represent to themselves their (usually subjugated) others, autoethnographic texts are those the others construct in response to or in dialogue with those metropolitan representations." In fact, when autoethnographic texts are *mis*read as "'authentic' self-expression or, conversely, as 'inauthentic' assimilation, their transcultural character is obliterated and their dialogic engagement with western modes of representation is lost."[8] Clearly, Synge is not a "colonized subject" in the sense that Pratt means it; but his desire for identification with the Aran Islanders allows him to take such a position with respect to anthropological discourses. To the extent that he succeeds in challenging these discourses, he acts in a productive dialogue with them; to the extent that he fails in doing so, his text slips into the unreflective attitude of the ethnographer, but without the objectivity that would give the lack of reflection a certain scientific justification.

The West of Ireland became for Synge an opportunity for self-exploration and self-expression, and *The Aran Islands* reflects this in a hybrid structure that is in part the effect of an autoethnographic confrontation with conventional assumptions about primitive peoples. In the end, writing about the Aran Islands involved more for Synge than redeeming a primitive community from the threat of extinction; it involved redeeming himself as well.

The Aran Islands is unique in the Revivalist canon in that it aspires to the kind of "total picture" that academic ethnographers like A. C. Haddon and C. R. Browne were attempting to cobble together from secondhand sources and new scientific methods of anthropometry (the measurement of physical features like head size, eye color, skin pigmentation, and the like). Haddon and Browne were doing field-work in the West of Ireland throughout the 1890s and conducted an ethnographic survey on the Aran Islands in 1891–3, just a few years before Synge's series of sojourns there between 1898 and 1901.[9] It is important to recall that in the 1890s anthropology and even more so ethnography were emergent disciplines still very much determined by the natural sciences out of which they evolved. In the 1870s and 1880s, British ethnology and social anthropology derived their authority from evolutionists like E. B. Tylor who "attempted a universal ordering of ethnographic data in terms of *time*."[10] The evolutionary anthropologist conceived of history in Hegelian terms as a progression from the primitive East to the civilized West and regarded primitive societies as lacking the historical development that characterizes the civilized cultures of Europe.[11] Tylor was not himself a fieldworker (relying, as so many of his generation did, on secondhand sources), nor did he train graduate students in fieldwork; nevertheless, he influenced the next generation of British anthropologists – especially A. R. Radcliffe-Brown and Malinowski – who were less interested in using empirical data about native psychology, physiology, and social and economic systems to create general theories of evolutionary development, aspiring instead to use such data in the functional analysis of social institutions.[12]

With ethnographers like Haddon, whose training in the natural sciences led to an emphasis on the taxonomic arrangement of data, anthropology moved away from the evolutionism of Tylor, acquiring its authority increasingly from the fieldworker immersed for extended periods in a single region. Authority was increasingly vested in the ethnographer's experience in the field, backed up by scientific methods of collection, organization, and analysis that quickly emerged in disciplinary forms analogous to those in the natural sciences. This sort of "intensive research" could not to be conducted by the "rapid collector"; rather, as George W. Stocking, has argued, Haddon emphasized "the urgent necessity not simply to gather 'specimens' but to take the time to 'coax out of the native by patient sympathy' the deeper meaning of the material collected."[13] Haddon is most famous for his involvement in the Torres Straits expedition, supported by money from Cambridge, scientific societies, and the British and Australian governments. And, while his work in the Torres Straits yielded a tremendous amount of ethnographic data, much of it was secondhand; Stocking notes that Haddon "culled extensively from missionary and travel accounts, and relied heavily on material provided by traders, missionaries, and government employees, either on the spot or in his extensive subsequent ethnography-by-mail." Such indirect procedures do not necessarily undermine the value of the ethnographic data collected (in either

Haddon's or Tylor's case); they do, however, point up the "distance from Torres Straits to fieldwork in what was to become the classic anthropological mode"[14] developed in the work of Radcliffe-Brown and Malinowski.

In subsequent anthropological adventures, Haddon was to acquire his information firsthand. Beginning in the 1890s, he took over as the principal investigator for the British Association's Ethnographic Survey of the British Isles. The first ethnography produced by Haddon and Browne, "The Ethnography of the Aran Islands, County Galway," illustrates the techniques and assumptions that characterize both the project as a whole and the emergent discipline of anthropology in the years before Malinowski's *Argonauts of the Western Pacific* established the norms for ethnographic fieldwork. The legacy of the natural sciences remains in their emphasis on empirical data, particularly the measurable features of the human body – hair and eye color, head, face, and body measurements; but they also include statistics concerning population, land use, language and physical and psychological health. Haddon and Browne's confidence in the possibility of achieving scientific objectivity and exactitude is reflected in their reliance on instruments that measure physical properties: the "Traveller's Anthropometer," the *compas d'épaisseur*, the *compas glissière*, and the Index of Nigrescence.[15] Written documentation (on small cards that "fit in a waistcoat pocket") facilitates the gathering of data later to be arranged in taxonomies and tables of measurements.[16]

In "The Anthropometry Laboratory of Ireland," Haddon and D. J. Cunningham describe the method of anthropometry in terms that reveal their empirical self-assurance:

It has therefore occurred to us that we might employ the anthropometric methods for the purpose of giving some assistance to the anthropologist in his endeavours to unravel the tangled skein of the so-called "Irish Race." With this end in view it is our intention when once we have fairly started to take excursions during the Long Vacation into the country, and with our apparatus, pitch our tent in different districts until at last we or our successors shall have traversed the entire extent of Ireland.[17]

It is ironic that the intention to traverse "the entire extent of Ireland" and to create an authoritative scientific text is realized in part with the aid of the stereotypical misrepresentations of an earlier generation of observers on the Aran Islands, principally J. T. O'Flaherty, John Beddoe, Dr. George Petrie, and Sir Samuel

Ferguson. What is remarkable about this kind of evidence is that it resembles so strongly Matthew Arnold's Celticism. Haddon and Browne cite at length Ferguson's "interesting sketch" of the South Island to support the conclusions they reach using the methods of anthropometry:

They are a handsome, courteous, and amiable people. Whatever may be said of the advantages of a mixture of races, I cannot discern anything save what makes in favor of these people of the pure ancient stock, when I compare them with the mixed populations of districts on the mainland. The most refined gentleman might live among them in familiar intercourse, and never be offended by a gross or sordid sentiment. This delicacy of feeling is reflected in their figures, the hands and feet being small in proportion to the stature, and the gesture erect and graceful.[18]

To give them credit, Haddon and Browne appear to be skeptical of any pure Irish race; but they are still ideologically committed to primitivist and racialist ideas about peasant culture. Their remarks about the "Irish race" together with their anthropometric taxo-nomies can be read "as an obsessive tabulation of desire" in which "theories of racial difference as degeneration themselves fused with the increasing cultural pessimism of the late nineteenth century and the claim that not only the population of cities but the world itself, that is the West, was degenerating."[19] This obsessive desire allows Ferguson, and Haddon and Browne after him, to make judgments about the "'superiority'" of the Aran natives to those of the "'mixed and planted districts.'"[20] And it is the same desire that leads E. W. Brabrook, President of the Royal Anthropological Institute of Great Britain and Ireland, to conclude that "the index of nigrescence [is] much lower in those who bear surnames indicating a mixture of race than in those who bear the ancient Irish tribal names."[21] However, the "homogeneity of strain" of the Aran population, attributed by Haddon and Browne to inbreeding, can be considered superior only with reference to the rest of Ireland.[22] The lack of comparison to other European populations suggests the racial alterity of the Aran Islanders, for whom Europe cannot supply a point of comparison. They are superior only in the sense of being a superior kind of primitive.

The desire for empirical knowledge – measurable, verifiable, capable of being recorded in taxonomic form – is accompanied (in the interest of completeness) by a desire for knowledge that is harder to gauge using instruments. Thus, while the "peripatetic"

Anthropometric Laboratory was designed primarily to gather information on physical characteristics, Haddon and Browne "exceeded the lines of research" proposed by the Anthropometric committee by considering "ethnical" information:

We have done so in the belief that the ethnical characteristics of a people are to be found in their arts, habits, language, and beliefs as well as in their physical characters. For various reasons we do not now propose to enter into all these considerations; but we hope that the following account will give a fairly accurate, though somewhat imperfect, presentment of the anthropography and mode of life of the inhabitants of the most interesting group of islands round the Irish coast.[23]

Here, as elsewhere, Haddon and Browne appear to acknowledge anthropology's "imperfection," its failure to achieve the accuracy and taxonomic completeness of a scientific text. But really being acknowledged are the limitations of a project that, given world enough and time, could exhaustively cover all areas of study.

This limitation is especially marked in the discussion of the psychology of the Aran Islanders, where the authors make the same claim to scientific authority and objectivity that they had made for their anthropometric measurements. "We believe the following to be a fair and unbiassed description of [the Islander's] psychology. This is a very difficult and delicate subject, but it must not be ignored in an investigation of this nature."[24] That it "must not be ignored" implies that it can be put to use in the development of a "total picture" of the "Irish race," which can then serve colonial administrations and anthropological institutions in their efforts to regulate and stabilize colonial territories. What is striking in this attempt at gaining psychological knowledge is that it is based almost exclusively on observations made by previous visitors like Ferguson and Petrie. Moreover, the tendency to qualify observations with phrases that suggest likelihood rather than empirical fact underscores the conjectural nature of their observations. A few examples will suffice to give a sense of the "fair and unbiassed" descriptions offered up as ethnographic data: "There are no indications that the aesthetic sense is well developed among the people. They appear to be distinctly non-musical, as is evidenced by the fact there is no piper, fiddler, or musician of any sort on the islands . . . The children, so far as we could see, do not appear to play games." In the interest of understanding what Petrie regards as a pure primitive race, one that "has hitherto wholly escaped contamination" and that "still retains all its delightful pristine purity," the authors must omit any mention of tramps, tinkers, and other itinerant travelers whose presence on the islands implies the very things (music, sport, commerce) whose absence marks the islanders as primitive.[25] (Synge himself proves to be just such a presence when he provides fiddle accompaniment at impromptu dances.) Indeed, what encroachments they are willing to admit from "outside" tend only to underscore the primitive purity of the population by effecting its diminishment. Again, the authority is secondhand:

The result of much inquiry and attentive observation [writes Petrie] was a conviction, that though from recent circumstances the brightness of this picture [primitive simplicity, ingenuous manners, and their singular hospitality] should now be somewhat lessened, and that the Araners can no longer be considered the simple race unacquainted with crime, such as they were generally depicted, yet that enough still remains of their former virtues to show that the representations of them were but little, if anything, exaggerated.[26]

Even when faced with evidence to the contrary, Haddon and Browne fall back on a decidedly unscientific primitivism according to which cultural purity is lost in an engagement with outsiders.

In the discussion of folklore, the authors must confess to having "scanty" information but are quick to call attention to the "ethnological importance" of the information they do in fact have and "to remind our readers that the lore is fast disappearing from the folk, and that no time should be lost in recording the vanishing customs and beliefs of old times."[27] Note the ethic of redemption that is so plainly evident here, grounded in the dubious assumption that something *essential* is lost in rapid social change, that the islanders are ineffectual guardians of their own culture and need outsiders to represent and thus redeem it. The characterization of the islanders as a credulous and simple people whose folklore may vanish at any time points up the primitivist distinctions that a redemptive ethnography inevitably invokes. Further, their reliance on secondhand information means that they are finally unable to avoid stereotypical and racialist attitudes about the Irish. They quote an Irish authority, O'Flaherty, to conclude that the Aran Islanders are a "primitive, simple, sequestered people," who are "credulous and superstitious," who occupy a land of "solitude and romantic wildness, whose "enthusiasm, credulity and second-sight" lead them to "believe in fairies, banshees, ghosts, &c."[28] And the inevitable Petrie is called upon to note that, at times of revelry, one is sure to find "instances of excess, followed by the usual Irish consequences of broken heads."[29] The cultural knowledge produced by the Ethnographic Survey ends up doing nothing more or less than repeating and reaffirming these attitudes and shoring up the authority of the primitivism that gave rise to them.

I have discussed Haddon and Browne at length largely to indicate some of the methods of observation that dominated British ethnography in the 1890s. The fact that Haddon and Browne and Synge performed fieldwork within a few years of each other in the same isolated region of Ireland indicates the importance of the West of Ireland for both anthropology and the Celtic Revival. I want to suggest that the similarities between ethnographers like Haddon and Browne and Revivalists like Synge point up a common investment in primitivism and a common desire for a "total picture" of the peasant society on the Aran Islands. Additionally, I want to suggest that Synge's autobiographical style and his willingness to articulate what conventional ethnographers ignored or suppressed makes possible an autoethnographic text, one that critiques even as it deploys colonialist and anthropological conceptions of the primitive and that shuttles ambivalently between detached observation of the islanders and intense emotional (at times imaginary) participation with them. Synge's text simultaneously articulates a desire for a "total picture" of Aran life and deconstructs that desire when sexual longing for Aran women effect the collapse of any clear distinction between primitive and civilized, observer and observed.

Much has been made of Yeats's famous advice, which he recalls in his preface to Synge's *The Well of the Saints* (1905): "Go to the Aran Islands. Live there as if you were one of the people themselves; express a life that has never found expression" (*CA*, 112). In recent years, critics have challenged the view that Yeats was solely or even mainly responsible for sending Synge to the Aran Islands. Declan Kiberd notes that Yeats had traveled there in 1896 before giving his advice, but was frustrated by his lack of Irish; his advice, therefore, should be seen "in terms of his own failure to master the Irish language which, he freely conceded, held the key to the life of the West."[30] David Greene has argued that "Synge was already prepared inwardly for the move westwards long before he had met Yeats."[31] As I have indicated above, part of this preparation was his

tutelage under Continental Celticists like Henri D'Arbois de Jubainville and Anatole le Braz, influences that were far more substantial
and, in Richard Fallis's words, "did a good deal more to send Synge
toward Aran than the famous meeting with Yeats at the Hotel
Corneille."[32] Recent assessments like Fallis's have tended to down-
play the importance of Yeats's meeting with Synge, suggesting that
the work he produced out of his experience on the Aran Islands
constitutes a reaction to "the attitudes toward [its] subject found in
. . . Yeats's *Celtic Twilight*."[33] Some critics, in fact, have gone as far as
Nicholas Grene, who calls the account made by Yeats a "marve-
lously colorful but inherently unlikely story."[34] In any case, Yeats
regarded Synge's sojourn there in terms that reflected his own
artistic concerns. As Robert O'Driscoll writes, "Synge was to
provide [Yeats] with a way of escape from [the dilemma posed by
the opposition between the material and the ideal], for Synge found
in the material world, and particularly in the life and language of the
west of Ireland, the 'metaphors and examples' by which he could
express his own emotion and thought."[35]

What has not been noticed is how well Yeats's advice sums up the
ethnographic imperative to immerse oneself in a native culture. *Live
there as if you were one of the people themselves* – what is this if it is not the
imperative to engage in "intensive research" of a single place? It is
the imperative to participate, to insinuate oneself into an Other
culture, to live "in daily contact with the people," to "acquire[] a
series of multitudinous impressions, each slight and often vague, that
guide [the ethnographer] in his dealings with them."[36] *Express a life
that has never found expression* – and what is this if it is not the
imperative to discover and describe unknown, "exotic" worlds, to
translate the terms of one culture into the terms of another? It is the
imperative to observe, to record the minutia of everyday life with
the impartiality of ethnographic detachment and to "formulate the
results in the most convincing manner."[37] Implicit in Yeats's advice
is a desire to redeem a primitive mode of life in a full representation,
a desire that Synge would come to share and to express in similar
terms. In a letter to Stephen MacKenna, he talked about the articles
he was writing for *The Manchester Guardian* on the Congested Districts
of the West of Ireland: "Unluckily my commission was to write on
the 'Distress,' so I couldn't do anything like what I would have
wished to do *as an interpretation of the whole life*."[38] This desire with
respect to the Aran Islands is ultimately thwarted, not by any

restriction on Synge's assignment but rather by his attempt to achieve a kind of intersubjective rapport that undermined the detachment necessary for "an interpretation of the whole life."

In "J. M. Synge and the Ireland of His Time," Yeats describes this rapport as a "correspondence" between Synge's temperament and the "harshness" of the Aran Islands:

> He loves all that has edge, all that is salt in the mouth, all that is rough to the hand, all that heightens the emotions by contest, all that stings life into a sense of tragedy; and in [*The Aran Islands*], unlike the plays where nearness to his audience moves him to mischief, he shows it without thought of other taste than his. It is so constant, it is all set out so simply, so naturally, that it suggests a correspondence between a lasting mood of the soul and this life that shares the harshness of rocks and wind. (*CA*, 153–4)

Yeats identified this "lasting mood of the soul" as the state of ecstasy "awakened by the presence before an ever-changing mind of what is permanent in the world" (*CA*, 96). And he was right to notice that Synge heroically threw his whole soul into the Aran adventure. Perhaps because he conceives of this "correspondence" in terms of a personality that authenticates experience in a "natural" representation, Yeats is not alert to Synge's "inconstant" relation to the ethnographic authority that subtends his text. He therefore fails to see that the correspondence he senses in *The Aran Islands* is the result of a process of ethnographic engagement in which the observer finds an analogue for his own suffering in the people and landscape he observes. In short, Yeats, like Synge, hovers ambivalently between criticizing and accepting the propriety of binomial primitivism and the superordinancy of the participant–observer.

Synge lived among the people of the Aran Islands and recorded what he saw in order to interpret their folkways for himself and for a metropolitan audience. He collected stories, songs, folktales, local histories, and anecdotes and described burial ceremonies, domestic arrangements, clothing (especially "pampooties," locally made shoes), and the rituals associated with work and recreation – diligently, though not always objectively, recording everything in notebooks. This information was later translated into a new textual form using the tense of the ethnographic present, a discursive mode that represented the behavior and activities of primitive people as a timeless iteration of tradition. Though he lived in close proximity to the islanders, boarding with a family on Inishmaan, and though his uncle, the Reverend Alexander Hamilton Synge, had served as the

Protestant minister on the islands in the 1850s, he remained for the most part distant and aloof. From his coign of vantage on the walls of the ancient ringfort or cashel, Dún Chonchúir, Synge reflects on his detachment:

When I look around from the top of these walls I can see the sea on nearly every side, stretching away to distant ranges of mountains on the north and south. Underneath me to the east there is the one inhabited district of the island, where I can see red figures moving about the cottages, sending up an occasional fragment of conversation or of the old island melodies. (*AI*, 70)

Synge returns again and again to this vantage-point, from which the islanders are little more than gashes of red or gray, their speech little more than a murmur of Irish rising up to him in a "world[] of mist" (*AI*, 73). It is a position very much like that which Mary Louise Pratt associates with early imperialist explorers who styled themselves "monarchs of all they surveyed" and who wrote in "a brand of verbal painting whose highest calling was to reproduce for the home audience the peak moments at which geographical 'discoveries' were 'won' for England."[39] In fact, Synge's uncle had once remarked about his position on the islands, "Here I am Lord of all I survey – surrounded by dirt and ignorance."[40] That Synge's authoritative position is recognized and to some degree legitimized by the islanders is evident in the fact that a "shanty" in which he used to sit – as Tim Robinson describes it, "a low, three-quarter-circle wall of massive stones on the brink of the highest cliff of Inis Meáin" – is still called Cathaoir Synge, "Synge's Chair." It is ironic that this ancient structure – "probably it was some sort of look-out post"[41] – should become the vantage-point of an ethnographic observer who captures the islanders in his sweeping, possessive gaze.

Synge was, of course, not the first to take such a position. We have seen that Haddon and Browne had taken the measure, so to speak, of the islanders and had relied for many of their conclusions on the authority of antiquarians and scholarly tourists. *The Aran Islands* pays a kind of homage to the latter, Synge noting early in his text that the islanders were well aware of their anthropological importance. "[Máirtín] told me that he had known [George Petrie] and Sir William Wilde, and many living antiquarians, and had taught Irish to Dr. Finck and Dr. Pedersen, and given stories to Mr. Curtin of America" (*AI*, 50).[42] From the outset, Synge positions himself within a tradition of linguistic, folkloric, archaeological and anthropological, inquiry in which an islander like old Máirtín moves with "great confidence in his own powers and talent, and in the superiority of his stories over all other stories in the world" (*AI*, 50). Máirtín goes on to become Synge's chief informant, supplying him with stories and anecdotes about the history of the islands and their inhabitants – supplying him, in other words, with the material to create a picture of the Aran Islands as an exotic, primitive locale that was saturated, like the Trobriand Islands as Malinowski understood them, "with myth and legendary tales, with the strange adventures, hopes and fears of generations of native sailors."[43]

Just after arriving on Aranmor, Synge decided, despite the "charm" of his teacher, to move on to Inishmaan, the middle island, "where Gaelic is more generally used, and the life is perhaps the most primitive that is left in Europe" (*AI*, 53). In keeping with a primitivist discourse that posits the cultural Otherness of native societies, Synge concentrates on those rituals and practices that mark the Irish-speaking islanders as a pre-historical, pre-industrial, pre-modern vestige of modern Europe. *The Aran Islands* is replete with descriptions of funerals and "keenings," of fishing, threshing, twisting rope, harvesting kelp, thatching cottages, and transporting horses and cattle to market on the mainland. Take, for example, the more or less objective description of the threshing of rye, which yields straw for thatching and rope:

In the autumn season the threshing of rye is one of the many tasks that fall to the men and boys. The sheaves are collected on a bare rock, and then each is beaten separately on a couple of stones placed on end one against the other. The land is so poor that a field hardly produces more grain than is needed for seed the following year, so the rye-growing is carried on merely for the straw, which is used for thatching. (*AI*, 130)

Such activities took place on the mainland, but they acquired for Synge a certain charm by virtue of having persisted in the harsh and isolated conditions of the islands. And, while he does not organize his data into categories or draw scientific conclusions, as Haddon and Browne had done, his point of view and his emphasis on the function and value of communal work looks forward to the approach of Conrad M. Arensberg and Solon T. Kimball in their influential study *Family and Community in Ireland*.[44]

I have been suggesting that, despite clear differences in style, *The Aran Islands* appears to be authorized by the same primitivism that underwrote Haddon and Browne's ethnographies. The difference is that, for Synge, the primitive is given a positive value over against decadent, hyper-civilized Europeans – a value linked to Rousseauean and Wordsworthian notions of the "noble savage":

The absence of the heavy boot of Europe has preserved to these people the agile walk of the wild animal, while the general simplicity of their lives has given them many other points of physical perfection . . . [T]hey seem in a certain sense to approach more nearly to the finer types of our aristocracies – who are bred artificially to a natural ideal – than to the labourer or citizen, as the wild horse resembles the thoroughbred rather than the hack or cart-horse. Tribes of the same natural development are, perhaps, frequent in half-civilized countries, but here a touch of the refinement of old societies is blended, with singular effect, among the qualities of the wild animal. (*AI*, 66)[45]

Synge's description, which leaves intact the Manichean structure of primitivism, isolates and elevates his subjects and give them an aura of idealized *natural* nobility. Not only does he regard the islanders (particularly those on the more isolated Inishmaan and Inishere) as culturally different from Europeans; they are also displaced spatially and historically, their lives possessing "the strange quality that is found in the oldest poetry and legend" (*AI*, 116) and their social organization lacking any division of labor recognizable to the civilized observer (see *AI*, 130–3). Here, Synge betrays the absence in his discourse of scientific methods of collection and description which would have allowed him to recognize, as Arensberg and Kimball did later, the complex division of labor to be found in Irish peasant communities.[46] His observations, like Yeats's, are guided less by strict conformity to ethnographic protocols than by a desire to find in the primitive Aran communities confirmation of and salvation from his own alienation. The dissociation of sensibility recorded in *The Aran Islands*, which anticipates that of modernists like T. S. Eliot, led Synge to make positive assessments of the islanders, even though he felt at times that their primitive simplicity was inaccessible to him: "I became indescribably mournful, for I felt that this little corner on the face of the world, and the people who live in it, have a peace and dignity from which we are shut for ever" (*AI*, 162). The same feeling registers in West Kerry: "Yet I know even while I was there I was an interloper only, a refugee in a garden between four seas."[47] Such statements occur more frequently in Synge's un-published fieldnotes, where a sense of cultural estrangement registers as linguistic anxiety: "I am not expert in carrying on a conversation with these primitive men and felt embarrassment at first among so many inquiring regards. My ignorance of ships and such like is here a hindrance I am not able to surmount and we remain mostly foreign to each other" (*MS*, 4385).[48]

For Synge, as for Revivalism generally, the primitive is equivalent to the natural: "In Inishmaan one is forced to believe in a sympathy between man and nature" (*AI*, 75). This view governs the representation of the peasant in *The Aran Islands* as well as in the journalistic essays collected under the title *In Wicklow, West Kerry and Connemara*. What Synge finds on the Aran Islands is a simple people who "talked continuously of the fairies and the women they have taken," an artless people whose language is a "primitive babble," as incomprehensible as the cries of birds, whose "language is easier than Gaelic," and which he seems to understand, "though [he is] not able to answer" (*AI*, 54, 79, 73–4). The islanders are a wild, sorrowful people who make "no distinction between the natural and the supernatural" and who have no conception of law (*AI*, 128). He finds women who "looked strangely wild and seal-like with the salt caked upon their lips and wreaths of seaweed in their hair" (*AI*, 108). In the talk of a young girl, he sees the noble primitive's disillusionment with the world:

I hear her voice going backwards and forwards in the same sentence from the gaiety of a child to the plaintive intonation of an old race that is worn with sorrow. At one moment she is a simple peasant, at another she seems to be looking out at the world with a sense of prehistoric disillusion and to sum up in the expression of her grey-blue eyes the whole external despondency of the clouds and sea. (*AI*, 114)

The identification of the girl with the despondency of a harsh natural world illustrates the peculiar nature of Synge's ethnographic realism, which derives from a need for accuracy that Kiberd associates with the struggle to represent the peasant's "folkloristic impersonality": "Synge records all this with a terrified and terrifying accuracy, because he knows that, however spare and beautiful such a culture may seem to the outsider, its costs in human terms are just too high."[49]

Paradoxically, however, it is Synge's awareness of the high cost of primitive nobility that motivates him to give expression to a desire that moves in the opposite direction from the need for accuracy. In his representations of peasant life, there is tension between, on the one hand, the ethnographic desire for an accurate representation of the terrifying costs exacted from a noble peasantry by a harsh environment and, on the other hand, the autobiographical desire that seeks to *misrepresent* these costs as reflections of his own alienated and fractured subjectivity. Even more damaging to the ethnographic authority that would enable an accurate representation is Synge's tendency to introduce the unmediated voices of his informants, principally the storytellers. When he allows "old Pat" Dirane to begin his contributions to *The Aran Islands* with the sentence, "Here is my story," (*AI*, 70), Synge effectively *dialogizes* his text, granting Dirane the kind of experiential authority usually reserved for the ethnographer himself, summed up in the implied assertion "I was there." In the paragraph following one of old Pat's stories, Synge notes, "[i]n stories of this kind he always speaks in the first person, with minute details to show that he was actually present at the scenes that are described" (*AI*, 72). A similar strategy is employed by Arensberg and Kimball in *Family and Community in Ireland* where they quote their informants directly on matters pertaining to kinship, the division of labor, and marriage customs.[50] Contemporary revisionist anthropology has seen in this tendency to grant authority to informants a sign of the ethnographer's willingness to share authority in the creation of a hybrid or dialogical text. The critical problem for Synge, as for revisionist anthropologists, is to avoid reinscribing his own authority and thereby "confirming the final virtuoso orchestration by a single author of all the discourses" in his text.[51]

The hybrid nature of *The Aran Islands* – ethnographic in its mode of observation and collection and data, literary in its tendency to resignify ethnographic realism as autobiography – produced uneasiness and consternation from the start. One early reviewer of *The Aran Islands* politely derided Synge as a "peasant addict" while another accepted the book on what appeared to be its own terms – that is, as an exotic travelogue.[52] For many readers, *The Aran Islands* was caught up in the retrogressive revivalism Frantz Fanon describes:

You will never make colonialism blush for shame by spreading out little-known cultural treasures under its eyes. At the very moment when the native intellectual is anxiously trying to create a cultural work he fails to realize that he is utilizing techniques and language which are borrowed from the stranger in his country. He contents himself with stamping these instruments with a hallmark which he wishes to be national, but which is strangely reminiscent of exoticism. The native intellectual who comes back to his people by way of cultural achievements behaves in fact like a foreigner.[53]

The exotic text is produced in the revivalist phase of a developing native intelligentsia, and it is in this phase that many of Synge's contemporaries believed he had halted. They found his exoticism deeply problematic, straddling as it did the line separating two world views: the primitive Celt and the civilized European. As an anonymous reviewer noted in the *Times Literary Supplement* in 1907, Synge was a "sympathetically gifted man," who heard from the lips of the primitive Irish "stories as rude and fresh as anything in medieval Celtic literature, and these he has set down just as they were spoken. They are the best part of the book; for the rest, it is a thought too objective, albeit inspired by the kindliest sympathy and admiration of a simple folk."[54]

The problem for this reviewer is not that Synge engaged in a project of ethnographic exoticism, but that he had done it so well. The reviewer's uneasiness may in part be a reaction to the scrupulousness of an ethnographic gaze that took in the details of clothing, domestic life, rituals, customs, and other cultural phenomena and put them forward as part of an affirmative, if melancholy picture of a "simple folk." Though, generally speaking, ethnographic knowledge benefited colonial administrators who could use every bit of information about native life they could find, it was not always the case that citizens of the metropolitan center wanted more information. Indeed, the anonymous reviewer suggests that he or she would rather stick with stereotypes – "The people are primitive, talking a good deal of English but more Gaelic, and believing still in fairies" (that "still" clinches it) – than know more about the islanders. J. B. Yeats, writing in *Harper's Weekly* in 1911, may have put his finger on the real reason for his contemporaries' anxiety when he suggested that Synge had unveiled the imaginative power of the illiterate peasant: "[Synge] stands apart from them all, because he portrays peasant poetry and passion, and a humor which cuts deep into the mystery and terror of life."[55] Perhaps it is this understanding of the "mystery and terror of life," that the *Times* reviewer thought was represented "a thought too objectively," when what was wanted, evidently, was a stereotypical *mis*representation of the peasant as exotic anthropological artifact.

Synge, of course, had more at stake in *The Aran Islands* than providing, as the *Times* reviewer might have wished, "rude and fresh" stories to mollify a metropolitan audience hungry for things primitive. But it was not always clear what that stake was, for even Synge's fellow Revivalist, Lady Gregory, was reputed to have "wished it dreamier and less specific."[56] The reaction against objective or specific representation in the remarks of Lady Gregory and the *Times* reviewer raises important questions about genre and generic expectations. What sort of text did people think they were reading when they picked up *The Aran Islands*? Though readers today may criticize it for being too stylized to be of much use as an ethnography, a contemporary may have found less fault with Synge's style, which resembled the popular genre of the travelogue.[57] In some ways, it resembles the "prose topographies" of Pierre Loti's *Pêcheur d'Islande* and Le Braz's *Au Pays des Pardons*.[58] However, as Kiberd points out, there was an Irish model closer to home: "Those who make this claim [that Synge was influenced by Loti and Le Braz] have ignored the most likely model of all – [Arthur] Symons's essay on 'The Isle of Aran.'" Since Yeats had only recently accompanied Symons on a writing assignment to Aran, Kiberd finds it "unthinkable that [Yeats] did not mention Symons's article as a model of the work to be done."[59]

Kiberd's argument about sources implicitly underscores the agreement of most critics on the early modernist romanticism that is Synge's *métier*. But this agreement masks a *valze hesitation* around increasingly fine literary judgments. James Knapp, for example, referring to Synge's "decadent Parisian fantasy" *Étude Morbide*, calls his sensibility "urban romanticism" and links it to the attitude proper to colonialism and anthropology: "Although he would regret this pose, Synge [in *Étude Morbide*] is the weary aesthete, fleeing a world of 'agony' in search of the kind of joyful spontaneity that presumably still exists in this simple, natural world. He makes the peasants dance like puppets, a gesture that reveals the radical Otherness he sees in them."[60] The work of Le Braz and Loti and the kind of romanticism described by Knapp are frequently invoked by critics of Synge in an attempt to describe the genre of *The Aran Islands* and to account for its odd medley of ethnographic, folkloric, literary, autobiographical, and even spiritual discourses. We are reminded in such attempts of Edward Hirsch's description of *The Celtic Twilight* as a generic anomaly, a "curious hybrid of the story and the essay, the accurate notation of the folklorist and the fictional reminiscence of the imaginative writer."[61] John Wilson Foster attempts to understand this anomalous quality in terms of *spiritual exoticism*, a common enough influence in *fin de siècle* Paris and Dublin. According to Foster, Synge's text, like Loti's *Pêcheur d'Islande*, possesses "a strong documentary and folkloristic underpinning" and seeks

to convey the folkways and mind of an intensely local, coastal, and Celtic peasantry, a people presented as devout, shy, hardy, quietly heroic, loyal, proud, poor, superstitious, and, in their own way, passionate. The strangeness of the subjects, to writer and reader, is part of the charm of both books. We have in each, however, not just the appeal of remoteness to the traveler and folklorist, but also the *appeal of exoticism* to a romantic sensibility.[62]

Foster goes on to analyze this appeal in terms of the relatively banal "jottings" of the traveler and the spiritual implications of legend: "*The Aran Islands* is a remarkable and closely observed travel book which emerged from notebooks crammed with impressions and anecdotes" but it goes beyond "the journeyings and jottings or a traveler with both ears and both eyes open" – "it bears a passing resemblance to the old Irish voyage tales."[63] Despite the appeal to exoticism, Foster desires, as do other critics (like Ann Saddlemyer), to assimilate Synge's texts to an indigenous tradition of spiritual travel and to read *The Aran Islands* as a kind of prose *immram*. There is, of course, something to be said for this claim, considering the presence in Synge's text of certain elements (spiritual questing, wandering among islands) typically found in *immrama*. Even so, we would still have to account for Synge's melancholy inwardness and the intensity of his desire for reciprocity with the peasants with whom he sojourns. Perhaps, as some critics have suggested, the Wordsworthian tradition of autobiography, in which subjectivity is keyed to a spiritualized Nature, is closer in form and method to Synge's work than the native Irish tradition of travel narratives.

What both Knapp and Foster leave unanalyzed is the extent to which Synge's essentially Romantic sensibility – a sensibility characterized by spirituality, morbidity, musicality, vision, dream, and a sense of deracination that makes everything a little melancholy – comes into contact with and begins to mimic an ethnographic attitude. Indeed, the way Foster slights the anthropological significance of *The Aran Islands* tells us much about critical resistance to its hybrid form and Synge's equally hybrid social authority. He notes that "Synge had to be conscious of his own apartness while on the islands, and in doing so he was little different from other Irish Revival writers."[64] Foster refers, of course, to the sense of deracination common among Anglo-Irish Revivalists, especially those, like Synge and Yeats, whose work depended on a certain anthropological validity. However, for Foster

[t]he anthropological validity of Synge's observations is not at issue here, but rather *his perception* of island life. Medieval, prehistoric, pagan, illiterate: these are the recurring descriptions; most frequently does the word "primitive" occur: Synge came to see gradations of primitiveness on the islands, and came to hold in half-contempt the more "civilized" portions, moving from Aranmor to Inishmaan for this purpose.[65]

Note that Foster shifts the terms of discussion from anthropological to perspectival validity without recognizing that it is precisely perspective – the "hegemony of the visual"[66] – that in large measure authorizes ethnographic inquiry. Foster himself cannot help noting that "one cultural geographer has quoted Synge's observations with approval."[67] But these scientific considerations are less important than the literary style that transforms his observations into literature. Perhaps, like the *Times* reviewer, Foster finds anthropological validity "a thought too objective."

Nicholas Grene is more helpful when he charts Synge's stylistic development in order to account for the literary valence of *The Aran Islands*. He argues that Synge seeks less to achieve an objective report than to construct a "characteristic" Irish idiom. An analysis of his notebooks leads Grene to speculate that Synge's earliest published article (1898), which included a transcription of a tale he heard on the Aran Islands, revealed a writer unpracticed "in the difficult business of recording dialect accurately." In the short span separating his fieldwork and the composition of *The Aran Islands*, a transition occurs "from conventional travel reportage to a more dramatic presentation."[68] Through "a process of selection and revision," Synge's ethnographic inquiries are transformed into aesthetic representations:

What appears in the original manuscripts of the stories Synge heard on Aran is a peculiar combination of arch storybook English with occasional barbaric-looking pieces of translation from Irish. The final versions look much more authentic, much more convincing, even though in particular cases the actual words used may have been dropped. For the language of the stories in *The Aran Islands* is consistent; it is virtually the language of the characters in a Synge play.[69]

For Grene, a literary style succeeds where an ethnographic method failed: it created a text that "looks" authentic. Where Foster sees the anthropological element of Synge's text as irrelevant, Grene sees it as a stage in a developmental process that culminates in a literary work: the "dilettante dabbling in amateur folklore collection, musing sentimentally on the environment around him, becomes an artist capable of presenting directly and dramatically significant impressions of what he sees."[70] As the next chapter will demonstrate, Synge recognized and exploited the performative dimension of his challenge to ethnographic realism.

Grene is vigorously seconded by Malcolm Kelsall, who regards Synge's claims to have given "a direct account of [his] life on the islands" (*AI*, 48) with jaundiced skepticism: "He lied." Synge, according to Kelsall, was unaware that he was writing an "autobiographical portrait of the artist," "for *The Aran Islands* is in the main an artistic creation written, like many romantic works of art, to reveal the *weltanschauung* of its author."[71] Kelsall is not alone in regarding Synge's "artistic creation" in autobiographical terms; but such readings tend to see the problems I am here associating with an ethnographic imagination in aesthetic terms only, as if the particularities of Aran social life were secondary, part of a plausible "exotic" background for the development of an artistic consciousness.[72] To some degree, these critics appear to elaborate on Yeats's conception of Synge in "John M. Synge and the Ireland of his Time," where Yeats astutely describes *The Aran Islands* as a negation of observation in the "overflowing" of self (*CA*, 153). Paradigmatic is an evaluation by Ann Saddlemyer who, taking her cue from Synge's random notes on aesthetics, claims that Synge "allowed the world outside to play on his feelings and emotions as a violinist handles his violin, reflecting and intensifying the mood and atmosphere to which he is attuned. All his work was subjective, coming out of moods in his own life."[73]

Robert Welch advances a more complex analysis of the self who observes, seeing it as part of a dialectic of self and world, a "struggle to balance self with history, subject with object" in which "the relation between [Synge's] own inner being and the external world was a baffling and frightening one."[74] In Welch's view, Synge in *The Aran Islands* attempts "to change our method of looking, of apprehension" by writing in "a style in which the life of the islands, in all its severity, intermingles with his own impressions. The method is disciplined attentiveness, a meditative transfigured realism that gives its due value to the objective and subjective impulses."[75] The method of "disciplined attentiveness," which is a good way of describing ethnographic fieldwork, is here transformed into an aesthetic perspective capable of conferring value on "objective and subjective impulses." Seamus Heaney makes a similar point when he argues that Synge's description of a funeral in *The Aran Islands* "is as much revelation as observation" and then goes on to extol the "irresistible" aspect of "the Aran world," "its sense of form and ritual" capable of invoking something like Yeats's "unity of culture" which would abolish class and sectarian difference:

At that moment [i.e., of the keening], there was no need for Synge to feel that he was a member of the Established Church intruding upon a congregation of Roman Catholics: these incidental and slightly vulgar distinctions are consumed and abraded as Synge and keening women perne in the gyre of race and whirl in the vortex of inner consciousness out of the ebb and flow of the modern tide.[76]

The racial identity of the Aran Islanders becomes one with the Synge's "inner consciousness," both serving as anodynes for modernity.

The tendency in criticism to read the autobiographical element of *The Aran Islands* at the expense of its ethnographic inflections has the curious effect of suppressing the putative content of the book, the folkways of the islanders. Consequently, Synge's ethnographic imagination is subsumed unnoticed within the limits of something more conventionally literary and recognizably romantic. "*The Aran Islands,*" writes Foster, "is neither mere fieldwork for the plays nor mere record of rural retreat, much less a mere manifesto of union with an archaic society, but a romantic document in its own right."[77] Any claim that romanticism might rest on anthropological authority would be deemed irrelevant – or a lie – for romanticism (not, incidentally, foreign to classic ethnographic discourse, as Malinowski's *Argonauts* attests) would negate any "technical" affiliation with ethnography. Indeed, the emphasis on spirituality that often accompanies such assessments seems calculated to achieve just this effect. Hence, Foster can assert that "however partial a record is *The Aran Islands* from an anthropological point of view, it is from the literary critic's point of view a profound spiritual autobiography." Note the odd parallelism (partial/profound), which implies that a profound experience of the self is full and present for representation, while ethnographic practice is negligible because it is *un*profound and offers only a partial representation. This romanticist privileging of the autonomous self leads ultimately to a willful rejection of Synge's hybrid *social* authority. "Under the fieldwork and documentary attentiveness," Foster continues, "are pattern and direction as Synge abandons the more advanced, sociable, and, in a metaphoric sense, 'eastern' parts of the islands for the more primitive, isolated, and 'western' parts, all the while freeing the self from all social forces until at last it is at the mercy of the elements of existence."[78] Even what Foster believes to be "under" ethnography turns out to be at the heart of it – for what is this "abandonment" of the east for the west but an expression the ethnographer's desire to discover a pristine culture to redeem?

Equally significant is the inverse tendency to see autobiographical experiences as irrelevant. Tim Robinson's introduction to a recent edition of *The Aran Islands* puts the matter in terms of a complex relation that suppresses Synge's personal experience in his representation of the islands:

The life-currents that bring him repeatedly to the islands and carry him off again are virtually unrepresented in the book, which suggests that progressive, autobiographical time is as irrelevant as history to the truths he is conveying. And in listening for these truths, one has to be aware of variable distances between his islands and the Aran of our geographies, as well as between the visitor he projects on the islands and the Synge of the biographies. Synge the writer, for instance, had to put down thousands of words on that spray-encrusted paper while in Aran; the visitor's mind retains the most complex sensations and intuitions in their pristine perfection.[79]

Robinson resolves the vexed question of the role of Synge's experience on Aran by positing *two* Synges: one who writes, for whom the Aran Islands are an expression of personality, and one who visits, for whom the islands retain a "pristine perfection" (presumably this perfection is uncontaminated by autobiographical interference). Still, despite invocations of "variable distance" and the suppression of "progressive, autobiographical time," Robinson, like so many others, cannot help but regard Aran as somehow an emblem of Synge: "That double-natured and sphinx-like creature, Synge-on-Aran, still proposes its riddle, which is that of our own mortal stance on earth."[80] For Robinson, the contours of external space are grafted on to the mind of the observer, creating a Wordsworthian unity of sensibility and Nature. Though Robinson may not wish it to become an emblem of an autobiographical ethnography, the image of Synge as a "double-natured and sphinx-like creature" aptly figures the fusion of author and milieu in which consciousness is spatialized, as if in the alembic of an ethnographic imagination Synge becomes himself a part of Aran's primitive culture and geography. Heaney's "Synge on Aran" evokes a similar image of a participant–observer who becomes the landscape he seeks to pre- serve: "There / he comes now, a hard pen / scraping in his head; / the nib filed on a salt wind / and dipped in the keening sea."[81] Both Robinson and Heaney locate the radical ambivalence of Synge's text precisely in the annihilation of the distinction between observer and observed, in the monstrous, "sphinx-like" hybridity of "Synge-on- Aran."

New developments in revisionist ethnography that acknowledge the value and inevitability of autobiographical desire in ethno- graphic discourse can shed light on Synge's ambivalent position on the Aran Islands. The central question is whether the sovereign authority of the participant–observer is annulled or enriched by autobiographical representation. In the preface to their collection of essays, *Anthropology and Autobiography,* Judith Okely and Helen Callaway, pose the problem of the participant–observer in terms of an experiential specificity "lost or generalized in the standard monograph which tends to present the society [under study] through the overarching authority of the named author." The turn to autobiography permits the retrieval of "individual voices" – those of the author as well as of the native subjects of ethnographic dis- course.[82] Autobiography paradoxically enables a more accurate assessment of the experience of fieldwork by granting legitimacy to the "whole being" of the fieldworker. "Anthropologists," Okely writes, "immersed for extended periods in another culture or in their own as participant–observer, learn not only through the verbal, the transcript, but through all the senses, through movement, through their bodies and whole being in a total practice."[83] This "totalizing" experience "has not been theorized because it has been trivialized as the 'collection of data' by a dehumanized machine. Autobiography dismantles the positivist machine."[84] Kirsten Hastrup, writing in the same volume, argues that fieldwork is "situated between auto- biography and anthropology" and that "ethnographers and infor- mants are equal."[85] The crux of the problem for revisionists concerned with the role of autobiography is a conflict between disciplinary and experiential authority – or, as Johannes Fabian puts it, a "conflict between theoretical–methodological conventions and lived experience." He is inclined to see autobiography as a helpful, even a necessary element in an otherwise scientific discourse, for while "[a]nthropological writing may be scientific[,] it is also inherently autobiographic" – and he *does* mean autobiographical in the trivial sense "that ethnographic reports are sometimes cluttered with anecdotes, personal asides, and other devices apt to enliven an otherwise dull prose."[86] Certainly this is true for Malinowski's *Argonauts of the Western Pacific*, where descriptions of the ethnographer's voyages in the Melanesian archipelago are "cluttered" with concerns about books, papers, and photographic equipment. The ethnographer experiences culture *through time*, Fabian argues, and this involves the subjective analysis of data: "[t]he object's present is founded in the writer's past. In that sense, facticity itself, that cornerstone of scientific thought, is autobiographic."[87]

The authority of classic ethnography, grounded on principles of scientific objectivity, cannot bear the challenge of subjectivity advanced by Fabian, Okely, and Callaway, even if the ethnographer is willing to concede, as Malinowski does, "that in current and intuitive practice we react and respond to the behavior of others through the mechanism of our own introspection."[88] The more serious challenge to ethnographic authority comes in the form of an autobiographical impulse that both multiplies the subjects of ethnographic scrutiny and threatens to turn the ethnographer into an object of that scrutiny. This latter possibility, which James Clifford calls *self-ethnography*, is not, strictly speaking, autobiography but "an act of writing [one's] existence in a present of memories, dream, politics, daily life," a mode of self-fashioning in which "ethnography encounters others in relation to itself, while seeing itself as other."[89] This mode of self-fashioning has a number of historical precedents, for, as David Spurr points out, writers like Chateaubriand, Lamartine, Flaubert, and Nerval "make[] the experience of the non-Western world into an inner journey, and in so doing render[] that world as insubstantial, as the backdrop of baseless fabric against which is played the drama of the writer's self."[90] But it is Michel Leiris, the French poet, autobiographer, and ethnographer, who, in the 1930s, developed the implications for ethnography of an explicitly auto-biographical style. Speaking of the works of native artists in Western museums, he notes that "[h]owever far they have come, they speak to us – and what is more extraordinary, they speak to us about ourselves."[91] Leiris's *L'Afrique Fantôme*, which combines ethnography with an autobiographical journal style, resembles in some ways Malinowski's *Dairy in the Strict Sense of the Word*, but it is not a "private" text. Rather, it is a deliberate attempt, through a mode of self-ethnographic expression, to deconstruct ethnography in the creation of something that is *not* ethnographic. As Marianna Torgovnick puts it, "the juxtaposition between documentary data and subjective impressions mounts an attack on the traditional assumptions of ethnography: who is to say that the day-dreams are not as valid as the ethnographic observations, [*L'Afrique Fantôme*] seems to ask." Leiris's encounters with jazz in 1920s Paris and his "partial replications" of an Edenic Africa, allowed him to "rewrite himself by rewriting his relationship to Africa."[92] The paradox of self-ethnography lies in the fact that the same autobiographical desire that subverts ethnographic objectivity by moving beyond the object of ethnography leads the observer to a new understanding of what it is he does – leads him, in short, "beyond Africa, to ethnography."[93]

In this final section, I want to suggest that Synge's autoethnographic expressiveness incorporates the kind of self-fashioning noted above and that these two impulses – one toward a productive dialogue with metropolitan representations of the primitive and one toward a self-reflexiveness that posits Aran women as an eroticized space on which Synge maps the resolution of his own anomie and dissociation – redefine and refine the tension between tradition and modernity characteristic of the Revival's anthropological modernism. Thus Synge's desire for a sexualized native subject salves the alienation he feels in the modern cities of Europe, but it also marks him as irredeemably modern precisely because of his difference from the native subject whose primitive traditionality he desires.

In a general sense, Synge differs very little from the conventional ethnographer who requires some form of rapport in order to gather data; but he differs to the extent that he wishes to belong *within* the community he observes. On his second visit to the islands, Synge writes, "[l]ast year when I came here everything was new, and the people were a little strange with me, but now I am familiar with them and their way of life, so that their qualities strike me more forcibly than before" (*AI*, 106). His desire to belong is at least partly satisfied once he is established in the cottage of his host family, where he not only overhears but is invited to listen to and be part of the community. He is included in the rounds of *poitín*, and provides fiddle accompaniment at dances. But he nevertheless feels that the islanders, despite any affinity they might have with "the moods of varying rapture and dismay that are frequent in artists, and in certain forms of alienation" (*AI*, 30), are fundamentally different – in a word, primitive. The ambivalence of his position thus results in contradictory perceptions: on the one hand, the "men and women seem strangely far away," yet, on the other hand, "[t]here is hardly an hour I am with them that I do not feel the shock of some inconceivable idea, and then again the shock of some vague emotion that is familiar to them and to me" (*AI*, 113). After registering his shock of recognition – which is, in a sense, the shock of kinship or oneness with the Other – he goes on to write, "On some days I feel this island as a perfect home and resting place; on other days I feel that I am a waif among the people . . . and while I wander among them, they like me sometimes, and laugh at me sometimes, yet never know what I am doing" (*AI*, 113). Counterposed to this shock is one that Synge associates with the terrifying strangeness of the landscape:

It would be an interesting if cruel experiment to bring some sensitive native from the central portion of Ireland who had never seen the seas[,] to carry him blindfolded to Aran on a tranquil calm day and keeping [him] in confinement till a great storm arose lead him on the cliff and take away the cloth from his eyes. I am not able to imagine any shock more great. (*MS*, 4385)

The shocking quality of the Aran Islands and their inhabitants marks the contradiction at the heart of Synge's autoethnographic text: he keeps his distance from a primitive race in need of ethnographic redemption, but he also desires an intimate rapport with a people whose wild and lonely temperament seems to coincide with his own.

Nowhere is this contradiction more evident and more expressive of the constitutive instability of ethnographic authority than in Synge's depictions of Aran women and his desire for their "remote sexual sympathy" (*MS*, 4344). Significantly, Synge seems to have followed an ethnographic imperative when he composed *The Aran Islands*, for many of his remarks about Aran women in his field notebooks do not appear in the finished text. To some degree, the intertextual relations between *The Aran Islands* and the typescript drafts and notebooks are similar to those that obtain between

Malinowski's *Argonauts* and *A Dairy in the Strict Sense of the Term*. The difference lies in the fact that Synge's finished text retains significant traces of what ethnographic protocol would ordinarily disallow: a sexual desire for the subject of ethnography. For Malinowski, the illicit quality of this desire is apparent:

A pretty finely built girl walked ahead of me. I watched the muscles of her back, her figure, her legs, and the beauty of the body so hidden to us, whites, fascinated me. Probably even with my own wife I'll never have the opportunity to observe the play of back muscles for as long as with this little animal. At moments I was sorry I was not a savage and could not possess this pretty girl.[94]

The stance of the participant–observer is simultaneously under-scored *and* undone in the presence of young native women. In Malinowski's case, the experience, which is frankly, even crudely sexual, is relegated to a private diary, which indicates the ethnographer's sense that it has no proper place in his scientific account.

In Synge's case, the question of including eroticized images of native women in an ethnographic text is not one of propriety; rather it is one of aesthetics or, more specifically, the refinement of literary representations that attempt to capture the strange spiritual sensuality of Aran women. The following passage appears in Synge's notebook but not in *The Aran Islands*:

The women on this west coast seem to belong to two very distinct types, one tall, red-haired or blond with high round heads and a coarse skin and voice, the other finely made with black hair, blue eyes, a wonderfully fair skin and a low musical voice, that form altogether a radiantly spiritual expression that I have never seen equalled in other places. This girl I speak of was of the latter type and her face haunted me all day on the rocks. (*MS*, 4344)

Synge sees the same girl later and he describes her in the florid style of the *fin de siècle* aesthete: "I saw suddenly the beautiful girl I had noticed on the pier and her face came with me all day among the rocks. She is madonna-like yet has a rapt soul-wrought majesty as far from earthly exaltation as from the maternal comeliness of Raphael's later style" (*MS*, 4385). Descriptions in *The Aran Islands* tend to be less overheated. At the conclusion of the description of the threshing of rye cited above, Synge describes a young girl sitting on a heap of straw: "A ray of sunlight fell on her and on a portion of the rye, giving her figure and red dress with the straw under it a curious relief against the nets and oilskins, and forming a natural picture of exquisite harmony and color" (*AI*, 130). The difference is clear: the published passage emphasizes the woman's harmony with nature, while the passage in the notebook too patently reveals the author's longing for the girl as well as the primitivism that allows him to differentiate among "distinct types." It is interesting to note that, while elsewhere he writes that Aran women "looked strangely wild and seal-like with the salt caked upon their lips and wreaths of seaweed in their hair" (*AI*, 108), he suppresses the racialist language of types. It is quite the opposite with an ethnographer like Malinowski, who suppresses his erotic and aesthetic responses (save the few "light touches" he adds to *Argonauts*) in the interests of a scientific discourse of racial types.

In the eroticized, literary descriptions in *The Aran Islands*, Synge combines the iterative modality of ethnographic description with the voyeuristic tendencies of early modernist aestheticism, a combination that crops up whenever the quest for sensual liberation intersects with a desire for things primitive. In a passage that anticipates the famous bird-girl scene of Joyce's *A Portrait of the Artist as a Young Man*, Synge evokes an image of a girl whose birdlike sensuality disturbs his native guide:

I often come on a girl with her petticoats tucked up round her, standing in a pool left by the tide and washing her flannels among the sea-anemones and crabs. Their red bodices and white tapering legs make them as beautiful as tropical seabirds, as they stand in a frame of seaweeds against the brink of the Atlantic. Michael, however, is a little uneasy when they are in sight, and I cannot pause to watch them. (*AI*, 76)[95]

The modesty that Michael so evidently evinces is alien to Synge; still, though he "cannot pause to watch" the girls, he has evidently paused often enough before in order to give this detailed portrait "in a frame of seaweeds." In a passage from the notebooks, this ambivalence signals a more general sense of alienation, which comes increasingly to determine the nature of his attitude toward the islanders: "I seem shut out from the world upon this lonely rock and shut out again from the people who are on it. In these moments I am drawn to the girls of the island, for in even remote sexual sympathy there is an interchange of emotion that is independent of ideas" (*MS*, 4344).

It is tempting to regard this "remote sexual sympathy" as a kind of ethnographic voyeurism, in which the racial distinctions inherent in the ethnographic situation are recoded as sexual difference. As

Robert Young writes, "sexual difference [in colonial contexts is] translated into the sexual division of race, so the white male's object of desire has been relocated across the racial divide."[96] In the Irish context, this process is complicated by the fact that there is no racial difference other than the phantasmic one created by imperialist ethnologists like Matthew Arnold; hence the signal importance of the kind of gendered difference that marks the feminized Irish in opposition to the masculine English. Synge's desire to find in the alterity of Aran women evidence of sympathy with his own moody and passionate sexuality betrays a level of complicity with this colonialist mode of differentiation. On one level, he creates an image of Aran women – exotic and sexual in a vaguely transgressive way – that conforms to the discourse of primitivism; but, on another level, he presents a quite different image – of a redemptive sexual naturalness – that deeply colors not only his sense of the Irish "race" but also his sense of himself as Irish. In his responses to Aran women, he attempts to resolve the ambivalence of his position as an Anglo-Irish Revivalist doing fieldwork on the Aran Islands and struggles with his contradictory attitudes toward women who are the subjects, by turns, of an "ethnography of colonial desire"[97] and the spiritualized autobiography of an alienated modern artist who seeks salvation by observing their sensuous, primitive beauty.

Synge seeks the eroticized primitive in part because he can no longer bear the burden of an alienated subjectivity. This is a common enough motif in modernist literature, one that Joyce exploited in *Ulysses*, where Leopold Bloom's Orientalist fantasies compensate for his sense of emasculation at the hands of his fellow Irishmen. In both Synge's and Bloom's cases, the desire for the primitive offers salvation from what Marianna Torgovnick calls "transcendental homelessness": "Whatever form the primitive's hominess takes, its strangeness salves our estrangement from ourselves and from our culture."[98] But this salvation introduces a contradiction, for two mutually exclusive rhetorical modes structure the desire for the primitive. A "rhetoric of control and domination," which belongs as much to anthropology as to the discourses of colonialism, "exists alongside (behind) a rhetoric of more obscure desires: of sexual desires or fears, of class, or religious, or national, or racial anxieties, of confusion or outright self-loathing. Not just outer-directed, Western discourse on the primitive is also inner-directed – salving secret wounds, masking the controller's fear of losing control and power."[99]

In the notebooks and the draft versions of *The Aran Islands*, the two strategies appear together, the latter undermining the ethnographic authority of the former. Especially telling in this regard is Synge's compulsion to link Aran women, with their characteristic red petti-coats, to the isolation and violence of the islands. In a passage struck from an early typescript draft of *The Aran Islands*, Synge adopts both the attitude and the frame of reference of the participant–observer, invoking a primitivist discourse in order to explain the significance of their "unceasing red" (*MS*, 4385):

The natives have of course a halfsavage fondness for ornament such as cheap jewelry and ribbons yet the bright colors they are fond of fit well with the scheme of their dress. No one who has not passed months among these gray clouds and seas can realize the hungry joy with which one follows the red dresses of the women. If they were dressed in blue also the island would be hardly habitable and one would be ready to commit murder to gloat a moment upon red. (*MS*, 4344).

While references to red petticoats also occur in *The Aran Islands*, they carry little overt erotic significance. The notebooks and drafts, however, reveal the extent to which the "unceasing red" of the petticoats and the "halfsavage fondness" for ornament are the indisputable mark of Aran women's Otherness. The red petticoats indicate, perhaps, the association of women with the body in birth, menstruation, distress, and death (this association is explicit in plays like Synge's *Riders to the Sea*); but, more important, they represent for Synge, according to Luke Gibbons, an "ominous association between violence and sexuality."[100] They emerge, in a torturous network of associations, as the sign of pure difference as well as of a redemption worth murdering for. They signal a potential for vio-lence in Aran men that would erupt only in the absence of that which marks women *as* women. Women ameliorate life on the islands; by wearing red, they prevent men from murdering for it. But it is not women per se that make life bearable, for Synge suggests that, "dressed in blue," the island would hardly be habitable. Blue, evidently, is too close chromatically to the grayness Synge sees everywhere; what is needed is the utterly different color red, opposed to gray and suggestive of the absolute difference of women from men and from the desolate nature of Aran itself. What is more, the origin of the choice or directive to wear red remains a mystery: "What has guided the women of grey-brown western Ireland to color them in unceasing red?" Synge asks in his notebook

(*MI*, 4385). The possibility that the women themselves, guided by some unknown agency, choose the color red suggests that they alone hold violence at bay.

It is important to emphasize that Synge's desire for Aran women and their utter difference is not his alone, for it would be shared by *anyone* who has "passed months among these grey clouds and seas." In such remarks Synge replicates the tendency in classic ethnography to generalize from particular evidence and personal experience, to "search[] for the universal in the local, the whole in the part."[101] Synge's ethnographic voyeurism replicates what Jenny Sharpe, in her discussion of the symbolic significance of English women in India, calls the "discourse of rape": "a specifically sexual form of violence which has as its aim an appropriation of women as 'the sex.' This appropriation takes place through the objectification of women as sexualized, eroticized and ravaged bodies."[102] Sharpe goes on to suggest that Anglo-Indian women are transformed "into an institution, the 'English Lady,'" and that their violation (real or imagined) converts the "English Lady" into a symbol of colonial authority under siege. As such, a colonialist discourse mobilizes them into service as national icons, creating "a slippage between the violation of English women as the object of rape and violation of colonialism as the object of rebellion."[103] Synge describes a similar process, though the Aran women are clearly not to be taken as symbolic of English or Anglo-Irish womanhood nor of colonial authority. But they are reduced in a similar way to an imaginary status, their gender difference elevated to the foreground as a symbolic resignification of violence. They become the visible sign of the West of Ireland, the purity of being of a people whose violence is barely contained by the mere presence of women in red.

Synge's representations of Aran women point up the contradictions at the heart of Revivalist ethnography and indicate the erotic valence of an anthropological modernism that posits a native Other as the salvation of a dissociated subjectivity. On the one hand, the Aran Islands and their inhabitants belong to a strange natural world that often appears to Synge, as it did to Yeats, as the objective correlative of his own cultural estrangement. "It was a coincidence for Synge," writes John Wilson Foster, "happy artistically, less happy emotionally, that he found a people whose moods and way of life (their nocturnal activities, for example) were so complementary to his own – complementary yet inescapably other."[104] But, on the other hand, he fears the correspondence of "the strange beauty of [Aran] women" with his own waif-like sensibility. The sense of estrangement, of arriving and sojourning in a desolate land far from home, the difficulties of language and custom, the disturbing paradox of finding in an exotic locale a sense of "hominess," the reduction of the self to the status of waif, barely noticeable, moving among Others – all these elements foreshadow "a new 'ethnographic subjectivity'" as Clifford describes it, a "condition of off-centeredness in a world of distinct meaning systems."[105] Synge's *Aran Islands* dramatizes this "off-centeredness" even as it employs methods, resources, and attitudes of ethnographic discourse, and even as its narrator occupies the position, albeit in a highly self-conscious fashion, of the participant–observer. To ignore the ethnographic imperative in Synge's work is to miss not only an important facet of its representational method (its commitment to a realistic rendering of social and cultural "facts"), but also the critique of that imperative that literary and autobiographical discourses make possible. The desire for Aran women, even as it reinscribes certain primitivist notions of gender and race, nevertheless challenges colonialist and anthropological misrepresentations by drawing out the voyeuristic desire latent in the ethnographic situation. Indeed, the very possibility of their "strange beauty" in the desolate environment of Aran – "a mass of wet rock, a strip of turf, and then a tumult of waves," a place where the islanders "shriek with pitiable despair before the horror of the fate to which they all are doomed" (*AI*, 72, 75) – is a potent criticism of such representations, though as we shall see in the next chapter, Synge's alternatives were often regarded as a new kind of stereotype.

Like Yeats, Synge articulated the dilemma of native intellectuals in an epoch of decolonization who must work through a tangled net of complicities to "introduce into their readers' or hearers' consciousness the terrible ferment of subversion."[106] By assimilating his own subjective responses to the Aran Islands and their inhabitants into the discursive space of ethnography, by allowing the contradictions and tensions of ethnographic discourse to unfold in a dialogic play of voices and cultural authorities, Synge calls into question the most basic assumption of cultural representation: that there is a singular and essential "culture" and that it can be represented and preserved – in a word, *redeemed* – by a discourse essentially foreign to its participants. Synge's Revivalist text stands as a harbinger of both a revisionist anthropology that seeks to break down the barriers between the ethnographer and the primitive society he observes and an instance of an anthropological modernism that exploits the constitutive tension between tradition and modernity. This modernism aspires to new levels of critical and "indigenous" authority in Synge's dramatic work, especially *The Playboy of the Western World* (the focus of the next chapter), and in Joyce's *A Portrait of the Artist as a Young Man* and *Ulysses*. Of particular importance for all of these texts is the reconfiguration of the cultural authority of the participant–observer, who is liberated in the new cathexes opened up by new modes of representation and new styles of cultural belonging. The Ireland that Yeats, Synge, and Joyce seek to invent is in many ways symbolized by Synge's experience on the Aran Islands, for in place of the "real" Aran that so many readers despaired of finding in Synge's text we find the sphinx-like "Synge-on-Aran," a man who has written himself into a landscape: "a hard pen / scraping in his head; / the nib filed on a salt wind / and dipped in the keening sea."[107]

CHAPTER 4

Staging ethnography: Synge's 'The Playboy of the Western World'

I'll tell you a story – the kings have story-tellers while they are
waiting for their dinner – I will tell you a story with a fight in it,
a story with a champion in it, and a ship and a queen's son that
has his mind set on killing somebody that you and I know.

W. B. Yeats[1]

It is a paradox of the ethnographic imagination of the Revival that
Synge's *Playboy of the Western World* is in some ways a more disciplined
attempt to deal with the complex problems of cultural representation
than *The Aran Islands*. This is due largely to the dramatic structure of
The Playboy, which leaves Synge little opportunity for the expression
of an autobiographical desire. But, in some very important ways,
these two texts are linked, for Synge's dramatic development of
folklore material in *The Playboy* constitutes a further *performative* phase
of an ethnographic enterprise that began with *The Aran Islands*.
Moreover, the structure of this continuing enterprise extends beyond
the performance of the play to include public reactions to it. By
staging his ethnographic fieldwork in *The Playboy*, often in exorbitantly unrealistic terms, Synge effectively challenges the primitivism
on which he had himself relied in *The Aran Islands* and develops
further the contours of an Irish anthropological modernism by
calling into question the way tradition typically furthers the aims of
the modern artist. No longer content to accept the redemptive
promise of a primitive traditionality, Synge in *The Playboy* makes the
traditional modern by demonstrating that both tradition and modernity suffer from the same debilitating absence of authenticity.
Another way to frame this problem, which for Terry Eagleton is
constitutive of Irish modernism, is to restate the distinction between
tradition and modernity as a distinction between reality and representation. As *The Playboy* demonstrates, the assumption that the

traditional is somehow more real or more authentic fails to consider the role of representation in the construction of tradition. In this sense, Synge reveals the modernity of tradition at the same time that he reaffirms the fundamental importance for the Celtic Revival of traditional material and themes.

Understanding the mechanism of Synge's performative reenactment of ethnographic knowledge may help us understand the tensions between tradition and modernity, representation and reality. For *The Playboy*, understood in the context of its inaugural productions and the responses to it from audience members and critics, reveals that these tensions arose from a misunderstanding of the nature of artistic production and the artist's relation to tradition. Far from seeking to advance a Revivalist representation of the Irish peasantry that would displace or annul more authentic alternatives – a situation that for many readers constituted the crisis behind *The Playboy* – Synge's play departs from the protocols of ethnographic realism and challenges the assumption, as much anthropological as it is aesthetic, that a faithful (that is to say, mimetic) representation of culture is possible. To see the problem solely in terms of representational fidelity is to obscure the fact that it is not a question of the *right* representation but rather of the *right to represent*. The tendency for nationalists to misapprehend the nature of the two questions, seeing in the first an answer to the second, is critiqued in an autoethnographic performance that challenges assumptions about race, identity, and nationalism by exposing the constructedness of any representation of authenticity. In a sense, Synge grants himself the right to represent precisely by refusing to conform to existing (mis)representations.

It is important to understand Synge's autoethnographic project in the context of Revivalist theatre and its various obligations to cultural nationalism. For a number of reasons that are not always obvious to today's readers of *The Playboy* but which were notoriously so to Synge's audiences, the Irish National Theatre was not primarily a *nationalist* project; this was especially true in the early years of the Abbey Theatre, which opened in 1904. Playwrights like Synge, Yeats, and Lady Gregory produced dramatic works under constraints that led them to the creation of a national style that avoided explicitly nationalist sentiments, a style that was recognizably Irish, that drew on folklore, myth, and legend, but that avoided the partisan, polemical, and propagandistic tendencies of various nationalist factions. Critical responses to performances during the

early years of the Literary Theatre (1898–1901) and the Irish
National Drama Society (1902) – particularly the 1899 performances
of *The Countess Cathleen* and the 1902 performances of that signature
Revivalist play, *Cathleen Ni Houlihan* – suggest a defensive reaction on
the part of nationalists who felt that a national theatre ought to form
not challenge national identity. Many nationalists resented what they
considered to be negative portrayals of the Irish peasantry, preferring
instead to see plays that dramatized political sentiments and represented myth and legend as revolutionary and patriotic allegory.[2]
Nationalist pressures, even the possibility of such pressures, occasionally led the Abbey Theatre directors to withhold production of
plays like Synge's *The Tinker's Wedding* for fear of the kind of violent
public reaction that eventually greeted *The Shadow of the Glen* and *The
Playboy of the Western World*. As Yeats wrote to Lady Gregory, "the
tinker play" was considered "with a view to performance and
publication in *Samhain* but [he and Synge] decided that it would be
dangerous at present."[3] Compounding this fear of public reaction
was the influence of Annie Horniman, the Englishwoman who built
and financed the Abbey Theatre and was its sole patron from 1904
to 1910. As Adrian Frazier and others have shown, Horniman (often
with Yeats's blessing) was untiring in her struggle to keep the Abbey
Theatre from staging any kind of nationalist drama.[4] The combined
forces of Horniman's injunctions and an apolitical aestheticism,
voiced most stridently by Synge, led to the formation of a purport-
edly ideologically neutral "folk drama," which by 1917 had become,
as Yeats put it in a letter to James Joyce, a reliable "type" that
"keeps the Theatre running."[5]

The fact that the Abbey Theatre directors were Anglo-Irish
certainly contributed to this state of affairs, primarily because their
privileged positions as members of an intelligentsia set them apart
from the native Catholic Irish of which they wrote. Though Yeats at
this time identified himself with the Celtic bard – that powerful
amalgam of historian, genealogist, poet, courtier, educator, scholar,
and wanderer – his sympathies were turning, as I have shown in
chapter 2, in a new direction. By 1907, when *The Playboy* was first
staged, Yeats and Synge were engaged in an attempt to distance the
Revival from its origins in folkloristic fieldwork and to define (rather
than to obscure) their social difference from the Irish peasantry and
to do so in terms of aesthetic autonomy. Synge articulated this
perspective when he rejected Lady Gregory's dream of a national

drama that would "get at the highest and most disinterested feelings and passions of the people," preferring instead a primarily literary theatre: "The whole interest of our movement," he wrote to Frank Fay in 1904, "is that our little plays try to be literature first – i.e., to be personal, sincere and beautiful – and drama afterwards."[6] Like Yeats, Synge combined a Romantic temperament with a tendency to idealize the Irish peasantry from a position of sympathetic detachment. But this detachment, really a specific form of a more pervasive Anglo-Irish deracination, together with the compromises necessitated by Horniman, which mostly took the form of injunctions against political plays, did not necessarily negate the oppositional potential of Revivalist dramatic productions. We might go so far as to say that Yeats, Synge, and Lady Gregory, despite their Anglo-Irish backgrounds, managed to produce a corpus of folk plays that can be regarded as an early example (though severely conventional) of resistance theatre – if only because it so effectively countered the stage Irishmen of the Queen's Royal Theatre and the crude, racist stereotypes of British propagandists. As David Cairns and Shaun Richards have recently written, "the Irish were racially and culturally located to a subordinate position in the Imperial community through, amongst other elements, [Matthew] Arnold's typifications of 'Celtic' personality as feminine, irrational, impractical and childlike, and social-darwinist stereotyping of the Irish as inferior racially to the Aryan Anglo Saxons."[7] Against a colonialist and anthropological tradition of primitivist Celticism and despite the conditions imposed by Horniman and Dublin Castle (chiefly through the power of granting patents), the Revivalists succeeded in creating an *imaginary* Ireland rooted in a distinctly Anglo-Irish social authority but ultimately transcending that authority. Certainly this was Yeats's understanding when he wrote, referring to himself, Synge, and Lady Gregory, that "[w]e three have conceived an Ireland that will remain imaginary more powerfully than we have conceived ourselves."[8]

But Revivalist dramatists did not create this "imaginary" Ireland *ex nihilo*. The principal writers – Yeats, Lady Gregory, and Synge – drew on a folk tradition that provided plots, themes, and characters for their plays, many of which, though breaking new ground by offering non-traditional dramaturgical styles, were more or less faithful dramatizations of this tradition. Synge alone, it seems to me, went beyond this practice of faithfully retelling stories and legends to challenge the anthropological authority behind the retellings. This is not to say that other Revivalist playwrights did not issue similar challenges. For example, Lady Gregory, in her representations of peasant characters and traditional folkloristic and legendary stories, undercuts what Lucy McDiarmid and Maureen Waters call the "double plot" of eighteenth- and nineteenth-century Irish drama, "challeng[ing] colonial attitudes" by placing "historically marginalized figures of Irish country people at the center of the new drama." For them, Lady Gregory's plays critique "the way nineteenth-century comic fiction and drama were used to debase and disenfranchise the Irish peasant to please an English audience."[9] Her most famous peasant comedies, like *Hyacinth Halvey* and *Spreading the News*, made comic capital out of Irish cultural traits, particularly the peasant's propensity to spin yarns that had no basis in reality; but they do not go very far toward a critique of the primitivist categories that persist just beneath the surface of her seemingly sympathetic portrayals of tramps, constables, peasants, and republican outlaws. McDiarmid and Waters are right to emphasize Lady Gregory's importance as a Revivalist playwright and folklorist; but the fact that she repositions peasant characters "at the center of the new drama" is critically insignificant as long as the role of a redemptive ethnography in the construction of that drama is left unquestioned.

Yeats presents us with a similar problem, one that reveals a fundamental distinction between his and Synge's use of folklore in dramatic productions. As I have indicated in chapter 2, Yeats's Revivalist project until about 1897 was dedicated primarily to a method of creative evocation in which "fair equivalents" of folklore were the goal of a redemptive ethnographic project. I have also shown that a shift took place in the mystical stories of 1897, in which "divine substances" displaced "fair equivalents" as the object of a new social authority that combined the visionary capacity of the mystic with the modern artist's increasing interest in personality as the mediating filter for any representation of the "real" world outside the observer's consciousness. The dramatic works that Yeats began to produce in the 1890s in some ways evince aspects of both "fair equivalents" and "divine substances," with the latter prevailing as he became more interested in non-representational drama. Though Yeats continued to use traditional materials, he tended to borrow them rather than collect them; as a result, these plays do not reflect the folkways of the peasantry as he once experienced them as a folklorist doing fieldwork. By and large, the plays that focus on legendary and folk material performed in the years 1899–1910 do not appear to derive from or contribute to the anthropological modernism that yielded works like *Fairy and Folk Tales* and *The Celtic Twilight*, nor do they produce "new originals" in Talal Asad's sense of "transformed instances of [an] original." Even an early play like *The Land of Heart's Desire*, which is concerned with the fairy-faith of the peasantry, is not drawn from Yeats's own experience in the field but reflects a folkloric tradition transformed by the poet's imagination. And, while I do not wish to gainsay the imaginative element in the texts that emerged out of Yeats's folkloristic fieldwork, it is the experiential authority of those texts that provided the opportunity for a productive engagement with and resistance to the misrepresentations of anthropological and colonialist discourses. The goal of creating "fair equivalents" is superseded in the plays by what Deborah Fleming calls "new mythologies." In her comparison of the dramatic methods of Yeats and Synge, Fleming points to the difference I am here trying to sketch:

While Yeats created new mythologies from old folk motifs and legends, Synge wrote plays derived from his experience on the Aran Islands. Like Yeats he was a traditionalist, but he was far more a primitivist, for he celebrates in his prose and drama the peasants' way of life, which he believed to be more virtuous and meaningful than the 'civilization' of eastern Ireland . . . Their work reveals quite different purposes, for while Yeats's undisguised lyricism emphasizes the connection of the natural world to folkloristic motifs, Synge focuses on direct experience of the peasants' difficult lives.[10]

As I argue throughout this chapter, it is Synge's focus on "direct experience" and the problems of representing that experience that opens up an opportunity for a more self-consciously critical perspective on the anthropological authority that underwrites the modernist sensibility of the Celtic Revival.

One result of this critical perspective was the discovery that representations of culture have a powerful ability to install themselves as truths. Synge learned early on the implications of challenging these cultural truths, as the controversy surrounding *The Shadow of the Glen* indicates. Early in his stay on the Aran Islands, Synge recorded a tale told to him by Pat Dirane about a man who feigns death in order to trap his wife with her lover.[11] In the version included in *The Aran Islands*, the lover is hit by the husband "so that the blood out of him leapt up and hit the gallery" (*AI*, 72). There is a certain wild justice to the violence depicted here that Synge associated with the peasantry of the West of Ireland. In *The Shadow of the Glen*, a quite different form of justice transpires. Instead of fighting, the husband toasts the lover. "I was thinking to strike you, Michael Dara," says the husband, "but you're a quiet man, God help you and I don't mind you at all." They each take up a glass of whiskey and Michael replies, "God reward you, Daniel Burke, and may you have a long life and a quiet life, and good health with it."[12] In addition to this striking change in the relation between lover and husband, Synge appears to articulate a modernist sensibility with respect to Nora Burke, who asserts her independence and sexual autonomy by walking out on her husband in order to travel the roads with a tramp. Synge's frank treatment of what he considered to be the reality of an Irish peasant woman is certainly an improvement on the ambivalent fantasies he entertained while writing *The Aran Islands*. But it was precisely this reality that provoked his audience to charge him with casting aspersions on the piety and purity of Irish womanhood. Maud Gonne, among others, walked out of the first performance in 1903 as a public protest, and the scandal was still trumpeted in the press, primarily in Arthur Griffith's *United Irishman*, the following year when the play opened at the Abbey Theatre.

The *Shadow of the Glen* laid bare the reality behind the nationalist idealization of Irish women, but the nationalists themselves, particularly Griffith, preferred to be outraged – after all, the reality of an Irishwoman's life was less useful in nationalist propaganda. It is ironic, of course, that in preserving a pure and pious ideal of Irish womanhood, in constructing female icons of the Irish nation, nationalists were duplicating the gendered typology of imperial apologists like Matthew Arnold.[13] As I will argue below with respect to *The Playboy of the Western World*, Synge's refusal to perpetuate the misrepresentations of Irish life and identity not only provoked nationalist outrage, but inaugurated a self-critical mode of performative justice that in Synge's case also amounted to a refusal of the very ethnographic authority that enabled him to write *The Aran Islands*. In order to clarify the development of this performative justice, I will draw on Victor Turner's anthropological theory of social drama to illustrate the extent to which *The Playboy* is both an autoethnographic text as well as an ethnographic event in its own right, an event in which the play and audience reactions to it come together in a single "cultural performance." It is important to stress here that Synge seeks to revise not only colonialist and anthropological attitudes and stereotypes of the Irish, but also those attitudes and stereotypes developed in the Revival's own projects of ethnographic redemption. In fact, once we understand Synge's commitment to revising his *own* assumptions about Irish peasant culture, we will be in a position to see precisely how his failure to conform to his audience's expectations constitutes his chief success. By staging ethnography, Synge confronts the problem of representing national self-determination and national identities and the right to represent both; he becomes, as Fanon puts it, "an awakener of the people," and *The Playboy* takes its place in the canon of "a fighting literature, a revolutionary literature, and a national literature."[14]

As I argued in the previous chapter, *The Aran Islands* was governed to a significant degree by an ethnographic imperative to redeem a primitive society from the encroachment of modernity. I also argued that the ethnographic imperative in Synge's text is reconfigured, if not annulled, by an autobiographical desire that confounds ethnographic authority by privileging intersubjective experience and by making the participant–observer both subject *and object* of the ethnographic text.

The ambivalence of Synge's position on the Aran Islands is, in part, a function of his own personal anxieties, which tempted him to regard the islanders, especially the women, in terms of a primitivist discourse in which they function as exotic pretexts for the psychosexual development of an Anglo-Irish interloper. In this sense, Synge illicitly wields ethnographic authority in order to circumvent the debilitating effects of modernity; moreover, his very presence among the islanders, his immersion in their day-to-day lives and his rejection of the urban centers of Europe, can be regarded as a version (problematic, to be sure, given Synge's Anglo-Irish background) of Fanon's call for native intellectuals to base their revolutionary activities in rural areas where they might have greater influence over the peasantry: "They fall back toward the countryside and the mountains, toward the peasant people. From the beginning, the peasantry closes in around them, and protects them from being pursued by the police."[15] Unlike Yeats, whose periodic forays in the Irish countryside lacked the element of long-term immersion, Synge sought in the desolation of Connemara, West Kerry, and the Aran

Islands a mode of life free from the corrupting effects of European modernity, a mode of life in which he might express himself wholly and heroically. However, because he did not quite surrender the modality of ethnographic inscription, with its "obsessive tabulation of desire,"[16] and because he did not reach the level of political solidarity with the peasantry that Fanon advocates, he remained caught within a lived experience he could neither embrace fully nor represent adequately. In Fanon's terms, he stops just short of the "fighting literature" that would enable him to challenge the colonialist and anthropological authorities responsible for the denigration and disavowal of the Irish peasantry. This is possible only when he transforms ethnographic knowledge into a dramatic performance that makes representation and the *right* to represent an open question.

As is well known, Synge based his major plays on fieldwork done in County Wicklow and the West of Ireland. Typically, the plays elaborated on folklore and anecdotes he had collected or heard and observations he had made, with the result that his dramatic works embody a good deal of ethnographic data. His decision to redeploy ethnographic knowledge in dramatic form offers just the modality of expression that would allow him "to give the reality, which is the root of all poetry," as he put it in the preface to *The Playboy* (53), and to avoid contributing to an exoticism that would sustain the authority of a primitivist discourse. Yeats was astute in recognizing how the plays tended to reconfigure ethnographic knowledge:

As I read *The Aran Islands* right through for the first time since he showed it me in manuscript, I come to understand how much knowledge of the real life of Ireland went to the creation of a world which is yet as fantastic as the Spain of Cervantes. Here is the story of *The Playboy*, of *The Shadow of the Glen*; here is the ghost on horseback and the finding of the young man's body of *Riders to the Sea*, numberless ways of speech and vehement pictures that had seemed to owe nothing to observation, and all to some overflowing of himself, or to some mere necessity of dramatic construction. (*CA*, 152–3)

Yeats acknowledges that Synge's plays derived from a "knowledge of the real life of Ireland," but only once he has seen this knowledge expressed in the ethnographic realism of *The Aran Islands*. He notices that the plays transform that knowledge to such a degree that its ethnographic character is obscured in the assertion of personality or the "necessity of dramatic construction." But it is interesting to note that elsewhere Yeats insists on the role played by the Aran Islands as a reflection of Synge's melancholy character. The implication is that even knowledge of "real life" is inevitably mediated by the personality of the observer.

It is important at this point to emphasize what Synge meant when he spoke of "the reality" he sought to capture in his plays. As I noted in chapter 3, Robert Welch described Synge's style in *The Aran Islands* as a form of "transfigured realism that gives its due value to the objective and subjective impulses."[17] For the plays, precisely because they eschew the ethnographic realism at work in *The Aran Islands*, required a representational strategy that would effectively move beyond realism, even a "transfigured" form that permits the breakdown of distinctions between subject and object, and beyond the strong determinate presence of a subjective impulse. Thus Synge developed "a comprehensive and natural form" of writing that would both preserve what was essential about peasant culture while at the same time demonstrate that the essential element was, in fact, "the root of all poetry." In other words, he created or "gave" a reality that was comprehensive and natural, an imaginative style that could adequately reflect the reality of an imaginative people: "[I]n countries where the imagination of the people, and the language they use is rich and living," he writes in the preface to *The Playboy*, "it is possible for a writer to be rich and copious in his words, and at the same time to give the reality, which is the root of all poetry, in a comprehensive and natural form." He goes on to indicate that an ethnographic perspective was essential to his understanding of that reality. Speaking of his experience writing *The Shadow of the Glen*, Synge writes, "I got more aid than any learning could have given me, from a chink in the floor of the old Wicklow house where I was staying, that let me hear what was being said by the servant girls in the kitchen" (*Playboy*, 53). Significantly, Synge subtly undermines the authority of the participant–observer when he reveals the voyeuristic character of his own observations. The effect of this challenge to the superordinancy of objective observation is to expose the ambivalence of the observer's position, for Synge is both a guest in the house he describes and a detached and secretive observer of what transpires in it. Synge's voyeuristic position is therefore both a betrayal of the people with whom he seeks to establish a meaningful rapport and an exposé of the fundamentally unscientific nature of ethnographic observation. The implications of this minor anthropological allegory are developed, as we shall see, in Joyce's *Ulysses*, where Leopold Bloom refashions the objectivity of ethnographic observation, recasting it as self-conscious voyeurism, formulating on-the-spot fantasies of participation in communities from which he is debarred.

In a sense, the voyeuristic perspective limned in the preface to *The Playboy* is a refusal of the ethnographic realism governing *The Aran Islands*. The dramatic re-enactment of ethnographic knowledge deliberately eschews the position of observer-narrator that so strongly characterizes *The Aran Islands* and thereby shifts the responsibilities of representation from the observer – whose anguished solitude signals his ambivalent *right* to represent – to the members of the audience of *The Playboy*, who must infer for themselves both the nature and the rightness of what the play represents. Accordingly, the problems of identity and representation that Synge confronts in *The Playboy*, as well as the social texts that emerge in reaction to the play, can be understood as part of a metadrama of cultural crisis. Ginger Strand has argued along similar lines, writing that *The Playboy* "self-consciously addresses questions of enactment and theatricality."[18] This is certainly an apt description as far as it goes, but I want to suggest that Synge's metadramatic self-reflexivity extended well beyond the contexts that "shap[ed] his work and its reception"[19] and included the anthropological traditions he drew on and contributed to in *The Aran Islands*. To be sure, Synge does bring into prominence the problem of representation and the social power behind it, which Strand identifies as "the representative status attributed to the Irish National Theatre."[20] What she and other commentators fail to note, however, is that the power behind Synge's representations, as well as the "representative status" of much of what was produced by the Irish National Theatre, is specifically anthropological. By translating ethnographic knowledge into dramatic performance, Synge criticized the very Revivalist mode of redemptive ethnography that had authorized Yeats's and his own fieldwork in the West of Ireland. Furthermore, by creating a context in which ethnographic knowledge could be resignified and recontextualized, used not to redeem or preserve primitive social institutions but rather to recreate them in a "new original," Synge radically transformed the ethnographic protocols and primitivist assumptions that made *The Aran Islands* such a deeply problematic text. This reappropriation resulted in a self-critical mode of anthropological modernism that negated the very ethnographic authority it presupposed.

The self-critical mode of Synge's anthropological modernism

derives from his ability to create a performative context in which the social authority of the ethnographic text is contested by the subjects of it. The text of *The Playboy*, together with its opening performances and the audience's response to it, constitutes a kind of performative justice that seeks to redress the discursive violence perpetrated by Revivalist, nationalist and anthropological representations. This justice is described by Victor Turner as a self-perpetuating loop of crisis and redressive cultural performance, a bi-directional flow of performative energies in which social crisis becomes formalized in a redressive drama, which can, in turn, afford the opportunity for new crises (for example, the riots attending the opening week of *The Playboy*) and further redressive performances. In social drama, Turner's term for this process, public performance of ritual metes out justice by seeking to reinstate social harmony or to demarcate the limits of mutual exclusion, following a four-phase process of breach, crisis, redress, and resolution/separation:

[A] social drama first manifests itself as the breach of a norm, the infraction of a rule of morality, law, custom or etiquette in some public arena . . . [A] mounting crisis follows, a momentous juncture or turning point in the relations between components of a social field . . . The phase of crisis exposes the pattern of current factional struggle within the relevant social group . . . In order to limit the contagious spread of *breach* certain adjustive and redressive mechanisms, informal and formal, are brought into operation . . . The mechanisms may range from personal advice and informal arbitration, to formal juridical and legal machinery, and, to resolve certain kinds of crisis, *to the performance of public ritual* . . . The final phase consists either in the reintegration of the disturbed social group . . . or the social recognition of irreparable breach between the contesting parties.[21]

A model of agonistic social processes, the social dramatic structure can be found at all levels of human society, and encompasses a tremendous variety of social phenomena, including (to give a few examples relevant to Synge's work) scenes of storytelling, public performance of plays, riots, reviews, newspaper articles, speeches, letters to editors, and parodies, all of which can function as redressive measures for a social crisis. A social drama can be elaborated in complex textual inscriptions and/or performances or in informal social relationships; it can be repeated interminably or consist of a single enactment. The division into phases remains a constant, however, and this constancy suggests a "well-nigh universal processual form, representing a perpetual challenge to all aspirations to perfection in social and political organization."[22] Turner looks expressly to dramatic performance in order to surmount the discursive limitations of traditional ethnographic discourse, especially when it comes to translating "eccentric" or "marginal" rituals. Synge, I would argue, turns to drama for precisely the same reason.

The social dramatic structure of *The Playboy* consists of a series of crises, each one necessitating a form of redress that, in its turn, initiates another crisis. The first crisis occurs in Synge's own ethnographic representation of the traditional culture of the Aran Islands, which can be regarded as a breach of the very reciprocity that he most desired but which his position as a participant–observer undermined. Specifically, this breach occurs in the ethnographic treatment of an anecdote about a "Connaught man" who had killed his father, which Synge heard from "an old man, the oldest on the island" (*AI*, 95) and which became the basis of *The Playboy*. Unlike Pat Dirane, who sat with him "in the chimney-corner, blinking with the turf smoke" (*AI*, 61), telling folktales that he had inherited from storytellers before him, the old man insists on the veracity of his information: he tells "anecdotes – not folktales – of things that have happened here in his lifetime":

He often tells me about a Connaught man who killed his father with the blow of a spade when he was in a passion, and then fled to this island and threw himself on the mercy of some of the natives with whom he was said to be related. They hid him in a hole – which the old man has shown me – and kept him safe for weeks, though the police came and searched for him, and he could hear their boots grinding on the stones over his head. In spite of a reward which was offered, the island was incorruptible, and after much trouble the man was safely shipped to America. (*AI*, 95)

When Synge retells the anecdote as an example of the local custom of protecting criminals (generalized as a trait "universal in the west" [*AI*, 95]), he effectively implicates his own text in an ethnographic discourse in which "the Connaught man" and the islanders generally are branded as a lawless primitives. The anecdote is consigned to the discourse of primitive sociology, along with such useful information as George Petrie's observation that "'instances of excess'" are "followed by the usual Irish consequences of broken heads."[23]

The problem Synge confronts in translating the anecdote into a dramatic form is a familiar one in ethnographic theory. As Tiraswini Niranjana argues, "[i]mplicitly or explicitly, ethnography always conceived of its project as one of *translation*."[24] Ethnographic translation creates asymmetrical relations of power in which the "universal" language of the sovereign Western observer assimilates and (mis)represents native societies in terms foreign to those who belong to them. Of course, the form of translation at issue here is not limited to language–language translation, but includes any attempt to represent non-Western cultural artifacts in Western terms. In whatever specific sense we construe translation, we find a common result: the creation of uneven relations of linguistic competence and production that duplicate discursively the inequalities of socio-political power. Relevant here is Talal Asad's idea of authorized or "implicit" meanings that emerge in the process of translation. These are "not the meanings the native speaker actually acknowledges in his speech, not even the meanings the native listener necessarily accepts, but those he is 'potentially capable of sharing' with scientific authority 'in some real situation.'"[25] The hypothetical possibility that a native listener will accept the ethnographer's meaning in translation "in some real situation" is connected to another possibility, less hypothetical because far more likely given the imbalance of power between the ethnographer and the native, that the translated text will become "a privileged element in the potential store of historical memory" for the native culture in question.[26] The kind of privilege to which Asad alludes attaches to the scientific texts produced by professional anthropologists, though it is not hard to see that an amateur ethnography like *The Aran Islands*, because of its strong residual investment in ethnographic realism and its *fin de siècle* aesthetic sensibilities, results in a privileged representation that *speaks for* the Aran Islanders – and this despite the islanders' self-consciousness of anthropological curiosity about their way of life and the ability of those who know English to read Synge's text. For the question in the Irish context is not that of a Western observer translating utterly foreign customs into a language that makes them familiar, but that of a "native outsider" who seeks to embrace as familiar what is essentially foreign. As the reception of *The Playboy* suggests, Synge's *Aran Islands* might have been greeted by the islanders not with incomprehension but with a polite refusal to accept an Anglo-Irish vision of their own community.

But ethnography need not result in privileged representations, as anthropologists like Asad and Turner affirm when they adduce alternatives to classic ethnographic realism that can more effectively translate cultural texts and practices:

Indeed, it could be argued that "translating" an alien form of life, another culture, is not always done best through the representational discourse of ethnography, that under certain conditions a dramatic performance, the execution of a dance, or the playing of a piece of music might be more apt. These would all be *productions* of the original and not mere interpretations: transformed instances of the original, not authoritative textual representations of it.[27]

Asad's concept of a performative translation radically undermines the mimetic capacity of ethnography: in doing so, it instates an ideal of *productivity* that generates new cultural originals over and above an ideal of *preservation*, one that presupposes the kind of "representational discourse" that seeks to quantify and stabilize ethnographic knowledge in scientific texts. I might add that this performative mode of cultural production lends itself most readily to the indigenous ethnographer who seeks to contest and resist stereotypical representations and reductive theories of primitive culture.

The cultural translation at work in *The Aran Islands* requires a performative mode of redress that will more closely approximate the native context from which the original ethnographic datum was extracted. What Synge seeks in translating material already used in *The Aran Islands* into dramatic form is not the preservation or redemption of an essence, but a "new original" crafted out of traditional material, faithful (but not in mimetic terms) to the "real life" of the Irish peasant. Part of this process is the creation of a Hiberno-English dialect that aspires to avoid the assimilative impulses of anthropology, colonialism, and nationalist groups like the Gaelic League. As James Knapp writes, "[t]he Hiberno-English that writers such as Lady Gregory and Synge attempted to shape was . . . constituted in the space between two languages, each aspiring to command the total assent of a 'monologia.' "[28] Synge's Hiberno-English offers a hybrid alternative to the opposed primary languages of English and Irish that refuses the authority of either and implicitly refuses the binomial alignments of civilized and primitive that their opposition implies. In a sense, the Hiberno-English of his plays reflects the productive hybridity of a text that combines ethnographic knowledge and dramatic performance in a process of translation that invites a native audience to contest the ways in which ethnographic knowledge is used. However, as I will argue in the last section of this chapter, the audience for *The Playboy*, due to its ideological heterogeneity, demonstrates the problematic complexity of the very notion of a native audience. Despite (perhaps because) of this complexity, Synge's self-reflexive cultural performance affords the opportunity for the kind of symbolic redress that Turner describes, one that leads to effective resistance to an array of social authorities. Understood in this way, the contradictions inherent in the play and its audience, which have posed problems for critics who try to understand Synge's nationalist loyalties, may be regarded as the onset of a new crisis which will entail the construction of new modes of redress. Moreover, the representation of these contradictions registers the modernist's desire for primitive purity at the same time that it undermines that desire by exposing the primitivity of the Irish peasant as a fiction emanating from a complex network of anthropological, colonialist, and nationalist idealizations.

The point of departure for Synge's critique of these misrepresentations is the concept of the hero or "playboy." In an early draft of *The Playboy*, Pegeen Mike laments the dearth of heroic men. "A good job to be living with no fighting or dancing or good works at all, and hardly a fellow left in it with the heart in him to make a keg of poteen and to dare the law" (*Playboy*, 60). Though Synge eventually struck this passage from the final version of the play, the sentiment it expresses – that the Irish peasantry attaches a high value to the violence of the outlaw – remained at the heart of the play's theme and action. It was also one of the elements of the play that attracted immediate and vocal resistance by nationalist members of the audience. While early spectators and reviewers found it morally and politically necessary to decry Synge's representation of a peasantry so easily seduced by Christy Mahon's parricidal violence, recent critics have had a considerably more difficult time interpreting Synge's attitude. G. J. Watson, for example, has written that "[v]itality or energy or 'wildness' was to be a cardinal virtue in all of Synge's plays" and that their "rhetoric of violence" was meant to communicate this virtue, which Synge regarded as evidence of the Irish peasant's distance from the enervation of civilized Europe.[29] Heidi Holder articulates a similar view, arguing that Synge's plays enact ritualistic "dramas of spiritual violence."[30] Such assessments, even as they attempt to explain the representation of violence in an affirmative way, very nearly fall into the kind of cultural stereotyping of which Synge himself was accused. Luke Gibbons is considerably more cautious in his estimation, arguing that Synge saw violence for what it was, even as he used it in order to celebrate a superior way of life:

Synge's preoccupation with lawlessness and violence is central to his overall conception of the western world, for in throwing off the shackles of discipline and constraint, he is undermining one of the main requirements of modernization as exemplified in nineteenth-century Ireland – the centralization of law, ideology and the state apparatus.[31]

For Gibbons, nationalist reactions to Synge's representation of the peasantry were directed not only at the representations as such, but also at the questions of political power that they raised for different constituencies. The confrontation between Synge and the Catholic nationalists was not merely a disagreement over ethnographic accuracy but a "struggle over access to a dominant ideology, to a controlling vision of Irish life."[32]

It is not altogether clear whether Synge's "soft primitivism," as Gibbons styles it, which represents violence in order to invoke a better time prior to the "disenchantment" of modernity, can win the struggle for a "controlling vision of Irish life." Gibbons points out that Synge's representation of violence had analogues in pre-Famine Ireland and cites George Cornewall Lewis's 1836 book *On Local Disturbances in Ireland*, which recounts an episode in County Tipperary that exemplified "a general hatred of the law" and "a sympathy with criminals 'so great as to be scarcely credible.'" Gibbons then wonders whether "Synge had read Cornewall Lewis before he embarked on his own, not so pure fiction."[33] The problem, then, lies in Synge's *attitude* toward the violence he represents and how he wished his audience to interpret his representations of it. Ginger Strand suggests, with some reservations, that Synge's depiction of the violence in *The Playboy* was not embraced by the nationalists in the audience primarily because they felt they had been tricked into assenting to Revivalist stereotypes. "The audience protested what they found to be an ugly depiction of Irish behavior," she writes. "Crucially, this was an image not only presented by Synge but invested by him with the authority of a self-representation – an image created with the collaboration of the Irish themselves."[34] Once the audience found, like the Mayo villagers in *The Playboy*, that they had "invested the powers of representation in a 'likely gaffer,'" they turned on Synge, much as the villagers turn on Christy: "Their displeasure was more complicated than a negative response to an ugly character. The role assigned to themselves offended them most."[35] I will return to the problem of the audience's reaction in the next section, but for now I want to suggest that critics who analyze that reaction, precisely because they refuse the unambiguous moral and nationalist positions taken by the Gaelic League and individuals like Patrick Pearse,[36] must negotiate between conflicting assessments: either Synge was complicit in a Revivalist project of cultural denigration or he rose above the partisan in-fighting among nationalist factions in order to comment, critically and metadramatically, on the problem of representation. But neither assessment seems satisfactory, and even the most astute commentators, like Gibbons and Strand, are forced either to leave the matter of Synge's politics teasingly unclarified, as Gibbons does in his short treatment of the play, or to grant that his politics were potentially, though perhaps unintentionally, progressive, as Strand does when she concludes that Synge's "disingenuous attempt to force the audience to validate his depiction of them" effectively acknowledges that the "immense powers of articulation he deploys are really in the hands of the audience."[37]

Strand's conclusion, echoed by other critics, suggests that Synge can critique Irish identity and self-representation only by surrendering his power of articulation. But this conclusion only makes sense if he were intent on providing the audience with what it appeared to want: a faithful representation of the peasantry. Rather than suppose that he provoked his audience into an awareness of their own critical capacity, perhaps we might assume that he failed to see such a capacity; certainly the public stance of the Gaelic League toward the Revival's dramatic productions left little room for critical self-examination. I would submit, then, that Synge's position was not that of a reactionary Anglo-Irish outsider whose representational authority depended on the unwilling complicity of his audience; rather, it was the position of the Fanonist native intellectual who has moved beyond the phase of revivalist exoticism (a phase in which some critics have placed the work of Irish–Ireland nationalists) to create a performative autoethnography that translated anthropological knowledge in a critical context and that did not require the abandonment of the power of articulation. I would submit further that Synge's *Playboy*, by virtue of its anti-realistic style, contested the primitivism that subtended stereotypes of the "stage-Irishman" and the ethnographic representations of people like Haddon and Browne, whose work contributed to the perpetuation of the idea that the Western Irish were the last bastion of a primitive race; it also called to account those nationalist discourses that celebrated an idealized, pre-modern, pre-colonial peasantry, the fantasy projection of an oppressed people driven to embrace uncritically an image of themselves prepared for them by anthropologists, antiquarians, and the "ascendant and idle class" (*FFT*, 6–7) of folklorists that Yeats set out to correct and supplant.

Heidi Holder has noted the tendency of nativist or Irish-Ireland nationalists to perpetuate certain stereotypical images and conceptions about the Irish people that were sometimes derived from or, as was more often the case, confirmed those found in colonialist discourses that relied on a primitivist distinction between the Irish and the European people. These images are perpetuated in the interests of national or racial reform and are part of a program of transformation which, as Holder argues,

had as its basic premise the notion that the Irish people were degraded, ignorant, and in perpetual danger of sliding further behind other European nations. The description of the Irish to be found in the writings of Irish nationalists was not flattering; in fact, these images of Ireland come perilously close at points to resembling the stereotypes and caricatures of anti-Irish propagandists.[38]

The "rhetoric of transformation" employed by nationalists like Sir Charles Gavan Duffy, Douglas Hyde, and Arthur Griffith insisted on the necessity for the moral improvement of the Irish peasantry. Synge's *Playboy* overcame this "transformative" vision by inviting the Irish people to reject an unflattering self-image precisely by presenting them with a patently constructed revision of it. Whether Synge intended it or not, this confrontation with the mechanisms of cultural image-making had the effect of contesting all forms of national identity, the paradoxical result of which, as Joyce demonstrates, is an authentically *inauthentic* vision of the Irish.

I want to go further and suggest that Synge contests his own representations in *The Aran Islands*, thus redressing the crisis brought on by his experiment in ethnographic redemption. The precise mode of this redress, the first phase of which is constituted by the performance of *The Playboy*, involved a departure from ethnographic realism and the strategic idealizations of nationalist propagandists. As Kiberd notes, Synge "depicted Ireland as she was after centuries of British domination, primitive and poor, yet colorful and poetic. The Irish nationalists were intent on changing all this and on achieving respectability; so they denounced Synge for his brutally frank portrait of the life produced by such oppression."[39] Ironically, Synge produces this brutally frank portrayal not by employing the scientific or mimetic methods of anthropology, but by turning these methods on their head. He relies on ethnographic data he had collected in his own fieldwork; but, unlike the classic ethnographer, he incorporated this data in an anti-mimetic dramatic form that subverted the ethnographer's scientific authority. By translating ethnographic knowledge into social drama, the West of Ireland is resignified and revalued as something other than a primitive culture in need of redemption.

Synge's treatment of peasant life in a Mayo village, despite the "anthropological fidelity"[40] that he maintained in matters of dress, dialect, and social custom, refused to conform to either the primitivism of anthropology or the idealizations of Irish-Ireland nationalism. Synge incorporated into *The Playboy* a number of ethnographic details concerning clothing, domestic practices, games, and races, as well as numerous phrases and styles of speech culled from notebooks that he kept while traveling throughout County Wicklow and the West of Ireland.[41] In ethnographic accounts like those of Haddon and Browne, such details would be dutifully recorded in the attempt to create an authoritative, objective, and totalizing account of peasant life. But Synge often altered the ethnographic data he used or left them out of his finished work. Perhaps by omitting or altering details like the washing of shirts in County Wicklow or the spoon-latch that he observed on the Blaskets and that appeared briefly in an early draft, Synge was attempting to subordinate anthropological fidelity to what Yeats called the "necessity of dramatic construction" (*CA*, 153). In any case, enough significant detail remained in the final draft to indicate that Synge wished his play to bear the mark of his fieldwork.

I have noted above that the origin of *The Playboy* was an anecdote about a Connaught man who had killed his father and "then fled to this island and threw himself on the mercy of some of the natives with whom he was said to be related" who then protected him from the police (*AI*, 95). This is perhaps the most famous example of Synge's practice of translating ethnographic knowledge into a dramatic context. What changes in *The Playboy* is that elements either absent or undeveloped in the anecdote become central to the dramatic structure of the play. *The Playboy* dramatizes the anecdote by imposing a concrete plot line, a cast of characters and actions (conversations, relationships, wakes, races, fights) that are more or less verifiable with reference to cultural "facts" that Synge had observed in his fieldwork. But the elaboration of the anecdote calls into question the value not only of an ethnographic discourse that interprets the "Connaught man's" actions as those of a primitive Irish peasant, but also of nationalist idealizations of a people distinguished, as Sir Charles Gavan Duffy put it, by the virtues of "purity, piety, and simplicity."[42] Synge's disapproval of this characterization is registered in his depiction of a credulous peasantry whose motives are far from pious or pure. At the beginning of the play, Christy Mahon tantalizes Michael Flaherty and his friends as he prolongs the revelation of his crime. Easily impressed with his bravery and audacity, the men curiously interpret his murderousness as evidence of his trustworthiness. As Jimmy Farrell says, leaving Pegeen Mike alone as he and Michael leave for the wake, "Now, by the grace of God, herself will be safe this night, with a man killed his father holding danger from the door" (*Playboy*, 77).

Perhaps the most important feature of Synge's critique of the stereotype of a pious peasantry is his depiction of Christy's heroism – or, better, the problem of style his heroism raises. By translating the anecdote into a dramatic idiom, the nameless, marginalized and banished peasant of *The Aran Islands* acquires a name and a heroic identity. In *The Playboy*, the "Connaught man" becomes a recognizable Irish hero, with all the wildness, passion and verbal dexterity of a bardic singer:

> CHRISTY. It's well you know what call I have. It's well you know it's a lonesome thing to be passing small towns with the lights shining sideways when the night is down, or going in strange places with a dog noising before you and a dog noising behind, or drawn to the cities where you'd hear a voice kissing and talking deep love in every shadow of the ditch, and you passing on with an empty, hungry stomach failing from your heart. (*Playboy*, 109)

As many critics have suggested, this kind of verbal display rings false; it would seem to be more appropriate to a man of greater linguistic power than Christy could possibly claim. However, we should bear in mind that, in early versions of the play, Christy was more overtly associated with the bardic tradition. In an early sketch of act one, Pegeen Mike tells of a man who "was a great warrant to tell stories of Holy Ireland" to which Christy replies, "*pricking his ears, jealous,*"

"Talking of Ireland is it. [*He pulls out papers from his pocket.*] If he was a warrant itself to tell stories you should hear me singing songs of Holy Ireland, till you'd think that would draw tears out of the moon" (*Playboy*, 336). Like Yeats's Red Hanrahan, this early version of Christy is a familiar figure, reminiscent of eighteenth-century bards like Anthony Raftery and Eoghan Rua Ó Súilleabháin. When Synge depicts his bardic hero as an inexperienced peasant boasting of murdering his father, when he has Pegeen admire him for his "bravery of heart" and his "savagery or fine words" (*Playboy*, 149, 153), he undercuts the folkloristic and nationalist conceptions of the bardic tradition long gone by the time of the play's action. In the dramatization of Christy's character, Synge is able to explore the cultural ramifications of the anecdote he left unexplained in *The Aran Islands*; by presenting the "Connaught man" as a facile constructor of his own identity, he underscores not only the inadequacy of the bardic model of the hero, but also what he sensed were the unpleasant realities of peasant life in the West of Ireland.

Those realities are revealed in another element of the anecdote that undergoes significant change in *The Playboy*. We should recall at this point that, for many spectators and subsequent critics, Synge's depiction of a murderous hero celebrated and fawned over by pious Irish peasants provoked outrage and cries of scandalous misrepresentation. But the anecdote as it was retold in *The Aran Islands* stressed the community's solidarity with the "Connaught man." For "[i]n spite of a reward which was offered, the island was incorruptible, and after much trouble the man was safely shipped to America" (*AI*, 95). In the third act of *The Playboy*, the Mayo villagers have a change of heart, with the result that Christy's murderous heroism is debunked and he his driven out of the village. This change did little to ameliorate Synge's critics; and the fact that it did not indicates a fundamental conflict within the audience itself. In this respect, Synge's dramatic translation of the anecdote marks an important shift in how the community itself is portrayed. "[T]he success of the community was precisely what Synge wrote out of the tale in adaptation," Harrington writes. "He altered the source in actual experience, which is ordinary procedure, but he did so to introduce failure, not success. That reverses the pattern of composition in nationalist, romantic, and even nineteenth-century popular melodramatic literature."[43] Harrington goes on to note that people like Maud Gonne decried Synge's depiction of communal failure as inappropriate for a national literature. This is an important point, one which was raised by other Irish-Ireland nationalists. But Ginger Strand points out that the failure of the community is less important than the failure of the villagers *and the audience* to distinguish clearly between two kinds of representation. The conflict lies in a distinction between a "true" story, which the villagers could applaud, if only because it took place in the "wide and windy acres" of a "naked parish" in faraway Munster (*Playboy*, 79) but which also turns out to be untrue, and another "true" story that took place in their own backyard. "The contradiction in the villagers' behavior," Strand writes, "resides not only in the difference between their approval of the story and their disapproval of the deed, but in their anger when they find the story was not true, and their even greater anger when they later find that it has been made true."[44] The *naïveté* of the villagers mirrors that of the audience which felt itself deceived by a Revivalist play that purported to represent the "truth" of the West of Ireland but that ended up undermining what the various factions of that audience had already decided *was* the truth.

It is Pegeen Mike who articulates the dilemma that critics have isolated as the "crisis" of *The Playboy*. Upon discovering that Christy had not in fact murdered his father, she utters the famous lines that point up both the hypocrisy of the villagers and the problem of representing them: "I'll say a strange man is a marvel with his mighty talk; but what's a squabble in your back-yard and blow of a loy, have taught me that there's a great gap between a gallous story and a dirty deed" (*Playboy*, 169). When Christy's purely fictional heroism is taken for the real thing – that is, when his linguistic *inventions* are taken for realistic representations of *actions* – Pegeen is confronted with the falsity of both Christy's heroism and of her own reactions to it. The problem, of course, is not that Christy has killed his "Da" but that he has *not* killed him in the heroic manner he advertised and that, moreover, his second attempt took place in such a way that implicates the villagers in the crime. This, as I have said, is the crisis of the play and the point at which so many critics prove so ambivalent; but, if we regard this crisis as part of a general critique of ethnographic stereotypes and nationalist idealizations, it might be more usefully regarded as a redressive maneuver for the kind of *mis*representations that took Irish violence as a sign of cultural essence.

A common complaint against Synge was that his plays distorted folk life, that his "exaggerated" realism misrepresented the simplicity and "purity" of the peasantry.[45] An anonymous writer for the *Freeman's Journal* articulated a popular position with respect to Synge's representational style: "The worst specimen of the stage Irishman of the past is a refined, acceptable fellow compared with that imagined by Mr. Synge, and as for his women, it is not possible, even if it were desirable, to class them."[46] The realism of Synge's drama was openly and vociferously contested from the start. Reactions to the first run of *The Playboy* (Saturday, Jan. 26–Saturday, Feb. 2, 1907) generally assumed that faithful imitation was the *raison d'être* of Irish drama. The *Freeman's Journal* ran a piece, "The People and the Parricide," that articulated a common assumption: "[I]t is essential to remember the mission for which the promoters of the Abbey Street theatre invited the sympathy of the Irish people. They were expected to fulfill the true purpose of playing – 'to hold as 'twere the mirror up to Nature,' to banish the meretricious stage, and give, for the first time, true pictures of Irish life and fulfillment of that pledge."[47] The allusion to Shakespeare here and in other commentaries emphasizes the stakes of dramatic performance: faithful representation of the "true" Irish life judged, as these articles suggest, by "true" Irish men and women. We can discern just how important the issue of realistic representation was for Synge's contemporaries if we consider those critics who took the opposite tack and championed Synge precisely for his accuracy. In one of the first major reviews of *The Playboy*, Patrick Kenny, in *Irish Times*, defended the play and Synge's representations of the peasantry against mainly nationalist reaction:

The merciless accuracy of his revelation is more than we can bear. Our eyes tremble at it. The words chosen are, like the things they express, direct and dreadful, by themselves intolerable to conventional taste, yet full of vital beauty in their truth to the conditions of life, to the character they depict, and to the sympathies they suggest. It is as if we looked in a mirror for the first time, and found ourselves hideous. We fear to face the thing. We shrink at the word for it. We scream.[48]

We are reminded of one of Oscar Wilde's aphorisms: "The nineteenth-century dislike of Romanticism is the rage of Caliban not seeing his own face in a glass."[49] In the present context, Caliban might stand for the nationalists who fail to see their ideal images of themselves in the mercilessly accurate mirror that Synge's anti-mimetic drama paradoxically holds up.

Daniel Corkery's critique of Synge raises the central question for those concerned with the "truth" of his work: "Is aesthetic pleasure preliminary to seeing into the life of things or is seeing into the life of things preliminary to aesthetic pleasure?"[50] Corkery appears to want to grant Synge his artistic *donnée* but, in the end, faults him for not seeing clearly enough into the life of things. But his criticism is pertinent *only* if Synge has been attempting to imitate faithfully a reality separable from his dramatic representation. Synge himself, in an interview with a reporter for the *Evening Mail* during the frenzy after the second performance, made clear that he was interested not in making "authoritative textual representations" of authentic peasant life but in creating "transformed instances" of that life.[51] When he was asked if the parricide depicted in *The Playboy* was probable, he responded "No, it is not; and it does not matter. Was Don Quixote probable? and still it is art." When the reporter asked whether his play "is not meant to represent Irish life," Synge responded, "I don't care a rap how the people take it. I never bother whether my plots are typical Irish or not; but my methods are typical." Finally, when Synge mentioned the actual event that inspired the play, the reporter pressed him, asking if the Aran girls had actually made love to the patricide. "No," he replied. "Those girls did not, but mine do."[52] Synge's responses clarify one of the most potent strategies of his play, for, instead of mirroring a "true" representation of West of Ireland life, it offers up a tactical falsehood, an improbability, that suggests something true about the Irish peasantry even as it points up the constructedness of primitivist stereotypes.

Whether we choose to see Synge's style as a departure from realism or a kind of "merciless accuracy," it is certainly a paradox that his play exaggerated character and incident in order to get at what he believed to be "real" or "true" about the Irish peasant. In his 1905 preface to *The Well of the Saints*, Yeats noted that "[p]erhaps no Irish countryman had ever that exact rhythm in his voice, but certainly if Mr. Synge had been born a countryman, he would have spoken like that. It makes the people of his imagination a little disembodied . . . all these people pass by as before an open window, murmuring strange, exciting words" (*CA*, 114). The implication of Yeats's remark, like that of Synge's preface to *The Playboy*, is that something real is captured in the palpable *un*reality of "strange, exciting words." During the first run of *The Playboy*, the Dublin critic, Stephen Gwynn, defended Synge in the *Freeman's Journal*, picking up on an idea that Yeats had put forward only days before – the idea that "all great literature deal[s] with exaggerated types" – arguing that exaggeration in *The Playboy* "is a distortion of life, literally speaking untrue, yet in a true relation to life."[53] This "double orientation," untrue but yet true, is a *will to style*, an anti-mimetic productivity that approximates what Homi K. Bhabha calls colonial mimicry, a discourse that *"repeats* rather than *represents,"* that is "at once resemblance and menace."[54] Synge's dramatic power stems largely from the blatant unreality of his representations, from a creative construction rather than an exacting imitation. The very "aesthetic pleasure" that Corkery is able to separate so confidently from "the life of things" was, for Synge, a fundamental part of that life: this is why he can "be rich and copious in his words, and at the same time to give the reality" (*Playboy*, 53). Synge's anti-realistic style, committed both to the "reality" of Irish life and to a "rich and copious" style of characterization and speech, violates the expectations of an audience seeking either ethnographic realism or nationalist idealizations masquerading as real. What was construed as a misrepresentation may be better understood as the production of a crisis within a social drama that "exposes the pattern of current factional struggle within the relevant social group," and that affords the opportunity to redress that crisis in "the performance of public ritual."[55] It should be noted that as social drama *The Playboy* requires the charge of misrepresentation, for it is the point around which "factional struggle" crystallizes into "public ritual."

The shift to a dramatic genre, particularly the emphasis on exaggerated character and dialogue, created an opportunity that *The Aran Islands*, with its residual commitment to ethnographic realism, could not exploit. The same person who might accept *The Aran Islands* as an accurate representation of peasant life in the West of Ireland might find much to deride in *The Playboy*. By throwing the audience's expectations into question, Synge's play points up the artifice (and thus the instability, even falseness) of nationalist and anthropological representations. As Tiraswini Niranjana writes, echoing Asad, "[r]evealing the constructed nature of cultural translations shows how translation is always producing rather than merely reflecting or imitating an 'original.'"[56] This is not to say that Synge did not claim a certain authority in his dramatic translation of ethnographic knowledge. During rehearsals for *The Well of the Saints*, he responded to criticism of his style by saying, "I write of Irish country life I know to be true and I most emphatically will not change a syllable of it because A, B or C may think they know better than I do."[57] Synge's claim, though it is based on the experiential authority of the ethnographer (whose texts resonate with the implied assertion, "I was there"), is fundamentally resistant to the *discipline* of ethnography, for he brooks no authority but his own, no anthropological theory of the primitive, no nationalist idealizations, only his own sense of what is "true." That he will not change "a syllable" indicates that this will to truth is finally a will to style.

In this context, Christy's heroism and Pegeen Mike's reaction to it emerge as the play's dominant theme, displacing the anecdote and its story of parricidal violence in favor of a repetition of it that foregrounds an exorbitant, unrealistic style at odds with ethnographic realism and nationalist idealizations, but one that nonetheless aspires to the condition of native utterance. Significantly, the act of violence related in the anecdote is not staged; the play concerns itself instead with Christy's elaboration of it in a series of retellings, in which it acquires a heroic grandeur:

CHRISTY [*impressively*] With that the sun came out between the cloud and the hill, and it shining green in my face. "God have mercy on your soul," says he, lifting a scythe; "or on your own," says I, raising the loy.
SUSAN. That's a grand story.
HONOR. He tells it lovely.
CHRISTY. [*flattered and confident, waving bone*] He gave a drive with the scythe, and I gave a lep to the east. Then I turned around with my back to the north, and I hit a blow on the ridge of his skull, laid him stretched out, and he split to the knob of his gullet. (*Playboy*, 103)

Neither the villagers nor the audience realize that Christy is elaborating or if they do, they do not seem to mind; but the responses of Susan and Honor clearly underscore the primary interest taken in this heroic young man: he tells a "grand story" in a "lovely" way. I have noted above that Christy's linguistic facility was originally meant to connect him with a native bardic tradition, and certainly the heroic tonality of the retelling makes that connection apparent in different ways to the villagers and the audience. The villagers readily accept his facility; it is, in fact, the basis of his swift acceptance into the life of the village. The audience, however, distracted by the scandalous spectacle of this acceptance, may have felt the bardic tradition sullied by Christy's murderous tale and hence felt justified in condemning him and Synge for proffering a *mis*representation.

The scene in act three in which Christy praises Pegeen, often cited as an example of Synge's "artistic" representation of peasant speech, can be adduced as evidence that Synge meant for Christy to be linked to a bardic tradition:

> CHRISTY. Isn't there the light of seven heavens in your heart alone, the way you'll be an angel's lamp to me from this out, and I abroad in the darkness spearing salmons in the Owen or the Carrowmore . . .
>
> PEGEEN. Yourself and me would shelter easy in a narrow bush, [*with a qualm of dread*] but we're only talking maybe, for this would be a poor thatched place to hold a fine lad is the like of you.
>
> CHRISTY [*putting his arm round her*] If I wasn't a good Christian, it's on my naked knees I'd be saying my prayers and paters to every jackstraw you have roofing your head, and every stony pebble is paving the laneway to your door. (*Playboy*, 149)

Synge expended considerable labor in successive drafts, perfecting the rhythm and images of Christy's speeches, a labor that attests both to the importance of the speeches in establishing Christy's bardic heroism and to their patently artificial nature.[58] But the fact that they are "untrue" in an ethnographic sense would not have detracted from their fidelity to the reality of peasant life as Synge understood it.

Ironically, Synge is a good deal closer to the essence of that life (as many nationalists imagined it) than his audience was willing to give him credit for. The exaggerated quality of the speeches has a precedent in Irish legends, where extravagance of utterance, like Emer's boasting of her six gifts or Mad King Sweeney's lamentations, is commonplace. Even the wording of the speeches, as Kiberd argues, owes a great deal to Revivalist translations of Irish poetry:

> It is one thing to parody the speech-patterns of interlocutors: it is quite another thing to appropriate the images, ideas and intensities of an entire literary tradition, as Christy does in wooing Pegeen. The dozens of borrowed lines deployed from [Douglas Hyde's] *Love Songs of Connacht* may testify to Synge's versatility as a new kind of writer, but, within the play itself, they also expose Christy's initial hollowness as a person, especially when declaring his love in phrases looted blatantly from the songs of the folk.[59]

Perhaps the audience was aware of the borrowings and shares Kiberd's criticism of Christy's "hollowness." In any case, it is clear that most people in the audience failed to recognize in Synge "a new kind of writer" who, in appropriating "the songs of the folk," issues a critique of Revivalism and its strategies of cultural redemption. Pegeen's sarcastic protestations to Shawn, her erstwhile lover, complement Christy's "hollowness" with a subversive refusal to play the part of an idealized Irish woman: "I'm thinking you're too fine for the like of me, Shawn Keogh of Killakeen, and let you go off till you'd find a radiant lady with droves of bullocks on the plains of Meath, and herself bedizened in the diamond jewelleries of Pharaoh's ma. That'd be your match, Shaneen" (*Playboy*, 155). The "radiant lady" suggests the young girl who "had the walk of a queen" in Yeats's and Lady Gregory's *Cathleen ni Houlihan*,[60] while the image of her "droves of bullocks" recalls Queen Medbh in the *Táin Bó Cuailgne*.[61] In her rejection of these potential models, Pegeen dissociates herself from the tradition of iconic women and warrior-queens, even as her verbal boasting with Christy, whose "poetry talk" inspires her to exert her own independence, aligns her not only with legendary women like Emer and Queen Medbh but also with Christy himself.

The picture of Christy as a bardic hero boasting of murdering his father and praising his lover in fine Irish style, together with the picture of Pegeen Mike accepting and then attacking him, upset the expectations of many people in the audience who wanted to be flattered or have their idealizations confirmed. What they got instead was a reminder that the images of themselves they cherished were as contradictory as those Synge presented on the stage. The conclusion of the play certainly drives the point home when it reveals Christy's heroism to be only "mighty talk" and his actions to be decidedly *un*heroic. But, at the same time, it suggests another form of heroism (and this is what rescues Christy in Pegeen's eyes): for Christy struts off stage with the boast that he will go "romancing through a romping lifetime from this hour to the dawning of the judgment day" (*Playboy*, 173). Like Yeats's Red Hanrahan, he is beaten, broken, even banished, an internal exile, but *heroically himself*. He is a far cry from the stage Irishman of the nineteenth century, though in some ways Christy's father, Old Mahon (once he arrives on the scene decidedly *not* dead), conforms to the stereotype. Ruth Fleischmann has remarked on the contrast between father and son, noting that, while Old Mahon resembles the kind of "shaming and distorted" images found in *Punch*, "the growth of Christy's self-confidence and the blossoming of his innate abilities and qualities resemble that of the nationalist movement during the period of the Irish Revival."[62] What Fleischmann does not note is that Christy's bardic heroism foregrounds the contradiction at the heart of a national identity formed, as Gibbons argues, in the *agon* of colonial oppression. Moreover, Pegeen Mike's tag line at the play's conclusion unveils a nationalist ideology that has, in its strategies of idealization, obscured its own complicity with that oppression and with an anthropological vision of the primitive Irish peasant. Though she rejects his "dirty deed" and his false "gallous story," Pegeen Mike nevertheless understands that, despite her distrust of his "poetry talk," she has discerned something authentic in Christy's heroism: "Oh, my grief," she keens in *"wild lamentations"* at the play's conclusion, "I've lost him surely. I've lost the only Playboy of the Western World" (*Playboy*, 173).

Pegeen Mike, as Gibbons notes, is "inextricably bound up with the darker impulses of cruelty and destruction" associated with Christy,[63] which is perhaps why she is able in the end to recognize the heroic struggle for an authentic subjectivity figured in his "gallous story." She dramatizes a sense of "nostalgic loss," which for Stephen Tifft is the source of the "self-contradictory positions to which the play solicits" the nationalists in the audience.[64] Their impotence is challenged by the spontaneity of a peasantry that, for Fanon, "gives concrete form to the general insecurity" of colonial oppression.[65] In Tifft's view, Christy's triumph absorbs "nostalgic loss" into an "empowering phantasy-scenario," while the crisis of identity arising out of Christy's exaggerated heroism and Pegeen Mike's reaction to it exposes the "ideology of nationalism" as a "phantasmatic uprising within actual submission" and unmasks the "intrapsychic self-betrayal implicit in nationalist rebellion."[66] Like Harrington, Tifft regards the success of Synge's play in terms of its failure, for "[p]ractical success would only be attained through the brilliant failure of a hopelessly, deliberately phantasmatic parricidal gesture."[67] Moreover, he allows that *The Playboy* might very well have been "made to order for the nationalists" precisely because it produces "the galvanizing effect of their resistance" to a "parricidal phantasy-scenario."[68] Like Ginger Strand, Tifft implies that Synge unintentionally grants the nationalists in the audience the power of critical articulation. And, while I generally agree with Tifft that *The Playboy* functions as a phantasmatic scenario, I would want to add that the crisis this scenario provokes doubles as a form of symbolic redress, at once challenging stereotypical representations and offering an alternative to mimetic representation *as such* in the form of an exaggerated, anti-mimetic heroism.

Obviously, *The Playboy* is caught in a bewildering tangle of conflicting discourses of national identity: nationalists confronting their own fantasies of betrayal and loss, metropolitan anthropologists caught up in an unacknowledged and "obsessive tabulation of desire," and Anglo-Irish Revivalists seeking to assert their own authority while balancing allegiances to both nationalism and the protocols of a redemptive ethnography. And while Tifft and Harrington correctly point to the virtues of failure in *The Playboy*, it is finally unclear in their accounts whether Synge's response to the identity crisis he dramatizes effectively redresses it. If *The Playboy* does, in fact, seek to redress a crisis of violated national identity, its efficacy can be determined only once we have considered the new crises it instates. For in the responses of Revivalist and nationalist alike, we find the continuation of a social drama that Synge himself came to understand as powerfully resistant to existing modes of cultural representation. If, as Strand argues, *The Playboy* deliberately provoked the audience, it was able to do so only insofar as the members of the audience were part of the performance itself, rather than mere spectators of it. By staging ethnography as a social drama in which the audience participates, Synge creates the opportunity for contestation and amendment. But this is not to say, as Strand implies, that Synge surrenders the power of articulating a critical point of view. The salient point of social drama is that all participants are given the power of articulation, all afforded the opportunity of contesting or affirming representations of national identity.

This power of articulation, granted to all participants in a social drama, crystallizes into a cultural performance when it is exercised in the arena of public debate. In this context, the first run of *The Playboy* is the point of departure for a new crisis of violated national identity and new redressive measures. The redressive phase, as Turner describes it, is "a liminal time, set apart from the ongoing business of quotidian life," a subjunctive mood, "a world of 'as if,' ranging from scientific hypothesis to festive fantasy."[69] Especially significant for *The Playboy* is the liminal space of what Turner calls cultural performance, a dramatic ritual that is " '*reflective* in the sense of showing ourselves to ourselves.' "[70] Synge's play, though it may thematize a certain liminal *space* in which Christy and the other villagers indulge in a "festive fantasy," enters into a more significant and problematic liminal *time* during which the audience seeks the means to redress the translation of peasant society into Western social text. "Indeed," writes Kiberd, "the recorded responses to [*The Playboy*] are, undeniably, extensions and imitations of its innermost theme": the contradiction borne out of the tension between the fantasy of cultural transformation "read into" Christy by the villagers and the "farce of revivalism, of fireside tales told about past heroes" that they "go back to."[71] Fantasy and Revivalist redemption intermingle in a cultural performance that contests existing representations of Irish identity.

The Playboy confronts head-on the slippery problem of identity formation; and it is precisely in this confrontation that the second redressive phase of Synge's social drama opens out into cultural performance, initiated by the word "shift."[72] Heidi Holder argues that the outcry leading to the riots "was not simply over the word 'shift' but concerned as well with conflicting notions of the true nature of the Irish peasant." Synge reveals to his audience "that their beloved image of the Irish country folk was a mere construction – a construction eminently open to challenge."[73] The precise nature of whatever insult the audience collectively felt is less important than the discourse that emerged in response to the often irreconcilable perceptions of it. Significantly, the outcry over the word "shift" was itself "staged," enacted dramatically in the newspapers as well as in the streets. One of many satiric verses generated by the crisis makes the point succinctly: "The stage became spectators / And the audience the players."[74] James Kilroy has documented the cultural performance of *The Playboy* riots, and his evidence indicates that they were widely understood, even by the "interrupters" ejected from the Abbey Theatre, as inherently dramatic. The *Freeman's Journal* ran a report by "one of the ejected" in which audience reactions and Yeats's use of police force make for

a better tragi-comedy than anything that could be conceived in the grotesquest fancies of the clever comic writers of [Yeats's] foredoomed theatre. How Moliere would have expanded on the spectacle of our dreamy poet swearing in the Northern Police Court that he distinctly heard a boo! What a spectacle for gods and men, the champion of a free Irish theatre calling in the police . . . What an instance of National topsy-turveydom in the picture of this Irish dramatist, this authority on the ways and speech of the Western peasant standing sick, silent, and ashamed when addressed in Irish.[75]

This account underscores the extent to which individuals at all levels – from the Abbey directors to the nationalist agitators – took part in a redressive cultural performance. It also makes clear what many took to be the general opinion of nationalists that the Anglo-Irish directors of the Abbey Theatre were ill-suited to represent the "Western peasant."

Cairns and Richards have suggested a way of reading the ideological lines of force that clashed during *The Playboy*'s first run and that forestalled the phase of reintegration or recognition of breach. The riots occurred, they argue, because *The Playboy* was "read" by very different audiences; the three most prominent groups were the Anglo-Irish, the Ulster Protestants, and the Catholic Nationalists, each with different reading protocols and different expectations of a play that they expected would represent West of Ireland life authentically. The "most influential lines of discourse" – the "derogatory Anglo-Saxonist discourse of the English press," with its formal instantiations in education, and "the essentially oppositional discourse of the Davisites and the more hard-line Irish-Ireland groups" – provided "the parameters within which a new text would be productively activated."[76] Resistance to *The Playboy* was strongest among what Cairns and Richards call the "Nationalist class-alliance":

All in all, then, even before the commencement of Act III, the particular form of the production and staging given to *The Playboy* left Nationalists within the audience with only one matrix within which they could place and productively activate the text – a framework which, in their own terms, was subversive of their oppositional views of the peasant man as nature's nobleman and of peasant woman as pious, virtuous and submissive.[77]

Once Synge's critique of representation is misperceived as a *mis*representation, once the question of authenticity is open for discussion and revision, even despite his protestations that mimetic fidelity was not his intent, there can be little chance for the reintegration of diverse social groups or for the peaceful recognition that such an integration is impossible, perhaps even undesirable.

It is interesting to note that Irish-Ireland nationalists were not the only ones to respond negatively to Synge's play and his Revivalist cohorts. George Russell, an advisor and friend to the

Abbey Theatre directors, was reputed to be the author of a parody published in *Sinn Fein* of Yeats's and Lady Gregory's *Cathleen Ni Houlihan*, called *Britannia Rule-the-Wave*, in which Yeats is depicted as "the Chief Poet of Ireland," and Kathleen is replaced by a "fat old lady" (perhaps an amalgam of the late Queen Victoria, Lady Gregory, and Annie Horniman) who leads the Chief Poet toward the harbor, where King Edward has landed. "Here's a holy sell," says the Chief Actor of Ireland. "Did you see a fat old lady going down the stairs?" The Scene-Shifter replies: "She was the very spit of the image on the new penny. And there was a mangey old lion from the Zoo walking by her side."[78] Here we find a signature piece of Revivalist drama deployed against its authors who are accused of complicity with the Empire. What the parody makes clear is that the problem of Synge's play cannot be reduced to a Manichean struggle between Revivalism and imperialism or between Revivalism and Irish-Ireland nationalism. Furthermore, it reveals that the final phase of the social drama inaugurated by Synge's play, in which we ought to find either the "reintegration of the disturbed social group . . . or the social recognition of irreparable breach between the contesting parties,"[79] is deferred in an interminable redressive phase that ensnares Synge, his defenders, and his detractors in a protracted battle for control of the representation of national identities and nationalist aspirations.

Synge's attempt at reintegration is the effect of a critical anthropological modernism that seeks to redefine the very primitivism that, in *The Aran Islands*, served as a salve for an alienated subjectivity. For reintegration, in this case, is an attempt to bridge the gap between the traditional and the modern that both instigated the feeling of alienation and created the binomial division of human societies in which one group (the primitive) is capable of "healing" another group (the civilized) by virtue of its simplicity, spirituality, naturalness, and lack of corrupting modern influences. This capacity to heal, however, does not do away with the division itself, and this is why the domination of the primitive by the civilized can go on unchecked; indeed, the condition of being dominated or being susceptible to domination, once it is redefined as primitive simplicity or feminine weakness or political *naïveté*, might be regarded as a virtue – just the kind of virtue that can heal the alienation and spiritual emptiness of the dominator. Synge's *Playboy* and, to a lesser extent, *The Aran Islands* sought to break down the binomial distinction that actuates this contradictory response by exposing the constructedness of the primitive and the historical conditions of that construction. As James Knapp argues, "Synge transformed the primitivism he first encountered in Paris and Brittany. He made of it a discourse of opposition that cannot be understood aside from the historical struggles of his time and nation."[80] By fusing primitive Ireland to modern Europe, Synge created "a language that is neither 'primitive' nor yet continuous with the high English of Ascendancy culture, English imperialism, and industrial modernization" and thereby revealed the "historical contingency of both nationalist rhetoric of racial nostalgia and the imperialist rhetoric of reason and progress."[81]

By making self-evident the historicity of Irish identity and the stereotypes of colonial, anthropological, nationalist, and Revivalist discourses that helped to determine it, Synge demystifies essentialist rhetoric by showing how easily it can be redeployed in the service of the *in*essential. The fact that *The Playboy* arrives at neither reintegration nor a recognition of breach but rather puts into motion a permanent social dissension is less a failure to satisfy one or another of the disputing factions than it is an inevitable response to an era of decolonization in which reintegration and recognition of breach are simply not possible. What is possible, however, is to raise the issue that representation, understood as a faithful imitation of cultural realities impervious to social and historical conditions, is a wholly inadequate means to the political ends of nationalism. "The anger provoked by Synge's work," writes Knapp, "expresses something deeper than frustrated aesthetic expectations. And it should be no surprise that he failed to win assent to the proposition that his primitivism inscribes: that men and women are constituted through language, contingently and historically."[82] Nevertheless, the seemingly endless and escalating series of redressive measures, however tedious and futile they may appear, creates the opportunity for the transformation of and resistance to primitivism wherever it might be found, with the result that Irish identities are forged in the very *mis*representations that throw them into question – they are forged, in short, under the authority of a poetics of inauthenticity.

In "John M. Synge and the Ireland of His Time," written three years after the riots, Yeats reenforces the interminability of the *Playboy* social drama in the sense that it serves as a deferred redressive response to the crisis provoked by the riots. "[L]ife became sweet again" Yeats writes, "when I had learnt all I had not learnt in shaping words, in defending Synge against his enemies" (*CA*, 142). It is significant that in Yeats's defense Synge emerges as a heroic figure (not unlike Christy Mahon), "full of passion and heroic beauty," whose "discovery of style" – purified of "insincerity, vanity, malignity [and] arrogance" (*CA*, 146, 142) – results from his own alienation and loneliness. In his celebration of Synge's tragic heroism, Yeats elaborates a theory of personality that appears to evolve from his earlier belief in "fair equivalents" and to complement and personalize his belief in "divine substances." He embraces a conception of the artist as the observer of life – "all that heightens the emotions by contest" (*CA*, 153–4) – whose personality is determined by his contact with that life and whose social authority is a distillation and refinement of that personality. The result is a "great art" that "chills us at first by its coldness or its strangeness, by what seems capricious" (*CA*, 172). Three years earlier, at the time of the riots, Yeats had defended Synge's strange and capricious style in the *Freeman's Journal* by noting that "All great literature dealt with exaggerated types, and all tragedy and tragi-comedy with types of sin and folly. A dramatist is not an historian."[83] It is just this sort of exaggeration that characterizes Yeats's heroic vision of Synge as an artist capable of producing a new work of art "not as it seems to eyes habit has made dull, but as we were Adam and this the first morning" (*CA*, 172). As Yeats was to discover in subsequent years, the Irish people were by and large not ready for such a vision or visionary, a sentiment he expressed in "On Those that Hated 'The Playboy of the Western World,' 1907," which takes the occasion of *The Playboy*'s performance as a decisive moment in the cultural history of Ireland. This poem, along with others like "September 1913" that criticize the Irish people for a lack of artistic principles, continues the symbolic redress inaugurated when, during a debate on *The Playboy* at the Abbey Theatre, Yeats lectured the audience on the need for "individual sincerity" and "the eternal quest for truth" (*E*, 228).

In his attempt to defend Synge, Yeats acts as his Horatio, promising to tell his story to whomever will listen. And many listened, or at least they heard something similar to what Yeats was trying to say. In *Synge and the Irish Language*, Kiberd cites approvingly from an article by an Englishman soon after the riots who wrote that one quality " 'which marks Mr. Synge's work as intensely national is its relation to Gaelic Literature' " and that " 'he accomplishes with a more perfect art what so many of the Gaelic poets attempted.' "[84] This is high praise, indeed, and was not restricted to English proponents of Synge's work, for as Kiberd notes further, by 1910 the staunchly republican journal, *An Claidheamh Soluis*, could claim that "Synge is a Gael among men. He is far more a Gael than Owen Roe O'Sullivan." A few years later, Patrick Pearse, stalwart critic of the Revival, "publicly repented of his part in the attacks on *The Playboy*" and conceded that Synge was "one of the two or three men who have in our time made Ireland considerable in the eyes of the world."[85] Kiberd himself affirms this judgment. "The mortal charm of Synge's dialect," he writes, "is the beauty that inheres in all precarious or dying things. Much of it is traceable to the Gaelic *substratum*, those elements of syntax and imagery carried over from the native tradition by a people who continue to think in Irish even as they speak in English."[86] Kiberd's assessment reflects a revisionist attitude that has its origin in the pre-1916 nationalist debates over Synge's representations that were conducted in a colonial context in which Revivalist projects were attacked for largely political reasons. It is not surprising that the influential work of Daniel Corkery, whose Catholic orthodoxy tended to obscure the kinds of concessions that Pearse and others were willing to make, still forms attitudes about what constitutes an authentically Irish tradition.

By staging ethnography, Synge's *Playboy* dramatizes the constructedness of any original or definitive representation of national identity and anticipates the critical anthropological fictions of writers like James Joyce. As social drama, *The Playboy* proffers alternatives to existing representations of culture and national identity and opens up avenues of resistance by opening up the theatre of representation. It confronts its audience with a world that resembles theirs but is curiously not theirs – a world transformed, a world whose patent inauthenticity serves as the most effective means of redress available for the crisis of violated national identity. In a curious way, the negative responses of Synge's Dublin audiences to his failure to conform to what was thought of as authentic in Irish life simply prove a salient point about the subversive power of his play and of the anthropological modernism of the Celtic Revival, for, if it misrepresents the folk life of the West of Ireland, it does so in order to create that life anew. In this sense, Synge resolves the conflict between traditional culture and modern techniques of representing it by producing a "new original," still redolent with turf smoke.

CHAPTER 5

"A Renegade from the Ranks": Joyce's critique of Revivalism in the early fiction

> "The English Language
> belongs to us. You are raking at dead fires,
>
> rehearsing the old whinges at your age.
> That subject people stuff is a cod's game,
> infantile, like this peasant pilgrimage."   Seamus Heaney[1]

As we have seen in the previous chapters, Yeats and Synge were instrumental in the development of an Irish modernist movement that sought to redefine the relationship between tradition and modernity. It is worth noting again Terry Eagleton's argument: "Modernism springs from the estranging impact of modernizing forces on a still deeply traditionalist order, in a politically unstable context which opens up social hope as well as spiritual anxiety. Traditional culture provides modernism with an adversary, but also lends it some of the terms in which to inflect itself."[2] One of the ways that traditional Irish culture lent itself to the modernism of the Celtic Revival was to provide Revivalists with the objects of a wide-ranging project of ethnographic redemption. Key elements of ethnographic practice – the reliance on a primitivist discourse, the predominance of fieldwork, and the objectivity of participant observation – emerge in the work of Revivalists like Yeats and Synge as hallmarks of an autoethnographic expressiveness capable of transforming these elements into a new mode of indigenous artistic production. In view of land legislation that from the 1880s at least benefited an emergent Catholic middle-class of "strong farmers" and the inevitable institution of some form of Home Rule, it is not difficult to imagine the anthropological modernism of the Celtic Revival as a cultural embodiment of Anglo-Irish marginalization and deracination and to interpret this social estrangement as a considerable barrier to the development of a national consciousness that would be something more than what Fanon describes as a "transfer into native hands of those unfair advantages which are a legacy of the colonial period."[3] It would seem, if the responses to Synge's *The Playboy of the Western World* are any indication, that the attempt by Anglo-Irish Revivalists to conduct the "political educa- tion" of the Irish fails to achieve a truly revolutionary national consciousness. Fanon writes, "political education means opening [the peoples'] minds, awakening them, and allowing the birth of their intelligence; as [Aimé] Césaire said, it is 'to invent souls.'"[4] Though I have argued in the preceding chapters that the Celtic Revival was capable of a limited form of autoethnographic resistance to an array of social authorities, Revivalism as a cultural practice conceived as "a borrowed aestheticism" (as Fanon puts it) that seeks to redeem primitive societies threatened by modernity proved inadequate for the articulation of an "authentic" Irish identity. And, while it is clear that Yeats and Synge succeeded in awakening the Irish people to a deeper sense of their national aspirations and national identities – and their right to represent these things – it is not clear that this awakening has led to the invention of a "soul." Perhaps the most that we can say is that the Revival succeeded primarily, and not insignificantly, in awakening the Irish to the need for such an invention.

Some influential critics of Joyce assume that his antipathy toward nationalism paralleled a similar antipathy toward the Revival.[5] To be sure, Joyce challenged the cultural assumptions of the Revival, especially its tendency to assume that the peasant somehow held out the hope of national virtue and cultural unity and its characteristic strategy, based on this primitivist assumption, of idealizing the Irish peasantry and locating cultural authenticity in folklore, legend, and mythology. He also challenged the redemptive mode of ethnography that characterized Revivalist attempts to represent or evoke the authenticity of the peasant's way of life. But it seems to me that we cannot understand the complexity of Joyce's attitude toward Revivalism if we place him outside its influence and lose sight of the fact that Joyce and Yeats desired the same thing: the creation of an imaginary Irish nation and race. Seamus Deane raises a question pertinent to both Revivalism and anthropological modernism, in so far as both seek to invent or "write" Ireland: how was Joyce "to create as literature something which would otherwise have no existence and yet was believed to exist already? The idea of Ireland still uncreated, awaited its realization."[6] Finding in Joyce a desire to realize the idea of Ireland provides powerful incentive for regarding him as a Revivalist; Deane goes so far as to argue that he was the one who most kept faith with the idea of *reviving* Irish culture: "whereas Yeats did indeed give up, to some extent, 'the deliberate creation of a kind of Holy City in the imagination' and replace it with images of enduring heroism and not-so-durable authority, Joyce remained faithful to the original conception of the Revival. His Dublin became the Holy City of which Yeats had despaired."[7]

The important point here, as Deane and others have noted, is that Joyce refused the mystic essentialism that underwrote Yeats's Revivalist aesthetics.[8] As we have seen, Yeats's mystical view of the Irish folk tradition, developed partly in response to Matthew Arnold's imperialist Celticism, was grounded in what Yeats called "our 'natural magic' [which] is but the religion of the world, the ancient worship of Nature and that troubled ecstasy before her, that certainty of all beautiful places being haunted, which it brought into men's minds" (*EI*, 176). But, as he developed his interest in mysticism, "natural magic" was transformed into something closer to alchemy, reflected in Robert Aherne's desire for the "transmutation of all things into some divine and imperishable substance" (*SRH*, 192). By the time Joyce was writing *Dubliners* (1904–7), Yeats's mystic essentialism, however much it might have attracted him when he was a student in the 1890s, was now the object of a critique that revealed it to be a mystification of oppressive social conditions. A problem arises, however, when we infer from this attitude toward essentialism that Joyce and Yeats had nothing in common. Emer Nolan has recently argued that Deane's view of a decisive difference of opinion between Joyce and Yeats on the questions of essence and authenticity tends to leave us with no credible argument to make regarding Joyce's view of Ireland and the Irish.[9] If Joyce rejected Yeats's essentialism, and the redemptive ethnographic imagination that authorized it, and if he rejected as well the Irish-Ireland nationalism of Arthur Griffith, D. P. Moran, and the Gaelic League, a view which until very recently has been something of a dogma in Joyce studies, what then are we to make of his attitude toward the Irish and his treatment of both nationalism and Revivalism? It is not my concern here to treat of Joyce's attitude toward the former, since Nolan's *James Joyce and Nationalism* has mounted a persuasive revisionist argument that opposes those critics who regard Joyce as indifferent to nationalism and to nationalist responses to the social conditions of colonial Ireland as well as those who regard him as espousing a "moderate" and or "pacifist" nationalism.[10] It will be the chief burden of this and the next chapter to analyze Joyce's attitude toward the Revival and Revivalism, specifically the ethnographic imagination that subtends its dominant practices and modes of textual expression, and consider the question of nationalism insofar as it shares ideas, theories, or practices with Revivalism.

Joyce and Yeats, each in different ways, epitomize the dilemma of the Irish writer faced with the necessity of constructing an imaginary nation from within a colonial context. While Yeats chose to revive an autochthonous folk tradition by evoking it using methods borrowed from anthropology and ethnography, Joyce chose to create a national literature by engaging in an immanent critique of Revivalism in which colonial and anthropological discourses are appropriated and criticized in a more sustained and consistent fashion than either Yeats or Synge were able to accomplish. In both cases, an ethnographic imagination comes into play, either as a method of cultural preservation and authentication (as with Yeats) or as a strategy of cultural critique (as with Joyce). This is not to say that Yeats was not critical, but rather that his criticism tended to focus on the subjects of his representations, the peasantry, and even himself among them; and, though he complained about the misrepresentations of his predecessors, he was not always aware of the extent to which his own work relied on classic anthropological assumptions and prejudices. Joyce's critique proceeds from this naive stage in the development of the Revival's anthropological modernism to arrive at a position from which he can challenge the theories and practices by which the Irish people are represented. In Yeats, the question of authenticity was pegged to the possibility of arriving at a "a fair equivalent for the gesture and voice of the peasant tale-teller" (*UP1*, 174). This possibility, as we have seen, is highly problematic, as Yeats knew intuitively, since he eventually abandoned that goal and moved first toward the goal of capturing "divine substances" and, ultimately, toward the elaboration of a spiritualized conception of artistic personality. In Joyce, however, the desire for authenticity finds expression not in redemptive strategies for the preservation of folk culture nor in "divine substances" or a spiritualized personality. I submit that, for Joyce, authenticity does not refer to an object to be redeemed by a kind of ethnographic realism but rather to a self-authenticating performance exemplified by Synge's *The Playboy of the Western World*. Energized by Synge's assault on nationalist pieties, Joyce wrote stories like "The Dead" which dramatized the ambivalence of Revivalist attitudes toward culture and the inevitably *in*authentic appeal to essence and wholeness that they entail. In fact, I would argue that the depiction of the experience of *in*authenticity is what Joyce seems to insist upon as the only irreducibly authentic representation he could make and that such representations could not be made without recourse to Revivalist strategies, positions, themes, and practices. Here Joyce departs from Synge, who remained convinced of the authenticity of his own experience even as he challenged his own representations of that experience.

Emer Nolan, in her revisionist critique of Joyce's nationalism makes a similar point, arguing that Joyce's "anti-nationalism" depends on the very rhetoric and tactics of nationalism that at least two generations of his critics have insisted were anathema to him. Her argument persistently illustrates the paradox that "Joycean modernism and Irish nationalism can be understood as significantly analogous discourses, and the common perception of them as unrelated and antagonistic begins to break down."[11] In the conventional view of his politics, according to Nolan, Joyce "did not believe in resuscitating outdated traditions." He criticized Irish national identity according to "implicitly cosmopolitan norms" and "rejected outright the cultural nationalism of Yeats and the Irish Literary Revival." But she is quick to point out that it is "seriously misleading to consider Joyce's relationship to Irish politics solely in these terms."[12] For Nolan, the only "truly" nationalist position is one that confronts both the traditionality of the local and the inevitability of modernist interventions to rescue or recuperate tradition. Tradition and modernity, localism and cosmopolitanism, periphery and metropole become intertwined; the primitive "peasant" infiltrates the center, while the metropolitan "citizen" in turn infiltrates the margins. And, while she does not explore the anthropological authority behind the Revival, she nevertheless insists that Joyce's critique of nationalism is unintelligible outside a Revivalist context. After all, she argues in her reading of "The Dead," Joyce was not "immune to revivalist romanticism and primitivism."[13] It is necessary to situate the apparently polarized positions of Yeats and Joyce in the same Revivalist context: "The gesture of commitment apparently offered by the work of Yeats, and the corresponding gesture of disengagement offered by Joyce, should be interpreted in the context of the historical and political milieu of the Irish Literary Revival."[14] By arguing that Joyce's autoethnographic texts transform and revalue Revivalism in an immanent critique of its characteristic perspectives, attitudes, and textual practices, I offer what I hope is a productive elaboration of Nolan's conclusion that Joyce's "supposed repudiation of the Literary Revival takes its place among competing notions of decolonization current in the Ireland of his time."[15]

Clearly, Joyce was not a Revivalist in the sense that he did fieldwork or sought to preserve, through translation or accurate and realistic accounts, the essence of Irish folk life. The project of redemption he regarded (as Fanon would) as an instance of incomplete repudiation of colonial rule. But Joyce did keep faith with the Revival's ideal of creating an imaginary Ireland by applying his style of "scrupulous meanness" to the critical analysis of this ideal, pushing the self-critical impulse we have seen in Synge's *Playboy* toward great effectiveness and exposing the Revival's investments in anthropological notions of a primitive Irish race. Whereas Yeats, and Synge in *The Aran Islands*, relied on anthropological methods to get at what was essential and true about Irish peasant life, Joyce, like Synge in *The Playboy*, deconstructs such methods in the production of anthropological fictions that are patently *in*essential and *un*true. This productivity in Joyce's texts takes place on two levels: on one level, it issues in an autoethnographic inquiry into the conditions of Dublin, a scrupulous record of the folkways of its inhabitants; on another level, it articulates a critique of such a view in depictions of disaffected "natives" like Gabriel Conroy and Stephen Dedalus, who exemplify the futility of a redemptive attitude toward peasant culture, and Leopold Bloom, whose ethnographic voyeurism illustrates the phantasmic dimension of participant observation. More successfully than Yeats's or Synge's, Joyce's texts reveal the fictiveness of anthropological knowledge while simultaneously insisting that in that fictiveness lies whatever truth we are likely to find about Irish culture. Paradoxically, Joyce's anthropological modernism, precisely by embracing the ambivalence that Revivalism sought to mask in its pretensions to cultural authority, arrives at something closer to an authentic representation of inauthentic social experiences. It acknowledges that the tension between the traditional and the modern is really a form of mutual determination whereby the traditional reveals its susceptibility to the intervention of modern political aspirations and the modern unveils its hidden desire to express its longing for totality and unity in traditional terms. Joyce anatomizes this mutually determining interaction in the early fiction, and is especially critical of the Revival's largely ineffective management of it. But it is in *Ulysses* that Joyce is able to recognize the productive power of this interaction and to transform a critique of Revivalism into a new revival, an awakening to the revolutionary possibilities of a "political education" in which both the traditional and the modern have a share in the invention of souls.

The first stage in this awakening is *Dubliners*, a text that is often regarded as a premier example of either realism or naturalism, part of a tradition that features European masters like Gustave Flaubert and Émile Zola. To be sure, this view of Joyce's first major work would not be out of place in a literary history of realistic fiction. However, as recent critics have begun to notice, *Dubliners* has complex ideological commitments to cultural nationalism and anti-colonial resistance, and its realist strategies are not strictly consonant with those of nineteenth-century practitioners, though Zola's interest in unmasking the hidden sources of social oppression is similar to what we find in Joyce.[16] In some cases, as in Nolan's discussion of "The Dead," Revivalism is identified as an important context for understanding these commitments. It hardly bears repeating the conclusion drawn by so many critics that Gabriel Conroy experiences a conflict over the values of cultural nationalism as they manifest themselves in Miss Ivors' enthusiasm for the Aran Islands. My discussion of Synge's own experience there indicates the extent to which the West of Ireland attained a nearly iconic significance for cultural nationalists and continued to hold that significance well into the opening decades of the twentieth century. Michael Levenson has drawn our attention to the significant fact that the *Playboy* riots of late January and early February of 1907 took place during the time Joyce was composing "The Dead." He writes that Joyce, "who was living out a few months of his exile in Rome, eagerly followed the controversy, clearly sensing that here was a foretaste of a feast being laid for him. The *Playboy* affair made clear that in the midst of an ongoing colonial struggle, the boundaries between art and politics were highly permeable, where they existed at all."[17] Joyce, then, picks up where Synge leaves off, exploring in his own anthropological fictions the permeability of boundaries that Synge had tested and exposed.

One thing Joyce might have taken from Synge is a sensitivity to the problems of the native artist for whom the dilemma of the participant–observer – is he inside or outside the culture he observers? – registers as a profoundly *aesthetic* problem. Seeing the kind of responses elicited by the representations of the peasant in Synge's plays, Joyce was reluctant to duplicate Revivalist representations of an Irish peasantry whose authenticity was all too often guaranteed by ethnographic means. Like Synge, Joyce developed an anti-mimetic style, especially in *Ulysses*, that privileged the artist's ability to enter into something like a natural process in which something new is produced. The idea is summed up in *Stephen Hero*, in a formulation that echoes Talal Asad's description of "transformed instances of the original, not authoritative textual representations of it":[18] "For Stephen art was neither a copy nor an imitation of nature: the artist's process was a natural process" (*SH*, 171). The emphasis on artistic process and the need to eschew imitation or copying (though not, I might add, the need to be realistic) are repeated in his letters to Grant Richards. As early as 1906, when he was composing *Dubliners*, Joyce saw that the liberatory potential of his writing depended on his success at representing Dublin as he knew it. Defending his stories and their "scrupulous meanness" to Richards, who was trying to get Joyce to revise some of the "scandalous" passages in *Dubliners*, Joyce wrote, "I fight to retain [the passages] because I believe that in composing my chapter of moral history in exactly the way I have composed it I have taken the first step toward the spiritual liberation of my country" (*D*, 270). I believe that this is one of those points in Joyce's career that explicitly marks his Fanonist position between the phase of revivalist recuperation of indigenous traditions and the phase of cultural awakening. That he conceives of liberation in terms of spirit testifies to his recognition that any genuinely anti-colonial position must incorporate the task of "inventing souls." That this invention paradoxically entails a scrupulous analysis of material social conditions, as opposed to an elaboration of anthropological fictions about the "natural magic" of the Irish peasantry, testifies to Joyce's unwillingness to succumb to the essentialism of the Revival's redemptive ethnographic imagination.

In part because of his concern with material social conditions, Joyce remained committed to a mode of realism that he treated less as a neutral instrument for social analysis than as a means by which to assert the social authority which granted him the right to represent those conditions. Like Synge, who resisted any suggestion that his experience with the Irish peasantry was illegitimate, Joyce insists on the authority of his own experience with the subjects of his analysis; and, also like Synge, his appeal to his own intimate knowledge of Irish society invokes a *personal* authority defined by interests that he clarifies to both Richards and his brother, Stanislaus. In a famous letter to Stanislaus, Joyce explicitly links his artistic justifications with his own "moral nature": "The struggle against conventions in which I am at present involved was not entered into by me so much as a protest against these conventions as with the intention of living in conformity with my moral nature" (*D*, 254). Here again, Joyce resembles Synge (especially the Synge of *The Playboy*) in that he refuses any authority other than his own "moral nature"; we do not see in Joyce's work the same confusion of ethnographic and autobiographical authority that we see in texts like *The Celtic Twilight* and *The Aran Islands*. When Joyce tells Richards that "I seriously believe that you will retard the course of civilization in Ireland by preventing the Irish people from having one good look at themselves in my nicely polished looking-glass" (*D*, 277), we are impressed with the extent to which Joyce has arrogated the authority of the cultural observer entirely to his own position as an artist.

We should not fail at this juncture to notice that Joyce, in flourishing his "nicely polished looking-glass," employs a metaphor that had been used against Synge during the *Playboy* controversy. A reviewer of *The Playboy* had lamented Synge's refusal to represent the Irish realistically, asserting that the Abbey Theatre directors "were expected to fulfill the true purpose of playing – 'to hold as 'twere the mirror up to Nature,' to banish the meretricious stage, and give, for the first time, true pictures of Irish life and fulfillment of that pledge."[19] Perhaps more effectively than Synge, Joyce reveals the complacency of those people whose faith in "true pictures" blinds them to the constructedness and the interestedness of realistic representation, as well as to the deleterious effects of Revivalist programs of cultural redemption that offer meager and ineffective alternatives to colonialist and nationalist idealizations whose reliance on a primitivist discourse was largely unexamined and uncriticized. Joyce's employment of the mirror-image, however, is both ironic and strategic, for, while it appears that Joyce's stories are meant to represent the social world realistically, we are constantly pulled, despite the narrators' scrupulous attention to detail, toward the subjective responses of characters to that world. This ironic deflection of the reader's gaze from the realistic detail to the subjective experience of characters who all too often simply fail *to see*, constitutes a strategic reversal of the aims of realistic discourse: to imitate through language the social and material relations of the external world. Joyce simply brings to the fore the ideological assumptions about what aspect of that world is "real" and proper for representation and how those assumptions fail individuals who abide by them.

A number of features of Joyce's realism alert us to the potentially subversive nature of his invocation of the mirror-image. First, the phrasing of his remark to Richards lends itself to an ironic reading: it is a *"nicely polished* looking-glass," which suggests a recognition on Joyce's part that the artist inevitably intervenes in the act of representation, transforming what is reflected with a scrupulous (that is to say, "nice") polishing of the image. (Compare Yeats's use of the same image – "I hold a clean mirror to tradition"[20] – which suggests a more conventional mimetic intention.) Whereas Synge, in *The Playboy*, reflected exaggerated characters in the mirror he held up to his audience, Joyce offers a different kind of distortion – the unreality of clarity, of a "good look" at what had been obscured by idealized images of what was "real" about Irish life. Another significant difference, but one that does not alter the similarity of effects between Synge's and Joyce's methods, lies in Joyce's choice of subjects – the urban proletariat, the lower classes, the petite bourgeoisie, the unemployed, single men and women, children – which underscored the double injustice done by the misrepresentations of both nationalists and Revivalists, for not only did they idealize or mystify the peasant, but the figure of the peasant had come to stand for *all* Irish people, regardless of the fact that many were increasingly residing in cities. Joyce recognized that this double injustice led to an equally doubled sense of inauthentic life for city dwellers; reality was twice-removed, as Gabriel Conroy, in "The Dead," realizes when he tries to vouch for his own authenticity through a self-serving vision of the specter of a peasant boy. If we regard his attempt as inauthentic, it should be no surprise, given the resources that Revivalism has made available for him.

Unlike Synge, who exaggerates the real to get at what he felt to be true about the Irish peasant's life, Joyce unveils the real as already a kind of exaggeration, especially for Dubliners who lack a ready

access to traditional folkways and must rely on representations
mediated by nationalist and Revivalist intellectuals. The effect is the
same for both Synge and Joyce: their art reveals the constructedness
of the real and the reality of constructions, a tautological relation
that we might say grows out of the increasingly mutually determining relation between tradition and modernity. Just as the Aran
Islanders could recite the names of previous anthropological adven-
turers to their shores, so the Dubliner could revel in the thoroughly
modern spectacle of the peasant on the stage of the Abbey Theatre –
a state of affairs which, paradoxically, Synge was signally responsible
for bringing about. Though Joyce as a student defended the Abbey
Theatre's production of *Cathleen ni Houlihan,* he soon grew wary of
the power such dramatic representations could carry; the *Playboy*
riots convinced Joyce that this power could be channeled into the
kind of political education that Joyce's "nicely polished looking-
glass" was meant to inaugurate. This may be why he could say that
the attempt on the part of publishers to withhold or alter his
representations would retard civilization in Ireland, for getting a
"good look" at themselves as phantasms, people who exist only in
the terms of a primitivist discourse with little or no relevance to their
daily lives, who see reality as a distortion of what may be real or
authentic about themselves, will lead his Irish readers to enter into a
"civilized" condition that would grant them the right to represent
themselves. Joyce holds a mirror up to *in*authentic lives and, while
the people he reflects may fail to amend their lives, to find a way to
live authentically, his stories accomplish an important first step
toward that goal by representing, with a kind of ethnographic
fidelity, the effects of Revivalism on the construction of an Irish
identity. So, while Joyce may appear to invoke the kind of ethnographic authority we see in Revivalists like Yeats and Synge, his
subversive application of its protocols marks his distance from
Revivalist practice and from the tradition of realism implied in the
reviewer's Shakespearean reference. As I have indicated above, this
application is both an appropriation and a critique, for the subversive effects of Joyce's ethnographic scrupulosity amount to the kind
of immanent critique that we have seen in variously nascent or
incomplete forms in Revivalist practice. Thus Joyce remains committed to a mode of realism that scrupulously exposes the inauthentic experience of Dubliners who are guided by Revivalist
ideals. But the revelation of inauthenticity – which characterizes a

good many of Joyce's famous epiphanies – becomes an empowering anthropological fiction in its own right, capable, for good or ill, of inventing Irish souls.

Joyce's representational strategy mimics the objectivity and detachment of the ethnographic participant–observer and functions on two interlocking levels: the narrator participates imaginatively in the lives of Dubliners whose experience is communicated from the position of a detached observer; but these experiences themselves are often ones of detached self-observation. What Roy Pascal says of Flaubert's style might be said of Joyce's: "Flaubert's realism did not imply the sort of objectivity that belongs to natural science, an objectivity founded on communicable skill and authoritative control over the (imaginary) object; on the contrary, it meant an imaginative self-submergence in the object, participation in the imagined character's experience, and communication of this intuitive experience."[21] We see this most powerfully in the access we are given to the subjectivity of characters like James Duffy, in "A Painful Case," whose pathological dissociation from himself and from the social world in which he moves converts objective observation into opportunities for regret and longing: "He began to doubt the reality of what memory told him" (*D*, 117). The tendency of characters like Duffy and Little Chandler, in "A Little Cloud," to regard themselves in the third person not only offers an ironic counterpoint to Joyce's scrupulous method, but also encodes a critique of the ethnographic imagination of the Revival. If *The Celtic Twilight* represents Yeats's attempt, by means of a redemptive ethnography, to represent an authentic peasant folk culture and to unify the artist with the peasantry by virtue of a shared belief in the reality of fairies, *Dubliners* might be read as a critique of that representation and the unity it celebrates, a critique in which Revivalism is shown to be a discourse that mystifies class and gender relations and offers no real alternative to oppressive social conditions.

The best illustrations of the pernicious effects of this mystifying discourse are "A Little Cloud" and "The Dead." In the former, Little Chandler's desire to sound "the Celtic note" and to "write something original" hinges on his ability to imitate the "Celtic school," to infuse the poems he has not yet written with a "melancholy tone" and "allusions" (*D*, 73–4). Joyce's lack of patience with the "Celtic school" is well known and can be gauged by his response to Lady Gregory's *Poets and Dreamers*, which he reviewed in 1903. "In fine, her book, wherever it treats of the 'folk,' sets forth in the fullness of its senility a class of mind which Mr. Yeats has set forth with such delicate scepticism in his happiest book, 'The Celtic Twilight.' ''[22] In this relatively rare, if guarded, expression of praise for Yeats, Joyce contrasts two ways of looking at the "folk": one that manages a "delicate scepticism," while another that appears gratuitous alongside it. Little Chandler, believing that the power of a cultural discourse like Revivalism will elevate him above his impoverished living conditions and confer upon him the authenticity that a "more Irish-looking" name would confer, lacks Yeats's saving skepticism. The inauthenticity of his position is all the more apparent, to the reader at least, when we learn of his habit of speaking of himself in the third person, "invent[ing] sentences and phrases from the notices which his book would get" (*D*, 74). Little Chandler engages in a detached self-observation; he makes himself the subject of a primitivist discourse that maintains an Arnoldian distinction between Celtic and English "notes." But the fiction of the Revivalist poet he conjures up, "T. Malone Chandler," fails to transform the ineffectual man who is terrorized by his own lack of authenticity. At the end of the story, he sinks back into the oppressive social conditions and "inauthentic consciousness"[23] that Revivalism has done nothing to alleviate – in fact, it has made things worse by leaving him with no alternative but a remorseful longing for an authenticity he can never attain. Like Mrs. Kearney, in "A Mother," who exploits her daughter's tenuous connections to the Revivalist movement in order to live vicariously through her musical achievements, only to discover that those connections are annihilated with the emergence of economic realities to which she has blinded herself, Little Chandler is ultimately the victim of Revivalism.[24]

In "The Dead," a story which, for many readers, serves as both culmination and summation of attitudes that have emerged more or less explicitly in the preceding stories, Joyce offers a far more trenchant and fully developed critique of Revivalism, specifically its reliance on a redemptive mode of ethnography. "The Dead" picks up on the detachment and anomie of other characters in *Dubliners* and links it explicitly with a set of essentially Revivalist attitudes toward the Irish "race" and the Irish language held by Gabriel and Gretta Conroy and Miss Ivors. As Levenson argues, "two strains of political discourse . . . leave visible marks on 'The Dead': the national autonomy movement of Sinn Fein, and the Irish language campaign."[25] Gabriel's ambiguous position also reflects the influence of the primitivism that subtends, albeit in a deeply sublimated fashion, the nativism of the Gaelic League and the Irish-Ireland nationalists. As Nolan argues in her reading of "The Dead," this context of cultural nationalism is vital, since it is the nationalist mythology of authenticity and its valorization of "the West," and not the encroachment of modernity, that precipitates Gabriel's "decenteredness." "Mortality – the occasion for Gabriel's reflections on identity is his meditation on death – in itself may be universal, but the particular ways in which it is apprehended . . . are intimately linked with the cultural situation in which the story is set."[26] In Joyce's depiction of Gabriel, we have an example of the compromised position Fanon describes in which the native intellectual engages in "the frantic acquisition of the culture of the occupying power" and "takes every opportunity of unfavorably criticizing his own national culture."[27]

Uncertain about his own cultural allegiances, Gabriel reacts defensively when he is playfully accused by Miss Ivors of being a West Briton:

It was true that he wrote a literary column every Wednesday in *The Daily Express*, for which he was paid fifteen shillings. But that did not make him a West Briton surely. The books he received for review were almost more welcome than the paltry cheque. He loved to feel the covers and turn over the pages of newly printed books . . . He did not know how to meet her charge. He wanted to say that literature was above politics. But they were friends of many years' standing and their careers had paralleled, first at the University and then as teachers: he could not risk a grandiose phrase with her. (*D*, 188)

This confrontation dramatizes Gabriel's sense of detachment from the Gaelic Ireland that she idealizes and aligns him with the West Britonism he so strenuously denies. His motives for writing for the pro-British *Daily Express* reveal that his complicity, far from artistic or subversive, turns out to be a pallid, unreflective mimicry of the bourgeois intellectual's rise to power in the metropolitan center.[28] His position within a nascent national bourgeoisie is camouflaged by his fetishization of books and by a blithe indifference to the situation of colonial Ireland. His "lame" response to Miss Ivors "that he saw nothing political in writing reviews of books" (*D*, 188) is an attempt to gloss over with an aesthetic justification what he half recognizes as a politically ambiguous pursuit.

Gabriel's contempt for Miss Ivors, who has unsettled his compla-
cent indifference to Irish culture, is a classic response of the native
intellectual whose scant share of the colonizer's power has been
held up for public censure. His response to the suggestion that
he learn Irish – "if it comes to that, you know, Irish is not my
language" – provokes Miss Ivors, who calls his national identity into
question: "And haven't you your own land to visit . . . that you know
nothing of, your own people, and your own country?" (*D*, 189). His
exasperated retort – "I'm sick of my own country, sick of it!" –
unveils his contradictory position. "For while Gabriel denies that
Irish is his language," writes Levenson, "he implicitly accepts
Ireland as his nation – 'my own country' – sick of it though he may
be."[29] This contradiction is duplicated in Gabriel's dinner speech, in
which he indicts Miss Ivors as part of a "new generation, educated
or hypereducated," that lacks "those qualities of humanity, of
hospitality, of kindly humour which belonged to an older day"
(*D*, 203). We are struck by his hypocrisy (they have had, after all,
"parallel" careers) and by his failure to see that he participates in the
same essentialist and primitivist attitude toward the West of Ireland
that characterizes the colonialist ruling classes.[30] By scorning the
invitation to visit the Aran Islands, Gabriel effectively scorns his
wife, Gretta, who is herself from Galway, and implicitly calls into
play a binomial primitivism similar to that which motivates Revivalist tourists like Miss Ivors.

Joyce's examination of people like Gabriel underscores the pervasive influence of anthropological attitudes, mediated by Revivalist
representations, toward the Irish-speaking peasantry. His ambivalent
position as an academic caught between nationalist and colonialist
interests is not unlike that of the Revivalist, for he is similarly caught
up in an identity crisis in which he cannot know himself without
confronting the specter of an Irish Other, someone more authentic,
more essential, rooted in the West of Ireland. But, perhaps because
of this ambivalent position with respect to his own Irishness, Gabriel
remains blind to the level of his own complicity with nationalist and
Revivalist projects of cultural redemption. Consequently, he gets
caught up in a process by which Michael Furey, a West of Ireland
boy his wife once knew, is marked as Other with respect to himself;
what he perceives to be the ascendancy, in his wife's remembrance,
of a more authentic Irishman, turns into a radical confrontation
with himself as *in*authentic. The dead West of Ireland boy becomes

the sign of a cultural authenticity from which Gabriel, the ambivalent insider, feels utterly estranged. He falls into a colonialist way of seeing the world in which his own ambivalent but privileged position in the native intelligentsia is defined by the existence of an unambivalent, purely Irish peasant. Gretta Conroy is also complicit in this half-conscious primitivism, for, in her memorialization of Michael Furey and in her self-image as a sacrificial sovereignty figure, she duplicates the legendary and folkloric tropes that Revivalism had made generally available as the signs of an authentic peasantry. Especially provocative in this regard is Gretta's answer to Gabriel about Michael Furey – "I think he died for me" (*D*, 220) – which echoes the answer given by the Old Woman in Yeats's and Lady Gregory's *Cathleen Ni Houlihan* to a query about "yellow-haired Donough that was hanged in Galway": "He died for love of me: many a man has died for love of me."[31] Bewitched by Bartell D'Arcy's rendition of "The Lass of Aughrim," the Conroys are seduced into a belief in their own authenticity, which is confirmed in their mutual adoration of Michael Furey, whose ghostly presence puts the lie to Yeats's famous claim that "Romantic Ireland's dead and gone" (*Poems*, 108). For, though it may be dead, the Romantic vision of Ireland is far from gone; it has merely become attenuated and ineffectual, exercising a kind of spectral influence from beyond the grave. Like the harp in "Two Gallants," which "seemed weary alike of the eyes of strangers and of her master's hands" (*D*, 54), Michael Furey is an exhausted symbol, signifying the inability of Revivalist discourse to offer meaningful alternatives to sentimental nostalgia and West Britonism. That Gabriel and Gretta have different emotional investments in him matters less than the fact that he serves the same psychic function for both: he provides the empty center for a hybrid identity caught in a vortex of conflicting demands: Revivalist mythologies, nationalist ideologies, Catholic confessionalism and the rewards of assimilation into an anglicized national bourgeoisie.

In the final scene of "The Dead," Gabriel undergoes a crisis in which he confronts the hybridized nature of his own identity; his response is simultaneously ambivalent and epiphanic and echoes similar responses by Little Chandler, with his *faux* Celtic Twilight sensibility and his inarticulate despair, and James Duffy, with his anemic emotional life and his well-nigh ethnographic distance from the sensual world in which he longs to participate: "He looked down the slope and, at the base, in the shadow of the wall of the Park, he saw some human figures lying. Those venal and furtive loves filled him with despair. He gnawed the rectitude of his life; he felt that he had been outcast from life's feast" (*D*, 117). In Gabriel's case, this "gnawing" takes the form of a "vague terror," an "impalpable and vindictive being" (*D*, 220) that assails him. It is significant that his "generous tears," which for many critics signal his epiphanic moment of self-consciousness, should be shed precisely when he imagines he sees a vision of the peasant boy: "The tears gathered more thickly in his eyes and in the partial darkness he imagined he saw the form of a young man standing under a dripping tree" (*D*, 223). For many readers, the "fading out" of Gabriel's identity and the "dissolving and dwindling" away of the "solid world" signal a "generosity of spirit" that proceeds, as Vincent Pecora argues, from a Christian tradition of self-sacrifice in which the autonomous subject is consolidated through a process of spiritual surrender: "[I]t is what Gabriel views as his generous self-sacrifice that proves and morally justifies [his] identity."[32] But, if Gabriel sacrifices himself to anything, it is to his own delusions, his mystified sense of what he is missing and what his wife evidently has access to: the "West of Ireland boy," whose authentic status is the product of his unwitting complicity in the redemptive desire of Revivalism. In the self-legitimating logic of ethnographic authority, Gabriel stabilizes his own position at the expense of a native Other whose authenticity he constructs, though he is not aware that it is a construction, in order to salve his own *in*authentic consciousness.

When Joyce turns to Stephen Dedalus, his critique of Revivalism appears at first glance to be subsumed within a larger critique of nationalism. This is certainly the common view of *Stephen Hero* and *A Portrait of the Artist as a Young Man*, a view which tends to regard Stephen as a renegade whose rejection of nationalism reflects Joyce's own rejection of the Gaelic League and Irish-Ireland nationalism generally.[33] Vincent Cheng's position is representative of this view: "Stephen recognizes that the emphasis on Irish language and culture is a misdirected nostalgia for a glorious Celtic past and purity which may have never really existed, [one that is] based . . . on the reaction of the oppressed group within a binary logic and structure imposed by the oppressors."[34] It seems to me that the problem here, as in other readings of Stephen's repudiation of nationalism, is the uncritical assumption of a Manichean model of colonial domination. By taking the view that Stephen's rejection of the Irish-Ireland nationalist agenda is equivalent to a rejection of Celticism, Cheng assumes that the Celticism in question is identical to the imperialist discourse of people like Matthew Arnold or the nationalist discourse of Gaelic Leaguers like Hughes (in *Stephen Hero*) and Madden/Davin (in *Stephen Hero* and *A Portrait*, respectively). To a certain extent, these discourses come into play in Stephen's political education; but the Manichean model leaves out of account the complicating factor of the Anglo-Irish Revivalists whose Celticism is significantly different from Arnold's and the Irish-Irelanders' and not so easily subsumed under the heading of "nationalism."

As I have indicated in previous chapters, this complication takes the form of the Anglo-Irish Revivalist's constitutive ambivalence with respect to the native Irish, an ambivalence akin to that which characterizes the classic ethnographer. And, as I have suggested in my discussion of *Dubliners*, this ambivalence is not restricted to the Anglo-Irish Revivalist but can be located in the Catholic-Irish intelligentsia whenever Revivalist discourse is drawn upon to authenticate their experience as Irish men and women. It seems to me that Stephen is no exception in this regard. In fact, I submit that his experience elaborates and develops, within the framework of a *Bildung*-plot, the kind of ambivalent and inauthentic national consciousness that we have already seen in Gabriel Conroy.[35] Stephen occupies a social position similar Gabriel's: both are what Seamus Deane calls "provincial intellectuals"[36] educated in the English language and European traditions, both are impatient with the linguistic policies of the Gaelic League, both are overly sensitive to accusations of inauthenticity, and both are complicit in the construction of an Irish Other indispensable to the formation of their own identities. Although Stephen's artistic sensibility alerts him to his own position within culture in a way vastly more sophisticated and critical than Gabriel could manage, both share a similar investment in Revivalism. Moreover, we see a significant shift in Stephen's attitude toward Revivalism as we move from *Stephen Hero* to *A Portrait*, and, finally, to *Ulysses*, a fact that is not marked in Cheng or in other critical assessments of Stephen's cultural politics. If we try to understand Stephen's attitudes toward the language question and the primitivism of the Revival in terms of ambivalence, then we might be able to avoid the very binary trap to which Cheng alerts us. The difference between Stephen and the Revivalists may not depend, finally, on the former being a Catholic and therefore more native than the latter; rather, it may depend chiefly on Stephen's ability to exploit the potential for critique (both of the attitudes he holds and of his own complicity in holding them) that an ambivalent position holds out – and to do so in a more sustained and critical fashion than the Revivalists (to their credit) attempted to do with limited success. From the detached observer of the peasantry in *Stephen Hero* to the detached observer of cultural observers like Haines in *Ulysses*, we witness a kind of political education of the native intellectual whose authenticity depends on his recognition of what is most inauthentic about himself. Joyce's ironic narrative method, then, often discussed in terms of aesthetic distance, might better be described in terms of the distance proper to ethnography; in this context, Joyce's irony falls squarely on Stephen's experience of inauthenticity and the role it plays in the creation of a racial conscience.

On many levels, *Stephen Hero* and *A Portrait* articulate similar themes and present Stephen's attitudes in similar ways. This is especially true with respect to nationalism and the Catholic Church. In *Stephen Hero*, the Gaelic Leaguer Mr. Hughes expresses a view of Stephen and his politics that remains relatively unchanged, though transferred to different speakers, in *A Portrait*: "Mr. Daedalus was himself a renegade from the Nationalist ranks: he professed cosmopolitanism. But a man that was of all countries was of no country – you must first have a nation before you have art" (*SH*, 103). Many of Stephen's attitudes in *Stephen Hero* toward the nationalist cause and the idea of an Irish nation are similar to those voiced in *A Portrait*, though the former lacks the subtlety and economy of expression we find in the latter. The belief that art and Stephen's own artistic development are of greater importance than the nation, implicit in *A Portrait* and later articulated in the drunken confrontation with the British soldiers at the conclusion of the "Circe" episode of *Ulysses*, is plainly expressed in *Stephen Hero*: "[m]y own mind . . . is more interesting to me than the entire country," Stephen says with sublime arrogance, while elsewhere the narrator notes that "[h]e acknowledged to himself in honest egoism that he could not take to heart the distress of a nation, the soul of which was antipathetic to his own, so bitterly as the indignity of a bad line of verse" (*SH*, 248, 146). It is this expression of the artist's antipathy toward the nation that has justified the belief that Stephen invested little or nothing in the nationalist cause. This is fair enough as far as it goes, but this same antipathy is often adduced as evidence that Stephen had little or no investment in Revivalism. However, other evidence points to the investments he did in fact make and continued to make in *A Portrait*. That they are for the most part uncriticized, that they exist as unacknowledged assumptions, indicates that Stephen's ambivalent attitude toward the culture he both observes and participates in, like that of the characters Joyce so trenchantly exposes in *Dubliners*, is determined in significant ways by the very Revivalist discourse that so many critics believe he repudiates.

Stephen's attitude toward the Revival in *Stephen Hero* might be said to begin and end with a few references to the fact that he admired Yeats's mystical stories of the late 1890s, particularly *The Tables of the Law*, "every word of which he remembered" and recited with "careful animation" to his friend Lynch (*SH*, 177). In my brief discussion of these stories in chapter 2, I suggested that they represent a turning-point for Yeats, a point at which he appears to have abandoned a belief in the efficacy of "fair equivalents" of folklore and to have embarked on a revision of Revivalism that no longer sought to represent an authentic Irish peasant culture but rather to legitimate an Anglo-Irish tradition by way of an appeal to "divine substances" that emerge in the visionary experience of the "Protestant magician."[37] But Stephen's admiration for these stories, with their descriptions of "incoherent and heterogeneous" rituals and the "strange mixture" of "trivialities and sacred practices" (*SH*, 178), is inconsistent with views stated elsewhere in the text. For example, he had earlier criticized the "romantic temper" in art for being "an insecure, unsatisfied, impatient temper which sees no fit abode here for its ideals and chooses therefore to behold them under insensible figures" which "are blown to wild adventures, lacking the gravity of solid bodies, and the mind that has conceived them ends by disowning them" (*SH*, 78). In a discussion of Shelley's "spiritual interpretation of landscape," Stephen notes that "[s]ome people think they write spiritually if they make their scenery dim and cloudy" (*SH*, 129). It is difficult not to discern in these criticisms an indirect attack on the "Celtic note," associated with Yeats's work in the 1890s, that Little Chandler strives to hit. What I think these references point to is a grudging investment in and identification with Yeatsian Revivalism, especially the form it began to take around

1897, the *annus mirabilis* of Yeats's folkloric fictions. It is, of course, unclear whether Stephen's view of Yeats reflects Joyce's but what is clear is that Joyce wished his hero to exhibit an ambivalent, perhaps even contradictory, attitude toward Yeats and Revivalism generally. We might gauge Joyce's ironic purpose in such an exhibition by considering that, with the exception of a single important reference to Michael Robartes, who is featured in Yeats's mystical stories, at the conclusion of *A Portrait*, there is little evidence to suggest that Stephen retains his ambivalent interest in Yeats or the Revival.

What does this add up to? For one thing, it indicates that Stephen's attitude toward the Revival cannot be taken as identical to or subsumed within his attitude toward nationalism. But the scanty references to Yeats are not the only evidence of Stephen's indebtedness to the Revival. His lingering dependence on primitivist cultural distinctions, for example, suggests at best an unconscious assent to the Revival's project of cultural redemption. This is not to say, however, that he does not explicitly reject certain elements of the Revival. The evidence in *Stephen Hero* and *A Portrait* support only the limited claim that Stephen rejects those elements of Revivalism – the language question, the fetishization of folklore, myth, and legend, complicity with colonial rule – that threaten his artistic freedom. In *Stephen Hero*, he explicitly denounces the Gaelic League for its complicity with colonial domination: "And how many relatives of Gaelic Leaguers are in the police and constabulary?" he asks Madden. "Even I know nearly ten of your friends who are sons of Police inspectors" (*SH*, 64). In *A Portrait*, this denunciation is generalized and aimed at the "indispensable informer" and the nationalist instinct for betrayal: "No honourable and sincere man," Stephen tells Davin, who has tried in vain to recruit him, "has given up to you his life and his youth and his affections from the days of Tone to those of Parnell but you sold him to the enemy or failed him in need or reviled him and left him for another. And you invite me to be one of you. I'd see you damned first" (*P*, 203). Such statements, indeed the nature of the entire dialogue between the two, has the effect of downplaying the importance of the Irish-language movement and of Revivalism generally, focusing on the corruptive effects of complicity on his own artistic ambitions.

Though primitivist discourse plays an enabling role in Stephen's artistic self-fashioning, it is represented in quite different ways in *Stephen Hero* and *A Portrait*. In a discussion of the role of the Church and the police in the Gaelic League, Madden defends the Church by saying that "our people have suffered for [it] and would suffer for [it] again" while the police are looked upon "as aliens, traitors, oppressors of the people." Stephen replies that "[t]he old peasant down the country doesn't seem to be of your opinion when he counts over his greasy notes and says 'I'll put the priest on Tom an' I'll put the polisman on Mickey'" (*SH*, 64). His recitation of what he sarcastically calls "Irish peasant wisdom" is met with an accusation that reminds us of Miss Ivors' retort to Gabriel Conroy: "No West-Briton could speak worse of his countrymen. You are simply giving vent to old stale libels – the drunken Irishman, the baboon-faced Irishman that we see in *Punch*" (*SH*, 64–5). Stephen's response, which, significantly, does not attempt to refute Madden's charge, invokes the authority of his own experience: "What I say I see about me." But it also invokes the experiential authority of the participant–observer that underwrites Revivalist representations of the Irish peasantry as well as ethnographies like those produced by A. C. Haddon and C. R. Browne, which drew upon stereotypes borrowed by previous visitors to the Aran Islands. In any case, the issue of Stephen's reliance on a primitivist discourse is sidestepped when he shifts the conversation to a critique of the economic hypocrisy of "[t]he publicans and the pawnbrokers who live on the miseries of the people" (*SH*, 65).

Vincent Cheng, who quotes exhaustively from L. P. Curtis's seminal work on stereotyped representations of the Irish, fails to see the implications of this dialogue, quoting only the first sentence of Madden's accusation and claiming, vaguely and tentatively, that Joyce was testing "the limitations of Stephen's attitudes toward his country."[38] Nor does Cheng examine the most damning evidence of Stephen's primitivist thinking, the "additional manuscript pages" appended to the text of *Stephen Hero* which depict his journey to Mullingar to visit his godfather, Mr. Fulham. These pages begin with Stephen's musings about the peasants in the third-class railroad carriage that takes him to Mullingar. He notes that

[t]he carriage smelt strongly of peasants (an odor the debasing humanity of which Stephen remembered to have perceived in the little chapel of Clongowes on the morning of his first communion) and indeed so pungently that the youth could not decide whether he found the odor of sweat offensive because the peasant sweat is monstrous or because it did not now proceed from his own body. He was not ashamed to admit to himself that he found it offensive for both of these reasons. (*SH*, 238)

The suggestion that the peasant is a species of "debased humanity,"
complicated by a characteristic egotism that prompts Stephen to
take offense at that which does not emanate from his own body, is
reinforced by the description of Mr. Fulham's neighbors as "primitive types" (*SH*, 241).[39] Joyce will later include the episode at
Clongowes in *A Portrait*, where the smell of "holy peasants" registers
in the young Stephen's consciousness as "a smell of air and rain and
turf and corduroy" (*P*, 18); but it is displaced from the adult Stephen's
memory in *Stephen Hero*, where it is contextualized by attitudes that
are far from childlike, and made to function in the later text as one
of a number of seemingly unrelated sensations. The implication, in *A
Portrait*, is that Stephen either outgrows a childish prejudice or that
the childish prejudice is really nothing of the sort: it is simply
another example of the incipient artist's sensitivity to sensations.

Stephen's musings, far more crudely and pejoratively couched
than what we find in Yeats or Synge, are nonetheless grounded in the
same primitivism that we find in both Revivalist and ethnographic
discourses. After hearing a "humorous story which was intended to
poke fun at countrified ideas" (*SH*, 242), a story which Stephen
thought had been told well and which makes him laugh, Mr. Fulham
notes "with conviction" that "[o]ur Irish peasantry . . . is the backbone of the nation" (*SH*, 244). The narrator then proceeds to situate
Stephen overtly within a context of ethnographic observation:

Backbone or not, it was in the constant observance of the peasantry that
Stephen chiefly delighted. Physically, they were almost Mongolian types,
tall, angular and oblique-eyed. Stephen whenever he walked behind a
peasant always looked first for the prominent cheek-bones that seemed to
cut the air and the peasants in their turn must have recognized
metropolitan features for they stared hard at the youth as if he were some
rare animal. (*SH*, 244)

Stephen here duplicates the characteristic position of the participant–observer who stands at a remove from the native subject and
who is utterly different from that subject – a "metropolitan" outsider
whose physiognomy throws the native's racial Otherness into relief.
He repeats as well the language of primitivism, with its binomial
structure and a typological rhetoric that makes a clear, physiological
distinction between civilized and primitive types. The careful description suggests the anthropometric methodology of Haddon and
Browne, while the "delight" Stephen takes in his "constant observance" suggests the "social authority" that his observation both

presupposes and confers. We are reminded of Bronislaw Malinowski's similar feelings of delight when he has emerged from the torpor induced by novels and erotic daydreams: "Once again upsurge of joy at this open, free existence amidst a fabulous [*sic!*] landscape, under exotic conditions, a real picnic based on actual work . . . This may have also been the cause of my joy at Nu'agasi, when suddenly *the veil was rent* and I began to collect information."[40]

Though they are isolated examples, the passages quoted above support other instances of Stephen's primitivist assumptions about the Irish peasantry. A problem arises, however, when we consider Joyce's treatment of Stephen's peasant friend Madden/Davin. In *Stephen Hero*, there is a clear separation between Stephen's attitude toward Madden and his attitude toward the peasantry during the trip to Mullingar. The primitivism so strongly evident in the passage relating that trip is a barely noticeable subtext in passages describing Madden: "Madden and [Stephen] were often together but their conversations were rarely serious and though the rustic mind of one was very forcibly impressed by the metropolitanism of the other both young men were on relations of affectionate familiarity" (*SH*, 52). Stephen makes here the same distinction he made between the Mongoloid peasant and the metropolitan observer; but the difference lies in the "affectionate familiarity" that allows Stephen to achieve a kind of intersubjective rapport and to overcome the distance that guarantees his "constant observance." The relationship with Madden, as with Davin in *A Portrait*, replicates in novelistic terms what Yeats attempted in folkloric terms in *The Celtic Twilight*: the artist–observer is allowed the seemingly contradictory privileges of distance and intimacy.

In *Stephen Hero*, Madden is represented in a specific social context that includes the Gaelic League, Irish-language instruction, and college life; he differs from Stephen's other friends in being a "rustic," but in every other ways he takes his place among his fellow students with little or no attempt on Stephen's (or Joyce's) part to romanticize his difference from them. In *A Portrait*, the blatantly primitivist discourse of *Stephen Hero* is excised, and the figure of Davin, with a few minor exceptions, remains the sole *locus* of Stephen's (and the text's) attitudes toward the peasantry; he condenses and crystallizes this attitude, emerging less as a character with whom Stephen interacts than as a type: "the peasant student" (*P*, 180). Stephen's description of him as a man in thrall to myth, legend, and an Irish-Ireland political ethos signals his racial and cultural difference:

Side by side with his memory of the deeds of prowess of his uncle Mat Davin, the athlete, the young peasant worshipped the sorrowful legend of Ireland. The gossip of his fellowstudents which strove to render the flat life of the college significant at any cost loved to think of him as a young fenian. His nurse had taught him Irish and shaped his rude imagination by the broken lights of Irish myth. He stood toward this myth upon which no individual mind had ever drawn out a line of beauty and to its unwieldy tales that divided themselves as they moved down the cycles in the same attitude as toward the Roman catholic religion, the attitude of a dullwitted loyal serf. Whatsoever of thought or of feeling came to him from England or by way of English culture his mind stood armed against in obedience to a password: and of the world that lay beyond England he knew only the foreign legion of France in which he spoke of serving. (*P*, 181)

To be sure, Joyce here criticizes nationalists' reliance on myth when he suggests that "no individual mind had ever drawn out a line of beauty" from it, and he undermines the picture of a noble and virtuous peasantry painted by Revivalists and Gaelic Leaguers alike when he asserts that the peasant's attitude toward myth was identical to his mindless subservience to the Church.[41] But the critical thrust of the passage is undermined by its invocation of the "dullwitted loyal serf" – either a Firbolg or a Milesian, both half-legendary candidates for the racial "origin" of the Irish Celts – which signals Stephen's sense that the Irish peasant remains trapped in Manichean opposition to metropolitan culture. His attitudes clearly reveal a residual investment in a primitivist discourse that constructs Davin as simple, guileless, and superstitious, the embodiment of provincialism and "the hidden ways of Irish life," a "peasant student" with "a dull stare of terror in the eyes, the terror of the soul of a starving Irish village in which the curfew is still a nightly fear" (*P*, 180–1). The irony, of course, is that Stephen takes an essentially Revivalist position even as he struggles to demythologize the peasant subject of the Revival's redemptive ethnography.

It seems to me that the transition from *Stephen Hero* to *A Portrait* reveals the ambivalent nature of Stephen's attitude toward the peasantry, for the rapport that he effects, or attempts to effect, with Davin in *A Portrait* is not simply the "affectionate familiarity" he felt for Madden but something closer to confessional intimacy.[42] Davin relates his unsettling encounter with a peasant women (*P*, 181–3), while Stephen confesses his desire to be free of nationalist and religious oppression in such a way that suggests earlier confessions: "The soul is born, he said vaguely, first in those moments I told you of" (*P,* 203). More important is Davin's consciousness of the impropriety of Stephen's confession: "I'm a simple person, said Davin. You know that. When you told me that night in Harcourt Street those things about your private life, honest to God, Stevie, I was not able to eat my dinner. I was quite bad. I was awake a long time that night. Why did you tell me those things?" (*P,* 202). The precise nature of Stephen's intimacies is unclear, though given his sexual experiences it is not hard to guess what they might be. But one small clue indicates that this confessional relationship, even as it instates a binomial distinction between metropolitan artist and primitive rustic, renders the distinction to some degree unstable, since, unlike any of Stephen's other friends, Davin calls him by the affectionately familiar "Stevie." Moreover, though in this intimate confessional relationship Davin is given a voice, what he speaks is a repetition of the very discourse that otherwise reduces him to a primitive type – "I am a simple person . . . You know that" – and that confers upon him an authentic social status. Ironically, part of what defines Stephen's relationship with him is his apparent desire for the authenticity that the peasant student represents. When Davin asks "What with your name and your ideas . . . Are you Irish at all?" Stephen responds with a defense of his Irishness: "Come with me now to the office of arms and I will show you the tree of my family." He clearly resents the implication that he is an inauthentic Irishman, yet he fairly bristles at signs of Davin's authenticity, especially his heavy boots, his simple credulous nature, and his naive commitment to Fenianism. Indeed, it is this authentic Irishness that within minutes Stephen will reject in his famous line about throwing off the nets of "nationality, language, religion" (*P,* 202–3). Perhaps nowhere else does Stephen's ambivalent desire for authenticity shade so markedly into contradiction.

Another important issue that undergoes transformation from *Stephen Hero* to *A Portrait* is the revival of the Irish language. The extended passages in *Stephen Hero* that describe Stephen's attendance at Irish-language classes and his open confrontations with Gaelic Leaguers on the question of reviving the Irish language give way in *A Portrait* to meditations that displace his struggle with language from a Revivalist to an imperialist context. Moreover, the object of his meditations shifts from the Irish to the English language. A new ambivalence is admitted into *A Portrait* that does not exist, or exists only implicitly, in *Stephen Hero*, for Stephen must now contend with a situation in which neither the English nor the Irish language appear authentic to him, neither appear to satisfy his desire for a language adequate to his artistic and emotional needs. The argument against learning Irish is clearly expressed in *A Portrait*: "My ancestors threw off their language and took another," he tells Davin. "They allowed a handful of foreigners to subject them. Do you fancy I am going to pay in my own life and person debts they made? What for?" (*P*, 203). The question of language easily slides into the larger question of colonial domination, of the "debts" incurred by ancestors who chose to give up their "mother tongue." His education and artistic sensibility have made him suspicious of the notion that the Irish language would somehow authenticate his experience as an Irishman. But he is equally suspicious of the English language, even as he continues to develop a masterful use of it. His meeting with the dean of studies articulates this suspicion and indicates the displacement from a Revivalist to an imperialist context:

The language in which we are speaking is his before it is mine. How different are the words *home, Christ, ale, master,* on his lips and on mine! I cannot speak or write these words without unrest of spirit. His language, so familiar and so foreign, will always be for me an acquired speech. I have not made or accepted its words. My voice holds them at bay. My soul frets in the shadow of his language. (*P*, 189)

The bitterness we discern in this passage is partly attributable to the anxiety of the colonial subject who must contend with a language that has been imposed rather than acquired. Stephen's discovery later that the word *tundish*, which he believed to be of Irish origin, turns out to be English after all, underscores the treachery of his situation. His response to the dean, recorded in his diary – "Damn him one way or the other" (*P*, 251) – signals the frustration that ensues once he realizes the interminable ambivalence involved in defining national identity in linguistic terms.

Patrick McGee argues that the ambivalent status of Ireland as a metropolitan colony created a unique set of social conditions in which writers like Joyce could be said to "anticipate the postcolonial writer precisely to the extent that they themselves, *as subjects*, have been colonized by hegemonic discourses to which they offer specific forms of linguistic resistance."[43] For an Irish intellectual like Stephen, who refuses on principle to embrace Irish as a "mother tongue" and who is hypersensitive to the denotative and connotative potentialities of language, English offers both the temptation of aesthetic satisfaction, as evidenced by the pleasure he derives from poetry and etymology, and the awareness of the inadequacy of what at times seems like an inauthentic mode of expression. But, even as he evinces the same impatience with the language question that characterizes Gabriel Conroy, he is capable of seeing that behind the question of whether Irish is *his* language lies a more pertinent one: why is a nearly dead language being used as a sign of authentic Irishness and the principal plank of a nationalist campaign? While Stephen may have a personal reason for not wanting to learn Irish ("Is it on account of that certain young lady and Father Moran?" Davin asks him [*P*, 202]), it is clear that his rejection is based chiefly on a conviction that the struggle for the future of Ireland, if it is to be fought on the battlefield of language, would take place in English, but an English that had been appropriated and resignified by the Irish artist. It is perhaps generally true that the Irish-Ireland movement, insofar as it adhered to a nativist ideal, insisted on the prominence of the Irish language on their political agenda; but, within the ranks of the Anglo-Irish intelligentsia, there was a decisive split between those like Douglas Hyde, who argued for the "de-anglicization" of Ireland,[44] and those like Yeats, Synge, and Lady Gregory who maintained that the future of Irish literature depended on the development of a Hiberno-English dialect. Stephen's resistance to the call for "de-anglicization" and his willingness to expand the expressive power of the English language places him within the tradition of the Celtic Revival, though he is critical of attitudes and practices often associated with a Hiberno-English dialect that readily lent itself to his parodic method. Nolan writes, "[l]ike his counterparts in the Literary Revival, Joyce concentrated on varieties of Hiberno-English, rather than on Irish, in his search for an alternative national vernacular. More explicitly than Yeats, Gregory, or Synge, however, Joyce's dialect also bears the weight of crucial political questions."[45] One of those questions bears directly on the anthropological modernism of the Revival, for, while Revivalists like Synge and Lady Gregory strove to use dialect forms of English to evoke a "fair equivalent" of an authentic folk culture, Joyce sought instead to subvert the reifying and essentializing effects of such equivalents in the production of a "national vernacular" whose inauthenticity is a function of a deliberate and liberatory *will to style*.

Intimately connected with the language question is Stephen's construction of Emma Clery as a parody of the traditional female sovereignty figure. Typically cast as Kathleen ni Houlihan, the sovereignty figure was developed in part as a response to the British image of Hibernia (a response which, not incidentally, can be regarded as a replication of colonialist iconography) but also, and perhaps largely, as a continuation of an indigenous tradition in which the sovereignty figure represents the political autonomy of the Irish people.[46] Yeats's *Cathleen ni Houlihan*, which reworks a folktale of an old woman who persuades the young men of Ireland to protect her from the strangers in her four fields, had become, by the time Joyce wrote *A Portrait*, both a powerful emblem of the aspirations of cultural nationalism and an obvious target of parody. And, while parodic manifestations of the sovereignty figure appear in *Ulysses*, Joyce's treatment of it in the early work is harder to characterize. Gretta Conroy's sense of her role in the death of Michael Furey certainly suggests the sovereignty figure, who seduces young men to sacrifice their lives, and the peasant woman in Davin's story of seduction serves a similarly conventional iconic function. Less conventional are the depictions of the bird-girl and E. C. in *A Portrait*. F. L. Radford and Anthony Roche have recently argued for the Celtic origins of the bird-girl, interpreting her as a figure of Irish sovereignty that embodies and resignifies Revivalist iconography in an aesthetic vision situated in the liminal time of the *sidhe*, a transitional zone of transformation and timelessness through which the artist passes, a space between this world and the Other world of *Tir na nOg* (Land of Youth).[47] As a reinterpretation of the Revivalist sovereignty figure, the bird-girl emerges less as a nationalist icon than as an "envoy" to the metropolitan artist on the eve of exile.

The image of sovereignty and seduction to which I now turn – E. C. refigured as the "bat-like soul waking to the consciousness of itself" (*P*, 183) – underscores both Stephen's ambivalence toward Revivalist iconography and the critical power of his parodic resignification of Revivalist myth. His reconstruction of the peasant woman in Davin's story and his conflation of her with Emma Clery together constitute a seductive tableau in which the sovereignty figure emerges as the symbol of an uncreated race with respect to which Stephen presides as priest and confessor.

The story Davin relates – the attempt to seduce him by a married peasant woman – duplicates the Revivalist trope of Kathleen ni Houlihan in such a way that reflects something of the reality of peasant life: Davin's lonely walk in the dark countryside, the woman's solitude and poverty, her husband's absence on market business. But, immediately after Davin relates the story, Stephen incorporates it as a repetition of his own experience – that is, of his habit of transforming "real" women into types of racial authenticity:

The last words of Davin's story sang in his memory and the figure of the woman in the story stood forth, reflected in other figures of the peasant women whom he had seen standing in the doorways at Clane as the college cars drove by, as a type of her race and his own, a batlike soul waking to the consciousness of itself in darkness and secrecy and loneliness and, through the eyes and voice and gesture of a woman without guile, calling the stranger to her bed. (*P*, 183)

Davin's story of the peasant woman becomes for Stephen an anthropological fiction that reconfigures the terms of binomial racialism into a monstrous representation of a native Other struggling through betrayal to awaken to a consciousness of herself and her race. It is significant that this manifestation of Irish sovereignty hovers at the threshold of adultery, for, as David Lloyd points out, "where the principal organizing metaphor of Irish nationalism is that of a proper paternity, of restoring the lineage of the fathers in order to repossess the motherland, Joyce's procedures are dictated by adulteration."[48] We should also note the way in which Stephen manages to undermine one kind of gendered icon (e.g., Kathleen ni Houlihan) only to create another in its place; for, although he rejects the idealized figure of sacrificial sovereignty in favor of a figure of vampiric sexual seduction, his rejection merely instates a more cynical version of previous icons: we are still confronted with a woman who seeks the sacrifice of young men who will save her from the violence of intruders and who holds out the promise of national self-consciousness. The tension between the opposed impulses to idealize and to demystify is sustained in nearly every encounter Stephen has with Irish women. Consider, for example, the passage immediately following his meditation on Davin's story in which Stephen comes upon a girl selling flowers who becomes still another repetition of his habit of iconizing peasant women: "The blue flowers which she lifted toward him and her young blue eyes seemed to him at that instant *images of guilelessness*." It is with a concentration of effort that he is able to vanquish these images and to see in their place "only her ragged dress and damp coarse hair and hoydenish face" (*P*, 183; my emphasis).

As part of a critique of Revivalist iconography, these passages are both powerful and original, instances of an autoethnographic expressiveness that retranslates a conventional figure of sovereignty into a new and subversive image, one that replicates an iconizing gesture while simultaneously dramatizing the process by which the gesture is deconstructed, leaving behind an image that suggests something of the material reality of poverty and oppression. We see something quite different in the representation of E. C. (Emma Clery in *Stephen Hero*) in Stephen's villanelle. The villanelle represents E. C. as a disembodied temptress in a profane interweaving of the sacrament of the Eucharist and sensual images of water, waves, and bodily warmth that effectively aestheticizes both religious adoration and sexual desire. What is not often noted about the passage is its framing context, for here we find one of those rare moments in *A Portrait* where the Gaelic Leaguers, so prominent in *Stephen Hero*, appear. But their appearance is so oblique, so much a function of Stephen's creative process (he appears to remember them in the intervals of composition), that we cannot help but notice how completely they and their cause have been diminished, serving now only as images of inadequacy and futility. Stephen recalls leaving the classroom where the Irish-language lessons are held, castigating himself for reviling and mocking Emma's image:

And yet he felt that, however he might revile and mock her image, his anger was also a form of homage. He had left the classroom in disdain that was not wholly sincere, feeling that perhaps the secret of her race lay behind those dark eyes upon which her long lashes flung a quick shadow. He had told himself bitterly as he walked through the streets that she was a figure of the womanhood of her country, a batlike soul waking to the consciousness of itself in darkness and secrecy and loneliness, tarrying awhile, loveless and sinless, with her mild lover and leaving him to whisper of innocent transgressions in the latticed ear of a priest. (*P*, 221)

The repetition of phrases he had earlier used to describe the peasant woman in Davin's story might lead us to think that she is merely another type of primitive Irish womanhood; but there is a key difference between the two passages, for here Stephen refers to *her* race, *her* country, whereas in the earlier passage he had referred to "her race and his own." As a result, E. C. is rendered absolutely Other with respect to Stephen. His latest reconstruction of the sovereignty figure as an image of the artist's profane sacramental desire, then, effects an uneasy balance between iconizing parody and mere repetition of conventional iconographic strategies.

It is this sacramental desire that critics leave out of their account of Stephen's construction of E. C. Vincent Cheng, for example, argues that "Emma *is* Hibernia" and that Stephen "is of course misogynistically essentializing Irish womanhood with the pejorative image of a 'batlike soul.' "[49] My interpretation takes a native sovereignty figure, rather than the imperialist Hibernia, as the more likely antecedent of Stephen's meditations. Moreover, Cheng does not pursue the link between this image of Emma and the Revivalist iconographic tradition, preferring instead to speak monolithically of "Irish Nationalism." He argues further that Joyce "imaginatively function[s] her as the seductive lure of Ireland and Irish Nationalism" and that she represents to Stephen "the very Irish Nationalist mind-set he must put aside."[50] Cheng is, of course, right about her seductive function, but I submit that Stephen's attitude toward the nationalist "mind-set" is more ambivalent than Cheng allows and that Stephen's sacramental desire is crucial to our understanding of E. C.'s function as an image of the Irish race.

When he is not imagining E. C.'s "shy nakedness," Stephen imagines himself as a "priest of eternal imagination, transmuting the daily bread of experience into the radiant body of everliving life." His acquisition, through a process of Nietzschean transvaluation, of the sacramental authority of the priest sets him apart from more "authentic" priests like Father Moran, the putative object of E. C.'s attention, who is described as "a priested peasant, with a brother a policeman in Dublin and a brother a potboy in Moycullen" (*P,* 221). Stephen's artistic priesthood, which we may regard as a further manifestation of his metropolitanism, reinstates the discourse of primitivism that we have seen numerous times before. In this way, he slyly implicates E. C. as sovereignty figure with the "priested peasant" in binomial opposition to the "priestly" aesthete that Stephen imagines himself to be. But, while his reconstruction of the sovereignty figure unveils the primitivist discourse at the heart of Revivalist iconography, it also has the unintended consequence of exposing his own residual investments in that discourse, which he has obscured in an eroticized aestheticism that redefines the "constant observance" of the native Other that so delighted him in *Stephen Hero* as "the human disposition of sensible or intelligible matter for an esthetic end" (*P,* 207).

Joyce's representation of Stephen's confrontation with Revivalism reaches a new level in the concluding section of *A Portrait* in which the point of view shifts abruptly from free indirect narration to the first-person immediacy of the diary entries, a shift that reflects an ironic detachment not only from the Revival but also from Stephen's own investments in it. This is reflected in his last conversation with Davin, whose curiosity about Stephen's imminent departure is met with the response that "the shortest way to Tara was *via* Holyhead" (*P,* 250) – a response that combines the metropolitan artist's desire for exile from a provincial milieu with the Revivalist's desire for mythic authenticity. The irony of his statement is perhaps double-edged, for it suggests either acquiescence in that authenticity, with the proviso that it can be acquired only by traveling the road of exile, or a recognition that Tara is knowable only through the distance afforded by exile.

In a curious way, the diary entries recapitulate the attitudes that we first discover in *Stephen Hero* and that are later modified and consolidated in the more tightly controlled point of view of *A Portrait*. Davin, Yeatsian Revivalism, the language question, the radical Otherness of the peasant, the participant–observer in the West of Ireland – all of these elements reemerge, asserting the irony of Stephen's position as an artist who has attempted to repudiate what the nationalist and Revivalist alike considered most authentically Irish. Though marked by a chronology that suggests the randomness of near-daily recording, the diary entries nevertheless create an effect of free association. For example, Davin's reappearance "at the cigar shop opposite Findlater's church" "in a black sweater [holding] a hurleystick" (*P,* 250) obliquely inscribes an Irish-Ireland ideal of robust peasant vitality. After this passage, Stephen invokes "swirling bogwater" and the "[e]yes of girls among the leaves. Girls demure and romping . . . Houp-la!" (*P,* 250). These images of rural Ireland direct our attention back to the "bat-like soul" of Davin's peasant temptress and E. C., creating a tension between Stephen's own myth-making and the Yeatsian vision of girls romping "among the leaves." Lynch's remark about women remembering the past seems to link these girls to a bygone time and provokes from Stephen an expostulation – "The past is consumed in the present and the present is living only because it brings forth the future" (*P,* 251) – that contextualizes, with its insistence on the primacy and immediacy of the present, his next remark about Yeats's mystical persona, Michael

Robartes, the central character of the stories Stephen had so admired. The remark is a kind of self-criticism, one that revises and restates his opinion of the "incoherent and heterogeneous" rituals (*SH*, 178) that characterize those stories:

Michael Robartes remembers forgotten beauty and, when his arms wrap her round, he presses in his arms the loveliness which has long faded from the world. Not this. Not at all. I desire to press in my arms the loveliness which has not yet come into the world. (*P*, 251)

Any hint of appreciation for the rituals of the Order of the Alchemical Rose is here displaced by a conviction that the Revivalist nostalgia for a beauty that requires redemption in mystical terms is as fruitless as the atavism that he identifies with Davin. But, at the same time, we are drawn back to the remark about Tara and the irony of the statement becomes more pronounced – indeed we wonder whether Stephen is capable of recognizing the ambivalence of his position. If his exile is to lead him to Tara, what then do we make of his desire for "the loveliness which has not yet come into the world"? Assuming that Stephen is not simply dismissing Davin and Tara – though it is tempting to regard his remark as a witticism in which he does not believe – we might conclude that this loveliness refers to the "conscience of his race" that Stephen desires to forge, which is in some ways represented both by the "bat-like soul" and by the mythic image of Tara. We might go further and conclude that what "has not yet come into the world" is in fact a "new original" produced in an autoethnographic conjoining of the Revivalism he rejects and his own "mild proud sovereignty" (*P*, 169).

Though his self-criticism appears still to be unsettled by contradiction and ambivalence, there is also an awareness that they are somehow unavoidable, that they may in fact be necessary for his artistic development. The business of the tundish returns Stephen to the question of language and reminds him with the force of a revelation that his frustration is less with the Gaelic League and its unrealistic agenda for linguistic authenticity than with the dean of studies who reminds him of his own anxiety in the shadow of the English language. "What did he come here for to teach us his own language or to learn it from me? Damn him one way or the other!" (*P*, 251). The point, of course, is that Stephen can neither learn it nor teach it, leaving him bereft of any social authority and of any mode of expression that could authenticate his own experience. His inarticulateness surfaces again in the entry that replays a scene from

Stephen Hero, in which a story is told of country life featuring an old man's wonder at the world beyond his peasant experience. Whereas in the early text this scene is played out in the context of Stephen's "constant observance" of the peasantry, it is now condensed into a vignette of Revivalist ethnography:

John Alphonsus Mulrennan has just returned from the West of Ireland. (European and Asiatic papers please copy.) He told us he met an old man there in a mountain cabin. Old man had red eyes and short pipe. Old man spoke Irish. Mulrennan spoke Irish. Then old man and Mulrennan spoke English. Mulrennan spoke to him about universe and stars. Old man sat, listened, smoked, spat. Then said:

– Ah, there must be terrible queer creatures at the latter end of the world. (*P,* 251)

This new version of the event undergoes a shift in context from the scene at Mullingar, where Stephen enjoyed the story as it was related by an officer, to one that can only be described as textual. The story no longer belongs to Stephen's experience, existing now as a self-conscious parody of Synge's *Aran Islands.* The clipped, telegraphic style of the entry parodies not Synge's style so much as the sovereign position of the participant–observer who uses his knowledge of Irish to establish a rapport with his native informant. Significantly, the old man's statement is rendered free of the dialect that we hear in *Stephen Hero* ("Aw, there must be terrible quare craythurs at the latther ind of the world" [*SH,* 243]), which may indicate Stephen's reluctance to "redeem" the old man's language and thus replicate the ethnographic gesture of Synge's text.

As if to underscore the contrast between Synge's position and his own, Stephen shifts out of a parodic mode and strives to articulate the ambivalent relation of the old man to his own experience. He admits that he fears him and his "redrimmed horny eyes": "It is with him I must struggle all through this night till day come, till he or I lie dead, gripping him by the sinewy throat till . . . Till what? Till he yield to me? No. I mean him no harm" (*P,* 252; Joyce's ellipsis). Though he does not condemn the peasant as monstrous, as he had in *Stephen Hero,* he nevertheless sustains a self-conscious anthropological fiction of the peasant as an opponent in his struggle for self-expression. Perhaps for the first time, Stephen articulates his desire to be free of the primitivist discourse that has tempted him into a Manichean struggle with a native Other. The detachment of the parody, with Mulrennan embodying the ethnographic attitude toward the peasantry, gives way to a personal struggle in which the metropolitan artist grips the old man's "sinewy throat." In this deadly intimacy, Stephen means him no harm; indeed, we are struck with the notion that this struggle is inextricably bound up with his desire to forge the "conscience of his race." The figure of the peasant, no longer trapped in Manichean opposition to him, reminds him of the inescapable fact of his hybridized identity, one that has incurred powerful and half-repudiated debts to Revivalism and its ethnographic imagination. Perhaps Stephen is here struggling with what he will later acknowledge, while walking along Sandy-mount Strand: the presence within him of "jerkined dwarfs, my people, with flayers' knives, running, scaling, hacking in green blubbery whalemeat. Famine, plague and slaughters. Their blood is in me, their lusts my waves" (*U*, 45). Unlike Gabriel Conroy, who regards Michael Furey as an implacable force, an Other that will beset and displace him, Stephen recognizes that the struggle with the old man and later the "jerkined dwarfs" is a fundamental part of his identity that he will not overcome so much as keep free from harm.

As I will show in the next chapter, Stephen has much to overcome, and Joyce is able to further his ends of criticizing Revivalist discourse in part because *Ulysses* allows Stephen to transcend his own limitations. This is partly a function of Joyce's self-reflexive narrative style, a signal feature of his modernism, one that more fully exploits a potential in Synge's *Playboy* and in some of Yeats's late work, specifically the revisionist reconstruction of Yeats's Red Hanrahan, poems like "The Fisherman," and plays like *Purgatory*. The realistic mode of representation that so strongly characterizes Joyce's early fiction and that suggests at certain points an affiliation with an ethnographic mode of representing the Irish peasantry undergoes a thorough revamping in *Ulysses*. This process, especially in the context of Leopold Bloom's ethnographic voyeurism, constitutes a form of immanent critique of both Revivalism and ethnography that is simultaneously a source of new, empowering anthropological fictions. In Joyce's modernism, the production of new fictions is always an opportunity to critique the process of fiction-making. And, in this relation of criticism and production, we find a complement to the tension between the archaic and the modern that characterizes Irish modernism generally.

CHAPTER 6

Joyce's modernism: anthropological fictions in 'Ulysses'

Slumming. The exotic, you see.   James Joyce[1]

James Joyce's modernism has always been something of a problem
for his critics, in part because the stylistic and narrative innovations
of a text like *Ulysses* comports uneasily with cultural attitudes toward
Ireland, nationalism, and race that determine characterization and
theme. Joyce's Irishness, when it is not subordinated to considerations
of style and narrative, frustrates those critics who wish to read his
work in the context of an Anglo-European tradition of modernism
that eschews the local in favor of a pan-historical universalism
typically marked by an emphasis on non-Western modes of religious
transcendence (which we see in T. S. Eliot's *The Wasteland*) or the
kind of "ply-on-ply" historicism that we see in Ezra Pound's *Cantos*
and Virginia Woolf's *Between the Acts*. The most famous attempt to
assimilate Joyce's work to this tradition of modernism, Eliot's review
of Joyce's *Ulysses*, interpreted the Homeric analogies signaled by the
title as evidence of its intention to propound a mythic method that
would order "the immense panorama of futility and anarchy which
is contemporary history."[2] More recent estimations of *Ulysses*,
especially those that focus on the political and cultural dimensions of
Joyce's Dublin, have advanced what we might call a historical
method concerned less with explicating mythic parallels than with
the problems of race, gender, class, colonialism, nationalism, and an
array of related topics. This work has considerably deepened and
complicated our ideas about Joyce's sense of history and culture and
has also refined our sense of what Joyce's modernism is and what it
sets out to accomplish.

As I have argued in the previous chapter, Joyce's early fiction
inaugurates a critique of the anthropological assumptions of the
Revival. This chapter explores the ways that *Ulysses*, by continuing

that critique, elaborates on the anthropological modernism we have already seen at work in Yeats and Synge and in texts like *A Portrait of the Artist as a Young Man*. My intention is not to gainsay other interpretations of Joyce's modernism; instead, I am interested primarily in supplementing those interpretations by considering aspects of Joyce's work that have not often been discussed. If we take seriously the idea put forward by Seamus Deane that Joyce was a Revivalist who alone kept faith with the project of the Revival,[3] then the role of anthropology in *Ulysses* acquires a new significance.

In an essay that explores the concept of "culture" in *Ulysses*, Marc Manganaro notes that "the early years of *Ulysses* criticism were marked by a professional resistance to reading the novel as ethnographically and metonymically mapping and representing a 'culture.'"[4] He goes on to point out that Bronislaw Malinowski's classic ethnography, *Argonauts of the Western Pacific*, was published in 1922, the same year as *Ulysses*, and suggests some affinities between the two texts. He notes that *Ulysses* resembles "in some generic but striking ways the organizational scaffolding of then emergent ethnography" as exemplified by Malinowski's *Argonauts*, the title of which, as Manganaro rightly points out, alludes to the same kind of mythic voyage that Joyce's title suggests.[5] But anyone who has read *Argonauts* will know that this analogy holds only in the most "generic" way, for Malinowski's text exhibits none of the stylistic or narrative experimentation that characterizes Joyce's, and it maintains a scientific decorum in the presentation of ethnographic data that Joyce nowhere attempts. (I might add incidentally that Synge's *Aran Islands* is a better example of a text organized, though much more loosely, along lines similar to *Argonauts*.) Manganaro is more persuasive when he argues that both Joyce and Malinowski invoke the same "master tropes" of culture to "organize and sculpt the massive array of ethnographic detail into the whole that we have come to call 'culture'":

for Malinowski, the *kula* as a comprehensive Trobriand system of trading and traveling that justifies and draws a "cultural" circle around, or makes "functional" in chaptered divisions, the welter of what Malinowski saw the Trobrianders doing; for Joyce, the Odysseus myth itself – so useful to "spatial" readings of the novel – as giving shape, in chronological chaptered form, to the seemingly chaotic ways of a people.[6]

While it is arguable that Joyce sought to give shape to the "ways of a people," Manganaro is right to see that Joyce and Malinowski shared certain assumptions about culture – and Manganaro means by "culture" an array of concepts harking back to Matthew Arnold and E. B. Tylor – and that he was not always as progressive in his invocation of culture as some of his critics have claimed.[7] But the affinities Manganaro points out ought not to obscure the manner in which a text like *Ulysses* critiques elements of the ethnographic attitude toward culture in Malinowski's theoretical work.

By the time *Argonauts of the Western Pacific* was published, the discipline of ethnography had developed an ensemble of normative practices, including long-term immersion in the field, competence in native languages, and methods of collecting and analyzing data governed by scientific principles. And, while Joyce could not have had access to Malinowski's work while he was writing *Ulysses*, he was just as familiar, in a general way, with the elements of ethnography as Yeats and Synge and perhaps for the same reason, since he came to intellectual maturity at a time when the Revival was exerting tremendous influence in the cultural life of Dublin. Like Yeats and Synge, Joyce foregrounded the problems of "doing" ethnography, free as he was from disciplinary constraints, and anticipated some aspects of the revisionist anthropology of recent years. The anthropological modernism of *Ulysses*, then, precisely because it foregrounds what ethnography deemed irrelevant to the scientific accounts of culture, anticipates and instantiates what Terence Turner identifies as a shift "in methodological and political stance from that of the objectively detached 'participant observer' to that of an observing and communicating actor, aware that [the ethnographer's] very activities of observation and communication had become integral parts of the process he was struggling to observe and understand."[8]

Critics of *Ulysses* have by and large ignored the anthropological character of *Ulysses*, just as they have underestimated Joyce's investments in Revivalism. Some studies have treated the figure of Haines in "Telemachus" as a comic symbol of ethnographic authority, while others, like Manganaro and David Spurr, have discussed the influence of anthropological theories of culture on Joyce's work.[9] But few critics have considered *Ulysses* in terms of a critique of the anthropological modernism of the Revival.[10] It is certainly not for the lack of a theoretical model for considering a text that functions auto-ethnographically in a "contact zone" comprising native and metropolitan spheres of social and cultural power and that does so critically, refusing the legitimization of nationalist, colonialist, anthropological, and Revivalist discourses. David Lloyd points us in this direction when he claims that "the processes of hybridization active in the Irish street ballads or in *Ulysses* are at every level recalcitrant to the aesthetic politics of nationalism and, as we can now see, to those of imperialism."[11] In my discussion of *Ulysses*, I will concentrate principally on the ways Revivalist and anthropological discourses contribute to these processes and on how they determine Joyce's texts and his attitudes toward nationalism. It is my belief that, like Synge before him, Joyce in *Ulysses* sought deliberately to provoke his audience into a spontaneous "political education" that would change the terms of the debate on national self-determination and national identity and on the manner of and right to represent both.

If we see the challenge in this way, then the "recalcitrance" of *Ulysses* can be regarded as a persistent refusal to adopt the model of autonomous and sovereign subjectivity presupposed as foundational for the authority of the ethnographic participant–observer and assimilated into Revivalist justifications of their experiential authority. The participant–observer who validates what he or she sees by claiming *I was there* relies on the same sovereign subjectivity that allows the colonialist to distinguish between civilized and primitive peoples. This same subjectivity, troubled by feelings of alienation and deracination, persists in Yeats's and Synge's quests for "personality" just as surely as it asserts itself in the *Bildung*-plot of *Stephen Hero* and *A Portrait of the Artist as a Young Man*, in which the development of a "mild proud sovereignty" resignifies and reinstates the ideal of the subject as autonomous and centered, unified in its relations to others (and, as we have seen, to a primitive Other). Yeats's emphasis on visionary experience (seconded and developed in a scientific register in W. Y. Evans-Wentz's ethnography of fairy-faith, which relies on "reliable seer witnesses") and his and Synge's insistence on their own experience as cultural observers imply the primacy of vision, or visualism, in Revivalist projects of ethnographic redemption. And, as Synge's *re*vision of his own representations of the peasantry attests, a critique of the "hegemony of the visual"[12] would be a crucial element in any critique of Revivalism. In this context, the gaze in *Ulysses*, which has been usefully analyzed by many Joyce critics in Lacanian terms, can be profitably reconsidered in terms of a parodic critique of ethnographic observation. This approach will be especially useful in a consideration of Leopold Bloom's ethnographic voyeurism, a mode of *re*vision (limned in Synge's *Aran Islands* and the preface to *The Playboy of the Western World*) that blurs the distinction between observer and observed and uncovers an erotic valence in participant observation. Bloom's "privatized" anthropological fictions travesty the social authority of the ethnographer's scientific text, undermining, in their evanescent performativity, any potential they might have to serve as "privileged element[s] in the potential store of historical memory" of native peoples.[13] I am not claiming that Bloom's travesty of ethnographic protocol necessarily means that Joyce privileges his experience or his self-representation of it; it is not as if Bloom's superior ability to dodge the responsibilities and limits of subjectivity triumphs over the ethnographer's principled observations. I am claiming, however, that even when he fails to dodge those limits, he creates opportunities for both himself and Joyce's readers to intervene critically into anthropological and Revivalist projects of cultural redemption, correcting or supplanting the misrepresentations that issue from them.

Stephen Dedalus presents us with a different set of problems. Hypereducated, perhaps, and by nature drawn to Revivalism despite his impatience with its mystic essentialism and redemptive desire, he focuses more acutely on the problem of national identity, for he recognizes the critical role of Revivalism in the politics of "inventing souls," in large measure because he feels unrecognized by and unjustly excluded from the Revival. He has a great deal more to overcome than Bloom, given the extent to which he is considered a traitor to the nationalist cause, but his experience nevertheless furthers the kind of "political education" that Fanon prescribes for the development of a revolutionary national consciousness. Bloom, too, educates in his way, but his politics are rather too "anything-arian" (*U,* 490); he proves all too willing to fold nationalist aspirations into generally bourgeois utopian fantasies. In the end, however, it is precisely Bloom's "anythingarianism" that leaves its mark most conspicuously on Joyce's anthropological modernism, because his way of seeing the world is both more capacious and transgressive, if not more critical, than Stephen's. In terms of critical acuity, Stephen's thinking is sharper and more incisive; but, in terms of uncovering the hidden assumptions about Irish culture in Revivalist, nationalist, and colonialist discourses, Bloom manages to create more opportunities for critical intervention on the social processes that determine personal and national identities. Like Synge, he casts a voyeur's gaze on a society with respect to which he feels an outsider; but unlike him he relishes the salacious pleasures of his outsider status, all the while cherishing the dream, as much anthropological as it is phantasmic, that he will find a way to get inside.

It is significant that *Ulysses* begins with an ethnographic encounter. In "Telemachus," Haines, the English friend of Buck Mulligan, tries to collect Stephen's sayings and appears to operate under the Arnoldean conviction of an essential difference between the English and the Irish races. His knowledge of Irish bespeaks not his solidarity with the Irish people but rather his difference from them, a fact that he ratifies in a remark to Stephen about "visit[ing] *your* national library today" (*U*, 15; my emphasis). He betrays an outsider's interest in someone whom he considers to be an exotic insider, saying to Stephen at one point, "I intend to make a collection of your sayings if you will let me . . . That one about the cracked lookingglass of a servant being the symbol of Irish art is deuced good . . . I was just thinking of it when that poor old creature came in" (*U*, 16). As Haines soon discovers, the "poor old creature," the milkwoman, does not know Irish; but, then again, he does not appear to realize, as Stephen and Mulligan clearly do, that her ignorance of Irish does not detract from her status as a symbol of Ireland, a version of the *bean bhean bhocht*, the poor old woman whose avatars include Kathleen ní Houlihan. The reader is let in on the secret through Stephen's interior monologue, in which she is described as "a witch on her toadstool, her wrinkled fingers quick at the squirting dugs" and "[a] wandering crone, lowly form of an immortal serving her conqueror and her gay betrayer, their common cuckquean, a messenger from the secret morning" (*U*, 13–14). She is "silk of the kine and poor old woman, names given her in old times" (*U*, 14) – names which identify her as a sovereignty figure, but a diminished one, a servant of Irish and English masters. Both the milkwoman and Stephen, "the bullockbefriending bard" (*U*, 132), amount to no more than occasionally frustrating curiosities, who "turn[] out not to be as exotic as [Haines] would have hoped."[14] In his unselfconsciously patronizing attitude, we recognize the disappointment of an ethnographer collecting material that fails to satisfy his desire for information that would explain the "mental attitudes" (as Malinowski put it) of a primitive race.

The general effect of critical discussions of Haines has been to isolate the scenes in "Telemachus" and treat them as set-pieces representing imperial attitudes toward the native Irish. For Vincent Cheng, these scenes depict "an ethnographic encounter with a 'native' population, in which the British anthropologist ventures out in the wilderness to study the primitive 'wild Irish' and their folkways, in the presence of a willing native informant (Mulligan) and the latter's semi-willing specimen of study (Stephen)."[15] The analogy drawn here between Haines and the "British anthropologist" seems overdetermined, and this is the problem with any interpretation that finds exact counterparts in a literary text to the individuals involved in an ethnographic encounter. For a crucial factor in Joyce's depiction of Haines is the fact that he is nothing like a "British anthropologist," if by that he means the likes of A. C. Haddon, A. R. Radcliffe-Brown, or Malinowski. Cheng is right about Stephen Dedalus being "a semi-willing specimen," but surely Mulligan is something less than a willing informant.

Enda Duffy advances a similar argument: "In Haines the 'innocuous Hibernophile' *Ulysses* launches in its first pages a scathing indictment of the apparently benevolent ethnographic interest in Irish folk life that was central to the *fin de siècle* Celtic revival."[16] He goes on to associate Haines with both "the never quite successful efforts of British well-wishers like the vicerne to ingratiate themselves with Irish culture, and the local highbrow ethnographers and folklorists of the Celtic revival, of whom Douglas Hyde and Lady Gregory were the outstanding representatives."[17] I would argue, however, that linking Haines to the Celtic Revivalists is misleading, for he and the other "British well-wishers" that Duffy mentions lack any desire to use ethnographic methods to challenge the representations of Irish culture put forward by anthropologists and imperial propagandists. I agree that the depiction of Haines is part of Joyce's indictment of ethnography. But to suggest that the British Haines is indistinguishable from the Revivalists is to gloss over the fact that the latter were, despite their Anglo-Irish background, committed (to varying degrees) to the nationalist cause. Indeed, the Revivalists themselves are objects of Haines's ethnographic curiosity, as is evident when he buys a copy of Hyde's *Love Songs of Connacht* and reappears in "Oxen of the Sun" brandishing "a portfolio full of Celtic literature in one hand, in the other a phial marked poison" (*U*, 412). By glossing over the distinction between Haines and the

Revivalists, Duffy and Cheng suggest that Stephen and Mulligan do not know the difference either.

What we see in "Telemachus" is not simply an "ethnographic encounter" but a performative critique of such an encounter, for Stephen is well aware of how far Haines's clumsy attempts to collect sayings falls short of Revivalist practice. Moreover, the Manichean structure of the encounter between Stephen and Haines is complicated by the presence of Mulligan, who restages Haines's attitude – an essentially colonialist attitude that, according to Bhabha, "produces the colonized as a social reality which is at once an 'other' and yet entirely knowable and visible"[18] – in half-ironic encouragement even while he draws out Stephen's criticisms of that attitude. Though in the end he emerges as the "gay betrayer," Mulligan begins by confusing the lines of distinction that make betrayal possible. By turns championing the cultural values of the civilized collector of native sayings and mocking or conspiring with Stephen to sell him bogus folklore, Mulligan introduces a new level of ambivalence into the ethnographic situation, one that complements Stephen's refusal to play along:

Cracked lookingglass of a servant. Tell that to the oxy chap downstairs and touch him for a guinea. He's stinking with money and thinks you're not a gentleman. His old fellow made his tin by selling jalap to Zulus or some bloody swindle or other. God, Kinch, if you and I could only work together we might do something for the island. Hellenize it. (*U*, 7)

Now here we see a point at which Revivalism does come into play in Joyce's critique of ethnography. The Revivalist desire for authenticity, for "fair equivalents," becomes in Mulligan's scheme, the desire to *forge* authenticity, to pass off Stephen's mordant witticisms as specimens of native culture. Moreover, Stephen's refusal to play along can be regarded as part of his growing critical awareness of the primitivism that led him to transform Madden/Davin and E. C. into idealized icons of "native" Ireland and to seek, in "the smithy of his soul," the "uncreated conscience of his race." It would be more fruitful, then, to regard Stephen and Mulligan not as willing dupes of a callow amateur ethnographer but as native intellectuals more or less aware of the complex ambivalence of their own social position, which resembles in some ways the position of the Anglo-Irish Revivalist.

As Fanon writes, the native intellectual in colonial situations is confronted initially with a choice – become a turncoat or a substantialist:

While the mass of the people maintain intact traditions which are completely different from those of the colonial situation, and the artisanal style solidifies into a formalism which is more and more stereotyped, the intellectual throws himself in frenzied fashion into the frantic acquisition of the culture of the occupying power and takes every opportunity of unfavorably criticizing his own national culture, or else takes refuge in setting out and substantiating the claims of that culture in a way that is passionate but rapidly becomes unproductive.[19]

Stephen's position, as we have seen, is that of an anti-substantialist, having rejected the nativism of Irish-Ireland nationalism with its emphasis on an essential Celtic substance. Mulligan, on the other hand, comically embodies the turncoat, who looks to the colonizer, in Albert Memmi's formulation, as to "a tempting model very close at hand" and who desires to "become equal to that splendid model and to resemble him to the point of disappearing in him."[20] When Stephen remarks that he sees little hope for money from the milkwoman or from Haines, from either Ireland or Britain, Mulligan replies, mockingly: "To tell you the God's truth I think you're right. Damn all else they are good for. Why don't you play them as I do? To hell with them all. Let us get out of the kip" (*U*, 16). Mulligan and Stephen complicate our understanding of the native intellectual, and it is this complication that warrants our attention, not Haines's transparently lame attempt to "do" ethnography.

Simultaneously ironic and clownish, Mulligan mocks the "tempting model" offered up in the figure of Haines. Selling a story to "the oxy chap" reduplicates, at the level of farce, the kind of rapport found in ethnographic situations; he is far from the docile informants upon which Malinowski relies or the "reliable seer witnesses" that Evans-Wentz found among the Irish peasantry and in Revivalist circles. Like Haines, Mulligan regards the Irish peasant as either an exotic or a fool but, in either case, as an object of ridicule. It is worth noting that his scheme to sell Stephen's witticism about the "cracked lookingglass" to Haines, because it will further his desire to "Hellenize" Ireland, reduplicates an Arnoldean distinction between the English and the Irish, although as Manganaro points out, we cannot assume that Mulligan's desire to Hellenize Ireland means that Ireland is not already Hellenized (as Arnold seemed to think) nor that Stephen would likely approve of the attempt.[21] Indeed, as Vincent Pecora argues, when Joyce "playfully manipulated the Hellene–Hebrew dichotomy as the basis of his great mock-epic" –

"Jewgreek is greekjew. Extremes meet" (*U,* 504) – he does so
"because, like many others around him, he accepted on some deep
level the ethnological assumptions it embodied."[22] These assumptions are structured by the kind of binomial opposition that characterizes primitivism and Orientalism, and Joyce's acceptance of
them testifies to their enduring power to determine the way
Europeans talked about culture. In the present context, the invocation of Arnold's culture theory illustrates the tenacity of binomial
structures, even in the anti-colonial discourse of Irish-Ireland nationalists who attribute the "failures" of Irish culture to "the race
diverging during this century from the right path, and ceasing to be
Irish without becoming English."[23] The divided, inconsistent, or
ambivalent position of the native intellectual is obscured by a
Manichean allegory in which Irish nationalism reveals its structural
complicity with colonialism. As I will show in the last section of this
chapter, this Manichean allegory is often invoked in discussions of
Ulysses to account for Joyce's depiction of nationalism.

In the ethnographic farce of "Telemachus," this allegory is
obliquely and ironically inscribed in Stephen's ambivalent reaction
to the "turncoat" Mulligan and the "substantialist" Haines. In
"Nestor" and "Proteus," his ambivalence deepens as he meditates
on race and national identity, spurred by the figure of Cyril Sargent,
the "ugly and futile" (*U,* 27) symbol of an oppressed race. As he
walks along Sandymount strand, Stephen constructs an anthropological fiction in which he imagines his "race" in terms of conquest
and assimilation:

Galleys of the Lochlanns ran here to beach, in quest of prey . . .
Danevikings, torcs of tomahawks aglitter on their breasts when Malachi
wore the collar of gold . . . Then from the starving cagework city a horde
of jerkined dwarfs, my people . . . Their blood is in me, their lusts my
waves. I moved among them on the frozen Liffey, that I, a changeling,
among the spluttering resin fires. (*U,* 45)

The primitivism that Stephen began to work through at the conclusion of *A Portrait*, subsists within this narrative of racial memory, but
the Manichean structure of colonial domination is destabilized by
the metropolitan intellectual's assertion of racial identity with the
"jerkined dwarfs." This destabilization does not eliminate primitivist
distinctions, clearly, but Stephen's refusal to give them pride of place
in this new stage of his racial self-fashioning makes it finally possible
for him to move beyond the redemptive ethnography of the Revival

and to reconsider the wisdom of his goal to forge the uncreated conscience of his race.

One aspect of this reconsideration is Stephen's revision of the feminizing trop of the "bat-like soul" that had governed his conception of Irish womanhood in *A Portrait*. As he walks along the strand, he conjures an image of woman as a vampiric scion of the moon: "tides, myriadislanded, within her, blood not mine, *oinopa ponton*, a winedark sea" (*U*, 47). While this image appears at first to develop the latent potential of the "batlike soul," we are soon struck by the way Stephen resignifies the blood imagery in masculine terms. The image of the "bridebed" shifts effortlessly into a fragment of the Introit of the Requiem Mass ("*Omnis caro ad te veniet*" [All flesh will come to thee]), which superimposes the figure of Christ on the "handmaid of the moon," before settling into an image of male vampiric desire drawn from Hyde's *Love Songs of Connacht*: "He comes, pale vampire, through storm his eyes, his bat sails bloodying the sea, mouth to her mouth's kiss" (*U*, 48). The original, "Mo bhrón ar an bhfarraige" ("Oh, my grief on the sea!"), reads: "And my love came behind me – / He came from the south – / With his breast to my bosom, / His mouth to my mouth."[24] In "Aeolus," Stephen recalls his own adaptation of these lines:

> *On swift sail flaming*
> *From storm and south*
> *He comes, pale vampire,*
> *Mouth to my mouth.*   (*U*, 132)

If his construction of a "batlike soul" implicated him in a practice of Revivalist iconography, in which a binomial primitivism underwrites the feminization of Ireland, his retranslation of Hyde's Revivalist text parodies this practice by reversing its gender polarity. Lloyd writes that Joyce here performs a practice of hybridization that makes folklore available for identity formation: "We may read in the gradual transformation of the folk-song a representation at several levels of the processes of hybridization as they construct individual consciousness."[25] Stephen's construction of himself as a native intellectual takes place in the context of a citational performance in which Hyde's "restored" folk song provides the opportunity for a critique of the Revival's "translational aesthetic."[26] By implicitly criticizing his own "monstrous" batlike version of the female sovereignty figure, he begins to free himself from such practices;

moreover, by incorporating vampire imagery within a reconfigured citation of a Gaelic folk song, Stephen draws attention to the Protestant mysticism or Gothicism latent in the Revivalist project. We find additional support for this in the appearance of Haines in the Gothic style of "Oxen of the Sun," holding the "portfolio full of Celtic literature" which most readers assume to be the copy of Hyde's *Love Songs* he had purchased earlier.

Stephen's intertextual engagement with Hyde anticipates his confrontation, in "Scylla and Charybdis," with the Anglo-Irish Revivalists. Like the ethnographic encounter in the Martello tower, this confrontation is really an extended performance in which normative attitudes about Shakespeare and the cultural authority of the Revival are subjected to citation and parodic resignification. "Scylla and Charybdis" begins with a pastiche of Revivalist motifs: "Cranly's eleven true Wicklowmen to free their sireland. Gap-toothed Kathleen, her four beautiful green fields, the stranger in her house. And one more to hail him: *ave, rabbi*. The Tenahely twelve. In the shadow of the glen he cooees for them. My soul's youth I gave him, night by night. Godspeed. Good hunting" (*U*, 184–5). Drawing mostly from the dramatic work of Yeats and Synge, Stephen conveys his own education in Revivalist mythmaking (linked significantly to his memory of his confessions to Cranly, another "gay betrayer"); but it also establishes the Revivalist context of the Shakespeare discussion that follows. In a sense, the discussion is provoked by the view of art put forward by AE, that most reliable of "seer witnesses": "Art has to reveal to us ideas, formless spiritual essences" (*U*, 185). The self-consciously provocative reading of Shakespeare that follows implicitly critiques the mystic essentialism of what H. L. Platt calls "revivalist romanticism."[27] Stephen's "idea of Hamlet" (*U*, 17) is both audacious and comical, as Mulligan's paraphrase in "Telemachus" indicates: "It's quite simple. He proves by algebra that Hamlet's grandson is Shakespeare's grandfather and that he himself is the ghost of his own father" (*U*, 18). Like Haines earlier, the men in the National Library miss Stephen's point about the "legal fiction" of paternity (*U*, 207) – "The Father and the Son idea." Haines remarks in "Telemachus." "The Son striving to be atoned with the Father" (*U*, 18) – and remain fixed on conventional notions of the relations between fathers and sons. As we discover when Stephen articulates his theory of "autopaternity," quite the opposite is the case. Speaking of Shakespeare's son Hamnet and his relation to the hero of *Hamlet*, he says that "he was not the father of his own son merely but, being no more a son, he was and felt himself the father of all his race, the father of his own grandfather, the father of his unborn grandson" (*U*, 208). It seems to me that Stephen is less interested in advancing a serious theory about Shakespeare than in revamping his own desire, determined, as we have seen, by a primitivist discourse, to create the "conscience of his race."

Stephen's challenge to the edifice of Shakespeare – "Rutland-baconsouthamptonshakespeare" as he calls him – is a challenge to paternalistic Revivalists like John Eglinton and Richard Best who fetishize an English playwright, holding him up as a model for "young Irish bards." Eglinton provides the provocation when he remarks that "[o]ur young Irish bards . . . have yet to create a figure which the world will set beside Saxon Shakespeare's Hamlet" (*U*, 185). When Eglinton quotes George Sigerson, intoning that "[o]ur national epic has yet to be written" (*U*, 192), we are struck with the irony of Stephen's position: the self-styled Hamlet is excluded from the charmed circle of "Irish bards," his artistic authority passed over by Revivalists who heed the call of the Danish Sigerson. When George Moore is suggested "as the man for it," Stephen can scarcely conceal his contempt for a movement that seeks within its own privileged ranks for a "national poet" and that excludes him, the "unclean bard," from their "sheaf of our younger poets' verses" (*U*, 15, 192). The Revivalists do not consider him a viable candidate because his ideas about Shakespeare are a foreign affectation ("a French triangle" [*U*, 213]). If this is the case, the irony of his position deepens, given that Best's chief contribution to Revivalism was a translation of *Le Cycle Mythologique Irlandais* by the French Celticist Marie Henri d'Arbois de Jubainville.

Stephen seeks to distance himself from the paternalism of Revivalist attitudes by parodying those attitudes in an audaciously implausible theory of autopaternity in which the son, rejecting the Father's agency, wills himself as the father of himself. But his overly subtle critique is not accessible to the Revivalists and requires Mulligan's mocking repetition of it. After being informed that the group has been discussing Shakespeare, Mulligan says, "Shakespeare? . . . I seem to know the name . . . To be sure, he said, remembering brightly. The chap that writes like Synge," a remark that provokes Eglinton to wonder why "no-one made [Shakespeare] out to be an Irishman" (*U*, 198). Sensing another opportunity to pillory Revivalists who try to regulate cultural authenticity by championing young Irish poets, Mulligan mimics Synge's peasant dialect, emphasizing the distance between Revivalist representations (which Eglinton, at least, credits as reasonable authorities on the question of "countryfolk" and their "chattels" – that is, "if our peasant plays are true to type" [*U*, 203]) and the authentic voice of the peasant: "It's what I'm telling you, mister honey, it's queer and sick we were, Haines and myself, the time himself brought it in. 'Twas murmur we did for a gallus potion would rouse a friar, I'm thinking, and he limp with leching. And we one hour and two hours and three hours in Connery's sitting civil waiting for pints apiece" (*U*, 199). Stephen's memory of a different Synge, one that he appears to have known in Paris – a "[h]arsh gargoyle face that warred with me over our mess of hash of lights" (*U*, 200) – allows him to distance himself from Mulligan's mockery and the self-importance of Best and Eglinton. But it is a memory closer to home, one that Mulligan sums up with his usual mocking wit, that exposes the violence of Revivalist attitudes toward the native Catholic Irish they seek to redeem: "The tramper Synge is looking for you, [Mulligan] said, to murder you. He heard you pissed on his halldoor in Glasthule. He's out in pampooties to murder you" (*U*, 200). Mulligan is, of course, aware that his own mockery is inauthentic, but it is precisely through its patent inauthenticity that we are able to discern both a scathing critique of Revivalist modes of representing Irish speech and an example of the very "exaggerated" reality that Synge proffered as a means by which to open up the possibilities for more authentic (because hybridized and self-critical) representations.

This, I am suggesting, is the point of Stephen's heretical talk of autopaternity and his psycho-sexual theory of Shakespeare's creative imagination, which are greeted with irritated bemusement by Eglinton, Best, and AE who may not be privy to Stephen's desire to forge a racial conscience. When Eglinton asks, "Do you believe your own theory?" (*U*, 213), he misses the point that it is not a matter of believing in a theory but of revising an attitude. And, while Stephen responds "promptly" (*U* 214) that he does not, it is clear that for him belief is not really the issue. His mock appeal for guidance – "I believe, O Lord, help my unbelief. That is, help me to believe or help me to unbelieve?" (*U*, 214) – exposes the ambivalence at the heart of the biblical authority from which he draws his appeal.[28] On the level of narrative, this discussion of belief pertains to Stephen's theory of Shakespeare; but his theory is not a theory at all but a performance, much like the one we have already seen in "Telemachus" – a performance that calls into question his own authority as an interpreter of Shakespeare. Mulligan again offers a paraphrase that clarifies Stephen's point while simultaneously deflating the Eglinton's and Best's paternalism: "Himself his own father, Sonmulligan told himself. Wait. I am big with child. I have an unborn child in my brain. Pallas Athena! A play! The play's the thing! Let me parturiate" (*U*, 208).

Mulligan's mockery is crucial because it sharpens the point of Stephen's critique of Revivalism. Disdainful and mildly contemptuous, Stephen seeks to assert his Irish identity against mainstream Revivalism, but the subtlety of his approach, which consists in a challenge to Shakespeare (as opposed to Yeats), is lost on his listeners. Mulligan's asides and comic banter bring his friend's criticisms to the surface, but only the reader, who has access to Stephen's interior monologues, can appreciate the counterpoint that Mulligan provides. In this way, Joyce underscores both the complexities and the complicities of native responses to Revivalism. Mulligan's anecdote about Stephen's failure to write a positive review of Lady Gregory's *Cuchulain of Muirthemne*, his most pointed and overt intervention in the novel, both mocks the Revivalists and castigates Stephen for not "play[ing] them as I do" (*U*, 17):

– Longworth is awfully sick, [Mulligan] said, after what you wrote about that old hake Gregory. O you inquisitional drunken jew jesuit! She gets you a job on the paper and then you go and slate her drivel to Jaysus. Couldn't you do the Yeats touch?
 He went on and down, mopping, chanting and waving graceful arms:
– The most beautiful book that has come out of our country in my time. One thinks of Homer. (*U*, 216)

The critical force of Mulligan's anecdote falls squarely on the Revivalists, who are depicted as a coterie with its own methods ("the Yeats touch") and a penchant for self-promotion. But it also falls on Mulligan himself, whose suggestion that Stephen should acquire the "Yeats touch" recalls his attempt in "Telemachus" to "touch [Haines] for a guinea" (*U*, 7). Joyce invites us to contrast Stephen's contempt for Revivalist versions of Irish authenticity with Mulligan's scheme to "forge" authenticity by toeing the Revivalist line. Mulligan may give voice to an incisive critique of Revivalism in this passage, but it is incisive only in the context of Stephen's own oblique and coded attack. In the end, it is Stephen who is able to criticize the Revival without allowing his ambivalence to shade into a kind of mercenary complicity and who is able to maintain an increasingly critical focus on his own investments in Revivalism.

With Bloom, a new mode of critical self-awareness emerges, one that, despite the lack of a sharp focus and a consistent object, aspires to a kind of autoethnographic expressiveness that transforms participant observation into parodic citation and performance. Robert Martin Adams, referring to "Lotus-Eaters," notes that Bloom attends "the performance of a mass where [h]e, as comparative anthropologist, reflects largely on the practice of god-eating in Christianity and elsewhere."[29] Bloom is also, like Stephen, a participant–observer, regarding his fellow Dubliners with an ethnographic detachment and invoking a discourse of primitivism ("Donnybrook fair more in their line," he says, thinking of the Irish inability to play cricket [*U*, 36]) that echoes Arnold's description of the "typical Irishman of Donnybrook Fair."[30] Bloom differs from Stephen primarily in the fictive uses to which he puts his observations. Lacking the frame of reference provided by a university education, his ethnographic imagination ranges over an array of diverse cultures, questioning assumptions about ritual, language, race, and religion in an undisciplined, sometimes confused but often enlightened and even progressive way. Moreover, he is far more successful in tapping the erotic potential of his "constant observance" (*SH*, 244), exploiting the distance necessary for observation in the development of private anthropological fictions.

One possible model for Bloom is the *flâneur* as described by Walter Benjamin, the detached observer of urban life, the happily deracinated European whose stream of consciousness, according to Enda Duffy, "shows itself to be a fresh and fertile ground for the creation of a radically new and independently narrating subject."[31] Like a good many other critics of Joyce, Duffy sees Bloom as an alternative to the Manichean thinking found so often in Revivalism and Irish-Ireland nationalism. Vincent Cheng's formulation is again representative: "What is interesting and distinctive about Bloom . . . (and thus about Joyce in choosing to depict Bloom thus), is his self-conscious and unceasing skepticism and questioning of such constructed images [as those produced by Orientalist discourse], repeatedly both absorbing and problematizing the propagated discourse."[32] According to Emer Nolan, Bloom's experience has been privileged by critics in part because he appears to be free from the influence of Revivalism and in part because this freedom enables him to occupy multiple social positions and to evince a destabilizing "multivocality."[33] To some extent, his voyeurism does permit him to destabilize the conventions of observation that underwrite the redemptive desire of the Revival; but, in other ways, his "constant observance" is determined by colonialist prejudice or the conventions of pulp fiction, so that images like the "blub lips" of Africans and the "opulent curves" of the woman in *Sweets of Sin* (*U*, 80, 236) remind us that an essentially binomial system of racial and gender stereotyping is at work, one that relies on visual evidence of difference. A *new* narrating subject, to be sure, but not an independent one in the sense that he is free from the kind of social and cultural pressures that so strongly determine characters like Stephen and Gabriel Conroy.

It would be useful at this point to consider the significance of visualism in anthropology and ethnography as it has been theorized by the metadiscourse of revisionism. James Clifford has noted that "[t]he predominant metaphors in anthropological research have been participant–observation, data collection, and cultural description, all of which presuppose a standpoint outside – looking at, objectifying, or, somewhat closer, 'reading,' a given reality."[34] This objectifying stance, this "reading" of reality, is beholden to the visual sense, which attains a well-nigh unquestioned authority in ethnographic accounts. Malinowski, for example, insists on the "unquestionable scientific value" of "direct observation."[35] Ethnographers must aspire not only to observe their native subjects but ultimately to appropriate the native's own vision of the world, "to enter into the soul of the savage and through his eyes to look at the outer world and feel ourselves what it must feel to *him* to be himself." This privilege is also granted to the reader of the ethnographic text: "I have tried to present everything as far as possible in terms of concrete fact, letting the natives speak for themselves, perform their transactions, pursue their activities before the reader's mental vision."[36] It is difficult to see how this goal of "grasp[ing] the native's point of view"[37] can allow the natives to speak for themselves, given the ideological commitment to Western science that authorizes it. Indeed, as Johannes Fabian argues, observation becomes problematic precisely when it "designate[s] an *ideological* current in Western thought."[38] Analyzing the problem of observation has led revisionist ethnographers like Stephen Tyler to challenge the "hegemony of the visual," the tendency of ethnography to reduce cultural phenomena to what can be seen. Tyler writes, echoing Fabian:

The hegemony of the visual, among other things: (a) necessitates a reductive ontological correlation between the visual and the verbal; (b) creates a predisposition to think of thinking/knowing as seeing; (c) promotes the notions that structure and process are fundamentally different and that the latter, which is only sequentiality, can always be reduced to the former, which is simultaneity, and thus being dominates becoming, actuality dominates possibility.[39]

Privileging the visual has resulted in a "fabulistic" ethnography that does not recognize itself as such. It posits "a 'doing together' which might include speaking together" but all too often results in a kind of betrayal: the "absence of dialogue signifies the subordination of participating to observing and the use of participation as a deception, as a means of establishing a position from which to observe."[40]

The question naturally arises whether Joyce can mount a critique against the visualist bias of ethnographic discourse if his hero's perspective is voyeuristic. One way of answering this question is to suggest that only by occupying, in a private and unregulated way, the privileged position of ethnographic observer can the native subject overcome "the hegemony of the visual." As Fabian points out, "some visual anthropologists affirm the importance of intersubjective experience of time and explore hermeneutic approaches to visual data."[41] Bloom's voyeurism, deplorable as it may be from the point of view of the moralist, acquires a critical valence when regarded from the point of view of the ethnographer sensitive to his or her own intersubjective experience and the conflicts it may generate whenever it contradicts the scientific principle of direct observation. For Bloom, vision must become *re*vision, in which the ethnographic gaze turns in on itself and contemplates the scientific authority that legitimizes it. In a generalized, abstract way, Stephen engages in just this kind of contemplation when, in "Proteus," he attempts to understand the limits of vision: "Limit of the diaphane in. Why in? Diaphane, adiaphane. If you can put your five fingers through it, it is a gate, if not a door. Shut your eyes and see" (*U*, 37). However much he manipulates his surroundings, however much he plays with the traditional notions of perception – that there is a "real" world out there, that there is only an ideal projection of a world – he nevertheless retains a fundamental binomialism in which the seen and the unseen are forever linked in significant opposition: "Ineluctable modality of the visible: At least that if no more, thought through my eyes. Signatures of all things I am here to read . . . colored signs" (*U*, 37). Though he tests the limits of vision, he never quite breaches them, and he certainly doesn't test the ethnographic situation in this way, though we do get a sense that he understands his own subjection to the "hegemony of the visual" when he acknowledges the futility of what he observes – the tide moving in "[t]o no end gathered: vainly then released" (*U*, 50) – and then turns away "rere regardant" (*U*, 51), half-expecting someone to be observing him.

Bloom is more successful in challenging the conventions of seeing, especially when he fastens on objects not in order to fix them in a representation but rather to circulate them in a purely subjective, phantasmic performance. His ethnographic voyeurism radicalizes the intersubjective experience to which Fabian refers, especially in episodes where mimesis itself is disavowed in a parodic resignification that phenomenologically levels the field, with stereotype and convention, fantasy and reality existing equally as objects in and for Bloom's gaze. But the very "multivocality" for which Bloom is so often praised, his "anythingarianism," undercuts the political significance of his *re*visioning and instates a perspectival ambivalence so openended that he is free to invent attitudes ("I'm as staunch a Britisher as you are, sir" [*U*, 457]) or equivocate (as he does in the famous passage in "Cyclops" on the Irish nation and later in the gender transformations of "Circe"). This inventiveness makes it difficult to discover any kind of ideological consistency; and this lack of consistency means that his attitudes are as often complicit with as they are resistant to the social authorities of colonialism, anthropology, and the Revival. His position, like the Revivalist's and the ethnographer's in the field, is both inside and outside the boundaries of a native culture; but he is also neither inside nor outside these boundaries because his perspective is so thoroughly ambivalent and willfully subjective. His voyeuristic meditations point up the instability of his position, in part by underscoring the subjective and fantastic nature of the point of view it enables, and in part by exploiting the libidinal economy at work in the observational nexus. By exposing the patently subjective, interminably ambivalent condition of participant observation, Bloom's voyeurism critiques the experiential authority at the heart of Revivalist and ethnographic discourse. Bloom's experience is a mimicry of fieldwork that distorts and confuses the distinction between observer and observed precisely by calling into question the possibility of seeing and knowing – and, ultimately of representing – cultural "facts." His "constant observance" expends itself in the field, so to speak; because it functions primarily as a way to gratify immediate sexual desire, there is no need for a written record, least of all a definitive one. We might say that, for Bloom, fieldwork is all in all.

Bloom's illicit observations dramatize, in an exorbitant fashion, the voyeurism latent in the participant–observer's position. In *The Sexual Life of Savages*, Malinowski appears to accept this latent possibility:

We shall follow several of them [the Trobriand Islanders] in their love affairs, and in their marriage arrangements; we shall have to pry into their domestic scandals, and to take an indiscreet interest in their intimate life. For all of them were, during a long period, under ethnographic observation, and I obtained much of my material through their confidences, and especially from their mutual scandal-mongering.[42]

It is significant that this admission should occur in an ethnography of sexual practices, for it suggests that the participant–observer cannot help but recognize the impropriety of his "indiscreet interest," which is justified by the necessity to state "simply and fully, though in a scientific language" the "essential facts of life" and by his confidence that "such a plain statement cannot really offend the most delicately minded nor the most prejudiced reader."[43] Of course, as his field diary indicates, Malinowski could not avoid the temptation to eroticize his "indiscreet interest" in his subjects: the "pretty, finely built" native girl who walks ahead of him, "the slender, agile bodies of little girls in the village," "the perennial whorish expression of the Kiriwina women."[44]

Bloom's voyeuristic meditations would not be out of place in Malinowski's *Diary in the Strict Sense of the Term*. When we first encounter him in "Calypso," he is watching a young woman leaving a shop: "To catch up and walk behind her if he went slowly, behind her moving hams. Pleasant to see first thing in the morning" (*U*, 59). A little later, in "Lotus-Eaters," he sees a woman alighting from an "outsider": "Careless stand of her with her hands in those patch pockets. Like that haughty creature at the polo match. Women all for caste till you touch the spot . . . Possess her once take the starch out of her" (*U*, 72). He is well aware of her social and economic distance from him: "Proud: rich: silk stockings" (*U*, 74). His desire to see, to catch a forbidden glimpse of stocking – we find out later from his wife, Molly, that he is "mad on the subject of drawers" (*U*, 746) – converts a chance encounter into an erotic fantasy. He is tantalized by the very distance he maintains, which has the curious effect of enabling his participation in a milieu from which he would otherwise be excluded. But even this pleasure is forbidden, as his phantasmic participation is forestalled, first by the "talking head" of M'Coy and then decisively by a "heavy tramcar honking its gong" and "slew[ing] between" him and the woman he observes.

At first, the "slewing" of the tramcar appears to cancel his opportunity to gaze: "Lost it. Curse your noisy pugnose. Feels locked out of it. Paradise and the peri. Always happening like that. The very moment" (*U*, 74). However, Bloom's voyeuristic fantasies permit the easy substitution of one object for another, much in the way that native subjects are more or less interchangeable for the ethnographer who studies the relationship between human behavior and social institutions. Because any chance encounter has the potential for fulfilling his sexual needs, he is able to compensate later while gazing, in a rapture of masturbatory desire, at Gerty MacDowell. In "Nausicaa," the observer/observed dyad, crucial to the stability and integrity of a binomial racial distinction, dissolves, and we are confronted with the spectacle of two observers observing each other observing.[45] Like Stephen, Bloom reflects on his own "constant observance," but he does so without the sophisticated philosophical paradigms that steer Stephen into heretical positions that leave the binomial relation of observer/observed in place. In "Proteus," as we have seen, Stephen can hardly bear the prospect of being observed and so pre-empts his own objectification by taking an aloof stance that, like James Duffy's, effectively cordons off a world that seems futile to him. Bloom, on the other hand, is all too willing to break the cord, to become himself an object of desire, to fall into someone else's anthropological fiction. In Stephen Tyler's formulation, he "rejects the ideology of 'observer-observed,' there being nothing observed and no one who is observer,"[46] and by so doing he rejects the "fable of participant observation" that, by subordinating participation to observation, converts participation into a "deception," "a deception, as a means of establishing a position from which to observe."[47]

By drawing our attention to the collapse of the distinction

between observer and observed, "Nausicaa" frames a parodic critique of the participant–observer that fetishizes distance as a space of fantasy and that exploits the eroticism latent in both the observer and the observed. This is one explanation for the bifurcated structure of an episode which offers not only Bloom's overdetermined observation of Gerty but also Gerty's equally overdetermined observation of Bloom, who emerges as a "manly man," a "foreigner" with "dark eyes and . . . pale intellectual face," a face "wan and strangely drawn" which "seemed to her the saddest she had ever seen" (*U*, 357, 356). Of this mysterious stranger – whose "story of sorrow" "[s]he would have given worlds to know" and who "couldn't resist the sight of the wondrous revealment half offered" (*U*, 357, 366) – she knows nothing. However, this does not prevent her from assuming that he is "a manly man" with a "deep passionate nature" "who had not found his ideal"; nor does it prevent her from authenticating her own desires by means of her phantasmic assumptions: "Yes, it was her he was looking at and there was meaning in his look" (*U*, 351, 357). Bloom, for his part, actively avoids "seeing" the essence that would authenticate his experience, self-consciously and spontaneously constructing an image of Gerty: "See her as she is spoil all. Must have the stage setting, the rouge, costume, position, music. The name too. *Amours* of actresses" (*U*, 370). So enthralled is he with his own construction that he assumes Gerty suffers some kind of lack because she cannot see herself as he sees her: "Pity they can't see themselves. A dream of wellfilled hose" (*U*, 368). But in a way she does, since she appears more than willing to conform to cultural stereotypes that refashion her as a conventional image of beauty: "The waxen pallor of her face was almost spiritual in its ivorylike purity though her rosebud mouth was a genuine Cupid's bow, Greekly perfect" (*U*, 348).[48] Her pastiche identity, her voyeuristic gaze, her exhibitionism and her appropriation of binomial typification in the service of her own desire for a "foreigner" whose secret "[s]he would have given worlds to know" (*U*, 357) confound not only our sense of what authenticity might be with respect to Gerty as an Irish woman but also our sense of what it is that Bloom actually sees. Paradoxically, the bivalent perspective of "Nausicaa" destabilizes the binomial structure of visualism by making the positions of observer and observed reversible, leaving no foundation upon which to ground an authentic representation. Like Synge, in the *Aran Islands*, Bloom exposes the erotic and voyeuristic potential of ethnographic observation; but, unlike him, he appears to recognize that this desire for the Other is purely phantasmic, a masturbatory reverie that leads not to a "fair equivalent" of a pious Irish Catholic woman but rather to an "*unfair* equivalent," an anthropological fiction, a "dream of wellfilled hose" (*U,* 368).

Bloom does indeed "ma[k]e up for the tramdriver" (*U,* 368) when he turns his voyeuristic gaze on Gerty, reduplicating the experience with the woman in silk stockings that he missed out on that morning. And clearly he can be indicted for a desire that manifestly and even exorbitantly objectifies women and relegates them to a subordinate status in his shameless, voyeuristic admiration of them in his masturbatory fantasies. But we should bear in mind that he is just as likely to be objectified himself, as we have see in "Nausicaa," or to subordinate himself to an Other. This latter possibility is dramatized in "Circe," where Bloom's power of observation goes into abeyance under the control of Bella/o Cohen ("Powerful being. In my eyes read that slumber which women love"), where observation is reduced to a kind of peep-show voyeurism ("You can apply your eye to the keyhole and play with yourself," Blazes Boylan tells Bloom, "while I just go through her awhile"), where he once again becomes an object of an Other's gaze, most notably when the Nymph, who had been for him an icon of beauty apprehended visually ("Your classic curves, beautiful immortal . . . a thing of beauty"), turns the tables and becomes herself an observer who is compelled to observe ("What have I not seen in that chamber? What must eyes look down on?") (*U,* 528, 539, 546–7). Like Stephen, who disturbs the placidity of binomial racialism in a self-identification that incorporates the "metropolitan youth" into a race of "jerkined dwarfs" (*U,* 45), Bloom disturbs the "hegemony of the visual" in a travesty of the ethnographic encounter. And, while he may lack the discipline and focus that Stephen brings to bear in his critical meditations, the stylistic permutations in episodes like "Circe" grant him a vaster field of opportunities for exercising whatever critical faculty he has.

We see something of this faculty in his desire for the Orient. According to Edward Said, the Orient was, for many Europeans, the source of a variety of images; indeed, it "was almost a European invention, and had been since antiquity a place of romance, exotic beings, haunting memories and landscapes, remarkable experiences."[49] Orientalism relies on a binomial distinction between "us" and "them" in which Europe strengthens its sense of identity "by setting itself off against the Orient as a sort of surrogate and even underground self."[50] Scholarly and anthropological analyses of language, literature, archaeology, and the arts furthered this process by creating "a set of institutions, a latent vocabulary (or a set of enunciative possibilities), a subject matter, and finally . . . subject races."[51] By the turn of the twentieth century, the Orient had come to be regarded by Europe as *the* space of cultural alterity, of sexual or criminal fantasy, of forbidden desires that could only be expressed in the form of Oriental strangeness and exoticism.

Bloom's eroticized fantasies of the East have come in for a good deal of criticism and for good reason, for in the very act of invoking Orientalist images, however critically, as a psychic defense against social conditions, he cannot avoid reduplicating the power relations configured in the opposition ours/theirs. His ethnographic voyeurism flaunts an Orientalist point of view, borrowing images of the East haphazardly found in popular accounts to trick out his desire for Molly and other women, situating them in a vaguely Eastern environment of sensual pleasure and danger, an environment that structures illicit desire: "Slumming. The exotic, you see" (*U*, 443). From the start, Bloom constructs his desire for Molly as part of an Oriental tableau of turbaned faces and dulcimer music:

Walk along a strand, strange land, come to a city gate, sentry there, old ranker too . . . Wander through awned streets. Turbaned faces going by. Dark caves of carpet shops, big man, Turko the terrible, seated crosslegged smoking a coiled pipe . . . The shadows of the mosques along the pillars: priest with a scroll rolled up . . . Night sky moon, violet, colour of Molly's new garters. Strings. Listen. A girl playing one of these instruments what do you call them: dulcimers. I pass. (*U*, 57)

The same binomial typification that led Bloom to imagine Gerty as a desirable exotic ("Hot little devil . . . Wouldn't mind. Curiosity like a nun or a negress or a girl with glasses" [*U*, 368]), leads him to transpose Molly into an eroticized Eastern milieu where her new garters become confounded with the strings of dulcimers.

Nowhere is this transposition more marked than in "Circe," where Molly is imagined as "*a handsome woman in Turkish costume stand[ing] before him. Opulent curves fill out her scarlet trousers and jacket slashed with gold*" (*U*, 439). As if she has known all along about Bloom's Orientalist fantasies, she flaunts her transformation and the power this seems to confer upon her: "So you notice some change?

(*Her hands passing slowly over her trinketed stomacher. A slow friendly mockery in her eyes.*) O Poldy, Poldy, you are a poor old stick in the mud! Go and see life. See the wide world" (*U*, 440). Needless to say, Bloom follows her advice, but only in the privacy of his imagination. When she announces a new creed in a Spanish–Arabic idiom – "Nebrakada! Feminimum!" (Blessed femininity) (*U*, 440) – she heightens the foreign exoticism and strangeness that triggers desire. And, just as Bloom was able to substitute Gerty for the woman in silk stockings, so he can find repetitions of his Orientalized wife wherever he chooses to look. When Bloom addresses the prostitute Zoe, quoting from Thomas Moore's *Lalla Rookh* – "I never loved a dear gazelle but it was sure to . . ." (*U*, 477; Joyce's ellipsis) – she instantly becomes part of an unreal Eastern tableau: "*Gazelles are leaping, feeding on the mountains . . . It burns, the orient, a sky of sapphire, cleft by the bronze flight of eagles. Under it lies the womancity, nude, white, still, cool, in luxury*" (*U*, 477). Bloom's Orientalizing desire constructs Zoe as a feminized Jerusalem ("*womancity*"), linking the sensuality of the Song of Solomon with the mercenary sexuality of the prostitute. But, in the phantasmagoria of "Circe," even an Orientalizing desire becomes aleatory and transgressive. The "rigidly binomial opposition of 'ours' and 'theirs,'" that governs Orientalist discourse, "with the former always encroaching on the latter (even to the point of making 'theirs' exclusively a function of 'ours'),"[52] breaks down, and we are just as likely to see "ours" becoming exclusively a function of "theirs." Because his chief pleasure lies in the immediacy of his fantasy, rather than in affirming the authority of "evaluative interpretations" of "languages, races, types, colors, mentalities" under which Orientalism organizes anthropological knowledge,[53] Bloom is able to appropriate and resignify images of the Other, privatizing a performance which makes use of them in an anthropological fiction that simultaneously posits the object of and gratifies desire.[54]

Bloom's pretensions to scientific knowledge – his "codology" (*U*, 304) – is well known. What I want to emphasize here is the anthropological tenor of that knowledge and his capacity to criticize it. Much of what he knows he acquires through "direct observation," and this is supplemented by the kind of knowledge he absorbs through the media and his haphazard reading. In a sense, he behaves after the fashion of early ethnographers like Haddon, who relied on second- and third-hand information, riddled with primitivist stereotypes; but, unlike them, he is aware that his fantasies feed on the fantasies of other men and is capable of spontaneously, if not always effectively, subjecting his sources to critical scrutiny. Half-informed by popularized anthropology, half-inclined to identity with the Other, Bloom inhabits and mimics both the position of participant–observer and the position of the native subject as the object of knowledge, an ambivalent capacity that throws into question binomial oppositions of ours and theirs, primitive and civilized. "Probably not a bit like it really," he muses, just after his first Orientalist fantasy. "Kind of stuff you read: in the track of the sun" (*U*, 57). "Wonder is it like that," he asks himself later, after imagining the Far East as a "[l]ovely spot," "the garden of the world, big lazy leaves to float about on, cactuses, flowery meads, snaky lianas" (*U*, 70). However, his inability to move beyond merely wondering, beyond merely marking the probability of mis-representation, disables his critical intentions and makes it impossible to sustain analysis.

Bloom's meditation on the Zionist colony Agendath Netaim illustrates the way critical analysis is forestalled. The flyer he had picked up at Dlugacz's butcher shop early in the day advertised shares in an agriculture venture that promised European investors that an exotic landscape could be delivered right to their doors: "Every year you get a sending of the crop. Your name entered for life as owner in the book of the union. Can pay ten down and the balance in yearly instalments." His reflections on the Agendath scheme indicate both his unwillingness to be taken in by it and his attraction to its putative rewards – the "[o]rangegroves and immense melonfields north of Jaffa" – both summed up in the guarded skepticism of his conclusion: "Nothing doing. Still an idea behind it" (*U*, 60). When he returns to the idea in "Lestrygonians," while pausing at the window of a silk mercers shop, Agendath Netaim takes its place in an Orientalist fantasy of sensual hunger:

High voices. Sunwarm silk. Jingling harnesses. All for a woman, home and houses, silk webs, silver, rich fruits, spicy from Jaffa. Agendath Netaim. Wealth of the world. A warm human plumpness settled down on his brain. His brain yielded. Perfume of embraces all him assailed. With hungered flesh obscurely, he mutely craved to adore. (*U*, 168)

Bloom's phantasmic meditation reappropriates images that had assailed him earlier in the day and generates within him a fleshy, hungry craving, an adoration that intoxicates him. In yielding to images that settle with a "warm human plumpness" into his consciousness, he substitutes an Orientalist fantasy for an all-too-real colonialist scheme. But any skepticism about the "idea" behind the scheme is overwhelmed by the thrill of imaginative participation in an imaginary tableau that saturates all sensation. He has in fact gotten the idea behind it, in a typically oblique and half-witting fashion, for his erotic appropriation of Orientalist imagery has the ironic effect of reproducing him as a kind of colonialist whose hegemonic fantasy reaps the "wealth of the world."

Bloom's consideration of missionaries in Africa further illustrates the limitations of a critical curiosity that seeks private rather than public expression. His meditation is provoked, appropriately, by a piece of textual flotsam, a notice on the backdoor of All Hallows church: "Sermon by the very reverend John Conmee S. J. on saint Peter Claver and the African mission. Save China's millions. Wonder how they explain it to the heathen Chinee. Prefer an ounce of opium" (*U*, 80). Bloom understands that religious conversion is connected intimately with imperial politics, a connection suggested by the pun on Gladstone's "conversion" to Parnell's Home Rule platform (*U*, 80). Moreover, he understands instinctively that the "big idea" behind the sacraments is connected, by a kind of anthropological cunning on the part of missionaries, to the practices of primitive people: "rum idea: eating bits of a corpse why the cannibals cotton to it" (*U*, 80). Indeed, he seems to discern a certain ecclesiastical calculation in the use of the sacrament of communion: "There's a big idea behind it, kind of kingdom of God is within you feel . . . Wonderful organization certainly, goes like clockwork . . . The doctors of the church: they mapped out the whole theology of it" (*U*, 81–3). But, despite his critical intervention, his understanding remains structured by the anthropological view of primitive people as passive, childlike, and easily duped. He calls to mind a "still life," in which white missionaries confront African natives in a parody of the ethnographic narrative of arrival: "He's not going out in bluey specs with the sweat rolling off him to baptise blacks, is he? The glasses would take their fancy, flashing. Like to see them sitting round in a ring with blub lips, entranced, listening. Still life. Lap it up like milk, I suppose" (*U*, 79).

To some extent, Bloom shares the ambivalent faith in a cultural ideal that we see in Marlow, the colonial explorer of Conrad's *Heart of Darkness*, who recognizes both the horror and the logic of an "imperial" idea:

"The conquest of the earth, which mostly means the taking it away from those who have a different complexion or slightly flatter noses than ourselves, is not a pretty thing when you look into it too much. What redeems it is the idea only. An idea at the back of it; not a sentimental pretense but an idea; and an unselfish belief in the idea – something you can set up, and bow down before, and offer a sacrifice to."[55]

Like Marlow, Bloom understands that an idea is an abstraction embodied in symbolic structures that exist purely to legitimate it. And, like Marlow, he is ambivalent about the nature of that legitimation primarily because he is ambivalent about the idea itself. But he is not interested in redemption or sacrifice, or, if he is, he is interested less in the idea behind them than in the rituals that play them out. His interest in the Latin liturgy – "Good idea the Latin. Stupifies them first" (*U*, 80) – resembles the ethnographer's interest in the structure of rituals. Like a good functionalist ethnographer, Bloom infers from the ritual specific social attitudes that may be obscure to the participants. And, like a good comparativist, he considers the rituals of the Catholic Church with the same easy equanimity that he considers the "savage" custom of cannibalism ("They don't seem to chew it; only swallow it down" [*U*, 80]), unaware that he may have challenged the "idea" behind the sacraments as he scrutinizes, with ethnographic zeal, the analogies between two cultural practices. That we have our doubts about him in the end, that we find his desires ambivalent and unsettling, can be attributed to a dehiscence in his social identity, a site of perpetual splitting where Orientalist and primitivist images coalesce briefly into fantasies that lack a coherent or stable ideological frame of reference.

One way of accounting for this lack is to recognize that Bloom's fantasies are self-regulating and self-validating anthropological fictions which submit ethnographic data (observed and borrowed) to a resignifying economy governed primarily by libidinal impulses. If there is an ideological commitment in this, it is to "anything-arianism," a worldview in which the desire for the Other frees itself from the institutional disdain that represses it and circulates anarchically in an undisciplined ethnographic imagination. And, while his fantasies fail to critique the discourses of primitivism and Orientalism in any sustained or incisive fashion, they nevertheless lend to Joyce's anthropological modernism a *frisson* of transgressive productivity. In this regard, we see something similar to the process already discussed with respect to Stephen's attitude toward primitivism – that is, Bloom's appropriation of discourses that deconstruct authenticity and essence, even while it implicates him in anthropological and colonialist attitudes, is sufficiently ambivalent to raise the possibility of a more thoroughgoing destabilization of those attitudes at the level of a metacommentary where Joyce invites his readers to engage in their own critical interventions. Having dissolved the observer/observed dyad in phantasmic performances that call the structure and ethics of observation into question, having broached a critical analysis of the "big ideas" behind colonialist and anthropological adventures, Bloom's ambivalent point of view yields a new set of values: a frank and sensual curiosity together with a self-consciousness of his own production of fantasy, a willingness to consider multiple perspectives and some capacity to criticize what he sees and what he desires. This point of view acquires its power initially from Bloom's position in Irish society – a "native" who comports himself like an outsider – and the specific contexts in which Joyce represents the ambivalence of that position. Like Synge's *Playboy*, the critical power of Joyce's representation of Bloom lies in an exorbitant *in*authenticity; Joyce offers his readers extravagant misrepresentations that do not guarantee the truth of any social reality but instead afford an opportunity for public debate on the nature of those realities and on the right to represent of them.

If Bloom's voyeuristic and Orientalist fantasies reveal the dangers of privatized anthropological fictions, his confrontation with the nationalists in "Cyclops" reveals an even greater danger, for in Barney Kiernan's pub his private fictions are articulated in a context that is determined by the public rhetoric of nationalism. As an abstemious, thrice-baptized Irishman of Hungarian Jewish descent, Bloom is an outsider who nevertheless tries very hard to situate himself within a Catholic nationalist milieu. The men in the pub, particularly the narrator, perceive Bloom as an outsider speaking an alien tongue: "argol bargol" (*U*, 336). The narrator reveals his *ressentiment* whenever he paraphrases Bloom's comments: "Bloom comes out with the why and the wherefore and all the codology of the business" and "starts with his jawbreakers about phenomenon and science and this phenomenon and the other phenomenon" (*U*, 304). His desire to know and understand the world in which he lives without insisting that everyone agree with his point of view contrasts sharply with the xenophobic nativism of those who, like the narrator and the citizen, appear to resent any sign of difference. Bloom's presence is construed as an affront, in part because it appears to privilege cultural difference over racial homogeneity, but also because his appeal to reason and universal love appears to the citizen and his cronies as frivolous. But there is also the ethnographic distance he maintains, which means that the "argol bargol" and "codology" that Bloom is thought to speak might reflect a nativist contempt for an outsider who attempts to explain them to themselves.

Ironically, by constructing Bloom as racially and sexually Other with respect to themselves, the men in the pub reveal an even greater commitment than Bloom to the primitivist discourses of their colonial and anthropological oppressors. Unable to be fixed securely within such discourses – "Is he a jew or a gentile or a holy roman or a swaddler or what the hell is he?" asks Ned Lambert (*U*, 337) – Bloom floats about the margins of the group like a wandering "perverted jew" or a "bloody dark horse" (*U*, 337, 335), his hybridized racial identity posing a threat that no one quite understands well enough to take seriously. The citizen's sense of Bloom as an outsider is further frustrated when John Wyse Nolan and Martin Cunningham confirm that he had a hand in the formation of Sinn Fein. The citizen's persistent refusal to respond to this confirmation and his tendency to veer into *ad hominem* attack (see *U*, 335ff.) reflect his anxiety that the "purity" of nationalism could be eroded from within by hybrid insiders who are also simultaneously and utterly outsiders. All the more reason that Bloom's conception of the nation be ridiculed, for, in claiming Ireland as his nation and himself as an Irishman, he contradicts what the citizen and his cronies believe to be the racial essence of the Irish nation. When asked by John Wyse Nolan, "What is it?" Bloom responds "A nation? . . . A nation is the same people living in the same place" (*U*, 331), which provokes a round of witticisms and laughter. "Ireland," he clarifies. "I was born here. Ireland" (*U*, 331) – as if by merely asserting the site of his birth he can obliterate his Otherness and guarantee his place in a nation that exists for all who are born or live in it.

Bloom is infuriatingly naive, to be sure, but what really escalates the hostilities and alienates him from the conversation is his appeal to race – "I belong to a race to," he says, "that is hated and persecuted. Also now. This very moment. This very instant" (*U*, 332) – and the universal triumph of love over "[f]orce, hatred, history, all that" (*U*, 333). The citizen and his cronies find Bloom's "anythingarianism" altogether too much to take, and the episode devolves into recrimination and, ultimately, violence directed at Bloom. Until the publication of Emer Nolan's *James Joyce and Nationalism*, interpretations of the cultural politics implicit in these reactions to Bloom tended to reiterate Joyce's antipathy to nationalism and to hail Bloom and his "anythingarianism" as a liberating alternative to a xenophobic nativism that seemed at times just as racist and intolerant as the colonialist disavowal of the native. Nolan traces this tendency to the influential work of Richard Ellmann and Dominic Manganiello. "These critics' attempt to make sense of what they interpret as Joyce's 'moderate' nationalism avails itself of the fact that there are generally believed to be two traditions in Irish nationalist history: the extremist and radical 'physical force' tradition and the reasonable, constitutional one."[56] In such an interpretation, the citizen's Irish-Ireland nationalism merely replicates the hegemonic desire of imperialism:

Where are our missing twenty millions of Irish should be here today instead of four, our lost tribes? And our potteries and textiles, the finest in the world! And our wool that was sold in Rome in the time of Juvenal and our flax and our damask from the looms of Antrim and our Limerick lace, our tanneries and our white flint glass down there by Ballybough and our Huguenot poplin that we have since Jacquard de Lyon and our woven silk and our Foxford tweeds and ivory raised point from the Carmelite convent in New Ross, nothing like it in the whole wide world! (*U*, 326)

The citizen expresses in an exorbitant style the same nostalgia for Ireland's national integrity that led Young Irelanders like Sir Charles Gavan Duffy to recall the successes of "small nations." "It is too true that our population is still diminishing," Duffy writes. "[G]enerations must perhaps pass before it regains the maximum it had reached fifty years ago; but let not that disastrous fact discourage us overmuch. It is not by the number, but by the intrinsic value of its men and women that a country becomes powerful and memorable. The true admeasurement, as we may learn from the inspiring story of small nations, is not geometrical but metaphysical."[57] But what in the eloquent address of Duffy, pillar of mainstream cultural nationalism, sounds like a noble expectation – that the Irish might return to a prior nobility and richness of resource and industry – in the citizen's Anglophobic rants sounds like an ignoble threat: "We'll put force against force, says the citizen. We have our greater Ireland beyond the sea" (*U*, 329).

As the "sinewyarmed hero" he becomes in one of the interpolated parodies of "Cyclops," the citizen makes audacious hegemonic claims on the world:

From his girdle hung a row of seastones . . . and on these were graven with rude yet striking art the tribal images of many Irish heroes and heroines of antiquity, Cuchullin, Conn of hundred battles, Niall of nine hostages, Brian of Kincora . . . Red Hugh O'Donnell . . . Goliath . . . the Village Blacksmith . . . Dante Alighieri . . . Patrick W. Shakespeare . . . Brian Confucius, Murtagh Gutenberg. . . Ludwig Beethoven, Adam and Eve . . . Herodotus . . . Gautama Buddha . . . (*U*, 296–7)

And the list goes on. The absurdity of the citizen's cultural hegemony is in part what Bloom (and to some extent J. J. O'Molloy) inadvertently reveals to the men about themselves: that their hatred of the English is trapped in a Manichean rhetoric and frame of reference. "Their syphilisation, you mean," the citizen says, responding to Bloom's and J. J. O'Molloy's "moderation and botheration" concerning English colonies and civilization. "To hell with them! The curse of a goodfornothing God light sideways on the bloody thicklugged sons of whores' gets! No music and no art and no literature worthy of the name. Any civilization they have they stole from us. Tonguetied sons of bastards' ghosts" (*U*, 325).

The condemnation of English "syphilisation" and the assertion of the superiority of pre-colonial Ireland is a version of what R. F. Foster calls "therapeutic Anglophobia," a display of rhetoric that masks political impotence.[58] For many Joyce critics, this impotence manifests itself in more than just rhetoric, however, seeing it in terms of a dangerous and ideologically suspect inversion of the racialism and violent disavowal characteristic of colonial discourse. In this reading, the citizen counters Bloom's "anythingarianism" with a rousing defense of the Irish nation and its patriots, simply inverting colonialist stereotyping. "As an ideology," writes Enda Duffy, "a force by which the subject is convinced of the naturalness of her position, nationalism, despite its role as vehicle of the new state, turns out invariably to have been always already a discourse of the former imperial culture, the very culture it would overcome."[59] By failing to conform to a type – he is neither a nationalist nor an informer nor an Anglo-Irishman nor an Englishman – Bloom reminds us that the binomial categories of nationalist/colonialist and native/metropolitan are themselves far from stable – indeed, they are constantly in danger of collapsing under the pressure of exceptions. In a similar way, he reminds us of the limits and dangers of ethnographic observation, even "from the inside." Without being aware that he is doing it, Bloom duplicates parodically the position of the participant–observer; he stands aloof from a native culture in which he belongs by right of birth and citizenship but from which he is estranged by virtue of religious and ethnic difference. His unwitting refusal to enter into the drinking culture of the pub marks him as a detached observer of the community rather than a native participant in it. It would not be unreasonable to imagine these men regarding Bloom's attempts at participation – even his bungled attempts at building rapport – as calculated solely to obtain a better vantage point from which to observe. We recognize here, albeit in an exaggerated form, not only the ambivalent position of the participant–observer, but also the characteristic stance of the Anglo-Irish Revivalist. Bloom's ethnic and religious differences from the citizen and his cronies put him in a position quite similar to that of the Revivalist, though the questions he raises among them are posed in a context of belligerence quite unlike the genteel antagonism Stephen experiences with the Anglo-Irish intelligentsia at the National Library. And, more important, while the Revivalists could claim that they were part of a larger social unity based on a long history of inhabitation and cultural contribution and were thus an integral part of the Irish nation, Bloom cannot make the same claim, given his Jewish and Hungarian background and the relatively recent arrival of his family in Ireland. It is this radical difference that leads him by way of compensation to conceive such grand, utopian visions of unity – "Union of all, jew, moslem and gentile . . . No more patriotism of barspongers and dropsical impostors. Free money, free love and a free lay church in a free lay state" (*U*, 489–90) – which are viciously parodied in "Cyclops" and with hallucinatory fervor in "Circe."

Following Emer Nolan, I do not think Joyce wished to suggest that Bloom's "anythingarianism" is preferable to the citizen's Irish-Ireland rants. In depicting Bloom and the citizen, he does not stage a Manichean endgame between nativist and the hybrid outsider in which the latter wins, in part because both rely to some degree on the binomial cultural oppositions embedded in colonial and anthropological discourses. The important question is whether nationalism, for Joyce, is irretrievably nullified by its structural similarities to colonialism. If the depiction of the citizen unveils this similarity, it does so not to invalidate nationalist aspirations as such, but rather to suggest the complacency and complicity of mainstream Revivalists like Yeats and Synge and of the "official" Irish-Ireland nationalism of Duffy, Sigerson, and Hyde. For, stripped of the "therapeutic Anglophobia" that characterizes his rants, the citizen's nationalist views are far from unreasonable, at least from a republican standpoint.

As I indicated at the beginning of this chapter, it has been until recently a critical commonplace that Joyce refused to associate himself with those nationalists who championed the revival of the Irish language and quintessentially Irish athletic events. In a similar way, critics have argued that he repudiated the fraudulent essentialism of extremists who justified violence in the name of cultural and racial purity. But, while Joyce deplored the violence of "physical force" nationalism, he did in fact approve of some Sinn Fein policies, especially economic autonomy, which he foresaw as the only way for Ireland to assert its independence.[60] Nolan's revisionist reading of Joyce's politics goes farther, claiming that in some cases the citizen's political attitudes may in fact be Joyce's:

For the moment, the observation that in some respects the views of Joyce and of the citizen may actually *coincide*, and the very fact that this has not been previously indicated, merely serves to illustrate further the inequality between extraordinarily generous critical estimations of Bloom and typical accounts of the citizen.[61]

The idea that Joyce's nationalism might exceed the "moderate" limits outlined by critics like Dominic Manganiello, Richard Ellmann, and Malcolm Browne, or that he might be sympathetic toward the citizen's views, modifies our understanding not only of Joyce's politics, but also of Bloom as the triumphant "hero" of "Cyclops," the persecuted "ben Bloom Elijah" who tears away in Martin Cunningham's carriage "like a shot off a shovel" (*U*, 345).

The issue, then, is not Joyce's repudiation of the aspirations of extreme Irish-Ireland nationalism and "hard men" like the citizen, but rather his recognition that these aspirations are doubly distorted, first by the hidden anthropological assumptions of mainstream nationalism and second by the rhetoric of hatred that seeks to radicalize that mainstream. It is significant that Joyce's exposé of the citizen's hatred and Bloom's unpredictable and ultimately inassimilable responses take place in the context of interpolated stylistic travesties of the Revival's ethnographic imagination. In "Cyclops," a capacious and mimic style reflects an anthropological modernism in which the redemptive, romanticizing strategies of Revivalist and nationalist alike are farcically reduplicated in exorbitant overstatements, gratuitous descriptions, and parodies that point up the failure of the Revivalists and other mainstream cultural nationalists to make credible representations of the Irish people and their political aspirations. Joyce targets second- and third-rate writers under the influence of Yeats's Celtic Twilight, writers who resemble Little Chandler who wants nothing more than to cash in on the success of "the Celtic school by reason of the melancholy tone" of the poems he has not yet written (*D*, 74). Throughout "Cyclops," Joyce parodies the Revivalist stereotypes of picturesque Ireland, particularly nineteenth-century translations (or versions) of Irish poetry, myth, and legend, that romanticized the plenitude of the Irish landscape: "A pleasant land it is in sooth of murmuring waters, fishful streams where sport the gunnard, the plaice, the roach, the halibut, the gibbed haddock, the grilse, the dab, the brill, the flounder, the mixed coarse fish generally" (*U*, 293–4).[62] Ironically, passages like these, according to Maria Tymoczko, place Joyce in the tradition of the Irish *senchaid*, "a 'reciter of lore, a historian' and later 'storyteller' . . . responsible both for providing entertainment and for safeguarding the knowledge of the tribe."[63] She goes on to conclude that "Joyce's fondness for lists and catalogues is therefore another feature linking *Ulysses* and the Irish narrative tradition."[64]

What Tymoczko misses is any sense that Joyce might be calling into question not the tradition itself, for which he had a great deal of respect, but rather its deployment by British and Anglo-Irish writers who, like nineteenth-century amateur anthropologists, contributed to and validated stereotypes of the Irish. But Joyce also targets "native" Irish orators like Dan Dawson, whose "picturesque" rhetoric, read and ridiculed in the "Aeolus" chapter of *Ulysses*, praises Ireland as *"unmatched . . . for very beauty, of bosky grove and undulating plain and luscious pastureland of vernal green, steeped in the transcendent translucent glow of our mild mysterious Irish twilight"* (*U*, 125). Particularly illuminating in this regard is the rather exorbitant title of a "native" text that appears to have adopted uncritically the persona of the "stage Irishman": *Real Life in Ireland: or, The day and night scenes, rovings, rambles, and sprees, bulls, blunders, bodderation and blarney, of Brian Boru, esq., and his elegant friend Sir Shawn O'Dogherty; exhibiting a real picture of the characters, manners, etc., in high and low life in Dublin and various parts of Ireland, embellished with humorous coloured engravings, from original designs by the most eminent artists / by a real Paddy.* It is fitting that this text was published in the same year (1904) in which Joyce set the events of *Ulysses* and represents in its own way a comic Odyssey in which the native tries on the stereotypes created by colonialism and anthropology, with his tongue in his cheek, perhaps, but with no apparent intention of undermining the basis of such stereotyping. Joyce's critical practice of juxtaposing inauthentic representations of Ireland with the citizen's nativist rants underscores the distance between "picturesque" misrepresentations and the harsh realities of modern Irish life – its poverty, its urban decay, its declining agriculture and industry, its social and political impotence.

As Fanon notes, it is in the colonialists' interest to sponsor stereotypical representations and to defend them as evidence of an authentic "native style."[65] Joyce attacks this false authenticity and holds up for censure the tendency of both Revivalists and nationalists to offer fictive representations of Irish culture that are not recognized as such. Though we may agree with Nolan that Joyce's politics are to some degree reflected in the citizen's discourse, it is also the case that he subjects that discourse to the same ironizing critique that so ruthlessly parodies the style of Revivalist Celticism:

From shoulder to shoulder he measured several ells and his rocklike mountainous knees were covered . . . with a strong growth of tawny prickly hair in hue and toughness similar to the mountain gorse (*Ulex Europeus*) . . . A powerful current of warm breath issued at regular intervals from the profound cavity of his mouth while in rhythmic resonance the loud strong hale reverberations of his formidable heart thundered rumblingly causing the ground, the summit of the lofty tower and the still loftier walls of the cave to vibrate and tremble. (*U*, 296)

This inauthentic "version" of the citizen is radically ambivalent in much the same way as Synge's Christy Mahon, for the citizen is simultaneously held up as a traditional Irish hero and reduced to a textual instance in Joyce's exaggerated parody. It is ironic that in both senses, as Tymoczko argues, such passages "reflect[] the formal qualities of Irish prose quite well; at the same time Joyce's exuberance, generally read as parody, can be seen as transposing the fun-loving qualities of the Irish adjectival style."[66] To the degree that Joyce "revives" traditional material in episodes like "Cyclops," we might say that he functions in ways similar to Yeats, Lady Gregory, Douglas Hyde, and other Revivalists. Where he differs is in his use of an exorbitant, parodic mode of representation that calls into question Revivalist projects of cultural redemption, which, as we have seen, rely to varying degrees on a mode of ethnographic realism. Joyce appears to address this question directly in his depiction of the citizen's dog, Garryowen, which is transformed into the poet Owen Garry, whose verse "bears a *striking* resemblance (the italics are ours) to the ranns of ancient Celtic bards" (*U*, 312). References to "Little Sweet Branch" (*An Craoibhin Aoibhinn*, Hyde's pen name) and "a more modern lyricist at present very much in the public eye" (perhaps Yeats) clearly indicate that the target here is not so much the citizen as the Revivalists who make folk culture into commodities for a metropolitan market. Like the "sinewyarmed hero," who reclaims all of the great figures of the world, as if they originated in Ireland and were stolen by other cultures, Owen Garry, with his bardic "curse" ("*The curse of my curses / Seven days every day / And seven dry Thursdays / On you, Barney Kiernan*" [*U*, 312]) travesties the picture of the Irish native constructed by Revivalism.

The citizen's chauvinistic ranting, far from reflecting Joyce's absolute intolerance for political extremism, may in fact be a sign of frustration with Revivalist representations, for his views, stripped of their extravagant rhetoric, reflect the economic and political (that is to say, the *material*) causes of Ireland's diminished status. If the citizen desires the kind of "small nation" to which Sir Charles Gavan Duffy alludes, he wants it on strictly Irish terms. But this raises the question of authenticity once again, for what exactly are the "Irish terms" upon which the citizen so strongly insists? Is it possible to discover these terms without succumbing to the Scylla of colonial discourse or the Charybdis of Anglo-Irish Revivalism? Here, I think, we can argue that Bloom issues a challenge to the binomial structure of cultural stereotyping by modeling hybrid national identities in fantasies that constitute a kind of performative autoethnography, the coming into being of a "narrating subject" in a contact zone on the shifting border between native insider and hybridized outsider, between nationalist rhetoric and anthropological fictions.

However, as we have seen, the critical value of this autoethnographic expressiveness is vitiated substantially by a voyeuristic desire that privatizes critique within aleatory fantasies and leaves little room for the creation of a *public* discourse that would address a credible future for Irish nationalism. Where are we to find such a discourse? I submit that we find it in Joyce's *will to style*, which opens up new possibilities – mediated by stylistic and narrative experimentalism, perspectivism, and "multivocality" – for developing new models of the native subject who rejects claims to authenticity based on the "fair equivalence" of an essence and embraces a deliberate *in*authenticity based in a self-critical production of anthropological fictions – *un*fair equivalents, as it were – that acknowledge the lack of essence, or at least the impossibility of representing it.

Nolan's conclusion is instructive, for it suggests that Joyce's modernism is inseparable from the kinds of questions I believe are central to the ethnographic imagination of the Revival:

At the simplest level, it is they [the men in Barney Kiernan's], after all, who make jokes, talk excessively and compose their own parodies: in their more global interests in imperialism and in politics they actually transcend the narrow focus of the novel itself on the Irish situation. Their very words bear the mark of their colonial experiences, and expose the grounding of the modernist textual experiments in a specific and brutally material history. We can see that Bloom does not bring "multivocality" to the scene, but that this is already there, produced by the colonial situation itself, but for the moment locked into that situation.[67]

Bloom's "multivocality" may comport well with Joyce's modernism, but that does not mean that we must therefore consign the citizen to the dust-heap of the "monological" and the "anti-modern." Neither is Ireland merely a local backdrop for local concerns. The importance for Nolan of a "high" modernist like Ezra Pound stems from his ability to move beyond this primitivist assumption and to express an "insistent belief that Joyce's critical assessment of the metropolis is *mediated through* his representation of Ireland. Whatever Pound's view of this critique, what matters is his assumption that Joyce's modernism is at loggerheads with modernity, as well as with provincial resistance to it."[68] Where Joyce finds fault with the Revival and Irish-Ireland nationalism is not in their complicity with a redemptive ethnography, but rather in their failure to transform this complicity, as Synge had done in *The Playboy of the Western World*, into a critical intervention into the practice of cultural representation. It is a failure, in Fanonist terms, to write a "fighting literature, a revolutionary literature, and a national literature" that "introduce[s] into [its] readers' or hearers' consciousness the terrible ferment of subversion."[69] To the extent that Revivalism and nationalism contribute to this failure by becoming bogged down in the romanticism of cultural redemption, they merely repeat, uncritically, the discourses of anthropological and colonial domination.

I would like to close this chapter by returning to my comparison of Bloom and Stephen and to emphasize the limits and potential of Joyce's anthropological modernism. We have seen how Bloom's ethnographic voyeurism destabilizes the binomial categories of observer/observed and primitive/civilized; however, the moment of decisive critique is forestalled in purely subjective responses that fail to consider the implications of such destabilizing gestures for the national struggle. We have also seen how "Cyclops" recontextualizes his "anythingarianism" and his private, aleatory practice of "constant observance" and makes it available, through Joyce's parodic and stylistic metacommentary, for a public critique of Revivalism and its redemptive vision of Irish culture. By refusing to occupy a single vantage point or perspective, Bloom is able to enjoy multiple fantasies of identity that resignify and revalue his hybridized colonial subjectivity. Stephen accomplishes much the same thing through a performative critique of the Revival, but his rhetorical and intellectual subtlety together with an unbearable contempt for his interlocutors disallow an overt articulation of his concerns. On the other hand, his meditations on Revivalism and primitivism tend generally to be more sustained and disciplined, thus opening up levels of critique that are unavailable to Bloom. An upstart native, Stephen resembles the frustrated militant who, in Fanon's words, "champs on his bit," dissatisfied with ineffectual leaders, left to wonder "whether the wind of history couldn't be a little more clearly analyzed."[70] If we find neither Bloom nor Stephen satisfactory as models for the native intellectual, if we suspect that their experience reflects a residual investment in ethnographic and Revivalist methods and practices, we do so because Joyce's "scrupulous meanness" makes available a rigorous exposé of the kinds of "inauthentic" discourses that assail them; but this same exposé affords new opportunities for critical intervention in the public debates on the future of the Irish nation and Irish national identities and on the nature of and right to represent them. And if we are willing to accept the representation of inauthenticity as itself authentic, as pointing toward the kind of "political education" Fanon talks about, we do so because Joyce's ironic recontextualization and stylistic metacommentary resignifies Bloom's and Stephen's experiences as part of a general critique of the effects of anthropological and Revivalist discourses on the formation of national identities.

By taking to task the very procedures that the Revivalists deployed with limited critical intentions, Joyce begins to pose searching questions about the validity of Revivalism and, at the same time, overtly reconfigures the structure of its complicity with anthropology into a more self-critical and productive modernism. Perhaps the most important effect of this reconfiguration is the emergence of a concept of national identity freed from the ignominy of primitivism and ethnographic redemption. In the end, Joyce makes explicit what Yeats and Synge could only imply: that cultural authenticity depends not on a redemptive vision of culture expressed in a reductive ethnographic realism, but rather on a mode of anti-mimeticism that confronts this vision and puts it under critical pressure. The possible future of an Irish nation inheres neither in Bloom's voyeuristic and utopian fantasies nor in Stephen's hyper-self-consciousness of his own ambivalence; if it exists at all in Joyce's texts it exists in a contact zone between private vision and public *re*vision, between the native in the making and the native always already made, between authenticity and inauthenticity, between ethnographic redemption and autoethnographic critique. The possibilities articulated in these contact zones point to what I think Seamus Deane means when he talks of Joyce's need to create an "idea of Ireland"[71] that his texts could freely presuppose, and what Stephen means when he writes, near the conclusion of *A Portrait*, that he desires not the faded "loveliness" of Romantic Ireland, dead and gone, but "the loveliness which has not yet come into the world."

Conclusion: After the Revival: "Not even Main Street is Safe"

> It all seems
> A little unreal now,
> Now that I am
>
> An anthropologist . . .   Derek Mahon[1]

This study began with a consideration of Yeats's redemptive Revivalism and it is difficult to say whether it does not end in the same way, for even Joyce's critique of the Revival harbors a desire to redeem Ireland from misrepresentations. Stylistically and ideologically, of course, a good deal separates Yeats's attempt to rescue folklore from rationalizations, stereotypes, and "the shallowness of an ascendant and idle class" (*FFT*, 7) and Joyce's similar attempt to rescue Dubliners from a tradition of Revivalist idealizations. In some ways, as we have seen, Synge serves as a bridge between these two powerful Irish writers, participating both in the project of ethnographic redemption – *The Aran Islands* stands as the quintessential Revivalist work in this regard – and in the critique of this project, which is limned in *The Playboy of the Western World*. What all three share is a commitment to an autoethnographic engagement or dialogue with an imperialist anthropology that in an important sense could not have been avoided, given that during the period covered by this study (1888–1922) the Celtic Revival emerged as a cultural movement just as anthropology entered into its modern phase of development, using Ireland as a laboratory, which, as D. J. Cunningham and A. C. Haddon believed, would "no doubt afford valuable information concerning the persistence or otherwise of racial characters."[2]

An important context for this coevality was that of decolonization, "a complete calling in question of the colonial situation," as Fanon describes it, a revolutionary time that "transforms spectators crushed with their inessentiality into privileged actors, with the

248

grandiose glare of history's floodlights upon them."[3] In an era of decolonization, resistance and complicity – with colonialism, with anthropology, with a nostalgic and primitivist Revivalism – become intertwined in the development of national consciousness, mutually determining representations of culture that demand, by virtue of their ambivalent relationship with "reality," a critical response. That this response was often itself stereotypical, an unreflective grasping after orthodoxy or party-line, only increased the sense among some Revivalists, Synge and Joyce particularly, that the education of the audience or reader would inevitably involve the painful process of forcing people to recognize the fictive nature of what they took to be reality. In the Irish context, awash with misrepresentations emanating from a metropolitan center only a few hundred miles away and from an Anglo-Irish class that claimed the same nativity as the indigenous Catholic Irish, this education proved an indispensable first step toward the revolutionary literature that Fanon postulated, the first step toward an awakening of the Irish people to the reality of their social conditions and thus to the reality of their national aspirations. It was, in a word, the first step in the process of "inventing souls."[4]

I have referred throughout this study to the tension between tradition and modernity which, for Terry Eagleton, constitutes the ideal conditions for the emergence of modernism. It would be useful to recall his formulation: "Modernism springs from the estranging impact of modernizing forces on a still deeply traditionalist order, in a politically unstable context which opens up social hope as well as spiritual anxiety. Traditional culture provides modernism with an adversary, but also lends it some of the terms in which to inflect itself."[5] To varying degrees, depending on the extent to which individual writers employed anthropological techniques and theories critically, Revivalism contributed to the formation of Irish modernism by exploiting a specific relation between the traditional and the modern, a relation determined by the technologies of anthropology and ethnography coming to bear on the traditional folkways and texts of the Irish peasantry. This autoethnographic engagement with anthropology at times resulted in a critique of Revivalism itself, whenever it could be shown that the Revival lacked a critical awareness of its own investments in anthropological or colonialist stereotypes and misrepresentations.

It is at this level that we can see still another strategy linking Yeats,

Synge, and Joyce, one that I have argued is definitive of the anthropological modernism of the Revival. As I have indicated in my discussions of Yeats's and Synge's redemptive ethnography of folk culture, representing authenticity was a primary goal of the Revival; Yeats's strategy of creative evocation, which yielded "fair equivalent[s] for the gesture and voice of the peasant tale-teller" (*UP1*, 174), and Synge's strategy of "transfigured realism," which approximated an accurate ethnographic account without dispensing with a subjective or literary style, sought in similar ways to represent cultural essences while retaining certain prerogatives of the artist. However, these strategies, because they lacked the important element of critical self-reflexiveness, forestalled the realization that the problem of authenticity is less one of finding the appropriate technique for unearthing cultural essences, and thereby arriving at what is authentic about culture, than it is one of coming to terms with the fact that authenticity is, in a sense, an impossible goal – for the Revivalist intent on representing it as well as for anyone who comes under the sway of (mis)representations claiming to have a purchase on it. When critical self-reflexiveness becomes part of Revivalist practice, as it does in Synge's drama (especially *The Playboy*) and in Joyce's fiction (especially *Ulysses*), then an autoethnographic critique makes possible the realization that the representation of *in*authenticity may in fact be the best way to arrive at an authentic expression of Irish national aspirations and the ambivalent process of Irish identity formation. The paradox that the *in*authentic is the authentic is not as paradoxical as it might appear, as my chapters on Synge and Joyce have attempted to show. For what is at issue is not so much the truth-value or essential nature of representations as the *right* to represent; and, as the debate over Synge's *Playboy* indicated, this right was not an exclusive one, it was not to be arrogated by a single nationalist constituency (much less by an imperialist anthropological mission). The result, as Joyce's *Ulysses* makes so playfully evident, is a debunking of anthropological fictions like those William Simmons describes – "purist notions that native cultures resist history, or that they disappear in its presence"[6] – and the creation of new, productive, and empowering fictions that testify to a pluralization of the right to represent Irish national self-determination and the vexed processes of identity formation.

Yeats and Synge were among the Anglo-Irish Revivalists who attempted to overcome with some success the ambivalence of their social position to contribute significantly to this critical impulse in Irish modernism, and the more so precisely because that position was, by the 1890s (and certainly in subsequent decades), radically destabilized. But we must not discount the extent to which Revivalist projects of cultural redemption created (or perpetuated) anthropological fictions of the "purist" type that Simmons describes. We can see this sort of thing in Yeats's tendency to consign the Irish peasant to a "timeless" realm – rooted, to be sure, in an Irish folk tradition and, for that reason, valued more highly than primitive peoples usually were in ethnographic accounts – or Synge's tendency to eroticize Aran Island women in order to salve his alienated subjectivity, a practice that was in keeping with contemporary notions of the primitive as an anodyne for modernity. We see it as well in Joyce's depiction of Gabriel Conroy, in "The Dead," and Stephen Dedalus, in *Stephen Hero* and *A Portrait of the Artist as a Young Man*, native intellectuals who must confront and overcome their investments in Revivalist primitivism. That Yeats, Synge, and Joyce were able, more or less successfully, to combat the stereotyped fictions put forward by Revivalism, nationalism, anthropology, and colonialist propaganda, despite their own complicity in sustaining them testifies not only to the critical potential of Revivalist discourses, but also to the inherent (if not constitutive) instability of the anthropological theories and ethnographic practices that so often subtended them.

To some degree, the increasingly critical direction of the Revival can be explained by considering the development of anthropology in the period with which this study is concerned. The empiricism of anthropologists like A. C. Haddon, which was grounded in the natural sciences, was concerned primarily with a tabular or taxonomic form of organizing ethnographic data and led eventually to a no less scientific approach increasingly governed by a realistic mode of representation that strove to provide "fair equivalents" of cultural phenomena. The "easy realism of natural history" (as Stephen Tyler formulates it[7]) can be seen in the descriptive chapters of A. R. Radcliffe-Brown's *The Andaman Islanders*, where social organization and ceremonial rituals are laid out with the painstaking care of a natural scientist; but, in the interpretive chapters (riddled as they are with the ethnographer's admissions that his knowledge is scanty or his methods inadequate), what we might call an *un*easy realism begins to take shape. This mode of ethnographic realism, as I have tried to show in chapter 1, characterizes Bronislaw Malinowski's *Argonauts of* *the Western Pacific* — a text that manages to reconcile the novelist's imperative to provide "a few light touches in order to produce a vivid and so-to-speak personal impression of the various type of natives, and countries and of cultures"[8] with the ethnographer's imperative to maintain strict scientific standards of objectivity and accuracy.

Malinowski's style, like Synge's in *The Aran Islands* and, to a lesser degree, Joyce's in *Ulysses*, is an attempt to capture the reality of cultural "wholes" which had been, since E. B. Tylor offered his famous definition of culture in 1871, the *raison d'être* of anthropology.[9] Moreover, his interest in the "mental attitudes" of his native subjects, as well as the "inponderabilia" of their actual life, corresponds to the interest of some Revivalists (principally Yeats in his later period) in expressing the fullness of the artist's personality. Malinowski's modernism, as I have argued in chapter 1, derives from conditions to some degree shared by ethnographers and Anglo-Irish Revivalists alike, conditions of deracination and anomie, a pervasive sense of alienation not only from their own culture, but also from any sense of stable or "sovereign" selfhood; it is this condition of "off centeredness" that led Malinowski and the Revivalists to desire, often strongly, an intersubjective rapport with their native informants. Now, it must be said that we can understand the full force of Malinowski's modernist sensibility only when we read his *Argonauts* alongside his *Diary in the Strict Sense of the Term*; but the necessity of this mode of reading does not invalidate the conclusions at which we might arrive. Indeed, it has been one of my chief contentions that such a mode of reading is essential if we are to understand not only the development of anthropology as a discipline, but also its influence on cultural movements like the Celtic Revival, which had a close — at times, intimate — relationship with anthropology. This relationship, constituted in part by parallel developments, in part by the Revival's ability to anticipate the problems of representation that anthropology, with its scientific self-assurance, tended not to address, is another key element of Irish modernism.

I would like to conclude this study with a brief consideration of some specifically Irish developments in both anthropology and Revivalism, and to suggest in what ways the critical impulse we discern in Synge's *Playboy* and Joyce's *Ulysses* continues to manifest itself "after the Revival." One thing we see happening after 1922 is an increased awareness on the part of the Irish people of their role (or lack of any) in anthropological accounts about them, and the relationship between those accounts and the reality of their lives. I have noted in chapter 3 that one of the things Synge discovered on the Aran Islands was that the inhabitants were very much aware of antiquarians and anthropologists who had come before him. One of his informants told him that "he had known [George Petrie] and Sir William Wilde, and many living antiquarians, and had taught Irish to Dr. Finck and Dr. Pedersen, and given stories to Mr. Curtin of America" (*AI*, 50). Conrad Arensberg, over thirty years later, makes a similar observation, with which he begins his study of the "Irish countryman." After noting that "the arrival of a stranger in a west country Irish town is still an event," he goes on to say that

time brings acceptance to most mysteries. It finds a formula for them that gives them a familiar ring. So, the anthropologist gradually found acceptance. Even his formidable title grew easier as its translation spread. The Irish today are a very literate people. And a sudden increase in the circulation of books on anthropology from the county library helped very quickly to establish the anthropologist as "looking for old customs."[10]

Significantly, neither Synge nor Arensberg are surprised at the knowledge of the Irish people, though Arensberg does regret that the country people persist in thinking of anthropologists as collectors of "old customs." Writing in 1937, Arensberg is aware that some people might think that Ireland, as a modern nation, is no longer a fit subject for anthropological study. He defends his decision to study it by adducing the advances in anthropology as a discipline, particularly the functionalism of Malinowski, which made possible the study of "dynamic functions of a whole social system," the social forces of which are "as controllable and as demonstrable as a study of chemical interaction."[11] What was learned in "primitive" places like the Trobriand Islands could be usefully applied to "civilized" countries like Ireland. Looking forward to developments that would change anthropology's warrant, Arensberg notes, "not even Main Street is safe from the ethnographer's prying eye."[12]

Arensberg, like many anthropologists of his generation, exhibits a curious mix of progressive intentions and retrograde attitudes. On the one hand, he wishes to treat Ireland seriously as a modern nation, noting that "[t]he barrier between the barbarian and the civilized man . . . is no longer conceivable in simple terms."[13] Like Malinowski, he appears to believe that "[t]he time when we could tolerate accounts presenting us the native as a distorted, childish caricature of a human being [is] gone."[14] But alongside such seemingly progressive notions is a stalwart faith in the ethnographer's ability to stand outside the culture under observation and acquire a total picture. After distinguishing among "four Irelands" Arensberg claims that "[I]f we are to make an attempt at a whole view, we must see the country whole."[15] Indeed, the problem of "old custom," which, for Arensberg, is something more than "dying survivals of an age-old habit," only makes sense when it is contextualized within "a larger whole, a whole which in its total is coextensive with the total-pattern of the life of which old custom is still a part."[16] For its time (1940), Arensberg and Solon Kimball's influential study, *Family and Community in Ireland* (from which the lectures constituting *The Irish Countryman* were derived), was a progressive work of anthropology combining a functionalist approach with a sophisticated statistical apparatus. However, as Lawrence J. Taylor points out, there has been little advance since that time, which has resulted in "a curious and instructive asymmetry between the role of anthropology in Irish academic life and its part in the public imaginary and self-knowledge of the Irish."[17]

For Taylor, the problem is twofold: on the one hand, there is a tendency among Irish anthropologists to construct narrow local studies "too mired in the western bogs, namely, endless variations on Arensberg and Kimball." On the other hand, there is little attempt on the part of anthropologists, Irish or otherwise, to reflect "on the Irish public's occasionally vituperative reaction to anthropology."[18] He cites a number of studies in recent years – notably Robin Fox's *Encounter with Anthropology* and Nancy Scheper-Hughes's *Saints, Scholars, and Schizophrenics* – that provoked reactions pointing up the gap between "Irish self-image and Irish reality."[19] Especially provoking was Scheper-Hughes's book, which "struck at the very heartland in the symbolic geography of Irish identity: the west of the west, the seaboard of Kerry."[20] In view of these provocations and the potential they afford for critical self-reflection, Taylor advocates an anthropology that would take its role in these crises of national identity seriously. In his preference for an "interpretative anthropology that attends both to the textual qualities of the rhetorical idioms elaborated in the warring discourses and to the specific social formations and political agendas that invent themselves in the process," we can discern the kind of critical interventions in the processes of national-identity formation that characterizes Revivalist texts like Synge's *Playboy* and Joyce's *Ulysses*. I would suggest that what Taylor calls for is precisely the kind of national discourse that can proffer a sense of authentic Irishness grounded, as it were, in the *agon* of contesting narratives of identity and in an interpretive freedom that, for an earlier generation of anthropologists, could only have been called *in*authentic.

Another legacy of the Revival was an indigenous tradition of amateur self-ethnography, if this is not too strong a description for texts like Maurice O'Sullivan's *Twenty Years A-Growing*, Peig Sayers's *The Autobiography of Peig Sayers of the Great Blasket Island*, Tomas Crohan's *The Islandman*, and Pat Mullen's *Man of Aran*.[21] O'Sullivan's *Twenty Years A-Growing*, the first and perhaps most famous of these texts, is fascinating in large part because of the discrepancy between the intentions of the author (who wrote it "by himself for his own pleasure and for the entertainment of his friends, without any thought of a wider public"[22]) and the interpretations that cluster around it. The story is simple, episodic, and, for the most part, unselfconsciously written. However, in some passages, as in the chapter "Ventry Races," in which the young narrator and a friend sneak off to watch the curragh races, we detect something of the poetic peasant that Synge produced on the Abbey Theatre stage:

Away we went down the roads, leaping now as light as goats, we were so fresh after the meal. The sun had gone down in the west after bidding farewell to the big world, sheep-shearings in the sky overhead, the old men of the parish stretched out on the top of the cliff giving their breasts to the fragrant sea air and talking together after the day, a heat haze here and there in the bosom of the hills moving slowly among the valleys, a colt whinnying now and then and asses braying.[23]

We could easily imagine Synge's Christy Mahon uttering these lines, and this possibility makes the question of authenticity in texts like O'Sullivan's a complicated one indeed, for the translators, who attest to the author's intentions, also attest to the authenticity of the style by invoking the authority of the Revival: "[W]e have freely used the Irish dialect of English as being the nearest to our original, and in this respect we are following the example of Synge, who of all writers in English had the deepest understanding of the Irish-speaking peasantry."[24]

Certainly, the popularity of Synge's *Aran Islands* had as much to do with his authority as the plays, which are the source of his version of Hiberno-English. For the "deep understanding" the translators evince reminds us of Radcliffe-Brown's assertion that the ethnologist comes to understand the natives by "acquir[ing] a series of multitudinous impressions, each slight and often vague, that guide him in his dealings with them."[25] Indeed, the more general ethnographic understanding that Synge acquired on the Aran Islands subtends the translators' remarks as well as E. M. Forster's "Introductory Note," which invites the reader to take an essentially ethnographic position with respect to O'Sullivan's world: "[I]t is worth saying 'This book is unique,' lest [the reader] forget what a very odd document he has got hold of. He is about to read an account of neolithic civilization from the inside. Synge and others have described if from the outside, and very sympathetically, but I know of no other instance where it has itself become vocal, and addressed modernity."[26] Forster's note manages to compress into three sentences an affirmation of primitivism, a description of ethnographic participant–observation, a critique of the Revivalist's "outsider" status, and a recognition that authenticity rests on the productive tension between the traditional and the modern. Elegant and economic, it testifies to the extent to which the Revival's anthropological modernism had become available, by 1933, to mainstream European intellectuals.

But there is another kind of indigenous response to this anthropological modernism, a tradition based not in the West of Ireland but in the North. Space permits only the briefest of discussions, so I will restrict myself to just a few examples – the poetry of Seamus Heaney and Derek Mahon. For many writers in Northern Ireland, like those in the West, the land is a repository of memories and history: the "shards / Of a lost culture," as John Montague put it in *The Rough Field*.[27] Heaney, especially in his early poetry, exploited the archaeological richness of the "symbolic geography" of Northern Ireland, making the essentially Revivalist argument that authenticity could be evoked through a poetry that unearthed "fair equivalents" of the Irish past. In "Feeling into Words," a lecture given at a meeting of the Royal Society of Literature in 1974, Heaney notes that implicit in Wordsworth's *Prelude*

is a view of poetry which I think is implicit in the few poems I have written that give me any right to speak: poetry as divination, poetry as revelation of the self to the self, as restoration of the culture to itself; poems as elements of continuity, with the aura and authenticity of archaeological finds, where the buried shard has an importance that is not diminished by the importance of the buried city; poetry as a dig, a dig for finds that end up being plants.[28]

In the archaeological tenor of these remarks, we find the emphasis on digging beneath surfaces for something essential which, in historical terms, entails privileging the past over the present or, to put my point another way, understanding the present through uncovering artifacts of the past. As Seamus Deane remarks, "the poet comes more fully to grips, not with the past, but with its recovery and incorporation into the present."[29] This emphasis on *un*covering and *re*covering artifacts reveals a strong affiliation with the redemptive ethnography of Revivalism.

In the late 1960s and early 1970s, the period during which Heaney composed and published *Wintering Out* and *North*, his "archaeologizing imagination" (as Neil Corcoran described it) was being energized by events in Dublin: "When I came down here there were excavations going on, and the revisionism about the Vikings was in the air. I had a sympathetic interest in it – not very systematically reading upon it, but I knew [the Irish archaeologist] Tom Delaney and through him I got some little flicker of an intimacy with it."[30] Some readers have criticized this "archaeologizing imagination," especially as it is manifested in Heaney's so-called bog poems. In these poems, this imagination becomes politicized when the poet confronts head-on the problem of tribal loyalties and his obligation to literary traditions (English and Revivalist). Referring to Heaney's "Kinship," which relates the poet's reactions to an Iron Age body preserved in a bog – "Kinned by hieroglyphic / peat on a spreadfield / to the strangled victim, / the love-nest in the bracken, / I step through origins . . ."[31] – Ciaran Carson points out the contradiction between the poem's sensibility and its methods of archaeological inquiry:

The two methods [the local-Irish and the mythic-European] are not compatible. One gains its poetry by embodiment of a specific, personal situation; the other has degenerated into a messy historical and religious surmise – a kind of Golden Bough activity, in which the real differences between our society and that of Jutland in some vague past are glossed over for the sake of the parallels of ritual.[32]

Carson's criticism centers on Heaney's apparent reliance, in poems like "Kinship" – and we might generalize to include most of the other bog poems – on a comparative anthropology (as mystifying as it is mythologizing) insufficiently sensitive to cultural and historical difference. Elsewhere, Carson criticizes Heaney for celebrating sacrificial violence and becoming "an anthropologist of ritual killing, an apologist for 'the situation,' in the last resort, a mystifier."[33] Edna

Longley echoes this criticism when she accuses Heaney of "plundering . . . the past for parallels" – a practice which insists on "'territorial piety,' on a religious–anthropological, even slightly glamorous way of apprehending the conflict" in Northern Ireland.[34] She adduces the sequences in *North* – "Viking Dublin: Trial Pieces," "Bone Dreams" and "Kinship" – in order to suggest that, "the further back Heaney pushes, in default of a specific impulse, the more specialized and specialist he in fact becomes; so that the sequences exaggerate the book's anthropological, archaeological and philological tendency."[35]

The attentiveness to the pressures of colonial and anthropological violence that Longley calls "archaeological awe"[36] is a paradoxical attitude of engaged participation and detached observation – "I am the artful voyeur // of your brain's exposed / and darkened coombs" the poet writes of a woman dug out of a bog[37] – that reveals an ambivalent desire to redeem a traditional culture from obliteration. This attentiveness also reconfigures the tension between the traditional and the modern characteristic of the Revival, but Heaney does so in terms that reflect the unique ways that the modernizing technologies of anthropology have come to bear on life in Northern Ireland. What Seamus Deane says of Derek Mahon might also be said of Heaney: "Belfast is [for Mahon] a dark country, an archaeological site, bleak monuments of men, hard flints of feeling"; he notes further how often "the figure in his poems is that of a spectator; or in the love poems a man brought in from the outside to share a basic warmth."[38] Given the similarities between the Protestant Mahon and the Catholic Heaney, it is fitting that Mahon's "Lives," which depicts the Northern Irish poet in explicitly anthropological terms and is dedicated to Heaney, should serve as an envoi to this study.

The speaker of the poem begins by identifying himself with archaeological artifacts: "First time out / I was a torc of gold," then "a bump of clay // In a Navaho rug" and then "a stone in Tibet, // A tongue of bark / At the heart of Africa // Growing darker and darker."[39] Inevitably, it seems, the "unreality" of the poet's position with respect to his homeland slides effortlessly into the unreality of the modern anthropologist:

> It all seems
> A little unreal now,
> Now that I am

An anthropologist
With my own
Credit card, dictaphone,
Army-surplus boots
And a whole boatload
Of photographic equipment.

I know too much
To be anything any more . . .[40]

The attitude toward culture expressed here is tied to certain forms of cultural privilege ("Credit card, dictaphone") that serve to mark the complicity of the Irish writer with an anthropology fully in step with the technologies of late modernity. This complicity with high-tech ethnographic intervention suggests an even more troubling complicity with the particular variety of panoptic observation the British occupying forces use to keep track of republican activity in the North. The "hegemony of the visual,"[41] with its obsessive desire for proof and verification ("a whole boatload / Of photographic equipment"), is invoked in order to underscore the utter paucity of being ("I know too much / To be anything any more") that results from ethnographic surveillance. The poet's position is, finally, irresolvably ambivalent, his object of study, like himself, unknowable; the poem closes by issuing a warning to those who might regard him with the same kind of ethnographic curiosity:

And if in the distant

Future someone
Thinks he has once been me
As I am today,

Let him revise
His insolent ontology
Or teach himself to pray.[42]

The insolence that comes from knowing the way another exists must be revised, since to do otherwise is to repeat the arrogant self-assurance of anthropology and, by implication, the worst tendencies of Revivalism. The other alternative, prayer, is particularly troubling, since it suggests both the absence of any ability to pray (one must teach oneself to do so) and the utter lack of any rational solution to "the situation" in the North.

In the closing decade of the twentieth century, Irish writers are still engaged with some of the same problems of cultural and political power that occupied the Anglo-Irish Revival at the turn of the century and that led to the development of an anthropological modernism. In a sense, my argument comes full circle, for Heaney's "archaeological awe" with respect to the land and its natives brings us back to the concerns of the Revival. However, this return is a return with a difference, for not only is the political landscape utterly unlike that of Dublin before 1922, but sensibilities have changed. Northern writers (like their counterparts in the Republic) no longer feel compelled to create universalizing narratives about Ireland and the Irish; the legends of Cuchulain and Fionn MacCumhaill are no longer taken as foundational or even relevant. In the 1990s, Irish writers are more likely to explode such narratives and legends; but they are also likely to return to the seedbed of the Revival – to their own turf, there to fight local battles in the north and south, east and west, town and village, bog and shore. In the end, Irish literature persists in its engagement with colonialism and anthropology, in its entanglements with a divided and betrayed Revivalism, in its expression of an ethnographic imagination, and in its preparation for new revivals.

Notes

I THE CELTIC MUSE: ANTHROPOLOGY, MODERNISM, AND THE CELTIC REVIVAL

1   Ambrose Bierce, *The Devil's Dictionary* (Cleveland and New York: World Publishing Company, 1944), p. 88.
2   Terry Eagleton, *Heathcliff and the Great Hunger: Studies in Irish Culture* (London and New York: Verso, 1995), p. 274.
3   Ibid., p. 297.
4   Ibid., p. 298.
5   Ibid., p. 300.
6   Sir Charles Gavan Duffy, "The Revival of Irish Literature," in *The Revival of Irish Literature: Addresses by Sir Charles Gavan Duffy, K.C.M.G., Dr. George Sigerson, and Dr. Douglas Hyde* (London: Fisher Unwin, 1894), pp. 9–10.
7   Ibid., p. 47.
8   Ibid., p. 20.
9   Douglas Hyde, "The Necessity for De-Anglicizing Ireland," in *The Revival of Irish Literature: Addresses by Sir Charles Gavan Duffy, K.C.M.G., Dr. George Sigerson, and Dr. Douglas Hyde* (London: Fisher Unwin, 1894), pp. 128, 118.
10 Robert O'Driscoll, "The Aesthetic and Intellectual Foundations of the Celtic Literary Revival in Ireland," in Robert O'Driscoll (ed.), *The Celtic Continuum* (New York: Braziller, 1982), pp. 405, 407; see also O'Driscoll, "'A Greater Renaissance': The Revolt of the Soul against the Intellect," in Wolfgang Zach and Heinz Kosok (eds.), *Literary Interrelations: Ireland, England and the World* 3 (Tübingen: Gunter Nass, 1987), pp. 133–44.
11 See Declan Kiberd, *Inventing Ireland* (Cambridge, MA: Harvard University Press, 1996) and Seamus Deane, *Celtic Revivals: Essays in Modern Irish Literature 1880–1980* (Winston-Salem: Wake Forest University Press, 1987), especially pp. 38–50, 92–107. For other discussions of the Celtic Revival, see Désirée Hirst, "The Sequel to 'The Irish Renaissance,'" *Canadian Journal of Irish Studies*, 12.1 (June 1987), 17–42; Ronald Schleifer (ed.), *The Genres of the Irish Literary Revival* (Norman, OK: Pilgrim Books; Dublin: Wolfhound Press, 1980); Kiberd, "Anglo-Irish Attitudes," in *Ireland's Field Day: Field Day Theatre Company* (London: Hutchinson,

1985), pp. 81–105 and "The Perils of Nostalgia: A Critique of the Revival," in Peter Connolly (ed.), *Literature and the Changing Ireland*, Irish Literary Studies 9 (Gerrards Cross: Colin Smythe; Totowa, NJ: Barnes and Noble, 1982), pp. 1–24; Lorna Reynolds, "The Irish Literary Revival: Preparation and Personalities," in Robert O'Driscoll (ed.), *The Celtic Continuum* (New York: Braziller, 1982), pp. 383–99.

12   Kiberd, *Inventing Ireland*, p. 107.

13   I wish to note that my use of the words "peasant" and "peasantry" throughout this study should be understood as in quotation – that is to say, as under suspicion. I use these terms to refer not to specific social classes (small farmers, tenant farmers, landless laborers) but to the imaginary constructions of these classes created in Revivalist discourses. For an analysis of the Revival's deployment of the concept of the peasantry, see Edward Hirsch, "The Imaginary Irish Peasant," *PMLA* 106 (1991), 1116–33.

14   On the Manichean model of colonial domination, see Abdul R. JanMohamed, "The Economy of Manichean Allegory: The Function of Racial Difference in Colonialist Literature," *Critical Inquiry* 12 (1985), 59–87.

15   Michael Hechter, *Internal Colonialism: The Celtic Fringe in British National Development, 1536–1977* (Berkeley and Los Angeles: University of California Press, 1975), p. 9.

16   Matthew Arnold, *On the Study of Celtic Literature*, in *The Works of Matthew Arnold*, vol. v (1867; rpt. London: Macmillan, 1903), p. 83.

17   David Cairns and Shaun Richards, "Reading a Riot: The 'Reading Formation' of Synge's Abbey Audience," *Literature and History* 12.2 (Autumn 1987), 222.

18   On the Protestant Ascendancy, see R. F. Foster, *Modern Ireland: 1600–1972* (London: Penguin, 1989), pp. 168–94.

19   See Kevin Whelan, *Fellowship of Freedom: The United Irishmen and 1798* (Cork University Press, 1998).

20   R. F. Foster, "Protestant Magic: W. B. Yeats and the Spell of Irish History," *Proceedings of the British Academy* 75 (1989), 243–66. See also Foster, *Modern Ireland*, pp. 400–28.

21   James Clifford, "On Ethnographic Allegory," in James Clifford and George E. Marcus (eds.), *Writing Culture: The Poetics and Politics of Ethnography* (Berkeley: University of California Press, 1986), pp. 112–13.

22   William S. Simmons, "Culture Theory in Contemporary Ethnohistory," *Ethnohistory* 35.1 (1988), 7.

23   Bronislaw Malinowski, *The Sexual Life of Savages in North-Western Melanesia* (New York: Eugenics Publishing Company, 1929), p. 101. See also Malinowski, *Argonauts of the Western Pacific* (London: Routledge; New York: Dutton, 1932), p. 11.

24   Malinowski, *Sexual Life of Savages*, p. 76.

25   Claude Lévi-Strauss, *Structuralist Anthropology*, trans. Claire Jacobson and Brooke Grundfest Schoepf (New York: Basic Books, 1963), p. 11.

26 Bronislaw Malinowski, *A Diary in the Strict Sense of the Term*, trans. Norbert Guterman (Stanford University Press, 1989), pp. 69, 225, 140; see also p. 278.

27 Edward Said, "Representing the Colonized: Anthropology's Interlocutors," *Critical Inquiry* 15 (Winter 1989), 211–12.

28 E. W. Brabrook, "President's Address," *Journal of the Anthropological Institute of Great Britain and Ireland* 26 (1897), 428.

29 Beddoe, John. "Anniversary Address," *Journal of the Anthropological Institute of Great Britain and Ireland* 20 (1891), 358.

30 Edward Said, *Culture and Imperialism* (New York: Vintage-Random, 1993), p. 152.

31 E. W. Brabrook, "Anniversary Address," *Journal of the Anthropological Institute of Great Britain and Ireland* 25 (1896), 384.

32 Mary Louise Pratt, "Fieldwork in Common Places," in James Clifford and George E. Marcus (eds.), *Writing Culture: The Poetics and Politics of Ethnography* (Berkeley: University of California Press, 1986), p. 27.

33 Pratt, ibid., pp. 25, 27.

34 E. B. Tylor, *Primitive Culture*, vol. 1 (1871; rpt. New York: Harper, 1958), p. 22.

35 Ibid., p. 37.

36 Ibid., p. 68.

37 Ibid., p. 1.

38 See Franz Boas, "History and Science in Anthropology: A Reply," *American Anthropologist*, n.s. 38 (1936). See also Boas's *Race, Language and Culture* (New York: Macmillan, 1940).

39 Lévi-Strauss, *Structuralist Anthropology*, p. 9.

40 A. R. Radcliffe-Brown, *The Andaman Islanders* (1922; rpt. New York: The Free Press, 1964), p. vii.

41 A. C. Haddon, *The Study of Man* (New York: Putnam's; London: Bliss, Sands, 1989), p. 371.

42 Stephen A. Tyler, "Post-Modern Ethnography: From Document of the Occult to Occult Document," in James Clifford and George E. Marcus (eds.), *Writing Culture: The Poetics and Politics of Ethnography* (Berkeley: University of California Press, 1986), p. 130.

43 Radcliffe-Brown, *The Andaman Islanders*, p. 234.

44 Ibid., pp. 230–1.

45 Bronislaw Malinowski, "Culture," in Edwin R. A. Seligman and Alvin Johnson (eds.), *Encyclopaedia of the Social Sciences*, vol. IV (New York: Macmillan, 1930–5), p. 625.

46 Malinowski, ibid., p. 645.

47 Bronislaw Malinowski, *A Scientific Theory of Culture and Other Essays* (Chapel Hill: University of North Carolina Press, 1944), p. 5

48 Malinowski, *Argonauts*, pp. 18–19.

49 Ibid., p. 454.

50 Ibid., p. 509.

51 Lévi-Strauss, *Structuralist Anthropology*, p. 12.

52 Malinowski, *Argonauts*, p. 6.
53 Radcliffe-Brown, *The Andaman Islanders*, p. 69, n. 1.
54 Malinowski, *Argonauts*, p. 6.
55 Malinowski, *The Sexual Life of Savages*, p. 101.
56 Malinowski, *Argonauts*, p. 454.
57 Ibid., p. 25.
58 Ibid., p. 11; see also pp. 60, 156.
59 Malinowski, "Culture," p. 634; see also Malinowski, *Theory of Culture*, pp. 9–10, 197–8.
60 Tylor, *Primitive Culture*, p. 68.
61 Lévi-Strauss, *Structuralist Anthropology*, p. 26 n. 24. Lévi-Strauss quotes from Malinowski, "Culture as a Determinant of Behavior," in *Factors Determining Human Behavior* (Cambridge, MA: Harvard University Press, 1937), p. 155.
62 Malinowski, *Diary*, pp. 178, 279.
63 On the significance for Malinowski of Joseph Conrad's work, see James Clifford, *The Predicament of Culture: Twentieth-Century Ethnography, Literature, and Art* (Cambridge, MA: Harvard University Press, 1988), pp. 92–113 and Michael North, *The Dialect of Modernism: Race Language, and Twentieth-Century Literature* (New York: Oxford University Press, 1994), 37–58.
64 Malinowski, *Diary*, p. 122.
65 Ibid., p. 175.
66 Ibid., pp. 122, 249.
67 Ibid., p. 165.
68 Clifford, *Predicament*, pp. 25–6.
69 Malinowski, *Argonauts*, pp. 115, 465; on the degradation of the *tasasoria* (trial running of canoes before a Kula expedition), see pp. 154–5.
70 Malinowski, *Diary*, p. 236.
71 Malinowski, *Argonauts*, p. 4.
72 Ibid., p. 55.
73 Ibid., p. 4.
74 Ibid., p. 6.
75 Ibid., p. 80.
76 Clifford Geertz, *Works and Lives: The Anthropologist as Author* (Cambridge: Polity, 1988), p. 96. For a discussion of "literary anthropology" that quotes generously from practitioners and theorists, see Nigel Rapport, *The Prose and the Passion: Anthropology, Literature and the Writing of E. M. Forster* (Manchester and New York: Manchester University Press, 1994).
77 Malinowski, *Diary*, p. 110.
78 Ibid., p. 268.
79 Ibid., p. 277.
80 Ibid., p. 219.
81 The mental attitudes of natives is also important for Malinowski's theorization of the role of magic in culture generally; see "Culture," pp. 634–40.

82 Malinowski, *Diary*, pp. 126, 284, 186.

83 The English "lack reflection, continuous systematization" (ibid., p. 126).

84 Ibid., pp. 112–13.

85 Ibid., p. 119. Bracketed words in the original.

86 Mary Louise Pratt, *Imperial Eyes: Travel Writing and Transculturation* (London and New York: Routledge, 1992), p. 7.

87 Malinowski, *Theory of Culture*, p. 71.

88 Malinowski, *Diary*, p. 135.

89 Ibid., p. 131.

90 Ibid., p. 219.

91 Ibid.

92 Ibid., p. 255.

93 See David Spurr, "Myths of Anthropology: Eliot, Joyce, Lévy-Bruhl," *PMLA* 109 (March 1994), 226–80. Other relevant texts include Marc Manganaro (ed.), *Modernist Anthropology: From Fieldwork to Text* (Princeton University Press, 1990); Paul Benson (ed.), *Anthropology and Literature* (Urbana and Chicago: University of Illinois Press, 1993); and Arnold Krupat, *Ethno-Criticism: Ethnography, History and Literature* (Berkeley: University of California Press, 1992).

94 Malinowski, *Argonauts*, p. 13.

95 Clifford, *Predicament*, p. 9.

96 On the "new" modes of authority, see Clifford, *Predicament*, pp. 34–54. On dialogism and multiple narratives, see Richard Handler, "On Dialogue and Destructive Analysis: Problems in Narrating Nationalism and Ethnicity," *Journal of Anthropological Research* 41 (Summer 1985), 171–82; and Dennis, Tedlock, "The Analogic Tradition and the Emergence of a Dialogical Anthropology," *Journal of Anthropological Research* 35 (1979), 387–400 and "Questions Concerning Dialogical Anthropology," *Journal of Anthropological Research* 43 (Winter 1987), 325–44.

97 Francesco Loriggio, "Anthropology, Literary Theory, and the Traditions of Modernism," in Marc Manganaro (ed.), *Modernist Anthropology: From Fieldwork to Text* (Princeton University Press, 1990), p. 219.

98 David Chioni Moore, "Anthropology is Dead, Long Live Anthro(a)-pology: Poststructuralism, and Anthropology's 'Nervous Present,'" *Journal of Anthropological Research* 50 (1994), 351.

99 Tyler, "Post-Modern Ethnography," p. 126.

100 Stephen Tyler, *The Unspeakable: Discourse, Dialogue, and Rhetoric in the Postmodern World* (Madison: University of Wisconsin Press, 1987), p. 98.

101 Tyler, "Post-Modern Ethnography," p. 126.

102 W. D. Ashcroft, argues that deconstruction or "grammatological philosophy itself is positioned within patriarchy" and reflects the usual trajectory of both patriarchal and Eurocentric intellectual hegemony" ("Intersecting Marginalities: Post-colonialism and Feminism," *Kunapipi* 11.2 [1989], 24).

103 Kamala Visweswaran, *Fictions of Feminist Ethnography* (Minneapolis: University of Minnesota Press, 1994), pp. 78–9.

104 Said, "Representing the Colonized," p. 212.

105 Ibid., p. 208.

106 Ibid., p. 217.

107 Ibid., p. 220.

108 Edward Said, "Third World Intellectuals and Metropolitan Culture," *Raritan* 9.3 (Winter 1990), 29.

109 Immanent critique disallows any "Archimedean" position outside the culture under analysis. According to Theodor Adorno, immanent critique "takes seriously the principle that it is not ideology in itself which is untrue but rather its pretension to correspond to reality." The immanent method is "more essentially dialectical," by which he means that contradictions and aporias are embodied in the "innermost structure" of the object under analysis and that "the dialectical critic of culture must both participate in culture and not participate. Only then does he do justice to his object and to himself." Immanent criticism, as Adorno warns us, "cannot take comfort in its own idea" (*Prisms*, trans. Samuel and Shierry Weber [Cambridge, MA: MIT Press, 1981], pp. 32–3).

110 Talal Asad, "The Concept of Cultural Translation in British Social Anthropology," in James Clifford and George E. Marcus (eds.), *Writing Culture: The Poetics and Politics of Ethnography* (Berkeley: University of California Press, 1986), p. 159.

111 Benita Parry, "Problems in Current Theories of Colonial Discourse," *Oxford Literary Review* 9 (1987), 43–4. Cf. Clifford on revisionist ethnographers who respond to the radical imperative "to stage authenticity *in opposition to* external, often dominating alternatives" (*Predicament*, pp. 11–12).

112 Homi Bhabha, *The Location of Culture* (London and New York: Routledge, 1994), p. 86.

113 Frantz Fanon, *The Wretched of the Earth*, trans. Constance Farrington (New York: Grove Weidenfeld, 1963), pp. 36–7.

114 Said, "Representing the Colonized," p. 219; Said, *Culture and Imperialism*, p. 226.

115 Said, *Culture and Imperialism*, p. 226.

116 Fanon, *Wretched of the Earth*, pp. 222–3, 68.

117 Ibid., p. 223.

118 Tyler, "Post-Modern Ethnography," p. 126.

2 "FAIR EQUIVALENTS": YEATS, REVIVALISM, AND THE REDEMPTION OF CULTURE

1 W. B. Yeats, *Essays and Introductions* (New York: Collier-Macmillan, 1968), p. 174.

2 See Jonathan Allison (ed.), *Yeats's Political Identities: Selected Essays* (Ann

Arbor: The University of Michigan Press, 1996); Marjorie Howes, *Yeats's Nations: Gender, Class, and Irishness* (Cambridge, Engl.; New York: Cambridge University Press, 1997); Elizabeth Cullingford, *Gender and History in Yeats's Love Poetry* (Cambridge University Press, 1993); and *Yeats, Ireland and Fascism* (London: Macmillan, 1981).

3 Stephen Myers, *Yeats's Book of the Nineties: Poetry, Politics, and Rhetoric* (New York: Peter Lang, 1993).

4 W. Y. Evans-Wentz, *The Fairy-Faith in Celtic Countries* (1911; rpt. New Hyde Park, NY: University Books, 1966), p. 477.

5 Ibid., p. 27.

6 On the "ethnographic present," see Johannes Fabian, *Time and Other: How Anthropology Makes its Object* (New York: Columbia University Press, 1982), pp. 81–7.

7 James Clifford, *The Predicament of Culture: Twentieth-Century Ethnography, Literature, and Art* (Cambridge, MA: Harvard University Press, 1988), p. 202. See also Clifford, "On Ethnographic Allegory," in James Clifford and George E. Marcus (eds.), *Writing Culture: The Poetics and Politics of Ethnography* (Berkeley: University of California Press, 1986), pp. 98–121.

8 Bronislaw Malinowski, *Argonauts of the Western Pacific* (London: Routledge; New York: Dutton, 1932), pp. 464, 35.

9 Ibid., p. 65.

10 Clifford, "On Ethnographic Allegory," p. 113.

11 Howes, *Yeats's Nations*, p. 18.

12 Ibid., p. 43.

13 Terry Eagleton, *Heathcliff and the Great Hunger: Studies in Irish Culture* (London; New York: Verso, 1995), p. 297.

14 See Homi Bhabha, *The Location of Culture* (London and New York: Routledge, 1994), pp. 86–8.

15 Seamus Deane, *Celtic Revivals: Essays in Modern Irish Literature 1880–1980* (Winston-Salem: Wake Forest University Press, 1987), p. 38.

16 Edward Said, "Yeats and Decolonization," in *Nationalism, Colonialism and Literature* (Minneapolis: University of Minnesota Press, 1990), p. 86.

17 E. B. Tylor, *Primitive Culture*, vol. I (1871; rpt. New York, 1958), p. 1. For a study of culture as it was defined and used in eighteenth- and nineteenth-century anthropology, see George W. Jr. Stocking, *Race, Culture and Evolution: Essays in the History of Anthropology* (New York: Free Press; London: Collier-Macmillan 1968).

18 Deborah Fleming, *"A man who does not exist": The Irish Peasant in the Work of W. B. Yeats and J. M. Synge* (Ann Arbor: University of Michigan Press, 1995), p. 21.

19 Edward Said, *Orientalism* (London: Peregrin–Penguin, 1985), p. 227.

20 Marianna Torgovnick, *Gone Primitive: Savage Intellects, Modern Lives* (University of Chicago Press, 1990), p. 8.

21 Fabian, *Time and Other*, p. 121.

22 Torgovnick, *Gone Primitive*, pp. 9, 18.

23 Marc Manganaro, "'Beating a Drum in a Jungle': T. S. Eliot on the Artist as 'Primitive,'" *Modern Language Quarterly* 47 (December 1986), 393–421.

24 Ibid., p. 410.

25 Torgovnick, *Gone Primitive*, p. 18.

26 Ernest Renan, *Poetry of the Celtic Races and Other Essays* (1859; rpt. London and Felling-on-Tyne: Walter Scott, 1896), pp. 3, 8, 14, 10, 22.

27 Ibid., pp. 6–7, 58.

28 Matthew Arnold, *On the Study of Celtic Literature*, in *The Works of Matthew Arnold*, vol. v (1867; rpt. London: Macmillan, 1903), p. 83.

29 Ibid., p. 84.

30 Ibid.

31 Howes, *Yeats's Nations*, pp. 22–3.

32 Arnold, *Celtic Literature*, pp. 12–13; Arnold's emphasis

33 Vincent Pecora, "Arnoldean Ethnology," *Victorian Studies* 41.3 (Spring 1998), 362. On Arnold's ethnology, see Frederic E. Faverty, *Matthew Arnold: The Ethnologist* (Evanston: Northwestern University Press, 1951) and Robert Young, *Colonial Desire: Hybridity in Theory, Culture and Race* (London: Routledge, 1995), pp. 55–89.

34 Arnold, *Celtic Literature*, p. xx.

35 Ibid., p. viii.

36 Pecora, "Arnoldean Ethnology," p. 363.

37 Arnold, *Celtic Literature*, p. 90.

38 Ibid.

39 Ibid., p. 131–2.

40 Ibid.

41 R. F. Foster, *W. B. Yeats: A Life. Vol. I: The Apprentice Mage 1865–1914* (Oxford University Press, 1997), p. 53.

42 Arnold, *Celtic Literature*, p. 84.

43 Declan Kiberd, *Inventing Ireland* (Cambridge, MA: Harvard University Press, 1996), p. 124.

44 Howes, *Yeats's Nations*, pp. 32–3.

45 See Edward Hirsch, "The Imaginary Irish Peasant," *PMLA* 106 (1991), 1116–33; Fleming, *"A Man who does not Exist"*; and L. P. Curtis, *Apes and Angels: The Irishman in Victorian Caricature* (Washington, D.C. : Smithsonian Institution Press, 1996).

46 Richard J. Loftus, *Nationalism in Modern Anglo-Irish Poetry* (Madison and Milwaukee: University of Wisconsin Press, 1964), p. 41.

47 Ibid., pp. 50, 52.

48 Hirsch, "The Imaginary Irish Peasant," 1122.

49 See Phillip L. Marcus, *Yeats and the Beginning of the Irish Renaissance*, 2nd edn (Syracuse University Press, 1987); Mary Helen Thuente, *Yeats and Irish Folk-lore* (Dublin: Gill and Macmillan, 1980); Edward Hirsch, "'Contention Is Better Than Loneliness': The Poet as Folklorist," in Ronald Schleifer (ed.), *The Genres of the Irish Literary Revival* (Norman, OK: Pilgrim Books, 1980), pp. 11–25.

50 The edition I quote from – W. B. Yeats (ed.), *Fairy and Folk Tales of Ireland* (New York: Macmillan, 1986) – incorporates both *Fairy and Folk Tales of the Irish Peasantry* (1888) and *Irish Fairy Tales* (1892).

51 On Yeats's sources, see Thuente, *Yeats and Irish Folk-lore*, pp. 32–105.

52 Marcus, *Irish Renaissance*, p. xv.

53 See Malinowski, *Argonauts*, pp. 428–63.

54 Edward O'Shea, *Yeats as Editor* (Dublin: Dolmen Press, 1975), p. 20.

55 Ibid. On Yeats's editorial practice in the folklore collections, see Thuente, *Yeats and Irish Folk-lore*, pp. 85–97; Marcus, *Irish Renaissance*, especially chapters 1 and 5; Hirsch, "The Poet as Folklorist."

56 Thuente, *Yeats and Irish Folk-lore*, p. 74.

57 On the "Irishness" of Yeats selections, see Steven D. Putzel, "Towards an Aesthetic of Folklore and Mythology: W. B. Yeats, 1888–1895," *Southern Folklore Quarterly* 44 (1980), 111–13.

58 Hirsch, "The Poet as Folklorist," p. 14.

59 Frank Kinahan, *Yeats, Folklore, and Occultism: Contexts of the Early Work and Thought* (Boston: Unwin Hyman, 1988), p. 63.

60 Ibid., pp. 63–4.

61 Evans-Wentz, *Fairy-Faith*, pp. xxiv, 469.

62 Arnold, *Celtic Literature*, p. 134.

63 See Foster, *Yeats*, pp. 48–52.

64 Fleming, *"A Man who does not Exist,"* p. 71.

65 R. F. Foster, "Protestant Magic: W. B. Yeats and the Spell of Irish History," *Proceedings of the British Academy* 75 (1989), 260.

66 Ibid., 259.

67 Marcus, *Irish Renaissance*, pp. 24–5.

68 Evans-Wentz, *Fairy-Faith*, pp. 5, 471.

69 Ibid., pp. 22, 357.

70 Talal Asad, "The Concept of Cultural Translation in British Social Anthropology," in James Clifford and George E. Marcus (eds.), *Writing Culture: The Poetics and Politics of Ethnography* (Berkeley: University of California Press, 1986), p. 163.

71 Edward Hirsch, "Coming Out Into the Light: W. B. Yeats's *The Celtic Twilight* (1893, 1902)," *Journal of the Folklore Institute* 18.1 (January–April 1981), 13.

72 W. B. Yeats, *The Celtic Twilight* (Lawrence and Bullen, 1893), p. 1. Unless otherwise noted, all other citations are to the 1902 edition of *The Celtic Twilight*, which contains substantial additions and revisions made to the first edition.

73 Lady Augusta Gregory, *Visions and Beliefs in the West of Ireland* (Gerrards Cross: Colin Smythe, 1970), p. 202.

74 Clifford, *Predicament*, p. 35.

75 A. R. Radcliffe-Brown, *The Andaman Islanders* (1922; rpt. New York: The Free Press, 1964), pp. 230–1.

76 At about the same time, Lady Gregory was fostering similar relationships with informants in her native Kiltartan region of County Galway.

Her most famous informant, known to Yeats as well, was Biddy Early, who is the subject of many anecdotes and stories in her *Visions and Beliefs in the West of Ireland*.

77 W. B. Yeats, *Poems* (London: Fisher Unwin, 1895), 139. This poem underwent significant revision after 1912.

78 W. B. Yeats, *The Variorum Edition of the Poems of W. B. Yeats*, ed. Peter Allt and Russell K. Alspach (New York: Hudson River-Macmillan 1987), p. 799.

79 Asad, "Cultural Translation," p. 163.

80 Mary Louise Pratt, *Imperial Eyes: Travel Writing and Transculturation* (London and New York: Routledge, 1992), p. 6.

81 Lucy McDiarmid and Maureen Waters, "Introduction," in Lucy McDiarmid and Maureen Waters (eds.), *Selected Writings* by Lady Augusta Gregory (London: Penguin, 1995), p. xxi.

82 Lady Augusta Gregory, *Poets and Dreamers: Studies and Translations from the Irish* (New York: Oxford University Press, 1974), p. 33.

83 McDiarmid and Waters, "Introduction," p. xxii. Yeats's articles are reprinted in *Uncollected Prose*, vol. ii, pp. 54–70, 74–87, 94–108, 167–83, 219–36, 267–82.

84 W. B. Yeats, *Memoirs*, ed. Denis Donoghue (New York: Macmillan, 1972), pp. 250–1. George Sigerson makes similar claims in "Irish Literature: Its Origin, Environment, and Influence," in *The Revival of Irish Literature: Addresses by Sir Charles Gavan Duffy, K.C.M.G., Dr. George Sigerson, and Dr. Douglas Hyde* (London: T. Fisher Unwin, 1894), pp. 79–92.

85 It is worth noting here the parallel between Yeats's desire to interpret "the spirit of Ireland to itself" and Clifford Geertz's theory that, for the Balinese, the cockfight was "a story they tell themselves about themselves" (*The Interpretation of Cultures* [New York: Basic, 1973], p. 448).

86 Richard Fallis, *The Irish Renaissance* (Syracuse University Press, 1977), p. 63. For a more critical view of O'Grady's work and influence, see Declan Kiberd, "The Perils of Nostalgia: A Critique of the Revival," in Peter Connolly (ed.), *Literature and the Changing Ireland*, Irish Literary Studies 9 (Gerrards Cross: Colin Smythe; Totowa, NJ: Barnes and Noble, 1982), 18–20. According to Kiberd, O'Grady wrote his *History* "in hopes of interesting his fellow-landlords in the culture of the folk, but failed to read the ominous signs when he was forced to pay for the cost of publication himself. He was a propagandist without a significant audience and even his few disciples [e.g., Yeats] scarcely understood the implications of what he said" (18).

87 Standish O'Grady, *The History of Ireland*, vol. i (London: Sampson Low, Searle, Marston and Rivington; Dublin: E. Ponsonby, 1878), p. vi.

88 Osborn Bergin, *Irish Bardic Poetry*, ed. David Greene and Fergus Kelly (1912; rpt. Dublin: Dublin Institute for Advanced Studies, 1970), p. 4.

89 Daniel Corkery, *The Hidden Ireland: A Study of Gaelic Munster in the Eighteenth Century* (1924; rpt. Dublin: Gill and Macmillan, 1967),

pp. 76–7, 72. See also Sigerson, "Irish Literature," pp. 103–8. According to Corkery, "*Filí* and not *bards* it was that both conducted and used [the bardic] schools, the bards, as compared with the *filí*, being a lower order, *untrained* poets – singers of songs, reciters of verse, strolling jongleurs" (*The Hidden Ireland*, p. 76). I follow Bergin in using "bard" to refer to both figures.

90 Loftus, *Anglo-Irish Poetry*, p. 45.

91 Marcus, *Irish Renaissance*, p. xviii.

92 Said, "Yeats," p. 92.

93 Frantz Fanon, *The Wretched of the Earth*, trans. Constance Farrington (New York: Grove Weidenfeld, 1963), p. 240.

94 First published in 1897, *The Secret Rose* included, without separate heading, a series of stories about the wandering bard Red Hanrahan, which Yeats published separately in 1905 and thereafter as *Stories of Red Hanrahan*. Separate publication obscured the historical sequence of the original ordering, in which the Hanrahan stories served as a visionary conclusion to the history of the bardic tradition. I will be referring both to the first edition of *The Secret Rose* and to the 1914 American edition of *Stories of Red Hanrahan*, in which the Hanrahan cluster precedes the stories of *The Secret Rose*, a reversal of the implied history told in the stories in their original ordering. I have relied on the American edition because it incorporates numerous revisions of the 1913 London edition with the same title and contents. These later editions omit some material from the first edition and reflect revisions Yeats undertook with Lady Gregory's assistance. On the publishing history of these texts, see Richard Finneran, *The Prose Fiction of W. B. Yeats: The Search for "Those Simple Forms"* (Dublin: Dolmen Press, 1973) and Yeats, *The Secret Rose, Stories by W. B. Yeats: A Variorum Edition*, 2nd edn, ed. Warwick Gould, Phillip L. Marcus, and Michael Sidnell (London: Macmillan, 1992), pp. xv–xlvii.

95 Victor Turner, *From Ritual to Theater* (New York: Performing Arts Journal Publications, 1982), pp. 75, 83.

96 Kinahan, *Yeats, Folklore, and Occultism*, pp. 63–4.

97 Gregory, *Visions and Beliefs*, p. 34.

98 On Hanrahan's genealogy, see Augustine Martin, "*The Secret Rose* and Yeats's Dialogue with History," *Ariel* 3.3 (July 1972), 98–9.

99 Martin, "Yeats's Dialogue with History," 97–8.

100 Yeats discovered associations between the Holy Grail in Christian legend and the four sacred objects (the cauldron, stone, spear, and sword) often found in Irish folklore. See W. B. Yeats, *The Speckled Bird*, ed. William H. O'Donnell (Toronto: McClelland and Stewart, 1976), pp. 201–7.

101 See Yeats, *Secret Rose, Variorum*, p. xviii and Finneran, *Prose Fiction*.

102 Evans-Wentz, *Fairy-Faith*, pp. xxiv, xxxiii.

103 Ibid., p. 232.

104 Malinowski, *Argonauts*, pp. 18–19.

105 Evans-Wentz, *Fairy-Faith*, p. 20.

106 Ibid., p. 300.

107 Ibid., p. 21, 59.

108 Foster, "Protestant Magic," 265–6.

109 W. B. Yeats, *Mythologies* (New York: Collier-Macmillan, 1969), p. 346.

110 The note is reprinted in *Mythologies*, p. 1. The 1914 edition of *Stories of Red Hanrahan* includes a much shorter version of this note, praising Lady Gregory's rendering of the "beautiful country speech of Kiltartan" (p. 2).

111 Kiberd, *Inventing Ireland*, p. 153.

112 Yeats, *Variorum Poems*, p. 803.

113 Kiberd, *Inventing Ireland*, p. 125.

114 Ibid.

115 Ibid., p. 118.

116 See Robert O'Driscoll, "Yeats's Conception of Synge," in S. B. Bushrui (ed.), *A Centenary Tribute to John Millington Synge 1871–1909: Sunshine and The Moon's Delight* (New York: Barnes and Noble, 1972), 159–71. R. F. Foster emphasizes the influence of Synge in the years between *The Playboy* riots in 1907 and Synge's death in 1909; see *Yeats*, pp. 359–401. Kiberd sees the influence in another, though not unrelated, way, noting that "Synge's extraordinary influence on the middle period of Yeats's poetry was attributable to his insistence that violence and poetry went hand in hand" (*Inventing Ireland*, p. 169).

117 O'Driscoll, "Yeats's Conception of Synge," p. 164. O'Driscoll incorporates quotations from "Discoveries."

118 Evans-Wentz, *Fairy-Faith*, pp. 365, 335.

119 Bronislaw Malinowski, *A Diary in the Strict Sense of the Term*, trans. Norbert Guterman (Stanford University Press, 1989), p. 219.

120 Kiberd, *Inventing Ireland*, p. 213.

121 Ibid., p. 124.

122 Quoted in Richard Ellmann, *Yeats: The Man and the Masks* (New York: Norton, 1978), pp. 252–3.

123 Ibid., p. 252.

124 Bronislaw Malinowski, "Culture," in Edwin R. A. Seligman and Alvin Johnson (eds.), *Encyclopaedia of the Social Sciences*, vol. IV (New York: Macmillan, 1930–5), p. 628.

125 Ibid., p. 297.

126 In the first edition of *On the Boiler*, the line reads "I killed that lad because he had grown up." Subsequent editions make the correction I have indicated in brackets.

3 "SYNGE-ON-ARAN": *THE ARAN ISLANDS AND THE SUBJECT OF REVIVALIST ETHNOGRAPHY*

  1 Seamus Heaney, "Synge on Aran" in *Death of a Naturalist* (London: Faber, 1966), p. 52.

2 On Synge's Irish teachers and his experience in Brittany, see David Greene, "Synge and the Celtic Revival," *Modern Drama* 4 (1961), 292–9.

3 Ibid., 296.

4 Fallis, Richard. "Art as Collaboration: Literary Influences on J. M. Synge," in Edward A. Kopper, Jr. (ed.), *A J. M. Synge Literary Companion* (New York: Greenwood Press, 1988), p. 147.

5 Susan Sontag, "The Anthropologist as Hero," in *Against Interpretation and Other Essays* (New York: Delta, 1967), p. 77. On the "ethnographic hero," see George W. Jr. Stocking, *The Ethnographer's Magic and Other Essays in the History of Anthropology* (Madison: University of Wisconsin Press, 1992), pp. 51–9.

6 Talal Asad, "The Concept of Cultural Translation in British Social Anthropology," in James Clifford and George E. Marcus (eds.), *Writing Culture: The Poetics and Politics of Ethnography* (Berkeley: University of California Press, 1986), p. 163.

7 Mary Louise Pratt, *Imperial Eyes: Travel Writing and Transculturation* (London and New York: Routledge, 1992), p. 6.

8 Ibid., pp. 7, 102.

9 Haddon and Browne produced ethnographies of Gorumna, Lettermullan, Inishbofin and Inishshark in Country Galway, the Mullet Peninsula, Ballycrag, Clare Island and Inishturk in County Mayo, and the parish of Moyrus in Connemara. The results of the survey, conducted throughout the 1890s and concluded in 1902, were published in the *Proceedings of the Royal Irish Academy*.

10 Fred Eggan, "One Hundred Years of Ethnology and Social Anthropology," in J. O. Brew (ed.), *One Hundred Years of Anthropology* (Cambridge, MA: Harvard University Press, 1968), p. 122.

11 See G. W. F. Hegel, *Introduction to The Philosophy of History*, trans. Leo Rauch (Indianapolis and Cambridge, MA: Hackett, 1988).

12 See Stocking, *The Ethnographer's Magic*, pp. 17–21.

13 Ibid., p. 27.

14 Ibid., p. 24.

15 A. C. Haddon and C. R. Browne, "The Ethnography of the Aran Islands, County Galway," *Proceedings of the Royal Irish Academy*, third series, vol. 2 (1891–93), 773, 776.

16 Ibid., 772.

17 A. C. Haddon and D. J. Cunningham, "The Anthropometry Laboratory of Ireland," *Journal of the Anthropological Institute of Great Britain and Ireland* 21 (1892), 36.

18 Haddon and Browne, "Ethnography of the Aran Islands," 781.

19 Robert Young, *Colonial Desire: Hybridity in Theory, Culture and Race* (London: Routledge, 1995), p. 178.

20 Haddon and Browne, "Ethnography of the Aran Islands," 781.

21 E. W. Brabrook, "President's Address," *Journal of the Anthropological Institute of Great Britain and Ireland* 27 (1898), 548.

22 Haddon and Browne, "Ethnography of the Aran Islands," 798.

23 Ibid., 769.
24 Ibid., 800.
25 Ibid., 800, 803.
26 Ibid., 801; the second bracketed insertion appears in the original.
27 Ibid., 816.
28 Ibid., 817–18.
29 Ibid., 801.
30 Declan Kiberd, "Synge, Symons, and the Isles of Aran," *Notes on Modern Irish Literature* 1 (1989), 32. More recently, Kiberd has suggested that Yeats did, after all, "send" Synge to Aran (see *Inventing Ireland* [Cambridge, MA: Harvard University Press, 1996], p. 169).
31 Greene, "Synge and the Celtic Revival," 3.
32 Fallis, "Art as Collaboration," 150.
33 Ibid., 151.
34 Nicholas Grene, "Yeats and the Re-making of Synge," In Terence Brown and Nicholas Grene (eds.), *Tradition and Influence in Anglo-Irish Poetry* (London: Macmillan, 1989), p. 48.
35 Robert O'Driscoll, "Yeats's Conception of Synge," in S. B. Bushrui (ed.), *A Centenary Tribute to John Millington Synge 1871–1909: Sunshine and The Moon's Delight* (New York: Barnes and Noble, 1972), p. 162.
36 A. R. Radcliffe-Brown, *The Andaman Islanders* (1922; rpt. New York: The Free Press, 1964), p. 231.
37 Bronislaw Malinowski, *Argonauts of the Western Pacific* (London: Routledge; New York: Dutton, 1932), p. 23.
38 Quoted in Ann Saddlemyer, "Synge and Some Companions, with a Note Concerning a Walk through Connemara with Jack Yeats," *Yeats Studies: An International Journal* 2 (1972), 27; my emphasis. The essays written for *The Manchester Guardian* and other periodicals were later collected under the title *In Wicklow, West Kerry and Connemara*.
39 Pratt, *Imperial Eyes*, p. 201.
40 Quoted in Tim Robinson, "Place/Person/Book: Synge's *The Aran Islands*," in J. M. Synge, *The Aran Islands*, ed. Tim Robinson (London: Penguin, 1992), p. 138, n. 4.
41 Ibid., p. 143, n. 47.
42 For a discussion of this tradition, see Robinson, "Place/Person/Book," pp. xv–xxii. Petrie, "the father of Irish archaeology" (p. xv) first arrived on the Aran Islands in 1821 and was well remembered by the islanders, as Synge recounts in Part I of *The Aran Islands*.
43 Malinowski, *Argonauts*, p. 221.
44 Conrad M. Arensberg and Solon T. Kimball, *Family and Community in Ireland*, 2nd edn (1940; Cambridge, MA: Harvard University Press, 1968).
45 On the peasant as noble savage, see Deborah Fleming, *"A Man who does not Exist": The Irish Peasant in the Work of W. B. Yeats and J. M. Synge* (Ann Arbor: University of Michigan Press, 1995), ch. 3.
46 See Arensberg and Kimball, *Family and Community*, especially the

chapter "Family Labor," which details the precise and customary division of labor by gender and age-grade.

47 J. M. Synge, *In Wicklow, West Kerry and Connemara*, in *Collected Works*, vol. II, ed. Robin Skelton (New York: Oxford University Press, 1962–68), p. 258.

48 I am grateful to Stewart Ó Seanóir, Keeper of Manuscripts at Trinity College, for allowing me access to Synge's notebooks. I wish to thank especially Felicity O'Mahony, who helped me transcribe Synge's hand.

49 Kiberd, *Inventing Ireland*, p. 172.

50 See also Conrad M. Arensberg, *The Irish Countryman: An Anthropological Study* (1937; rpt. Gloucester, MA: Peter Smith, 1959). This text brings together a series of lectures that offer in a somewhat informal fashion the ethnographic data that are presented in statistical and taxonomic form in *Family and Community in Ireland*. In the absence of the technical apparatus that we find in the latter text, *The Irish Countryman* tends to emphasize the informants' accounts, if only because there is less competition from scientific evidence.

51 Clifford, *Predicament*, p. 50.

52 See V. S. Pritchett, "Current Literature," *The New Statesman and Nation* (Apr. 19, 1914), 413 and Maurice Bourgois, "Synge and Loti," *The Westminster Review* 179 (May 1913), 532–6.

53 Frantz Fanon, *The Wretched of the Earth*, trans. Constance Farrington (New York: Grove Weidenfeld, 1963), p. 223.

54 Anonymous, "The Aran Islands," *The Times Literary Supplement* (June 28, 1907), 202.

55 J. B. Yeats, "Random Reflections on a Much-Discussed Dramatist From the Standpoint of a Fellow-Countryman," *Harper's Weekly* 55 (Nov. 25, 1911), 17.

56 Fallis, "Art as Collaboration," 151. On Lady Gregory's suggestion that Synge make his text "dreamier," see David H. Greene and Edward M. Stephens, *J. M. Synge 1871–1909* (New York: Macmillan, 1959), pp. 120–1. See also letters between Yeats and Synge in Ann Saddlemyer (ed.), *Theatre Business* (University Park and London: Pennsylvania State University Press, 1982), pp. 32–4.

57 For examples of travelers' accounts of exotic, picturesque Ireland, see William Stevens Balch, *Ireland, As I Saw It: The Character, Condition, and Prospects of the People* (New York: G. P. Putnam, 1850); William Steuart Trench, *Realities of Irish Life* (London: Longmans, Green and Co., 1869); Alexander Innes Shand, *Letters from the West of Ireland, 1884* (Edinburgh: Blackwood, 1885); Edith Somerville and Martin Ross, *Through Connemara in a Governess Cart* (London: W. H. Allen, 1893); M. F. Mansfield and B. McM. Mansfield, *Romantic Ireland* (1904); and G. K. Chesterton, *Irish Impressions* (Boston: L. C. Page and Co., 1919).

58 Bourgois, "Synge and Loti," 533.

59 Kiberd, "Synge, Symons," 34.

60 James F. Knapp, "Primitivism and Empire: John Synge and Paul Gaugin," *Comparative Literature* 41 (Winter 1989), 66.

61 Edward Hirsch, "Coming Out Into the Light: W. B. Yeats's *The Celtic Twilight* (1893, 1902)," *Journal of the Folklore Institute* 18.1 (January–April 1981), 13.

62 John Wilson Foster, "*The Aran Islands* Revisited," *University of Toronto Quarterly* 51.3 (Spring 1982), 255.

63 Ibid., 260.

64 Ibid., 256.

65 Ibid., 246.

66 Stephen Tyler, *The Unspeakable: Discourse, Dialogue, and Rhetoric in the Postmodern World* (Madison: University of Wisconsin Press, 1987), p. 150.

67 Foster, "*The Aran Islands* Revisited," 262, n. 3.

68 Nicholas Grene, "Synge's Creative Development in *The Aran Islands*," *Long Room* 10 (1974), 31–2. Hilary Pyle writes that Synge and Jack B. Yeats, while traveling through Connemara gathering material for their *Manchester Guardian* essays, "carried notebooks wherever they went and recorded what they saw, translating an incident, if it seemed possible creative material, into artistic form" ("*Many Ferries*: Jack B. Yeats and J. M. Synge," *Éire–Ireland* 18.2 [1983], 23).

69 Grene, "Synge's Creative Development," 36.

70 Ibid.

71 Malcolm Kelsall, "Synge in Aran," *Irish University Review* 5 (1975), 254.

72 On Synge's "spiritual autobiography," see Fallis, "Art as Collaboration," 151. For a discussion of *The Aran Islands* as a "fictionalized confessional autobiography," see Mary C. King, *The Drama of J. M. Synge* (Syracuse: Syracuse University Press, 1985), pp. 19–47. A more critical view of Synge's aestheticism can be found in Anthony R. Hale, "Framing the Folk: Zora Neale Hurston, John Millington Synge, and the Politics of Aesthetic Ethnography," *The Comparatist* 20 (1996), 50–61.

73 Ann Saddlemyer, " 'A Share in the Dignity of the World': J. M. Synge's Aesthetic Theory," in Robin Skelton and Ann Saddlemyer (eds.), *The World of W. B. Yeats* (Seattle: University of Washington Press, 1965; rev. edn 1967), pp. 207–8; see also Saddlemyer, "Art, Nature and 'The Prepared Personality': A Reading of *The Aran Islands* and Related Writings," in S. B. Bushrui (ed.), *A Centenary Tribute to John Millington Synge 1871–1909: Sunshine and The Moon's Delight* (New York: Barnes and Noble, 1972), pp. 107–20.

74 Robert Welch, *Changing States: Transformations in Modern Irish Writing* (London and New York: Routledge, 1993), pp. 80–1.

75 Ibid., pp. 85, 87.

76 Seamus Heaney, "A Tale of Two Islands: Reflections on the Irish Literary Revival," in P. J. Drudy (ed.), *Irish Studies* 1 (London: Cambridge University Press, 1980), p. 8.

77 Foster, "*The Aran Islands* Revisited," 256.

78 Ibid., 260.

79 Robinson, "Place/Person/Book," pp. xliii–xliv.

80 Ibid., p. xxxix.

81 Seamus Heaney, *Death of a Naturalist* (London: Faber, 1966), p. 52.

82 Judith Okely and Helen Callaway, Preface, in Judith Okely and Helen Callaway (eds.), *Anthropology and Autobiography* (London and New York: Routledge, 1992), p. i.

83 Judith Okely, "Anthropology and Autobiography: Participatory Experience and Embodied Knowledge," in Judith Okely and Helen Callaway (eds.), *Anthropology and Autobiography* (London and New York: Routledge, 1992), p. 16.

84 Ibid., p. 3.

85 Kirsten Hastrup, "Writing Ethnography: State of the Art," in Judith Okely and Helen Callaway (eds.), *Anthropology and Autobiography* (London and New York: Routledge, 1992), pp. 117, 122.

86 Johannes Fabian, *Time and Other: How Anthropology Makes its Object* (New York: Columbia University Press, 1982), p. 87.

87 Ibid., pp. 88–9.

88 Bronislaw Malinowski, *A Scientific Theory of Culture and Other Essays* (Chapel Hill: University of North Carolina Press, 1944), p. 71.

89 Clifford, *Predicament*, p. 14; Clifford, "Partial Truths," in James Clifford and George E. Marcus (eds.), *Writing Culture: The Poetics and Politics of Ethnography* (Berkeley: University of California Press, 1986), p. 23.

90 David Spurr, *The Rhetoric of Empire: Colonial Discourse in Journalism, Travel Writing, and Imperial Administration* (Durham and London: Duke University Press, 1993), p. 142.

91 Michel Leiris, "The Musée de L'Homme: Where Art and Anthropology Meet," interview with Jean Clay, *Realites* 182 (Jan. 1966), 62. On the self-ethnography of Leiris, see Clifford, *Predicament*, pp. 165–74.

92 Marianna Torgovnick, *Gone Primitive: Savage Intellects, Modern Lives* (University of Chicago Press, 1990), p. 105, 111.

93 Michel Leiris, *Manhood: A Journey from Childhood into the Fierce Order of Virility*, trans. Richard Howard (1939; rpt. University of Chicago Press, 1992), p. 109.

94 Bronislaw Malinowski, *A Diary in the Strict Sense of the Term*, trans. Norbert Guterman (Stanford University Press, 1989), p. 255.

95 For a discussion of Synge's and Joyce's descriptions, see Anthony Roche, "'The strange light of some new world': Stephen's Vision in *A Portrait*," *James Joyce Quarterly* 25.3 (Spring 1988), 323–32.

96 Young, *Colonial Desire*, p. 111.

97 Ibid., p. 174.

98 Torgovnick, *Gone Primitive*, p. 185.

99 Ibid., p. 192.

100 Luke Gibbons, *Transformations in Irish Culture* (University of Notre Dame Press; Cork University Press, 1996), p. 33.

101 Clifford, *Predicament*, p. 4.

102 Jenny Sharpe, "The Unspeakable Limits of Rape: Colonial Violence and Counter-Insurgency," in Patrick Williams and Laura Chrisman

(eds.), *Colonial Discourse and Post-Colonial Theory* (New York: Harvester Wheatsheaf, 1993), p. 229.

103 Ibid., p. 231.
104 Foster, "*The Aran Islands* Revisited," 259.
105 Clifford, *Predicament*, p. 93.
106 Fanon, *Wretched of the Earth*, p. 68.
107 Heaney, "Synge on Aran," p. 52.

4 STAGING ETHNOGRAPHY: SYNGE'S *THE PLAYBOY OF THE WESTERN WORLD*

1 W. B. Yeats, *On Baile's Strand*, in *The Collected Plays of W. B. Yeats* (New York: Macmillan, 1953), p. 163.
2 On propaganda and its role in dramatic productions in the Abbey Theatre, see Adrian Frazier, *Behind the Scenes: Yeats, Horniman, and the Struggle for the Abbey Theatre* (Berkeley: University of California Press, 1990), pp. 64–107.
3 Quoted in Ann Saddlemyer (ed.), *Theatre Business* (University Park and London: Pennsylvania State University Press, 1982), 80.
4 See Frazier, *Behind the Scenes* and R. F. Foster, *W. B. Yeats: A Life. Vol. I: The Apprentice Mage 1865–1914* (Oxford University Press, 1997), chs. 12–15.
5 Quoted in Saddlemyer, *Theatre Business*, p. 15.
6 The first quotation is from a letter Lady Gregory wrote to W. B. Yeats, June 13, 1904, quoted in Saddlemyer (ed.), *Theatre Business*, p. 12; the second can be found in Saddlemyer, Introduction, J. M. Synge, *Collected Works*, vol. III, ed. Robin Skelton (New York: Oxford University Press, 1962–8), p. xxvii.
7 David Cairns and Shaun Richards, "Reading a Riot: The 'Reading Formation' of Synge's Abbey Audience," *Literature and History* 12.2 (Autumn 1987), 222.
8 Quoted in Saddlemyer, *Theatre Business*, p. 23.
9 Lucy McDiarmid and Maureen Waters, "Introduction," in Lady Augusta Gregory, *Selected Writings*, ed. Lucy McDiarmid and Maureen Waters (London: Penguin, 1995), pp. xxx, xxxiv.
10 Deborah Fleming, *"A man who does not exist": The Irish Peasant in the Work of W. B. Yeats and J. M. Synge* (Ann Arbor: University of Michigan Press, 1995), pp. 100–1, 115.
11 Tim Robinson identifies the tale as "The Loving Wife," which he notes is found throughout Europe ("Place/Person/Book: Synge's *The Aran Islands*," in J. M. Synge. *The Aran Islands*, Tim Robinson (ed.) [London: Penguin, 1992], p. 142, n. 18).
12 J. M. Synge, *The Shadow of the Glen*, in *Collected Works*, vol. III, ed. Robin Skelton (New York: Oxford University Press, 1962–8), p. 59.
13 See David Cairns and Shaun Richards, "Tropes and Traps: Aspects of 'Woman' and Nationality in Twentieth-Century Irish Drama," in Toni

O'Brien Johnson and David Cairns (eds.), *Gender in Irish Writing* (Buckingham: Open University Press, 1991), pp. 105–35 and "'Woman' in the Discourse of Celticism: A Reading of *The Shadow of the Glen*," *Canadian Journal of Irish Studies* 13.1 (June 1987), 43–60. On the problems of iconographic representation in Revivalist discourse, see Amanda Yeates, "Cathleen in Service: Female Iconography in Lady Gregory, Yeats, Synge, and Joyce," Ph.D. diss., Arizona State University, December 1999.

14 Frantz Fanon, *The Wretched of the Earth*, trans. Constance Farrington (New York: Grove Weidenfeld, 1963), p. 223.

15 Ibid., p. 127.

16 Robert Young, *Colonial Desire: Hybridity in Theory, Culture and Race* (London: Routledge, 1995), p. 178.

17 Robert Welch, *Changing States: Transformations in Modern Irish Writing* (London and New York: Routledge, 1993), p. 87.

18 Ginger Strand, "*The Playboy*, Critics, and the Enduring Problem of the Audience," in Alexander G. Gonzalez (ed.), *Assessing the Achievement of J. M. Synge* (Westport, CT: Greenwood, 1996), p. 11.

19 Ibid., p. 12.

20 Ibid., pp. 20–1.

21 Victor Turner, *From Ritual to Theater* (New York: Performing Arts Journal Publications, 1982), pp. 70–1; my emphasis. It is worth noting that functionalist anthropology, as it was theorized by Bronislaw Malinowski, recognizes the significance for analysis of "ritual" and "pragmatic" performances within native cultures and of the "relation between a cultural performance and a human need" (*A Scientific Theory of Culture and Other Essays* [Chapel Hill: University of North Carolina Press, 1944], pp. 26, 38–9).

22 Turner, *From Ritual to Theater*, p. 71. On the "universals of performance," see Turner, "Are There Universals of Performance in Myth, Ritual, and Drama?" in Richard Schechner and Willa Appel (eds.), *By Means of Performance: Intercultural Studies of Theater and Ritual* (Cambridge University Press, 1990), pp. 8–18 and Herbert Blau, "Universals of Performance; or Amortizing Play," in the same volume (pp. 250–72).

23 A. C. Haddon and C. R. Browne, "The Ethnography of the Aran Islands, County Galway," *Proceedings of the Royal Irish Academy*, third series, vol. 2 (1891–3), 801.

24 Tiraswini Niranjana, *Siting Translation: History, Post-structuralism, and the Colonial Context* (Berkeley: University of California Press, 1992), p. 68.

25 Talal Asad, "The Concept of Cultural Translation in British Social Anthropology," in James Clifford and George E. Marcus (eds.), *Writing Culture: The Poetics and Politics of Ethnography* (Berkeley: University of California Press, 1986), p. 162.

26 Ibid., p. 163.

27 Ibid., p. 159.

28 James F. Knapp, "Primitivism and Empire: John Synge and Paul

Gaugin," *Comparative Literature* 41 (Winter 1989), 66. Tim Robinson makes a similar point, noting that Lady Gregory and Douglas Hyde "preceded Synge in the literary exploration of the borderzone between Irish and English inhabited by the folk-people of Ireland" ("Place/Person/Book," p. xxx).

29 G. J. Watson, *Irish Identity and the Literary Revival: Synge, Yeats, Joyce and O'Casey* (London: Croom Helm; New York: Barnes and Noble, 1979), p. 46.

30 Heidi J. Holder, "Between Fiction and Reality: Synge's *Playboy* and Its Audience," *Journal of Modern Literature* 14 (Spring 1988), pp. 529–30.

31 Luke Gibbons, *Transformations in Irish Culture* (University of Notre Dame Press; Cork University Press, 1996), p. 33.

32 Ibid., p. 35.

33 Ibid., pp. 33–4.

34 Strand, "Problem of the Audience," p. 14.

35 Ibid., p. 18.

36 On the Gaelic League's reaction to Synge's play and the Anglo-Irish Revivalists generally, see Declan Kiberd, *Synge and the Irish Language* (Totowa, NJ: Rowman and Littlefield, 1979), pp. 216–60. See also Stephen Tifft, "The Parricidal Phantasm: Irish Nationalism and the *Playboy* Riots," in Andrew Parker, Mary Russo, Doris Sommer, and Patricia Yaeger (eds.) *Nationalisms and Sexualities* (New York: Routledge, 1992), pp. 318–19.

37 Strand, "Problem of the Audience," p. 22.

38 Heidi Holder, " 'Stimulating stories of our own land': 'History Making' and the Work of J. M. Synge," in Alexander G. Gonzalez (ed.), *Assessing the Achievement of J. M. Synge* (Westport, CT: Greenwood, 1996), p. 140. See also Kiberd, *Synge and the Irish Language*, pp. 227–36.

39 Kiberd, *Synge and the Irish Language*, p. 245.

40 John P. Harrington, "Resentment, Relevance, and the Production History of *The Playboy of the Western World*," in Alexander G. Gonzalez (ed.), *Assessing the Achievement of J. M. Synge* (Westport, CT: Greenwood, 1996), p. 3.

41 From his travels in County Wicklow, Synge learned details of peasant clothing (*Playboy*, 82); on the Blasket Islands, he noted that spoons were sometimes used as door latches (*Playboy*, 94); throughout the Dingle peninsula and County Kerry, he learned of the games and races described in Act Three (*Playboy*, 132, 138); and he noted that in the small towns of Counties Kerry and Mayo, "[t]he town-crier is still a prominent person" (*Playboy*, 146).

42 Sir Charles Gavan Duffy, "The Revival of Irish Literature," in *The Revival of Irish Literature: Addresses by Sir Charles Gavan Duffy, K.C.M.G., Dr. George Sigerson, and Dr. Douglas Hyde* (London: Fisher Unwin, 1894), pp. 12–13.

43 Harrington, "Resentment, Relevance," p. 3.

44 Strand, "Problem of the Audience," p. 12.

45 Flann O'Brien derided Synge's depiction of the West of Ireland and the

exorbitant language of its inhabitants false and derogatory. For a discussion of O'Brien's and Corkery's criticism of Synge's style, see Edward Hirsch, "The Imaginary Irish Peasant," *PMLA* 106 (1991), 1127–9.

46 Anonymous, *Freeman's Journal*, Jan. 28, 1907, rpt. in James Kilroy (ed.), *The "Playboy" Riots* (Dublin: The Dolmen Press, 1971), p. 9.

47 Anonymous, *Freeman's Journal*, Jan. 29, 1907, rpt. in Kilroy, *The "Playboy" Riots*, p. 20.

48 Patrick Kenny, *Irish Times*, Jan. 30, 1907, rpt. in Kilroy, *The "Playboy" Riots*, p. 37–8.

49 Oscar Wilde, Preface, *The Picture of Dorian Gray: Authoritative Texts, Backgrounds, Reviews and Reactions, Criticism*, ed. Donald L. Lawler (New York: Norton, 1988), p. 3.

50 Daniel Corkery, *Synge and Anglo-Irish Literature: A Study* (1931; rpt. New York: Russell and Russell, 1965), 72.

51 Asad, "Cultural Translation," p. 159.

52 J. M. Synge, *Evening Mail*, Jan. 29, 1907, rpt. in Kilroy (ed.), *The "Playboy" Riots*, p. 24.

53 Stephen Gwynn, *Freeman's Journal*, Feb. 2, 1907, rpt. in Kilroy (ed.), *The "Playboy" Riots*, p. 73.

54 Homi Bhabha, *The Location of Culture* (London and New York: Routledge, 1994), pp. 88, 86.

55 Turner, *From Ritual to Theater*, pp. 70–1.

56 Niranjana, *Siting Translation*, p. 81.

57 J. M. Synge, *Collected Works*, vol. IV, ed. Robin Skelton (New York: Oxford University Press, 1962–8), p. xxiv.

58 Ann Saddlemyer describes Synge's style as "a complete re-creation, an artifice to give the *impression* of 'real' rhythm and phrasing" ("Synge's Soundscape," *Irish University Review* 22 [Spring/Summer 1992], 67).

59 Kiberd, *Inventing Ireland*, p. 180; see also p. 182.

60 W. B. Yeats, *Cathleen Ni Houlihan*, *The Collected Plays of W. B. Yeats* (New York: Macmillan, 1953), p. 54. *Cathleen Ni Houlihan* is now understood to have been co-written by Lady Gregory and Yeats. This claim was most recently made by Lucy McDiarmid and Maureen Waters in the Introduction to their edition of Lady Gregory's *Selected Writings*.

61 The *Táin Bo Cuailnge* (Cattle Raid on Cooley) relates the attempt of Queen Medbh of Connacht to carry off the bull of Cuailgne after an argument with her husband Aillel over who was richer. Medbh marched against Ulster, the most celebrated warrior of which was Cuchulain, and, though she did not win the battle against Cuchulain, she nevertheless managed to steal the celebrated bull.

62 Ruth Fleischmann, "Fathers Vanquished and Victorious – A Historical Reading of Synge's *Playboy*," in Michael Allen and Angela Wilcox (eds.), *Critical Approaches to Anglo-Irish Literature* (Gerrards Cross, Bucks: Colin Smythe, 1989), p. 68.

63 Gibbons, *Transformations*, p. 33.

64 Tifft, "Parricidal Phantasm," p. 324.

65 Fanon, *Wretched of Earth*, p. 116.
66 Tifft, "Parricidal Phantasm," pp. 325, 320–1.
67 Ibid., p. 328.
68 Ibid., pp. 321–2.
69 Turner, *From Ritual to Theater*, pp. 75, 83. Turner distinguishes between the liminal and the liminoid, the former "predominate in tribal and early agrarian societies" and issuing in "collective representations," the latter predominate in societies with "organic solidarity," bonded reciprocally by "'contractual relations'" and tending toward individual expression ("idiosyncratic, quirky"), even constituting "parts of social critiques or even revolutionary manifestos" (pp. 53–5). Needless to say, it is at times difficult to tell whether a given phenomenon or event or space is liminal or liminoid, especially given Ireland's colonial context, where the liminal exists side by side with the liminoid.
70 Turner, *From Ritual to Theater*, p. 75; Turner quotes Barbara Myerhoff.
71 Kiberd, *Inventing Ireland*, p. 181.
72 Tifft notes that it is only on the third instance of the word "shift" that the audience reacted violently ("Parricidal Phantasm," p. 316). See also Kiberd, who writes, "[t]he word 'shift' had been used without offense in Hyde's *Love Songs of Connacht* (in Irish, of course, as *léine*): but when Synge politely pointed this out in a newspaper interview, the point was left unexplored in the ensuing controversy" (*Inventing Ireland*, p. 183).
73 Holder, "Between Fiction and Reality," pp. 528–9.
74 Ginger Strand cites the complete poem as well as other examples; see "Problem of the Audience," pp. 19–20.
75 Anonymous, *Freeman's Journal*, Jan. 31, 1907, rpt. in Kilroy (ed.), *The "Playboy" Riots*, pp. 45–6.
76 Cairns and Richards, "Reading a Riot," p. 231. "Davisites" were people who upheld ideas associated with the *Nation*, a journal of the Young Ireland movement in which Thomas Davis played a pivotal role. On the politics of the Abbey Theatre audiences, see Frazier, *Behind the Scenes*, chapter 3. On Davis, see Sir Charles Gavin Duffy (ed.), *Thomas Davis; the Memoirs of an Irish Patriot, 1840–1846* (London, K. Paul, Trench, Trubner & Co., 1890).
77 Cairns and Richards, "Reading a Riot," p. 232.
78 Anonymous, *Sinn Fein*, Feb. 9, 1907, rpt. in Kilroy (ed.), *The "Playboy" Riots*, p. 94.
79 Turner, *From Ritual to Theater*, p. 71.
80 Knapp, "Primitivism and Empire," p. 67.
81 Ibid., p. 66.
82 Ibid., p. 67.
83 W. B. Yeats, *Freeman's Journal*, Jan. 30, 1907, rpt. in Kilroy (ed.), *The "Playboy" Riots*, p. 7.
84 George Roberts, quoted in Kiberd, *Synge and the Irish Language*, p. 225.
85 Ibid., pp. 258–9.
86 Kiberd, *Inventing Ireland*, p. 173.

5 "A RENEGADE FROM THE RANKS": JOYCE'S CRITIQUE OF
REVIVALISM IN THE EARLY FICTION

1 Seamus Heaney, "Station Island," in *Station Island* (London: Faber and Faber, 1984), p. 93

2 Terry Eagleton, *Heathcliff and the Great Hunger: Studies in Irish Culture* (London and New York: Verso, 1995), p. 297.

3 Frantz Fanon, *The Wretched of the Earth*, trans. Constance Farrington (New York: Grove Weidenfeld, 1963), p. 152.

4 Ibid., p. 197.

5 See Enda Duffy, *The Subaltern* Ulysses (Minneapolis: University of Minnesota Press, 1994), pp. 100–1. See also Vincent Cheng, *Joyce, Race, and Empire* (Cambridge University Press, 1995), pp. 51–7.

6 Seamus Deane, *Celtic Revivals: Essays in Modern Irish Literature 1880–1980* (Winston-Salem: Wake Forest University Press, 1987), pp. 99–100.

7 Ibid., p. 96. In "Irish Poetry and Irish Nationalism," in Douglas Dunn (ed.), *Two Decades of Irish Writing: A Critical Survey* (Chester Springs, PA: Dufour, 1975), Deane includes Joyce among the four principal Revivalists, along with George Moore, W. B. Yeats and J. M. Synge (p. 4).

8 See Seamus Deane, "Heroic Styles: The Tradition of an Idea," in *Ireland's Field Day* (London: Hutchinson, 1985), pp. 56–8.

9 Emer Nolan, *James Joyce and Nationalism* (London and New York: Routledge, 1995), pp. 17–18.

10 Ibid., pp. 1–22.

11 Nolan, *Joyce and Nationalism*, p. xii.

12 Ibid., p. 23.

13 Ibid., p. 32.

14 Ibid., p. 24.

15 Ibid.

16 On the revisionist attitude toward *Dubliners*, see Nolan, *Joyce and Nationalism*, pp. 24–35; Cheng, *Joyce, Race, and Empire*, pp. 77–147; Michael Levenson, "Living History in 'The Dead,'" in James Joyce, *Dubliners: Text, Criticism and Notes*, ed. Robert Scholes and A. Walton Litz (Middlesex: Penguin, 1996), pp. 421–38.

17 Levenson, ibid., p. 423.

18 Talal Asad, "The Concept of Cultural Translation in British Social Anthropology," in James Clifford and George E. Marcus (eds.), *Writing Culture: The Poetics and Politics of Ethnography* (Berkeley: University of California Press, 1986), p. 159.

19 Anonymous, *Freeman's Journal*, Jan. 29, 1907, rpt. in James Kilroy (ed.), *The "Playboy" Riots* (Dublin: The Dolmen Press, 1971), 20.

20 W. B. Yeats, *Uncollected Prose by W. B. Yeats*, vol. II (1897–1939), ed. John P. Frayne and Colton Johnson (New York: Columbia University Press, 1976), p. 69.

21 Roy Pascal, *The Dual Voice: Free Indirect Speech and Its Functioning in the*

Nineteenth-Century European Novel (Manchester University Press, 1977), p. 98.

22 James Joyce, *The Critical Writings of James Joyce*, ed. Ellsworth Mason and Richard Ellmann (1959; rpt. Ithaca: Cornell University Press, 1989), p. 104.

23 Trevor Williams, "No Cheer for the 'Gratefully Oppressed' in Joyce's *Dubliners*," *Style* 25.3 (Fall 1991), 426.

24 Recent criticism of "A Mother" has alerted us to the self-delusion of Dubliners who appeal to Revivalist attitudes in order to further their own ambitions. See Jane E. Miller, "'O, She's a nice Lady!': A Rereading of 'A Mother,' in James Joyce, *Dubliners: Text, Criticism and Notes*, ed. Robert Scholes and A. Walton Litz (Middlesex: Penguin, 1996), pp. 348–72, and Joseph Valente, *James Joyce and the Problem of Justice: Negotiating Sexual and Colonial Difference* (Cambridge University Press, 1996), pp. 49–66.

25 Levenson, "Living History," p. 425.

26 Nolan, *Joyce and Nationalism*, p. 35.

27 Fanon, *Wretched of the Earth*, p. 237.

28 Joyce's texts are replete with examples of a mimicry that remains unreflective, uncritical, and finally ineffective. See, for example, the *Dubliners* story "Counterparts," in which Farrington's habit of mimicking the accent of Alleyne, his Northern Irish employer, far from challenging or disrupting Alleyne's authority, succeeds only in jeopardizing his own position and pointing up his powerlessness. The enunciatory power of his mimicry diminishes gradually in facile repetitions for his friends' amusement in public houses.

29 Levenson, "Living History," p. 429.

30 "The bourgeois caste, that section of the nation which annexes for its own profit all the wealth of the country, by a kind of unexpected logic will pass disparaging judgments upon the other Negroes and the other Arabs that more often than not are reminiscent of the racist doctrines of the former representatives of the colonial power" (Fanon, *Wretched of the Earth*, p. 167).

31 W. B. Yeats, *Cathleen Ni Houlihan, The Collected Plays of W. B. Yeats* (New York: Macmillan, 1953), p. 54.

32 Vincent Pecora, "'The Dead' and the Generosity of the Word," *PMLA* 101 (1986), 239.

33 See Sandy Carlson, "James Joyce's Irish Nationalism, A Response to His Time: *A Portrait of the Artist as a Young Man*," *The Arkansas Quarterly* 2.4 (Oct. 1993), 282–98; Cheng, *Joyce, Race, and Empire*, pp. 57–76; and Dominic Manganiello, *Joyce's Politics* (London: Routledge, 1980), pp. 67–94.

34 Cheng, *Joyce, Race, and Empire*, p. 62.

35 I have discussed elsewhere the idea of the *Bildung*-plot and the role of the *Bildungsroman* tradition in Joyce's early fiction; see "The Book of Youth: Reading Joyce's Bildungsroman," *Genre* 22 (1989), 21–40, and "Confessing Oneself: Colonial *Bildung* and Homoeros in Joyce's *A*

Portrait of the Artist as a Young Man," in Joseph Valente (ed.), *Quare Joyce* (Ann Arbor: University of Michigan Press, 1998), pp. 157–82.

36 Deane, *Celtic Revivals*, p. 76.

37 See R. F. Foster, "Protestant Magic: W. B. Yeats and the Spell of Irish History," *Proceedings of the British Academy* 75 (1989), 243–66.

38 Cheng, *Joyce, Race, and Empire*, p. 67. See L. P. Curtis, *Apes and Angels: The Irishman in Victorian Caricature* (Washington, DC : Smithsonian Institution Press, 1996) and *Anglo-Saxons and Celts: A Study of Anti-Irish Prejudice in Victorian England* (Bridgeport, CT: University of Bridgeport Press, 1968).

39 Further on, Mr. Heffernan, a friend of Mr. Fulham's, "seemed to [Stephen] a typical Irishman of the provinces; assertive and fearful, sentimental and rancorous, idealist in speech and realist in conduct" (*SH*, 249).

40 Bronislaw Malinowski, *A Diary in the Strict Sense of the Term*, trans. Norbert Guterman (Stanford University Press, 1989), p. 257.

41 In *Stephen Hero*, Stephen claims that "The Roman, not the Sassenach, was for him the tyrant of the islanders: and so deeply had the tyranny eaten into all souls that the intelligence, first overborne so arrogantly, was now eager to prove that arrogance its friend" (*SH*, 53).

42 On the "confessional intimacy" that Stephen enjoys with Davin (as well as with Cranly), see my "Confessing Oneself," 177–9.

43 Patrick McGee, *Telling the Other: The Question of Value in Modern and Postcolonial Writing* (Ithaca and London: Cornell University Press, 1992), p. 139. See also Duffy, *Subaltern*, pp. 1–22.

44 See Douglas Hyde, "The Necessity for De-Anglicizing Ireland," in *The Revival of Irish Literature: Addresses by Sir Charles Gavan Duffy, K.C.M.G., Dr. George Sigerson, and Dr. Douglas Hyde* (London: T. Fisher Unwin, 1894), pp. 115–61. This essay was first delivered before the Irish National Literary Society in 1892.

45 Nolan, *Joyce and Nationalism*, p. 113.

46 For a discussion of the sovereignty figure and the iconization of women, see Richard Kearney, "Myth and Motherland," in *Ireland's Field Day: Field Day Theatre Company* (London: Hutchinson, 1985), pp. 61–80 and Amanda Yeates, "Cathleen in Service: Female Iconography in Lady Gregory, Yeats, Synge, and Joyce," Ph.D. diss., Arizona State University, December 1999.

47 See F. L. Radford, "Dedalus and the Bird Girl: Classical Text and Celtic Subtext in *A Portrait*," *James Joyce Quarterly* 24.3 (Spring 1987), 253–74 and Anthony Roche, " 'The Strange Light of some New World': Stephen's Vision in *A Portrait*," *James Joyce Quarterly* 25.3 (Spring 1988), 323–32.

48 David Lloyd, *Anomalous States: Irish Writing and the Post-Colonial Moment* (Dublin: Lilliput Press, 1993), pp. 105–6.

49 Cheng, *Joyce, Race, and Empire*, p. 71.

50 Ibid.

6 JOYCE'S MODERNISM: ANTHROPOLOGICAL FICTIONS
IN *ULYSSES*

1 James Joyce, *Ulysses* (1961; rpt. New York: Vintage-Random 1990), p. 443.

2 T. S. Eliot, "*Ulysses*, Order and Myth," in Frank Kermode (ed.), *Selected Prose of T. S. Eliot* (New York: Harcourt, Brace Jovanovich, 1975), p. 177.

3 Seamus Deane, *Celtic Revivals: Essays in Modern Irish Literature 1880–1980* (Winston-Salem: Wake Forest University Press, 1987), p. 96. See my discussion in the first part of chapter 5.

4 Marc Manganaro, "Reading 'Culture' in Joyce's *Ulysses*," *James Joyce Quarterly* 35.4/36.1 (Summer/Fall 1998), 776.

5 Ibid., 776–7.

6 Ibid., 776.

7 Manganaro refers to Cheryl Herr's *Joyce's Anatomy of Culture* (Urbana: University of Illinois Press, 1986) as an example of "culturalist criticism" that fails to reflect critically on the concept of culture that underwrites it.

8 Terence Turner, "Representing, Resisting, Rethinking: Historical Transformation of Kayapo Culture and Anthropological Consciousness," in George W. Stocking, Jr. (ed.), *Colonial Situations: Essays on the Contextualization of Ethnographic Knowledge*, History of Anthropology 7 (Madison: University of Wisconsin Press, 1991), p. 305.

9 See David Spurr, "Myths of Anthropology: Eliot, Joyce, Lévy-Bruhl," *PMLA* 109 (March 1994), 226–80. I will discuss those critics who consider Haines's role in "Telemachus" in the next section of this chapter.

10 L. H. Platt has done some important work on Joyce's treatment of the Revival, thought he does not explore the anthropological authority behind it. See "Joyce and the Anglo-Irish Revival: The Triestine Lectures," *James Joyce Quarterly* 29.2 (Winter 1992), 259–66 and "The Voice of Esau: Culture and Nationalism in 'Scylla and Charybdis,'" *James Joyce Quarterly* 29.4 (Summer 1992), 737–50.

11 David Lloyd, *Anomalous States: Irish Writing and the Post-Colonial Moment* (Dublin: Lilliput Press, 1993), p. 115.

12 Stephen Tyler, *The Unspeakable: Discourse, Dialogue, and Rhetoric in the Postmodern World* (Madison: University of Wisconsin Press, 1987), p. 150.

13 Talal Asad, "The Concept of Cultural Translation in British Social Anthropology," in James Clifford and George E. Marcus (eds.), *Writing Culture: The Poetics and Politics of Ethnography* (Berkeley: University of California Press, 1986), p. 163.

14 Enda Duffy, *The Subaltern* Ulysses (Minneapolis: University of Minnesota Press, 1994), p. 51.

15 Vincent Cheng, *Joyce, Race, and Empire* (Cambridge University Press, 1995), p. 152.

16 Duffy, *Subaltern* Ulysses, p. 47.

17 Ibid., pp. 47–8.
18 Homi Bhabha, *The Location of Culture* (London and New York: Routledge, 1994), p. 70.
19 Frantz Fanon, *The Wretched of the Earth*, trans. Constance Farrington (New York: Grove Weidenfeld, 1963), pp. 236–7.
20 Albert Memmi, *The Colonizer and the Colonized*, trans. Howard Greenfeld (Boston: Beacon, 1967), p. 120.
21 See Manganaro, "Reading 'Culture,'" 769.
22 Vincent Pecora, "Arnoldean Ethnology," *Victorian Studies* 41.3 (Spring 1998), 356.
23 Sir Charles Gavan Duffy, "The Revival of Irish Literature," in *The Revival of Irish Literature: Addresses by Sir Charles Gavan Duffy, K.C.M.G., Dr. George Sigerson, and Dr. Douglas Hyde* (London: Fisher Unwin, 1894), p. 118.
24 Quoted in Lloyd, *Anomalous States*, p. 103.
25 Ibid., p. 104.
26 For Lloyd, a "translational aesthetic" is one "for which the subject is formed in a continual appropriation of the alien to itself, just as translation, as opposed, for example, to interpretation or paraphrase, is seen as essentially a recreation of the foreign text in one's own language" (Ibid., p. 105). See also Lloyd, *Nationalism and Minor Literature: James Clarence Mangan and the Emergence of Irish Cultural Nationalism* (Berkeley: University of California Press, 1987), chapter 4.
27 Platt, "The Voice of Esau," 743–5.
28 See Mark 9:24, where a possessed boy appeals to Christ: "Lord, I believe; help thou mine unbelief."
29 Robert Martin Adams, "Hades," in Clive Hart and David Hayman (eds.), *James Joyce's* Ulysses: *Critical Essays* (Berkeley: University of California Press, 1974), p. 111.
30 See Matthew Arnold, *On the Study of Celtic Literature*, in *The Works of Matthew Arnold*, vol. v (1867; rpt. London: Macmillan, 1903), p. 83.
31 Duffy, *Subaltern* Ulysses, p. 62; see 53–92.
32 Cheng, *Joyce, Race, and Empire*, p. 175.
33 See Emer Nolan, *James Joyce and Nationalism* (London and New York: Routledge, 1995), pp. 94–119.
34 James Clifford, "Partial Truths," in James Clifford and George E. Marcus (eds.), *Writing Culture: The Poetics and Politics of Ethnography* (Berkeley: University of California Press, 1986), p. 11.
35 Bronislaw Malinowski, *Argonauts of the Western Pacific* (London: Routledge; New York: Dutton, 1932), p. 3.
36 Ibid., pp. 516–17.
37 Ibid., p. 25.
38 Johannes Fabian, *Time and Other: How Anthropology Makes its Object* (New York: Columbia University Press, 1982), p. 123.
39 Tyler, *The Unspeakable*, p. 150.
40 Ibid., 98.
41 Fabian, *Time and Other*, p. 123.

42 Bronislaw Malinowski, *The Sexual Life of Savages in North-Western Melanesia* (New York: Eugenics Publishing Company, 1929), p. 16.

43 Ibid., p. xxiii.

44 Bronislaw Malinowski, *A Diary in the Strict Sense of the Term*, trans. Norbert Guterman (Stanford University Press, 1989), p. 255, 253, 225.

45 I discuss the problem of the gaze in "Nausicaa" and its treatment by Joyce's critics in "Colonial Discourse and the Subject of Empire in Joyce's 'Nausicaa,'" *European Joyce Studies* 6 (1998), 115–44.

46 Stephen A. Tyler, "Post-Modern Ethnography: From Document of the Occult to Occult Document," in James Clifford and George E. Marcus (eds.), *Writing Culture: The Poetics and Politics of Ethnography* (Berkeley: University of California Press, 1986), p. 126

47 Tyler, *The Unspeakable*, p. 98.

48 On Gerty's self-construction, see Margot Norris, "Modernism, Myth, and Desire in 'Nausicaa,'" *James Joyce Quarterly* 26 (1988), 37–50 and Fritz Senn, "Nausicaa," in Clive Hart and David Hayman (eds.), *James Joyce's* Ulysses: *Critical Essays* (Berkeley: University of California Press, 1974), pp. 277–311.

49 Edward Said, *Orientalism* (London: Peregrin-Penguin, 1985), p. 1.

50 Ibid., p. 3.

51 Edward Said, *The World, the Text, and the Critic* (Cambridge, MA: Harvard University Press, 1983), p. 222.

52 Said, *Orientalism*, p. 227.

53 Ibid.

54 R. Brandon Kershner has argued that Bloom's Orientalist fantasies in "Circe" are public, by which he means that Bloom has ready access to a store of images that also turn up in Stephen's dream of "Haroun al Raschid" (*U*, 47). See "*Ulysses* and the Orient," *James Joyce Quarterly* 35.2/3 (Winter/Spring 1998), 273–96. Kershner concludes that this shared access amounts to a form of Orientalism that is "entirely and explicitly intertextual" (293). I agree in the main with Kershner's argument, though it does not alter the fact that Bloom's fantasies are *his* regardless of the shared source of the images he uses or their intertextual nature.

55 Joseph Conrad, *Heart of Darkness*, 3rd edn, ed. Robert Kimbrough (New York: Norton, 1988), p. 10.

56 Nolan, *Joyce and Nationalism*, p. 21. See Dominic Manganiello, *Joyce's Politics* (London: Routledge, 1980) and Richard Ellmann, *The Consciousness of Joyce* (London: Faber, 1977).

57 Duffy, "The Revival of Irish Literature," p. 53. Duffy goes on to name "little Athens," "little Rome," and "little Portugal" as examples of "small nations." In a similar vein, George Sigerson notes that the "Heroic age of Ireland" was comparable to Greece and Rome ("Irish Literature: Its Origin, Environment, and Influence," in *The Revival of Irish Literature: Addresses by Sir Charles Gavan Duffy, K.C.M.G., Dr. George Sigerson, and Dr. Douglas Hyde* [London: Fisher Unwin, 1894], p. 68).

58 R. F. Foster, "Anglo-Irish Literature, Gaelic Nationalism and Irish

Politics in the 1890's," in J. M. W. Bean (ed.), *The Political Culture of Modern Britain: Studies in Memory of Stephen Koss* (London: Hamish Hamilton, 1987), p. 100.

59 Duffy, *Subaltern* Ulysses, p. 33.

60 Joyce had a guarded respect for Arthur Griffith's Sinn Fein movement, especially when it concentrated on economic reform. See Joyce's article "Fenianism: The Last Fenian," published in the Trieste newspaper *Il Piccolo della Sera* in 1907 (rpt. *The Critical Writings of James Joyce*, ed. Ellsworth Mason and Richard Ellmann [1959; rpt. Ithaca: Cornell University Press, 1989], pp. 187–92). Malcolm Brown offers an anecdote that says less about Joyce's views than it does about his relation to "romantic Ireland, dead and gone": "watching [John] O'Leary make his myopic course through the Dublin bookstalls, [Joyce] saw in him the living reminder of the Fenian principle of 'physical force,' the persuasion that it was wasted time to broach the Irish issue to an Englishman without a gun in hand" (*The Politics of Irish Literature: From Thomas Davis to W. B. Yeats* [Seattle: University of Washington Press, 1972], pp. 7–8). See also Manganiello, *Joyce's Politics*.

61 Nolan, *Joyce and Nationalism*, p. 100.

62 For sources of these parodies, see the entries for "Cyclops" in Don Gifford and Robert J. Seidman (eds.), *Notes for Joyce: An Annotation of James Joyce's* Ulysses, rev. and expanded edition (University of California Press, 1988).

63 Maria Tymoczko, *The Irish* Ulysses (Berkeley: University of California Press, 1994), p. 141. Irish *senchas* (which can include "old tales, ancient history, tradition; genealogy, traditional law") "can be viewed as expanded or explicated lists, annotated with anecdote or narrative as the case may be," but, in any case, listing is "eminently consistent with narrative as a form of learning and lore" (p. 146).

64 Ibid., pp. 147, 149.

65 Fanon, *Wretched of the Earth*, p. 242.

66 Tymoczko, *The Irish* Ulysses, p. 150.

67 Nolan, *Joyce and Nationalism*, p. 119.

68 Ibid., p. 6.

69 Fanon, *Wretched of the Earth*, pp. 222, 68.

70 Ibid., p. 170.

71 Deane, *Celtic Revivals*, pp. 99–100.

CONCLUSION. AFTER THE REVIVAL: "NOT EVEN MAIN STREET IS SAFE"

1 Derek Mahon, "Lives," in *Selected Poems* (New York: Penguin, 1991), p. 36.

2 A. C. Haddon and D. J. Cunningham, "The Anthropometry Laboratory of Ireland," *Journal of the Anthropological Institute of Great Britain and Ireland* 21 (1892), 36.

3 Frantz Fanon, *The Wretched of the Earth*, trans. Constance Farrington (New York: Grove Weidenfeld, 1963), pp. 36–7.

4 See chapter 5 for a discussion of Fanon's idea that "political education means opening [the peoples'] minds, awakening them, and allowing the birth of their intelligence; as [Aimé] Césaire said, it is 'to invent souls'" (ibid., p. 197).

5 Terry Eagleton, *Heathcliff and the Great Hunger: Studies in Irish Culture* (London; New York: Verso, 1995), p. 297.

6 William S. Simmons, "Culture Theory in Contemporary Ethnohistory," *Ethnohistory* 35.1 (1988), 7.

7 Stephen A. Tyler, "Post-Modern Ethnography: From Document of the Occult to Occult Document," in James Clifford and George E. Marcus (eds.), *Writing Culture: The Poetics and Politics of Ethnography* (Berkeley: University of California Press, 1986), p. 130.

8 Bronislaw Malinowski, *Argonauts of the Western Pacific* (London: Routledge; New York: Dutton, 1932), p. 80.

9 "Culture or Civilization, taken in its wide ethnographic sense, is that complex whole which includes knowledge, belief, art, morals, law, custom, and any other capabilities and habits acquired by man as a member of society" (E. B. Tylor, *Primitive Culture*, vol. 1 [1871; rpt. New York: Harper, 1958], p. 1).

10 Conrad M. Arensberg, *The Irish Countryman: An Anthropological Study* (1937; rpt. Gloucester, MA: Peter Smith, 1959), pp. 1–2.

11 Ibid., p. 11. See also Conrad M. Arensberg and Solon T. Kimball, *Family and Community in Ireland*, 2nd edn (1940; Cambridge, MA: Harvard University Press, 1968), pp. xxv–xxxiii.

12 Ibid.

13 Ibid., p. 8.

14 Malinowski, *Argonauts*, p. 11.

15 Arensberg, *Irish Countryman*, p. 16. The four Irelands are (1) "the mystic land of the past," (2) "the happy-go-lucky present," (3) "a sober, hard-working land of minute towns and small farms," and (4) "the Ireland of the Faith, the Island of Saints and Scholars" (pp. 13–15).

16 Ibid., p. 179.

17 Lawrence J. Taylor, "'There Are Two Things that People Don't Like to Hear about Themselves': The Anthropology of Ireland and the Irish View of Anthropology," *The South Atlantic Quarterly, Ireland and Irish Cultural Studies* 95.1 (Winter 1996), 214.

18 Ibid., pp. 214–15.

19 Taylor, p. 220. See Robin Fox, *Encounter with Anthropology* (New York: Harcourt Brace Jovanovich, 1973) and Nancy Scheper-Hughes, *Saints, Scholars, and Schizophrenics: Mental Illness in Rural Ireland* (Berkeley: University of California Press, 1979).

20 Ibid., p. 219.

21 See Maurice O'Sullivan, *Twenty Years A-Growing*, trans. Moya Llewelyn Davies and George Thomson (New York: Viking Press, 1933); Peig

Sayers, *The Autobiography of Peig Sayers of the Great Blasket Island*, trans. Bryan MacMahon (Syracuse University Press, 1974); Tomas Crohan, *The Islandman*, trans. Robin Flower (Oxford: Clarendon Press, 1951); and Pat Mullen, *Man of Aran* (1934; rpt. Cambridge, MA: MIT Press, 1970). Mullen's *Man of Aran* was made into a documentary, directed by Robert J. Flaherty, in 1934. A 1935 edition of *Man of Aran* contains sixteen stills from the film.

22 Moya Llewelyn Davies and George Thomson, "Preface," *Twenty Years*, p. ix.

23 O'Sullivan, *Twenty Years*, p. 72.

24 Davies and Thomson, "Preface," *Twenty Years*, p. x.

25 A. R. Radcliffe-Brown, *The Andaman Islanders* (1922; rpt. New York: The Free Press, 1964), pp. 230–1.

26 E. M. Forster, "Introductory Note," *Twenty Years*, p. v.

27 John Montague, *The Rough Field*, 5th edn (1972; rpt. Winston-Salem: Wake Forest University Press, 1989), p. 34.

28 Seamus Heaney, *Preoccupations: Selected Prose 1968–78* (New York: Noonday-Farrar, Straus and Giroux, 1980), p. 41. On the archaeological quality of Heaney's work, see Jon Stallworthy, "The Poet as Archaeologist: W. B. Yeats and Seamus Heaney," *Review of English Studies*, n. s. 33 (1982), 158–74 and Ruth Niel, "Digging into History: A Reading of Brian Friel's *Volunteers* and Seamus Heaney's 'Viking Dublin: Trial Pieces,'" *Irish University Review* 16.1 (Spring 1986), 35–47. Other relevant works will be discussed below.

29 Seamus Deane, "Irish Poetry and Irish Nationalism," in Douglas Dunn (ed.), *Two Decades of Irish Writing: A Critical Survey* (Chester Springs, PA: Dufour, 1975), p. 13.

30 Quoted in Neil Corcoran, *Seamus Heaney* (London: Faber and Faber, 1986), pp. 33–4.

31 Seamus Heaney, "Kinship," in *North* (London: Faber and Faber, 1975), p. 33.

32 Ciaran Carson, quoted in Edna Longley, "*North:* 'Inner Emigré' or 'Artful Voyeur'?" in Tony Curtis (ed.), *The Art of Seamus Heaney*, 3rd edn (Chester Springs, PA: Dufour, 1994), p. 81.

33 Cairan Carson, quoted in Henry Hart, *Seamus Heaney: Poet of Contrary Progressions* (Syracuse University Press, 1992), pp. 76–7.

34 Longley, "*North:* 'Inner Emigré,'" p. 83.

35 Ibid., p. 86.

36 Ibid., p. 69.

37 Heaney, "Punishment," in *North*, p. 31.

38 Deane, "Irish Poetry," p. 12.

39 Mahon, "Lives," *Selected Poems*, p. 36.

40 Ibid.

41 Stephen Tyler, *The Unspeakable: Discourse, Dialogue, and Rhetoric in the Postmodern World* (Madison: University of Wisconsin Press, 1987), p. 150.

42 Mahon, "Lives," *Selected Poems*, pp. 37–8.

Adams, Hazard, *The Book of Yeats's Poems*, Tallahassee: Florida State University Press, 1990.

Adams, Robert Martin, "Hades," in *James Joyce's* Ulysses: *Critical Essays*, Clive Hart and David Hayman (eds.), Berkeley: University of California Press, 1974, 91–114.

Adorno, Theodor, *Prisms*, trans. Samuel and Shierry Weber, Cambridge, MA: MIT Press, 1981.

Allison, Jonathan (ed.), *Yeats's Political Identities: Selected Essays*, Ann Arbor: The University of Michigan Press, 1996.

Anderson, Benedict, *Imagined Communities: Reflections on the Origin and Spread of Nationalism*, London: Verso, 1983.

Anghinetti, Paul, "Berkeley's Influence on Joyce," *James Joyce Quarterly* 19 (Spring 1982), 315–29.

Anonymous, "The Aran Islands," *The Times Literary Supplement* (June 28, 1907), 202.

Arbois de Jubainville, Henri D', *Le Cycle Mythologique Irlandais et la Mythologie Celtique*, vol. II, Osnabruck: Zeller, 1969.

Arensberg, Conrad M, *The Irish Countryman: An Anthropological Study*, 1937, rpt. Gloucester, MA: Peter Smith, 1959.

Arensberg, Conrad M. and Solon T. Kimball, *Family and Community in Ireland*, 2nd edn, 1940; Cambridge, MA: Harvard University Press, 1968.

Arnold, Matthew, *On the Study of Celtic Literature*, 1867, in *The Works of Matthew Arnold*, vol. v, London: Macmillan, 1903, vii-xxi, 1–150.

Asad, Talal (ed.), *Anthropology and the Colonial Encounter*, New York: Humanities Press, 1973.

"The Concept of Cultural Translation in British Social Anthropology," in *Writing Culture: The Poetics and Politics of Ethnography*, James Clifford and George E. Marcus (eds.), Berkeley: University of California Press, 1986, 141–64.

Ashcroft, W. D, "Intersecting Marginalities: Post-colonialism and Feminism," *Kunapipi* 11.2 (1989), 23–35.

Bakhtin, M. M., *The Dialogic Imagination*, Michael Holquist (ed.), trans. Caryl Emerson and Michael Holquist, Austin: University of Texas Press, 1981.

Balch, Willaim Stevens, *Ireland, As I Saw It: The Character, Condition, and Prospects of the People*, New York: G. P. Putnam, 1850.

Beddoe, John, "Anniversary Address," *Journal of the Anthropological Institute of Great Britain and Ireland* 20 (1891), 348–59.

Benson, Paul (ed.), *Anthropology and Literature*, Urbana and Chicago: University of Illinois Press, 1993.

Bergin, Osborn, *Irish Bardic Poetry*, David Greene and Fergus Kelly (eds.), 1912; rpt. Dublin: Dublin Institute for Advanced Studies, 1970.

Bhabha, Homi, *The Location of Culture*, London and New York: Routledge, 1994.

Bierce, Ambrose, *The Devil's Dictionary*, Cleveland and New York: World Publishing Company, 1944.

Blau, Herbert, "The Myth of Ritual in the Marketplace of Signs," in *The Play and Its Critic: Essays for Eric Bentley*, Michael Bertin (ed.), Lanham: University Press of America, 1986, 305–39.

"Universals of Performance; or Amortizing Play," in *By Means of Performance: Intercultural Studies of Theater and Ritual*, Richard Schechner and Willa Appel (eds.), Cambridge University Press, 1990, 250–72.

Boas, Franz, "History and Science in Anthropology: A Reply," *American Anthropologist*, n.s. 38 (1936), 137–41.

Race, Language and Culture, New York: Macmillan, 1940.

Bourgois, Maurice, "Synge and Loti," *The Westminster Review* 179 (May 1913), 532–6.

Brabrook, E. W., "Anniversary Address," *Journal of the Anthropological Institute of Great Britain and Ireland* 25 (1896), 379–405.

"President's Address," *Journal of the Anthropological Institute of Great Britain and Ireland* 26 (1897), 416–32.

"President's Address," *Journal of the Anthropological Institute of Great Britain and Ireland* 27 (1898), 546–67.

Brown, Malcolm, *The Politics of Irish Literature: From Thomas Davis to W. B. Yeats*, Seattle: University of Washington Press, 1972.

Cairns, David and Shaun Richards, "Reading a Riot: The 'Reading Formation' of Synge's Abbey Audience," *Literature and History* 12.2 (Autumn 1987), 219–37.

"Tropes and Traps: Aspects of 'Woman' and Nationality in Twentieth-Century Irish Drama," in *Gender in Irish Writing*, Toni O'Brien Johnson and David Cairns (eds.), Buckingham: Open University Press, 1991, 105–35.

" 'Woman' in the Discourse of Celticism: A Reading of *The Shadow of the Glen*," *Canadian Journal of Irish Studies* 13.1 (June 1987), 43–60.

Writing Ireland: Colonialism, Nationalism and Culture, Manchester University Press, 1988.

Carlson, Sandy, "James Joyce's Irish Nationalism, A Response to His Time: *A Portrait of the Artist as a Young Man*," *The Arkansas Quarterly* 2.4 (October 1993), 282–98.

Castle, Gregory, "Colonial Discourse and the Subject of Empire in Joyce's 'Nausicaa,'" *European Joyce Studies* 6 (1998), 115–44.

"Confessing Oneself: Colonial *Bildung* and Homoeros in Joyce's *A Portrait of the Artist as a Young Man*," in *Quare Joyce*, Joseph Valente (ed.), Ann Arbor: University of Michigan Press, 1998, 157–82

"The Book of Youth: Reading Joyce's Bildungsroman," *Genre* 22 (1989), 21–40.

Cheng, Vincent, *Joyce, Race, and Empire*, Cambridge University Press, 1995.

Chesterton, G. K., *Irish Impressions*, London: W. Collins, 1919.

Clifford, James, "On Ethnographic Allegory," in *Writing Culture: The Poetics and Politics of Ethnography*, James Clifford and George E. Marcus (eds.), Berkeley: University of California Press, 1986, 98–121.

"Partial Truths," in *Writing Culture: The Poetics and Politics of Ethnography*, James Clifford and George E. Marcus (eds.), Berkeley: University of California Press, 1986, 1–26.

The Predicament of Culture: Twentieth-Century Ethnography, Literature, and Art, Cambridge, MA: Harvard University Press, 1988.

Clifford, James and George E. Marcus (eds.), *Writing Culture: The Poetics and Politics of Ethnography*, University of California Press, 1986.

Conrad, Joseph, *Heart of Darkness*, Robert Kimbrough (ed.), 3rd edn, New York: Norton, 1988.

Corcoran, Neil, *Seamus Heaney*, London: Faber and Faber, 1986.

Corkery, Daniel, *The Hidden Ireland: A Study of Gaelic Munster in the Eighteenth Century*, 1924; rpt. Dublin: Gill and Macmillan, 1967.

Synge and Anglo-Irish Literature: A Study, 1931; rpt. New York: Russell and Russell, 1965.

Crohan, Tomas, *The Islandman*, trans. Robin Flower, Oxford: Clarendon Press, 1951.

Cullingford, Elizabeth, *Gender and History in Yeats's Love Poetry*, Cambridge University Press, 1993.

Yeats, Ireland and Fascism, London: Macmillan, 1981.

Curtis, L. P., *Anglo-Saxons and Celts: A Study of Anti-Irish Prejudice in Victorian England*, Bridgeport, CT: University of Bridgeport Press, 1968.

Apes and Angels: The Irishman in Victorian Caricature, Washington, DC: Smithsonian Institution Press, 1996.

Davies, Moya Llewelyn and George Thomson, "Preface" to Maurice O'Sullivan's *Twenty Years A-Growing*, trans. Moya Llewelyn Davies and George Thomson, New York: Viking, 1933, vii-x.

Deane, Seamus, *Celtic Revivals: Essays in Modern Irish Literature 1880–1980*, Winston-Salem: Wake Forest University Press, 1987.

"Heroic Styles: The Tradition of an Idea," in *Ireland's Field Day*, London: Hutchinson, 1985, 45–58.

"Irish Poetry and Irish Nationalism," in *Two Decades of Irish Writing: A Critical Survey*, Douglas Dunn (ed.), Chester Springs, PA: Dufour, 1975, 4–22

Duffy, Enda, *The Subaltern* Ulysses, Minneapolis: University of Minnesota Press, 1994.

Duffy, Sir Charles Gavan, "The Revival of Irish Literature," in *The Revival of Irish Literature: Addresses by Sir Charles Gavan Duffy, K.C.M.G., Dr. George Sigerson, and Dr. Douglas Hyde,* London: Fisher Unwin, 1894, 9–59.

Duffy, Sir Charles Gavan (ed.), *Thomas Davis: The Memoirs of an Irish Patriot, 1840–1846,* London: K. Paul, Trench, Trubner & Co., 1890.

Eagleton, Terry, *Heathcliff and the Great Hunger: Studies in Irish Culture,* London; New York: Verso, 1995.

Eggan, Fred, "One Hundred Years of Ethnology and Social Anthropology," in *One Hundred Years of Anthropology,* J. O. Brew (ed.), Cambridge, MA: Harvard University Press, 1968.

Eliot, T. S., "*Ulysses,* Order and Myth," in *Selected Prose of T. S. Eliot,* Frank Kermode (ed.), New York: Harcourt, Brace Jovanovich, 1975, 175–8.

Ellmann, Richard, *The Consciousness of Joyce,* London: Faber, 1977.

Yeats: The Man and the Masks, New York: Norton, 1978.

Evans-Wentz, W. Y, *The Fairy-Faith in Celtic Countries,* 1911, New Hyde Park, NY: University Books, 1966.

Fabian, Johannes, *Time and Other: How Anthropology Makes its Object,* New York: Columbia University Press, 1982.

Fallis, Richard, "Art as Collaboration: Literary Influences on J. M. Synge," in *A J. M. Synge Literary Companion,* Edward A. Kopper Jr. (ed.), New York: Greenwood Press, 1988, 145–160.

The Irish Renaissance, Syracuse University Press, 1977.

Fanon, Frantz, *The Wretched of the Earth,* trans. Constance Farrington, New York: Grove Weidenfeld, 1963.

Faverty, Frederic E, *Matthew Arnold: The Ethnologist,* Evanston: Northwestern University Press, 1951.

Finneran, Richard J, *The Prose Fiction of W. B. Yeats: The Search for "Those Simple Forms,"* Dublin: Dolmen Press, 1973.

Fleischmann, Ruth, "Fathers Vanquished and Victorious – A Historical Reading of Synge's *Playboy,*" in *Critical Approaches to Anglo-Irish Literature,* Michael Allen and Angela Wilcox (eds.), Gerrards Cross, Bucks: Colin Smythe, 1989, 63–74.

Fleming, Deborah, "'*A Man who does not Exist*': The Irish Peasant in the Work of W. B. Yeats and J. M. Synge,* Ann Arbor: University of Michigan Press, 1995.

Forster, E. M., "Introductory Note" to Maurice O'Sullivan's *Twenty Years A-Growing,* trans. Moya Llewelyn Davies and George Thomson, New York: Viking, 1933, v-vi.

Foster, John Wilson, "*The Aran Islands* Revisited," *University of Toronto Quarterly* 51.3 (Spring 1982), 248–63.

Foster, R. F., "Anglo-Irish Literature, Gaelic Nationalism and Irish Politics in the 1890s," in *The Political Culture of Modern Britain: Studies in Memory of Stephen Koss,* J. M. W. Bean (ed.), London: Hamish Hamilton, 1987, 91–111.

Modern Ireland: 1600–1972, London: Penguin, 1989.

"Protestant Magic: W. B. Yeats and the Spell of Irish History," *Proceedings of the British Academy* 75 (1989), 243–66.

W. B. Yeats: A Life. Vol. I: The Apprentice Mage 1865–1914, Oxford University Press, 1997.

Fox, Robin, *Encounter with Anthropology*, New York: Harcourt Brace Jovanovich, 1973.

Frazier, Adrian, *Behind the Scenes: Yeats, Horniman, and the Struggle for the Abbey Theatre*, Berkeley: University of California Press, 1990.

Geertz, Clifford, *The Interpretation of Cultures*, New York: Basic, 1973.

Works and Lives: The Anthropologist as Author, Cambridge: Polity, 1988.

Gibbons, Luke, *Transformations in Irish Culture*, University of Notre Dame Press; Cork University Press, 1996.

Gifford, Don and Robert J. Seidman (eds.), *Notes for Joyce: An Annotation of James Joyce's* Ulysses, rev. and expanded edition, Berkeley: University of California Press, 1988.

Gregory, Lady Augusta, *Poets and Dreamers: Studies and Translations from the Irish*, New York: Oxford University Press, 1974.

Selected Writings, Lucy McDiarmid and Maureen Waters (eds.), London: Penguin, 1995.

Visions and Beliefs in the West of Ireland, Gerrards Cross: Colin Smythe, 1970.

Greene, David, "Synge and the Celtic Revival," *Modern Drama* 4 (1961), 292–99.

"Synge in the West of Ireland," *Mosaic* 5 (1971), 1–8.

Greene, David H. and Edward M. Stephens, *J. M. Synge 1871–1909*, New York: Macmillan, 1959.

Grene, Nicholas, "Synge's Creative Development in *The Aran Islands*," *Long Room* 10 (1974), 30–6.

"Yeats and the Re-making of Synge," in *Tradition and Influence in Anglo-Irish Poetry*, Terence Brown and Nicholas Grene (eds.), London: Macmillan, 1989, 47–62.

Haddon A. C., *The Study of Man*, New York: Putnam's; London: Bliss, Sands, 1989.

Haddon, A. C. and C. R. Browne, "The Ethnography of the Aran Islands, County Galway," *Proceedings of the Royal Irish Academy*, third series, 2 (1891–93), 768–830.

Haddon, A. C. and D. J. Cunningham, "The Anthropometry Laboratory of Ireland," *Journal of the Anthropological Institute of Great Britain and Ireland* 21 (1892), 35–9.

Hale, Anthony R, "Framing the Folk: Zora Neale Hurston, John Millington Synge, and the Politics of Aesthetic Ethnography," *The Comparatist* 20 (1996), 50–61.

Handler, Richard, "On Dialogue and Destructive Analysis: Problems in Narrating Nationalism and Ethnicity," *Journal of Anthropological Research* 41 (Summer 1985), 171–82.

Harrington, John P., "Resentment, Relevance, and the Production History of *The Playboy of the Western World*," in *Assessing the Achievement of J. M. Synge*, Alexander G. Gonzalez (ed.), Westport, CT: Greenwood, 1996, 3–9.

Hart, Henry, *Seamus Heaney: Poet of Contrary Progressions*, Syracuse University Press, 1992.

Hastrup, Kirsten, "Writing Ethnography: State of the Art," in *Anthropology and Autobiography*, Judith Okely and Helen Callaway (eds.), London and New York: Routledge, 1992, 117–33.

Heaney, Seamus, *Death of a Naturalist*, London: Faber, 1966.

  Preoccupations: Selected Prose 1968–78, New York: Noonday-Farrar, Straus and Giroux, 1980.

  Station Island, London: Faber and Faber, 1984.

  "A Tale of Two Islands: Reflections on the Irish Literary Revival," in *Irish Studies* 1, P. J. Drudy (ed.), London: Cambridge University Press, 1980, 1–20.

Hechter, Michael, *Internal Colonialism: The Celtic Fringe in British National Development, 1536–1977*, Berkeley and Los Angeles: University of California Press, 1975.

Hegel, G. W. F., *Introduction to The Philosophy of History*, trans. Leo Rauch, Indianapolis and Cambridge, MA: Hackett, 1988.

Herr Cheryl, *Joyce's Anatomy of Culture*, Urbana: University of Illinois Press, 1986.

Hirsch, Edward, "Coming Out Into the Light: W. B. Yeats's *The Celtic Twilight* (1893, 1902)," *Journal of the Folklore Institute* 18.1 (January–April 1981), 1–21.

  " 'Contention Is Better Than Loneliness': The Poet as Folklorist," in *The Genres of the Irish Literary Revival*, Ronald Schleifer (ed.), Norman, OK: Pilgrim Books, 1980, 11–25.

  "The Imaginary Irish Peasant," *PMLA* 106 (1991), 1116–33.

Hirst, Désirée, "The Sequel to 'The Irish Renaissance,' " *Canadian Journal of Irish Studies* 12.1 (June 1987), 17–42.

Holder, Heidi J, "Between Fiction and Reality: Synge's *Playboy* and Its Audience," *Journal of Modern Literature* 14 (Spring 1988), 527–42.

  " 'Stimulating stories of our own land': 'History Making' and the Work of J. M. Synge," in *Assessing the Achievement of J. M. Synge*, Alexander G. Gonzalez (ed.), Westport, CT: Greenwood, 1996, 139–150.

Howes, Marjorie, *Yeats's Nations: Gender, Class, and Irishness*, Cambridge, Engl.; New York: Cambridge University Press, 1997.

Hyde, Douglas, "The Necessity for De-Anglicizing Ireland," in *The Revival of Irish Literature: Addresses by Sir Charles Gavan Duffy, K.C.M.G., Dr. George Sigerson, and Dr. Douglas Hyde*, London: Fisher Unwin, 1894, 115–61.

JanMohamed, Abdul R, "The Economy of Manichean Allegory: The Function of Racial Difference in Colonialist Literature," *Critical Inquiry* 12 (1985), 59–87.

Joyce, James, *The Critical Writings of James Joyce*, Ellsworth Mason and

Richard Ellmann (eds.), 1959; rpt. Ithaca: Cornell University Press, 1989.

Dubliners: Text, Criticism and Notes, Robert Scholes and A. Walton Litz (eds.), Middlesex: Penguin, 1996.

A Portrait of the Artist as a Young Man: Text, Criticism and Notes, Chester G. Anderson (ed.), New York: Penguin 1977.

Stephen Hero, John J. Slocum and Herbert Cahoon (eds.), Norfolk, CT: New Directions, 1959.

Ulysses, 1961; rpt. New York: Vintage-Random 1990.

Kearney, Richard, "Myth and Motherland," in *Ireland's Field Day: Field Day Theatre Company*, London: Hutchinson, 1985, 61–80.

Kelsall, Malcolm, "Synge in Aran," *Irish University Review* 5 (1975), 254–70.

Kershner, R. Brandon, "*Ulysses* and the Orient," *James Joyce Quarterly* 35.2/3 (Winter/Spring 1998), 273–96.

Kiberd, Declan, "Anglo-Irish Attitudes," in *Ireland's Field Day: Field Day Theatre Company*, London: Hutchinson, 1985, 81–105.

Inventing Ireland, Cambridge, MA: Harvard University Press, 1996.

"The Perils of Nostalgia: A Critique of the Revival," in *Literature and the Changing Ireland*, Peter Connolly (ed.), Irish Literary Studies 9, Gerrards Cross: Colin Smythe; Totowa, NJ: Barnes and Noble, 1982, 1–24.

Synge and the Irish Language, Totowa, NJ: Rowman and Littlefield, 1979.

"Synge, Symons, and the Isles of Aran," *Notes on Modern Irish Literature* 1 (1989), 32–40.

Kilroy, James (ed.), *The "Playboy" Riots*, Dublin: Dolmen Press, 1971.

Kinahan, Frank, *Yeats, Folklore, and Occultism: Contexts of the Early Work and Thought*, Boston: Unwin Hyman, 1988.

King, Mary C., *The Drama of J. M. Synge*, Syracuse University Press, 1985.

Knapp, James F., "Primitivism and Empire: John Synge and Paul Gaugin," *Comparative Literature* 41 (Winter 1989), 53–68.

Krupat, Arnold, *Ethno-Criticism: Ethnography, History and Literature*, Berkeley: University of California Press, 1992.

Leiris, Michel, *L'Afrique Fantôme*, Paris: Editions Gallimard, 1934.

Manhood: A Journey from Childhood into the Fierce Order of Virility, trans. Richard Howard, 1939; rpt. University of Chicago Press, 1992.

"The Musée de L'Homme: Where Art and Anthropology Meet," with Jean Clay. *Realites* 182 (January 1966), 57–62.

Levenson, Michael, "Living History in 'The Dead,'" in James Joyce, *Dubliners: Text, Criticism and Notes*, Robert Scholes and A. Walton Litz (eds.), Middlesex: Penguin, 1996, 421–38.

Lloyd, David, *Anomalous States: Irish Writing and the Post-Colonial Moment*, Dublin: Lilliput Press, 1993.

Nationalism and Minor Literature: James Clarence Mangan and the Emergence of Irish Cultural Nationalism, Berkeley: University of California Press, 1987.

Loftus, Richard J, *Nationalism in Modern Anglo-Irish Poetry*, Madison and Milwaukee: University of Wisconsin Press, 1964.

Longley, Edna, "*North:* 'Inner Emigré' or 'Artful Voyeur'?" in *The Art of*

Seamus Heaney, Tony Curtis (ed.), 3rd edn, Chester Springs, PA: Dufour, 1994, 63–95.

Loriggio, Francesco, "Anthropology, Literary Theory, and the Traditions of Modernism," in *Modernist Anthropology: From Fieldwork to Text*, Marc Manganaro (ed.), Princeton University Press, 1990, 215–42.

McDiarmid, Lucy and Maureen Waters, "Introduction," in Lady Augusta Gregory, *Selected Writings*, Lucy McDiarmid and Maureen Waters (eds.), London: Penguin, 1995.

McGee, Patrick, *Telling the Other: The Question of Value in Modern and Postcolonial Writing*, Ithaca and London: Cornell University Press, 1992.

Mahon, Derek, *Selected Poems*, New York: Penguin, 1991.

Malinowski, Bronislaw, *Argonauts of the Western Pacific*, 1922, London: Routledge; New York: Dutton, 1932.

"Culture as a Determinant of Behavior," in *Factors Determining Human Behavior*, Cambridge, MA: Harvard University Press, 1937, 133–68.

"Culture," in *Encyclopaedia of the Social Sciences*, Edwin R. A. Seligman and Alvin Johnson (eds.), vol. IV, New York: Macmillan, 1930–35, 621–45.

A Diary in the Strict Sense of the Term, trans. Norbert Guterman, 1967, Stanford University Press, 1989.

A Scientific Theory of Culture and Other Essays, Chapel Hill: University of North Carolina Press, 1944.

The Sexual Life of Savages in North-Western Melanesia, New York: Eugenics Publishing Company, 1929.

Manganaro, Marc, " 'Beating a Drum in a Jungle': T. S. Eliot on the Artist as 'Primitive,' " *Modern Language Quarterly* 47 (December 1986), 393–421.

"Reading 'Culture' in Joyce's *Ulysses*," *James Joyce Quarterly* 35.4/36.1 (Summer/Fall 1998), 765–81.

Manganaro, Marc (ed.), *Modernist Anthropology: From Fieldwork to Text*, Princeton University Press, 1990.

Manganiello, Dominic, *Joyce's Politics*, London: Routledge, 1980.

Mansfield, M. F. and B. McM. Mansfield, *Romantic Ireland*, Boston: L. C. Page and Co., 1904.

Marcus, Phillip L., *Yeats and the Beginning of the Irish Renaissance*, 2nd edn, 1970; rpt. Syracuse University Press, 1987.

Martin, Augustine, "*The Secret Rose* and Yeats's Dialogue with History," *Ariel* 3.3 (July 1972), 91–103.

Memmi, Albert, *The Colonizer and the Colonized*, trans. Howard Greenfeld, Boston: Beacon, 1967.

Miller, Jane E, " 'O, She's a nice Lady!': A Rereading of 'Mother,' " in James Joyce, *Dubliners: Text, Criticism and Notes*, Robert Scholes and A. Walton Litz (eds.), Middlesex: Penguin, 1996, 348–72.

Montague, John, *The Rough Field*, 5th edn, 1972; rpt. Winston-Salem: Wake Forest University Press, 1989.

Mullen, Pat, *Man of Aran*, 1934; rpt. Cambridge, MA: MIT Press, 1970.

Myers, Stephen, *Yeats's Book of the Nineties: Poetry, Politics, and Rhetoric*, New York: Peter Lang, 1993.

Niel, Ruth, "Digging into History: A Reading of Brian Friel's *Volunteers* and Seamus Heaney's 'Viking Dublin: Trial Pieces,'" *Irish University Review* 16.1 (Spring 1986), 35–47.

Niranjana, Tiraswini, *Siting Translation: History, Post-structuralism, and the Colonial Context*, Berkeley: University of California Press, 1992.

Nolan, Emer, *James Joyce and Nationalism*, London and New York: Routledge, 1995.

Norris, Margot, "Modernism, Myth, and Desire in 'Nausicaa,'" *James Joyce Quarterly* 26 (1988), 37–50.

O'Driscoll, Robert, "The Aesthetic and Intellectual Foundations of the Celtic Literary Revival in Ireland," in *The Celtic Continuum*, Robert O'Driscoll (ed.), New York: Braziller, 1982, 401–25.

" 'A Greater Renaissance': The Revolt of the Soul against the Intellect," in *Literary Interrelations: Ireland, England and the World* 3, Wolfgang Zach and Heinz Kosok (eds.), Tübingen: Gunter Nass, 1987, 133–44.

"Yeats's Conception of Synge," in *A Centenary Tribute to John Millington Synge 1871–1909: Sunshine and The Moon's Delight*, S. B. Bushrui (ed.), New York: Barnes and Noble, 1972, 159–71.

O'Grady, Standish, *The History of Ireland*, 2 vols. London: Sampson Low, Searle, Marston and Rivington; Dublin: E. Ponsonby, 1878, 1880.

O'Shea, Edward, *Yeats as Editor*, Dublin: Dolmen Press, 1975.

"Yeats's Revisions in *Fairy and Folk Tales*," *Southern Folklore Quarterly* 38.3 (1974), 223–32.

O'Sullivan, Maurice, *Twenty Years A-Growing*, trans. Moya Llewelyn Davies and George Thomson, New York: Viking, 1933.

Okely, Judith, "Anthropology and Autobiography: Participatory Experience and Embodied Knowledge," in *Anthropology and Autobiography*, Judith Okely and Helen Callaway (eds.), London and New York: Routledge, 1992, 1–28.

Okely, Judith and Helen Callaway, Preface, *Anthropology and Autobiography*, Judith Okely and Helen Callaway (eds.), London and New York: Routledge, 1992, i-xii.

Parry, Benita, "Problems in Current Theories of Colonial Discourse," *Oxford Literary Review* 9 (1987), 27–58.

Pascal, Roy, *The Dual Voice: Free Indirect Speech and Its Functioning in the Nineteenth-Century European Novel*, Manchester University Press, 1977.

Pecora, Vincent, "Arnoldean Ethnology," *Victorian Studies* 41.3 (Spring 1998), 355–79.

" 'The Dead' and the Generosity of the Word," *PMLA* 101 (1986), 233–45.

Platt, L. H., "Joyce and the Anglo-Irish Revival: The Triestine Lectures," *James Joyce Quarterly* 29.2 (Winter 1992), 259–66.

"The Voice of Esau: Culture and Nationalism in 'Scylla and Charybdis,'" *James Joyce Quarterly* 29.4 (Summer 1992), 737–50.

Pratt, Mary Louise, "Fieldwork in Common Places," in *Writing Culture: The Poetics and Politics of Ethnography*, James Clifford and George E. Marcus (eds.), Berkeley: University of California Press, 1986, 27–50.

Imperial Eyes: Travel Writing and Transculturation, London and New York: Routledge, 1992.

Pritchett, V. S., "Current Literature," *The New Statesman and Nation* (April 19, 1941), 413.

Putzel, Steven D., "Towards an Aesthetic of Folklore and Mythology: W. B. Yeats, 1888–1895," *Southern Folklore Quarterly* 44 (1980), 105–30.

Pyle, Hilary, "*Many Ferries*: Jack B. Yeats and J. M. Synge," *Éire–Ireland* 18.2 (1983), 17–35.

Radcliffe-Brown, A. R., *The Andaman Islanders*, 1922; rpt. New York: The Free Press, 1964.

Radford, F. L., "Dedalus and the Bird Girl: Classical Text and Celtic Subtext in *A Portrait*," *James Joyce Quarterly* 24.3 (Spring 1987), 253–74.

Rapport, Nigel, *The Prose and the Passion: Anthropology, Literature and the Writing of E. M. Forster*, Manchester University Press, 1994.

Real Life in Ireland: or, The day and night scenes, rovings, rambles, and sprees, bulls, blunders, bodderation and blarney, of Brian Boru, esq., and his elegant friend Sir Shawn O'Dogherty; exhibiting a real picture of the characters, manners, etc., in high and low life in Dublin and various parts of Ireland, embellished with humorous coloured engravings, from original designs by the most eminent artists / by a real Paddy, London: Methuen, 1904.

Renan, Ernest, *Poetry of the Celtic Races and Other Essays*, 1859; rpt. London and Felling-on-Tyne: Walter Scott, 1896.

Reynolds, Lorna, "The Irish Literary Revival: Preparation and Personalities," in *The Celtic Continuum*, Robert O'Driscoll (ed.), New York: Braziller, 1982, 383–99.

Rhys, John, *Lectures on the Origin and Growth of Religion as Illustrated by Celtic Heathendom*, London, 1888.

Robinson, Tim, "Place/Person/Book: Synge's *The Aran Islands*," in J. M. Synge, *The Aran Islands*, Tim Robinson (ed.), London: Penguin, 1992, vii–l.

Roche, Anthony, "'The Strange Light of Some New World': Stephen's Vision in *A Portrait*," *James Joyce Quarterly* 25.3 (Spring 1988), 323–32.

Saddlemyer, Ann, "Art, Nature and 'The Prepared Personality': A Reading of *The Aran Islands* and Related Writings," in *A Centenary Tribute to John Millington Synge 1871–1909: Sunshine and The Moon's Delight*, S. B. Bushrui (ed.), New York: Barnes and Noble, 1972, 107–20.

"'Infinite Riches in a Little Room' – The Manuscripts of John Millington Synge," *Long Room* 1 (1971), 23–31.

"'A Share in the Dignity of the World': J. M. Synge's Aesthetic Theory," in *The World of W. B. Yeats*, Robin Skelton and Ann Saddlemyer (eds.), Seattle: University of Washington Press, 1967, 207–19.

"Synge and Some Companions, with a Note Concerning a Walk

through Connemara with Jack Yeats," *Yeats Studies: An International Journal* 2 (1972), 18–34.

"Synge and the Doors of Perception," in *Place, Personality and the Irish Writer*, Irish Literary Studies 1, Andrew Carpenter (ed.), New York: Barnes and Noble, 1977, 97–120.

"Synge's Soundscape," *Irish University Review* 22 (Spring/Summer 1992), 55–68.

Saddlemyer, Ann (ed.), *Theatre Business*, University Park and London: Pennsylvania State University Press, 1982.

Said, Edward, *Culture and Imperialism*, New York: Vintage-Random, 1993.

"Intellectuals in the Post-Colonial World," *Salmagundi* 70–1 (Spring–Summer 1986), 44–64.

Orientalism, London: Peregrin-Penguin, 1985.

"Representing the Colonized: Anthropology's Interlocutors," *Critical Inquiry* 15 (Winter 1989), 205–25.

"Third World Intellectuals and Metropolitan Culture," *Raritan* 9.3 (Winter 1990), 27–50.

The World, the Text, and the Critic, Cambridge, MA: Harvard University Press, 1983.

"Yeats and Decolonization," in *Nationalism, Colonialism and Literature*, Minneapolis: University of Minnesota Press, 1990.

Sayers, Peig, *The Autobiography of Peig Sayers of the Great Blasket Island*, trans. Bryan MacMahon, Syracuse University Press, 1974.

Scheper-Hughes, Nancy, *Saints, Scholars, and Schizophrenics: Mental Illness in Rural Ireland*, Berkeley: University of California Press, 1979.

Schleifer, Ronald (ed.), *The Genres of the Irish Literary Revival*, Norman, OK: Pilgrim Books; Dublin: Wolfhound Press, 1980.

Senn, Fritz, "Nausicaa," in *James Joyce's* Ulysses: *Critical Essays*, Clive Hart and David Hayman (eds.), Berkeley: University of California Press, 1974, 277–311.

Shand, Alexander Innes, *Letters from the West of Ireland, 1884*, Edinburgh: Blackwood, 1885.

Sharpe, Jenny, "The Unspeakable Limits of Rape: Colonial Violence and Counter-Insurgency," in *Colonial Discourse and Post-Colonial Theory*, Patrick Williams and Laura Chrisman (eds.), New York: Harvester-Wheatsheaf, 1993, 221–43.

Sigerson, George, "Irish Literature: Its Origin, Environment, and Influence," in *The Revival of Irish Literature: Addresses by Sir Charles Gavan Duffy, K.C.M.G., Dr. George Sigerson, and Dr. Douglas Hyde*, London: Fisher Unwin, 1894, 61–114.

Simmons, William S., "Culture Theory in Contemporary Ethnohistory," *Ethnohistory* 35.1 (1988), 1–14.

Somerville, Edith and Martin Ross, *Through Connemara in a Governess Cart*, London: W. H. Allen, 1893.

Sontag, Susan, "The Anthropologist as Hero," in *Against Interpretation and Other Essays*, New York: Delta, 1967, 69–81.

Spurr, David, "Myths of Anthropology: Eliot, Joyce, Lévy-Bruhl," *PMLA* 109 (March 1994), 226–80.

The Rhetoric of Empire: Colonial Discourse in Journalism, Travel Writing, and Imperial Administration, Durham and London: Duke University Press, 1993.

Stallworthy, Jon, "The Poet as Archaeologist: W. B. Yeats and Seamus Heaney," *Review of English Studies*, n.s. 33 (1982), 158–74.

Stocking, George W. Jr., *The Ethnographer's Magic and Other Essays in the History of Anthropology*, Madison: University of Wisconsin Press, 1992.

Race, Culture and Evolution: Essays in the History of Anthropology, New York: Free Press; London: Collier-Macmillan, 1968.

Strand, Ginger, "*The Playboy*, Critics, and the Enduring Problem of the Audience," in *Assessing the Achievement of J. M. Synge*, Alexander G. Gonzalez (ed.), Westport, CT: Greenwood, 1996, 10–23.

Synge, J. M., *The Aran Islands*, Tim Robinson (ed.), London: Penguin 1992.

Collected Works, 4 vols., Robin Skelton (ed.), New York: Oxford University Press, 1962–8.

Synge Manuscript Collection, Trinity College, Dublin.

Taylor, Lawrence J, "'There Are Two Things that People Don't Like to Hear about Themselves': The Anthropology of Ireland and the Irish View of Anthropology," *The South Atlantic Quarterly, Ireland and Irish Cultural Studies* 95.1 (Winter 1996), 213–26.

Tedlock, Dennis, "The Analogic Tradition and the Emergence of a Dialogical Anthropology," *Journal of Anthropological Research* 35 (1979), 387–400.

"Questions Concerning Dialogical Anthropology," *Journal of Anthropological Research* 43 (Winter 1987), 325–344.

Thuente, Mary Helen, *The Harp Re-strung: The United Irishmen and the Rise of Irish Literary Nationalism*, Syracuse University Press, 1994.

Yeats and Irish Folk-lore, Dublin: Gill and Macmillan, 1980.

Tifft, Stephen, "The Parricidal Phantasm: Irish Nationalism and the *Playboy* Riots," in *Nationalisms and Sexualities*, Andrew Parker, Mary Russo, Doris Sommer, and Patricia Yaeger (eds.), New York: Routledge, 1992, 313–32.

Torgovnick, Marianna, *Gone Primitive: Savage Intellects, Modern Lives*, University of Chicago Press, 1990.

Trench, William Steuart, *Realities of Irish Life*, London: Longmans, Green and Co., 1869.

Turner, Terence, "Representing, Resisting, Rethinking: Historical Transformation of Kayapo Culture and Anthropological Consciousness," in *Colonial Situations: Essays on the Contextualization of Ethnographic Knowledge*, George W. Stocking, Jr. (ed.), History of Anthropology 7, Madison: University of Wisconsin Press, 1991, 285–313.

Turner, Victor, "Are There Universals of Performance in Myth, Ritual, and Drama?" in *By Means of Performance: Intercultural Studies of Theater and*

Ritual, Richard Schechner and Willa Appel (eds.), Cambridge University Press, 1990, 8–18.

From Ritual to Theatre, New York: Performing Arts Journal Publications, 1982.

Tyler, Stephen A, "Post-Modern Ethnography: From Document of the Occult to Occult Document," in *Writing Culture: The Poetics and Politics of Ethnography*, James Clifford and George E. Marcus (eds.), Berkeley: University of California Press, 1986, 122–40.

The Unspeakable: Discourse, Dialogue, and Rhetoric in the Postmodern World, Madison: University of Wisconsin Press, 1987.

Tylor, E. B., *Primitive Culture*, 2 vols., 1871, New York: Harper, 1958.

Valente, Joseph, *James Joyce and the Problem of Justice: Negotiating Sexual and Colonial Difference*, Cambridge University Press, 1996.

Visweswaran, Kamala, *Fictions of Feminist Ethnography*, Minneapolis: University of Minnesota Press, 1994.

Watson, G. J., *Irish Identity and the Literary Revival: Synge, Yeats, Joyce and O'Casey*, London: Croom Helm; New York: Barnes and Noble, 1979.

Welch, Robert, *Changing States: Transformations in Modern Irish Writing*, London and New York: Routledge, 1993.

Whelan, Kevin, *Fellowship of Freedom: The United Irishmen and 1798*, Cork University Press, 1998.

Wilde, Oscar, Preface, *The Picture of Dorian Gray: Authoritative Texts, Backgrounds, Reviews and Reactions, Criticism*, Donald L. Lawler (ed.), New York: Norton, 1988, 3–4.

Williams, Trevor, "No Cheer for the 'Gratefully Oppressed' in Joyce's Dubliners," *Style* 25.3 (Fall 1991), 416–38.

Yeates, Amanda, "Cathleen in Service: Female Iconography in Lady Gregory, Yeats, Synge, and Joyce", Ph.D. dissertation, Arizona State University, December 1999.

Yeats, J. B. "Random Reflections on a Much-Discussed Dramatist From the Standpoint of a Fellow-Countryman," *Harper's Weekly* 55 (November 25, 1911), 17.

Yeats, William Butler, *Autobiographies*, London: Macmillan, 1955.

The Celtic Twilight, Lawrence and Bullen, 1893.

The Celtic Twilight, Lawrence and Bullen, 1902.

The Collected Letters of W. B. Yeats. Vol. One: 1865–1895, John Kelly and Eric Domville (eds.), Oxford: Clarendon Press, 1986.

The Collected Plays of W. B. Yeats, New York: Macmillan, 1953.

The Cutting of an Agate, London: Macmillan, 1919.

Essays and Introductions, New York: Collier-Macmillan, 1968.

Explorations, New York: Macmillan, 1962.

Memoirs, Denis Donoghue (ed.), New York: Macmillan, 1972.

Mythologies, New York: Collier-Macmillan, 1969.

On the Boiler, Dublin: Cuala Press, 1939.

Poems, London: Fisher Unwin, 1895.

The Poems, Richard J. Finneran (ed.), vol. 1 of *The Collected Works of W. B. Yeats*, New York: Macmillan, 1983, 1989.

The Secret Rose, London: Lawrence and Bullen, 1897.

The Secret Rose, Stories by W. B. Yeats: A Variorum Edition, 2nd edn, Warwick Gould, Phillip L. Marcus, and Michael Sidnell (eds.), London: Macmillan, 1992.

The Speckled Bird, ed. William H. O'Donnell, Toronto: McClelland and Stewart, 1976.

Stories of Red Hanrahan / The Secret Rose / Rosa Alchemica, New York: Macmillan, 1914.

The Tables of the Law; and The Adoration of the Magi, Stratford-upon-Avon: Shakespeare Head Press, 1914.

The Variorum Edition of the Poems of W. B. Yeats, Peter Allt and Russell K. Alspach (eds.), New York: Hudson River-Macmillan 1987.

Uncollected Prose by W. B. Yeats, vol. 1 (1886–96), John P. Frayne (ed.), New York: Columbia University Press, 1970.

Uncollected Prose by W. B. Yeats, vol. II (1897–1939), John P. Frayne and Colton Johnson (eds.), New York: Columbia University Press, 1976.

Yeats, William Butler (ed.), *Fairy and Folk Tales of Ireland*, New York: Macmillan, 1986. This edition contains *Fairy and Folk Tales of the Irish Peasantry* (1888) and *Irish Fairy Tales* (1892).

Young, Robert, *Colonial Desire: Hybridity in Theory, Culture and Race*, London: Routledge, 1995.

Index

Yeats, William Butler (*cont.*)
  project of cultural redemption, 55, 61,
    66–7, 68, 74, 76, 78, 81–5, 88, 93, 95, 96,
    138
  response to Matthew Arnold, 49–52, 89–9,
    94
  Revivalism and, 1, 3, 5, 38, 41, 44, 55–6,
    70–1, 81–6, 89, 93, 95, 135–9, 167, 175–6,
    248
  works, *Fairy and Folk Tales of Ireland*, 53–60,
    61–2, 66, 89; *The Celtic Twilight*, 10,
    60–8, 86, 89, 90, 109, 117, 180, 183, 195;
    Stories of Red Hanrahan, 70–6, 81–3, 90;
    The Secret Rose, 5, 72–6, 80, 90, 271 n. 94;
    Autobiographies, 58, 63, 67, 68; *On the*

Boiler, 91–7; *Per Amica Silentia Lunae*, 80,
  85; "Rosa Alchemica," "The Tables of
  the Law," "Adoration of the Magi,"
  78–81, 95, 179, 191, 204–5; "The Celtic
  Element in Literature," 49–53, 67, 94;
  "John M. Synge and the Ireland of His
  Time," 84–5, 99, 108–9, 110, 120, 142,
  158–9, 169; "Swedenborg, Mediums,
  Desolate Place," 86; dramatic works,
  83–4, 91, 95–7, 136, 139, 162, 187, 200,
  207; poetic works, 83, 84–5, 87–91, 94–5,
  169, 207

Young, Robert, 105, 129
Young Ireland, 4, 8, 42, 70, 232, 282 n. 76